Absence and Memory in Colonial
American Theatre

"Palgrave Studies in Theatre and Performance History" is a series devoted to the best of theatre/performance scholarship currently available, accessible, and free of jargon. It strives to include a wide range of topics, from the more traditional to those performance forms that in recent years have helped broaden the understanding of what theatre as a category might include (from variety forms as diverse as the circus and burlesque to street buskers, stage magic, and musical theatre, among many others). Although historical, critical, or analytical studies are of special interest, more theoretical projects, if not the dominant thrust of a study, but utilized as important underpinning or as a historiographical or analytical method of exploration, are also of interest. Textual studies of drama or other types of less traditional performance texts are also germane to the series if placed in their cultural, historical, social, or political, and economic context. There is no geographical focus for this series, and works of excellence of a diverse and international nature, including comparative studies, are sought.

The editor of the series is Don B. Wilmeth (EMERITUS, Brown University), Ph.D., University of Illinois, who brings to the series over a dozen years as editor of a book series on American theatre and drama, in addition to his own extensive experience as an editor of books and journals. He is the author of several award-winning books and has received numerous career achievement awards, including one for sustained excellence in editing from the Association for Theatre in Higher Education.

Also in the series:

Undressed for Success by Brenda Foley
Theatre, Performance, and the Historical Avant-garde by Günter Berghaus
Theatre, Politics, and Markets in Fin-de-Siècle Paris by Sally Charnow
Ghosts of Theatre and Cinema in the Brain by Mark Pizzato
Moscow Theatres for Young People by Manon van de Water
Absence and Memory in Colonial American Theatre by Odai Johnson

Absence and Memory in Colonial American Theatre

Fiorelli's Plaster

Odai Johnson

First published in 2006 by
PALGRAVE MACMILLAN™
175 Fifth Avenue, New York, N.Y. 10010 and
Houndmills, Basingstoke, Hampshire, England RG21 6XS
Companies and representatives throughout the world.

PALGRAVE MACMILLAN is the global academic imprint of the Palgrave Macmillan division of St. Martin's Press, LLC and of Palgrave Macmillan Ltd. Macmillan® is a registered trademark in the United States, United Kingdom and other countries. Palgrave is a registered trademark in the European Union and other countries.

ISBN-13: 978–1–4039–7100–5
ISBN-10: 1–4039–7100–5

Library of Congress Cataloging-in-Publication Data

Johnson, Odai, 1959–
    Absence and memory in colonial American theatre : Fiorelli's plaster / Odai Johnson.
        p. cm. — (Palgrave studies in theatre and performance history)
    Includes bibliographical references and index.
    ISBN 1–4039–7100–5 (alk. paper)
        1. Theater—United States—History—17th century. 2. Theater—United States—History—18th century. I. Title. II. Series.

PN2237.J63 2006
792.0973'0903—dc22   2005053503

A catalogue record for this book is available from the British Library.

Design by Newgen Imaging Systems (P) Ltd., Chennai, India.

First edition: April 2006

10 9 8 7 6 5 4 3 2 1

Printed in the United States of America.

Contents ∾

List of Illustrations ∾

For T. G. Budley

Acknowledgments ◦◦◦

It is my great pleasure to acknowledge the kind and generous support of the Colonial Williamsburg Foundation for time spent as a resident researcher in Williamsburg, and in particular, my thanks go to Cary Carson and his office of Historical Research, to the Carl Loundsbury, Willie Graham, Ed Chapel, Tom Goyens, and Lisa Fischer for making the solitary act of writing pleasantly sociable. Gratitude is also extended to the staff at the Rockefeller Library, Gail Greve, George Yetter, and Del Moore.

I have had the good fortune of much kind assistance during the researches for this project, among which let me repay a debt of kindness to the delightful and knowledgeable Robert Hitchings at the Norfolk Public Library; Paula Felder at the Fredericksburg Historical Society; Jean Russo, and Glen Campbell at the Annapolis Historic Foundation; Jane McWilliams of the Annapolis Heritage Association; Ed Watson of the Museum of Fredericksburg; Gary Stanton of the Center for Historic Preservation, Mary Washington College; Connie King at the Library of Philadelphia; Elizabeth Fuller at the Rosenbauch Museum and Library; Annette Fern, Elizabeth Falsey, and Fredric Woolbridge Wilson at the Harvard Theatre Collection, Joseph Garver, at the Harvard Map Collection; Dorris O'Keefe at the American Antiquarian Society; Jan Hille at the New York Historical Society; Ansley Wegner at the North Carolina Office of Archives and History; Monica Moody of Historic Halifax, Stefan Bielinski at the Colonial Albany Social History Project; the invaluable James Fowler at the Covent Garden Theatre Museum for the James Winston material; the helpful Thomas Clark for the Jonathan Clark material; Peter Davis for kindly lending me his notes on the

Cruger family; David Wilmore and Ian Macintosh for their insights into the reconstruction of the Richmond Yorkshire playhouse; Dr. Glen Gordon, secretary, St. John's Lodge, Portsmouth, NH; Rhys Issac for many vibrant conversations at the carrels of the Rockefeller; Don Wilmeth, general editor, for reading and encouraging the project, and my colleague Barry Witham, for listening.

Finally, I must thankfully acknowledge that this current project began many years ago as an interpretive by-product that grew out of the production of *The Colonial American Stage 1665–1774: A Documentary Calendar* (AUP, 2001) and so many thanks are owed to that book's coauthor, William Burling.

Earlier versions and excerpts of some of the material have appeared in *Theatre Survey, Theatre Notebook*, and *New England Theatre Journal*.

Introduction: In the Cellars of the Vatican ✤

In the cellars of the Vatican, as narrow and winding as catacombs, there is a strange enormous graveyard. It is of parts of ancient statues, thrown on the ground in a rough classification, feet in one heap, then knees, then whole legs, and so on. There is something particularly poignant about the fingers and elbows. There are also parts of dogs and wild boars, and once the head of a Parthenon horse was found there.

Elanor Clark, *Roman Journal*

The past, it seems, is always awaiting ordering: sorting, assembling, reassembling, often in arbitrary ways. In the case of the ancient statues, the Vatican's criterion was anatomical: "feet in one heap, then knees." With only fragments to go on, one choice may be as informed or arbitrary as another, and often is. The ancient statues might just as well have been ordered by, say, sculptor, or century, or subject. Or the pieces might be left utterly unordered in some monstrously dismembered, postmodern Laocoön of feet, spears, and hydras. As it is, the elbows of Roman statuary coexist with Renaissance remakes, sharing only a common form, staring profusely and ambidextrously across the centuries.

I am intrigued by this compulsion to order and how the scant materials of the past have been roughly classified and arranged to tell what tales they will. What follows is also a reordering of sorts, a picking about in the bone pile of artifacts and absences of the colonial American theatre. It is my hope that the gesture is more than a random re-sorting—a moving of the material from one ordering to another, perhaps equally arbitrary, perhaps telling in the restacking. It is my hope that the reordering of the period somehow evokes the original in a more complete and authentic way. In practical terms, what follows is a two-fold project roughly broken into hemispheres of reading absence and memory. The reading of absence is an excavation into the ghosted materiality of performance that once was and is no more, yet whose residue and traces may yet be made legible, may yet be read for the materiality that once was, and the memory they yet contain.

A small, but pointed, example of reading absence and memory: when the recent excavations were underway in Williamsburg, Virginia, on the 1760 theatre site, below what was once the stage level in the bottommost strata of red clay, a small piece of grainy imprint was discovered. Held still legible in the earth itself was the indentation of the remains of a piece of the wooden stage floor. The wood, of course, had long since decomposed, but the imprint of the grain was left in the hardened clay. At one corner of this impression streaked a long, thin, and clearly defined stain of rust: a secondary layer of residue, this one of an iron spike.

A row of iron spikes lined the forestages of eighteenth-century English theatres, like those described by George Ann Bellamy in the Kelly riots at Smock Alley, and seen in the image of the Covent Garden, 1747, illustrating David Garrick's play *Miss in Her Teens*. London and provincial managers alike no doubt found such a formidable barrier occasionally very useful.[1] But there was no practical reason for iron spikes on the stage in Williamsburg; there were no riots there, no mention of any kind of disturbance at all among this polite Southern assembly. Yet they were part of an architectural tradition that served to evoke London playgoing for those more distant audiences, as a marker of recognition. It was a mark that in at least one case ruefully exceeded its application. One of the actors with Lewis Hallam's Company, Patrick Malone, was surprised in the playhouse late one night in Williamsburg, scuffled with the intruders, and was thrown on the spikes. Clearly they were a dangerous ornament for a genteel audience. None of these architectural oddities has survived from the circuit of colonial American theatres, but the impression of one has, and with it all that it evoked of London playgoing. This is the kind of absence I am interested in: the residue of the material, and hovering beyond that, the more distant memory of London and the immaterial desire for the familiar.

In many ways the two halves of the project, absence and memory, are reciprocal: what we call history—the narrative apparatus that forms the container of memory—is bound up with the surviving evidence and artifacts, even absent evidence and decomposed artifacts. But evidence also has a peculiar and sometimes pernicious way of surviving largely on its ability to conform to and endorse certain existing hegemonies and narratives, particularly well-shaped narratives. Both command a certain reserve of memory, and both are at work in this field. Memory first.

THE CHARISMA OF MEMORY

> *Lizzy Borden took an axe*
> *Gave her mother forty whacks*
> *When she saw what she had done*
> *Gave her father forty one.*

We recognize how certain well-shaped narratives have a way of coercing memory, creating what Paul Ricoeur has called in his obsession with this unjust allotment "an excess of memory here, and an excess of forgetting elsewhere."[2] This operation is more apparent when material evidence is absent and the subject thus resists its own recollection, a condition discussed below. To my mind, though, it is at its most interesting when evidence and narrative compete for memory and the competition remains highly visible. The infamous double-murder case of *Lisbeth Borden v. the State of Massachusetts* (mis)quoted above will stand for a petite and playful example of this competition and gravitational pull of narrative on memory. Historically—that is, according to the juridical record—Lisbeth Borden was acquitted of the murder of her parents, but (I would say "historically" here with equal conviction) we all know the story differently, and we know so on the strength of one delicious rhyme. Though legally acquitted, Lizzy Borden remains guilty in the public memory, axe and all, impaled upon an exquisite stanza of a child's rhyme, a distinction that should be borne in mind when one considers, among things, the quality of life that followed the accused. The history of performance (and politics) is filled with such contests of fact and form (the famous canard of the death of Percy Hammond, the critic who allegedly died from the witch doctor's spell after a poor review of Orson Welles's production of the "Voodoo Macbeth," or the stigma of misfortunes that follows other productions of Macbeth) in which the gothic shapeliness of the structure itself invites, indulges in an excess of memory, against which strains the unordered veracity of the event in the excess of forgetting that accompanies it. How history can "overly remember" certain events (the Holocaust, in Ricoeur's example; antitheatricalism in mine) while other events (the Armenian genocide, or performance itself) are historically less available is not the fault of the past, but rather of narrative and a certain unequal distribution of memory. I am both fascinated and troubled by these mechanisms through which certain figures, structures, and histories are made indelible—in part by their ability to seek remembrance—and against which the historical operation struggles to retrieve something authentic. The project that follows is such a struggle, devoted to this problem of how the history of one field was shaped by the availability and charisma of memory.

*   *   *

As I see it, there are two challenges to the historiography of the field of colonial American theatre: the first concerns a sizeable body of documentary evidence—particularly in the early period (1665–1752)—derived from the legal record and not from actual performance records. For material and ideologic reasons, the ephemera of theatrical production has not found repository in the cultural memory in the same way, or with the same weight, as the legal records have; thus, the second and far larger challenge, a curiously skewed and antagonistic narrative of the period—early and late—has emerged based on the prosecutors of theatre and not on the producers of it. Derived as it is from preserved legal records (legal suits, antitheatrical legislation, petitions against the introduction of theatre) and absent performance records (playhouses), one of the most persistent strategies to order the field of colonial American theatre has been to position theatre as a legal and moral alien that struggled against a community's opposition to arrive at its legitimacy. This narrative pattern—essentially a structuralist dyad of Puritan versus Player—has amassed early into a formidable cannon of works that form the core of the early American history of the stage, from William Dunlap's proto *History of the American Theatre* (1832), as an ontological defense of the theatre, to early twentieth-century studies, like Arthur Hornblow's *History of the American Stage*, as a justification of the ultimate triumph of the theatre, and had hardened into such a trope by mid-century studies, like Hugh Rankin's *The Theatre in Colonial America*, that opposition against the theatre had become a fundamental operating assumption of the field. Though subsequent studies have begun to erode the authority of the assumption and parse out a more nuanced profile of the opposition, even such revisions, nonetheless, betray the depth and persistent hold of this positioning.[3] The reliance of the field on this rhetorical, essentially dramatic device of pitting Puritans against players has informed the history of the discipline to such an extent that the story of the early theatre in America was not so much told as told against. And it has been this way since the very beginning.

THE VOICE OF EDWARD MARTIN

It is an unfortunate trope of colonial American theatre that the oldest evidence of any theatrical presentation in the British colonies comes to us from court records of detractors and not from actors, or even audiences, playbills, or costumes. On the complaint of one Edward Martin, three men—William Darby, Cornelius Watkinson, and Philip Howard—accused of having acted a play, *The Beare and the Cubb*, at Cowle's Tavern, Pungoteague, Virginia, were arraigned on November 16, 1665 and were ordered to appear in court, with costumes and script. We know neither the content of the play—the text has not survived— nor whether these men were in the habit of writing, acting, or producing other plays, nor how the play was received (beyond Martin's complaint), or even how often it was performed—the court records refer to it as "commonly called." In short, we have no material record of this performance. We only know that, much to the disappointment of Edward Martin, the justices found nothing offensive in the play, the actors were acquitted, and Martin was saddled with the court costs.[4]

This episode is an unfortunate opening of American theatre studies for exactly the two problems noted above. Our earliest evidence of

Anglophone performance in America is derived entirely from court records, and the recording of the event is itself antagonistic. It was framed not as an activity among other cultural activities—as, say, a tavern concert—but as a contest for legitimacy, and though the contest was ultimately hollow and the players exonerated, performance in colonial America arrived through the courtroom, through the persistent and, in the end, injurious voice of Edward Martin.

From the earliest accounts in 1665 to the second Congressional ban on theatres in 1778, the colonial American record is littered with a dense legal repository of evidence against the theatre, evidence that habitually overwhelms the actual performance records. The incident of *The Beare and the Cubb* is one example, but consider several other moments in that time line.

In Boston in 1714, Chief Justice Samuel Sewall heard about a play in rehearsal and rumored to be presented in the Senate house. This was to be a public performance in a civic building, but Sewall used his authority to suppress the play (reminding us the impulse to play precedes the impulse to prohibit). No record has survived about the play that was prepared, who had proposed it, who prepared it, or to what end these Puritans in Boston were undertaking a civic performance in the first place. As chief justice of the colony, Sewall's letters have been preserved and, consequently, his prohibition against the theatre.

We would do well to remember at this point that, as a British colony under the laws of Great Britain, there was nothing inherently illegal about theatre—that legally companies could play at the discretion of the governors, lieutenant governors, city councils, or mayors of each of the colonies and cities. We would also do well to remember that when prohibitions did occur, they were often met with immediate repeals, and as frequently as not prohibitions did little to prevent performances. Like Massachusetts, Pennsylvania had prohibited theatre three times by 1716 (each repealed in Great Britain), when at the annual meeting of the Quakers, leaders still "advised Friends against going to or being in any way concerned in plays, games, lotteries, music and dancing."[5] Clearly, in spite of repeated prohibitions, plays of some nature continued to be performed, but of these we have no performance records, only the injunctions against them. Indeed, the only hard evidence of an actual production in Philadelphia at this early period (1723) points up the very ineffectiveness of the prohibitions. It comes to us from a letter dated February 9, 1723 written by James Logan, the mayor of Philadelphia, to Henry Goldney:

> The Speaker, by appointment of the House, applied to the Govr. to discourage a Player who had Strowled hither to act as a Comedian. The Govr. excused himself from prohibiting it, but assured them he would take care good ord'r should be kept, and so the man went on to publish his printed bills, as thou wilt see by one of them inclosed, and to act accordingly.
>
> How grievous this proves to the sober people of the place, thou wilt easily judge, but it happens at p'sent to be more particularly so on me, having, unfortunately, been chosen Mayor of Philad [*sic*] for this year, there is an expectation that I should exert that authority to suppress their acting. But as they have chosen for their stage a place just without the verge of the City and ye Gov. himself resorts thither, I can by no means think it advisable to embroil myself with the governor to no purpose, or to raise a dispute between the Corporation and him in which nothing is to be gained.[6]

This unknown actor-manager had a company (also unknown), secured the governor's permission (unrecorded), erected or remodeled a playhouse of some nature outside the city's jurisdiction (undiscovered), printed and published his bills (which have not survived), and mounted something of a season of plays (whose titles remain unknown) that won favor with at least the governor, Sir William Keith. James Logan appended one of the playbills with the letter as evidence of the company. While the letter objecting to the performances has survived, the attached playbill announcing them has not.

Or consider the inaugural season of Lewis Hallam's company in Virginia, 1752–1753. That they were initially repulsed was recorded in the council minutes; that they ultimately secured permission was not. Of their season we know of twelve separate lawsuits for debt—including a detailed wrangling over the forfeiture and repossession of the playhouse—a break-in, an assault on an actor, several complaints and opposition to the players from the governor, the city council, and prominent citizens throughout the summer of 1752, and at least two very unkind epithets: "idle set of wretches," and "never were debts worse paid."[7] Of their actual performances, we have a prologue, titles of two plays and afterpieces, and a display of fireworks—this from the first fully outfitted London-trained professional company of actors after ten months of playing in a colony with local printers and newspapers.

At the later end of the colonial calendar: Preserved in the American Antiquarian Society in Worcester, Massachusetts, is an antitheatrical broadside on the back of which is handwritten a tantalizing note: "stuck up at Richmond close to the playbill for that date." This date was June 4, 1774. It was printed in Baltimore and posted in Richmond, Virginia, and the only known acting company in the colonies in 1774 was David Douglass's American Company, whose members had disbanded for the summer in mid-May at the close of the Charleston season, and their whereabouts accounted for.[8] Some company was playing in Richmond; who, we don't know, where, we don't know.[9] Again, the antitheatrical broadside was preserved while the playbill next to it was not.

Why it was thought memorable in each of the above cases to preserve evidence of the objections and not of the performance itself is central to the problem of constructing a performance history of the period based on performance, and not its detractors. A hegemony of preservation has played across the field, favoring the rich memory of the juridical record over the ephemera of performance, and recognizing it is central to how this culture chose to "over-remember" the theatre, central to how the history has subsequently been told, and central to this current project that seeks, against which, to reclaim a body of absent performance evidence.

Because it was not central to how theatre in colonial America actually happened. Players preceded prohibitions. Performances surpassed, bypassed, and outlived the legislation against it. Puritans and players shared the same cities, shared the same patrons, sometimes uneasily, sometimes indifferently, but shared nonetheless. Playbills and antitheatrical broadsides shared the same printers and were displayed on the same walls, and in several colonial cities, churches and theatres shared the same physical building.[10] While Quakers like James Logan opposed the idea of theatre, enough audiences, including the English-appointed governors like William Keith, John Penn, Horatio Sharpe, encouraged it, and more liberal-minded clergy, like James Sterling, wrote for it. In some colonies while severe legislation was enacted to prevent establishing the theatre, private letters of permission could (and often did) bypass the legislation, and clandestine performances evaded it entirely. If the Quakers made memorials of their opposition—legislation, hundred-signature petitions—the promoters of theatre were quietly attending in enough numbers to support a winter's season. The challenge is thus to recover the unpreserved voices of support in the attempt to acquire a more comprehensive understanding of theatre in the complexity of its culture.[11]

LOST AND FOUND

And here we are in luck. Over the last decade a good deal of new documentary and material evidence has been recovered, small things ("small things forgotten," to quote James Deetz's phrase), but taken together, they represent a large, diverse, and occasionally oblique body of performance evidence that gestures toward a monumental reorientation. Paramount among this new material are the remains of a 1760 playhouse unearthed in Williamsburg, Virginia. Less spectacular, but of equal importance, are the discovery of several new professional companies of itinerant players touring between America and the lower Caribbean circuit of playhouses on St. Croix, St. Kitts, Antigua, Barbados; a richly cultivated and deeply connected social network of itinerant actors preserved in the records of the Ancient and Honorable Freemasons; the receipt books of playgoer Thomas Jefferson; the discovery of an amateur company playing in and around Boston; unpublished playgoing diaries, a printer's receipts for running off playbills and tickets. "Small things forgotten," indeed, as small as ticket stubs. But even ticket stubs could be dense with history: used as currency to settle lodging debts, traded to printers on commission, forged on one occasion by a down-at-heels printer's apprentice, stolen on another from an actor's trunk, who, in turn for his benefit night, had them reprinted and marked with a special sign: the Masonic image of the builder's rule, the Grand Geometrician. By marking the ticket, the actor was not only speaking to a select society, announcing his affiliation, inviting the support of the Brotherhood, but was also marking out the illegitimate tickets that were still in circulation, creating currency of one image while devaluing another.

But much of the discussion of what follows involves the evocation of absent or immaterial evidence, the residue and traces of ghosted performance and performance culture the disappearance of which was never complete. Traces of its absence were left, and to some degree, remain legible, like the iron spike and the stage floor. The first half of the study that follows considers some of the more monumental fields of absence: a playhouse is reconstructed from the postholes it left in the ground, and with it is restored its position in the social landscape of a colonial capital; a circuit of theatres is reconstructed from a mapmaker's legend; spending patterns invite an exploration into the anatomy of a culture's desire for theatre; the social network of patronage extrapolated from the Masonic symbols left on ticket stubs; and finally, memory itself is evoked in the many preserved conventions of performance that were carried across the Atlantic, from London and the provincial stages; even through the medium of the antitheatrical campaigns theatre was made thinkable in the social imagination.

Unlike "small things forgotten," reading immaterial evidence—desire, memory, countenance, the social apparatus that allowed, encouraged, even expected a thriving and familiar theatrical circuit—has left no text. But occasionally the residue of the immaterial evidence—absence, desire, memory, the charisma of antitheatrical rhetoric—was potent enough to create a space for theatre in the cultural imagination and to find a repository in memory. Especially memory.

A distinction (and a debt) must be made here as this study is distantly akin to the work of other theorists of absence. Paul Ricouer, whose *Memory, History, Forgetting* cited above, offered the encouragement for tracing memory, and his huge presence was largely responsible for shifting the study from an investigation of evidence and narrative to one of absence and memory. Joseph Roach's work on the relationship of memory and forgetting found the residue of lost traditions surrogated back into circulation (*Cities of the Dead*). Although the kind of absence I am interested in needed no surrogation, as it itself left a mark, the problems posed were very useful in parsing out the many cavities performance has left behind. Another more distant absence is Peggy Phelan's concept of performance, who absence (disappearance) is essential to its being. Her reading of performance that "becomes itself through disappearance" requires its own erasure in ways this study resists (*Unmarked*, 146). For reading memory and its residues trapped in narrative structures, I look to Hayden White (*The Content of the Form*). Many historigraphical studies have also played a useful role in this project. For the evidence itself, I turn back to the material culture in which theatre lived in the attempt to recover something of the mental template of the times. I look to the work of social anthropologists to situate theatre in the market economy of genteel goods and the new Georgian order: Timothy Breen, Mark Leon, Parker Potter, Richard Bushman, and James Deetz.

Where the material is absent, I turn to the immaterial, whose residual traces where memory once lived offer more than a metaphor against the ephemeral disappearance of material culture. Ultimately, in its own curious way, what has not survived argues the loudest for its own endurance and a far higher degree of visibility for the idea of theatre than has hitherto been accorded it. Jean-Christophe Agnew is not alone when he concluded of colonial American theatre:

> Where colonial drama did make headway against the force of piety and prejudice, it was most often in the form of occasional entertainments by itinerant companies of English actors. Playhouses did spring up in Williamsburg, Charleston, and Annapolis during the eighteenth century, but they were mostly short-lived. (*Worlds Apart*, 150)

Rather, I am arguing for theatre's permanence, within the material marketplace, within the cultural imagination, and most potently, in the memory of colonial America. Playhouses did not "spring up" in Williamsburg by occasional strollers; they were built on the landscape because a certain desire propelled them into materiality—an enduring cultural memory of theatre and theatregoing preceded the materiality of theatre, occasionally standing in for it, even in the absence of professional players. Before the professionals arrived there were amateur companies, and before them were schoolboys keeping the desire and memory alive. William Byrd wrote of this desire and memory 25 years before the Hallams arrived in Williamsburg from London: "My young gentlewomen like everything in their own country, except the retirement, they can't get the plays, the operas, & the masquerades out of their heads."[12] Soliciting such immaterial evidence as memory and desire does not seek to re-create what is lost, but to return it to memory, to evoke it, if only to begin to dislodge something of the authority of the objectors and reassert the persistent presence of performance: playhouses, touring circuits, playbills, companies, patronage, all the once-but-absent markings of performance on the social landscape.

Part I. (Im)material Witnesses ✧

FIORELLI'S PLASTER

Is there a history of silence?

Derrida

As what follows is, in many ways, a history of absence, I want to begin with a poignant illustration of the virtues of a methodology that materializes something that was not there.

In 1860, when the young archeologist Giseppi Fiorelli was appointed as the new Director of Excavation for the sites of Herculaneum and Pompeii, his nomination to the post marked a sharp break with the tradition of what had been largely a honorary position that granted the recipient pirate rights to a percentage of whatever treasures the ancient sites would yield. Fiorelli's predecessor, for example, was Alexander Dumas, the novelist, who had little interest in the new science of archeology but a developed curiosity for the erotica and the pocketable prizes. Dumas was not unusual in this appetite. One earlier account of the discovery of the theatre in Herculaneum exampled the old pirate-practice: "The theatre must have been a fine one, as it is all encrusted with marble, which is carried off as fast as they removed the earth before it."[1]

The appointment of Giseppi Fiorelli marked the triumph of the new school of empirical knowledge. Fiorelli began a systematic dig, dividing the city into a grid of blocks to determine the parameters of the site, then carefully began removing and straining the dirt from the entire site, one layer at a time (what we call stratigraphy today). His mandate was not the retrieval of treasures, but rather to uncover the entirety of the town. As the topsoil receded, outlines of buildings began to emerge, artifacts were described in situ, labeled, and hand drawn. He prepared a catalogue of his findings—among the first of its kind—and began to map the ancient city.

There were, however, some troubling problems with his stratigraphy. Occasionally, as the dirt was removed and the ancient township exposed, holes would emerge that did not appear to have anything in them. They were, in essence, bubbles, gaps in the record, historically silent. At first the workers did nothing with them, dismissed the empty cavities as air pockets and continued digging. But as more of them began to appear, Fiorelli experimented with uncovering the size of the holes, as the cavities itself were part of the historic record. He mixed plaster of Paris, poured the wet compound into the holes, and allowed it to set. When the mixture dried and the dirt was chipped away, what was revealed was astonishing and poignant for its clarity. From the absence of the empty cavities of Herculaneum, human forms of white plaster emerged. These airholes turned out to be the citizens who lived there, the people who were at lunch that fateful early afternoon in AD 79 when Vesuvius erupted. The white plaster casts revealed the final detailed images of the families that died: of men hiding their heads from the ash, of mothers cradling children, a dog rolled up on his back, still on a chain. They had asphyxiated and their bodies were covered with molten ash and had hardened into casings. Under the ash their flesh and bones decomposed and the ashes solidified until all that was left was the precise outline of where a body used to be. It was, in essence, a death mask of the body, and those recovered holes the only evidence of the actual inhabitants of the two cities (figure 1).

Derrida asks, "Is there a history of silence?" Looking at the poignant forms as (im)material witnesses that emerged from the absence of Pompeii, such a history does indeed seem acutely possible, acutely necessary. What follows is an exegesis of another kind of absence, equally empty, equally necessary. Using a series of case studies (a recently uncovered site of a colonial American playhouse at Williamsburg, whose only physical remains are the empty postholes

Figure 1   Plaster casts from Pompeii

that once supported the structure; maps of playhouses no longer extant; printer's receipts of lost playbills; the burned library of a nineteenth-century historian), I offer a reading of absent and (im)material evidence. The intent is not to argue for the reconstruction of the theatre or playbills, or a company's roster, or a provincial circuit, but rather to evoke the potent ghost of performance and the desire for it where it left little material trace of itself, to reassert its absent presence back into the cultural landscape of colonial America, and back into the narrative of the history of performance in the period.

1. Working Up from Postholes ᴥ

There was once a circuit of theatres that extended along the eastern seaboard of British North America and across the Anglophone islands of the West Indies, from Halifax, Nova Scotia, to Fredericksted, St. Croix. Some were the permanent properties of the managers of professional London-trained acting companies who toured, performed during the court seasons and public times, and rented them out in their absence. Some were found spaces—converted warehouses, tobacco barns, Freemason lodges—bought, rented, and fitted up for a season and sold again at the player's departure. Some were the speculation of local merchants who built them because theatre could be a lucrative investment. They were all part of a North American provincial circuit loosely known as "America" to the eighteenth-century Anglophone world that made little cultural distinction between Bridgetown, Barbados, and Charleston, South Carolina; Providence, Rhode Island; or Halifax, Nova Scotia. The colonial capitals—Kingston, Philadelphia, New York, Williamsburg—tended to support the better companies for extended seasons and host permanent playhouses, while smaller hamlets, like New Bern, North Carolina, Fredericksburg, Virginia, or Frederickstead, St. Croix, saw only seasonal or occasional visits of rogue companies. In the interim between appearances, audiences kept up on their "theatrical intelligence": they read plays, formed amateur companies, discussed London theatre news that was circulated in American newspapers, and traveled great distances to the capitals when the professional companies appeared. All were important in the establishment of a permanent theatre culture between 1750 and 1774.

Next to nothing of this circuit has survived, and little of the theatre culture. There are, for example, no preserved colonial American playhouses and hardly even a reliable image of one.[1] But we are getting closer to recovering one.

As James Deetz has wryly and rightly observed, archeology is often a very expensive way to confirm what historians already know. But in the case of one colonial American playhouse, historians knew next to nothing prior to the discovery and excavation of the site. Through a recent and meticulous excavation, the remains of a 1760 playhouse, built in Williamsburg, Virginia, by David Douglass of the American Company, have been discovered and is currently under reconstruction. As difficult as it is to interpret material culture, in the case of much of the evidence that follows, we have not even the luxury of artifacts, but rather the residue where material culture once was, imprints of a stage floor, postholes where posts stood. We are working up from postholes, working back, from the (im)material to the material.

THE DISCOVERY OF A PLAYHOUSE

In 1999 archeologists from the Colonial Williamsburg Foundation (CWF) began a full-scale excavation on two lots adjacent to the capitol, bounded by Duke of Gloucester, Francis, and Eastern (now Waller) streets, as well as the Capitol Square. It was a major dig, covering so large an area because the exact location of their target was unknown. They were looking for a theatre known in its day as "the old playhouse near the Capitol." The most reliable plat map of the area, the so-called Frenchman's map of 1782, was created after the theatre had been pulled down, though the site was still known to residents at the time as "where the playhouse lately stood" four years later. Merchants on the Exchange—the east end of town—like William Willis, a gunsmith, might advertise as having "lately opened a shop near the playhouse," but "near" is nowhere to put a shovel.[2] So the dig was wide, large, and largely exploratory.

The playhouse was originally built by David Douglass in September of 1760 and was used by his American Company from 1760 to 1772. In the absence of the American Company, it was rented to other actors—William Verling's Virginia Company—as well as to itinerant preachers and once was fitted up for a school. But neither Douglass nor his tenants left any description of the building.

If archeologists knew little of its location, theatre historians knew less. Neither William Young, in his collection of early American playhouses, nor Brooks McNamara, in his study of eighteenth-century American playhouses, make any mention of it at all.[3] Earlier excavations on the same quest were ultimately daunted. James Knight undertook the first dig, cross-trenching two lots near the capitol in the late 1930s—he dug diagonal trenches a shovel-width wide and a shovel-length apart. By chance or good sense Knight partially uncovered the pit of the playhouse. But Knight's excavation turned north and found only nineteenth-century fence lines and the dig was abandoned as too disturbed to yield anything useful. In the process Knight uncovered three fragmentary sections of brick foundation, none of which appears to be related to the theatre.[4]

CWF returned to the project in 1999 with a more sophisticated team of archeologists. The first year of digging on the rear of the two lots next to Moir's Stable progressed slowly and evidence was meager. The picture, however, changed dramatically in June 2000 when the archeologists uncovered the first of a series of large, rectangular postholes, running a substantial length from east to west across lot 30, known as "Moir's lot." When the line finally turned sharply 90° to the north, forming the corner of the building, now with identifiable and recognizable dimensions, Williamsburg's elusive playhouse began to emerge.[5]

From the outline of postholes it was determined that the building was indeed the playhouse, whose exterior dimensions—72' in length and 44' in width—were similar to that of Douglass's other colonial playhouses. For example, the Queen Street Theatre that Douglass built in Charleston in 1763 was known to be 75' in length and 35' in width. Indeed, a surviving lease of the Queen Street Theatre offered valuable information upon which to base strong conjecture about the architecture of the Williamsburg site as the plot emerged.[6] Moreover, the dimensions were largely similar to many provincial English theatres of the period (Bath, Plymouth, Colchester, Margate, Worcester, Penzance, Richmond, Ipswich).[7] The postholes themselves were of a structurally substantial size. Measuring nearly 3' in depth, the rectangular posts that once occupied the postholes had supported a very large structure, at least two stories in height. Further research revealed a preserved purchase agreement dating from 1786 from a local contractor who obtained a large quantity of bricks from the theatre in that year.[8] It was thus posited that bricks were used in-between the posts on the first story of the building to form "a substantial foundation," while the posts supported the load of the wooden upper stories. This design seems to concur with the construction used later for the Southwark Theatre in Philadelphia that Douglass built in 1766, the second Annapolis Theatre, 1771, and the Church Street Theatre in Charleston, 1773.[9] All had a bricked-in foundation or ground floor and a framed-in wooden second story. The lease from the Church Street playhouse is preserved, documenting the construction as "a Brick foundation at least ten feet in height above the surface of the ground and thereupon a wooden frame of good and substantial materials to be filled up with Bricks and also covered with brick on the outside with proper Necessary and convenient doors, windows, locks, hinges, bolts, and other Materials."[10] The heavy post-in-ground and brick fill seem to suggest that Williamsburg's playhouse was built on a similar plan, and because it was built earlier than the other three, its success led Douglass to replicate it in subsequent colonial cities.

Brooks McNamara had wondered aloud whether "Douglass developed some sort of master plan for a theatre that he carried with him from place to place," and had noted the similarities of his later playhouses. Although McNamara made no mention of the 1760 playhouse (little was known of it), his impulses have indeed proved correct. It now appears that the Williamsburg theatre may have been the prototype, the model colonial theatre that Douglass would follow when building theatres in other cities (figure 2).[11]

The pit, 22' × 18.5' (north–south by east–west), sloped down slightly toward the stage. A robbed-out brick foundation separated the stage from the pit. The stage ran from the edge of the pit to the back of the theatre, a length of 33.5' × 30' (east–west by north–south), roughly half the interior size of the house. Further evidence indicates that part of the area below the stage (toward the pit) had also been dug out. Although not large enough to be dressing rooms, the space may have allowed access to grave-traps and perhaps even machinery, as machinery for changing scenes became an increasingly important part of the stage spectacle in Douglass's repertory.[12]

21

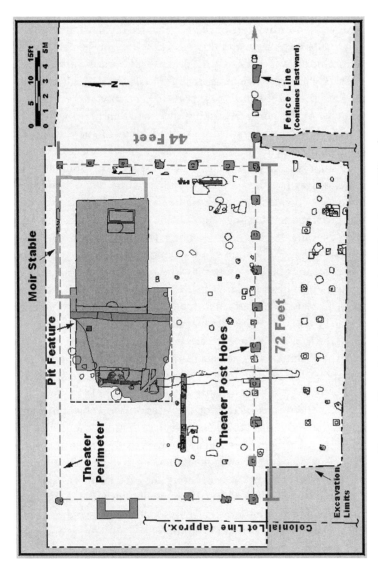

Figure 2   The archeological map of the 1760 playhouse, Williamsburg

Along the western exterior line of postholes, remnants of a C-shaped robbed-out foundation survive, which suggests support for the main entrance along the west wall and opening directly onto the Capitol Square. We know from the nota benes recorded on playbills that the theatre also had a stage door, and this was likely to be in the north wall, but the entire north wall (fronting the street) had been disturbed, and the location of the stage door thus unconfirmed. Interestingly, within the rectangular plan of the playhouse both the entrance and the pit appear to be offset to the north. Assuming that the auditorium was relatively symmetrical along its lengthwise axis and followed the dimensions of Douglass's subsequent theatres (70' × 30'), the south side of the building had approximately 14' of extraneous space. This southern "shed" was enclosed within the post-in-ground structure of the building, but architecturally divided by a brick wall, whose foundation survived, suggesting green rooms, dressing rooms, scene sheds, or even temporary residences for minor actors in the company during court season when lodging was tight.[13] The southern shed might also have served as storage for the company's bulkier properties when the actors hubbed out of the capital for their brief sojourns to the James River and Rappahonock hamlets, like Fredericksburg, Norfolk, or Petersburg. The presence of such storage rooms may suggest that this was their home theatre.

From the lean footprint a great deal of physical information has been gathered. The dimensions, the stage, the raked pit, the door and porch, the postholes for gallery support, the understage space, the southern shed. But beyond the shell of the building, playbills for this theatre supplement the reconstruction of the interior. We know, for example, there was the traditional box, pit, and gallery division, though the boxes have left no archeological residue. The boxes surrounded the pit, and the front box was directly over the entrance vestibule. These appear to have been rather narrow, at least along the pit's northern edge where they did not exceed 4' in width. There would have been a pit passage, leading from the vestibule, and a traditionally tight, winding stairwell that led up to the gallery that sat on top of the front boxes and was the area that offered the most affordable seating. We know that the stage did not offer direct access to the auditorium though there was a temptation toward stage sitting that the manager discouraged from the many admonitions affixed to the evening's bill, that "no one will be admitted at the stage door."

Where we are wanting solid archeological information, descriptions from other Douglass playhouses may be useful. For example, Philadelphia's Southwark Theatre, built in 1766, also seems to have been modeled on the 1760 Williamsburg playhouse. A hitherto unnoticed interior description has survived from a former resident of Philadelphia, Jacob Mordecai, who recalled entering the Southwark Theatre and immediately moving through "a long passage, not well lighted, to the pit, which opened by a door on one side, the left; the other was the west wall of the passage. British band formed the orchestra, 12 Regimental centinels stood near the stage. Boxes one on each side."[14] The Williamsburg playhouse likely contained many of these features: certainly a pit passage, side boxes, and a dedicated orchestra space, though none has left an archeological record. From other written descriptions, we learn that several of Douglass's playhouses underwent interior remodeling, usually involving the addition of a second tier of boxes, upper boxes, that were accessible from the stage. This was certainly true in Annapolis and the John Street Theatre in New York, and it may have been expedient for the Williamsburg playhouse as well, particularly in court season when the players could perform six nights a week, and sometimes in the afternoons as well.

From these findings, Douglass's 1760 Williamsburg playhouse can once again begin to take its place in the topography of the town. In the urban text of Williamsburg, the playhouse loomed large. In its day, the two- or three-story theatre would have been clearly visible along the length of the Duke of Gloucester Street, certainly the largest building on the Exchange (the eastern street of coffeehouses and taverns); it would have been a prominent feature punctuating the low-slung profile of the Williamsburg skyline.[15] As noted, at ground level the theatre's foundation was brick, but the upper story or stories were of frame construction and probably painted red, as many eighteenth-century playhouses were.[16]

SPACE AND PLACE

Of greater importance is what such a playhouse might have meant in the topography of colonial Williamsburg. This was not a temporary building, like the sail loft on Cruger's Wharf in New York that Douglass refitted for a season in the winter of 1758–1759 before it reverted back to storage or the 1751 Murray–Kean playhouse in Williamsburg that was later converted back to a dwelling. This was a permanent, purpose-built theatre, a substantial brick and timber edifice, situated, not on the fringes of the town, outside the city, but on Capitol Square, at the center of colonial power, and it was the seat of an emerging contest between British-appointed governors and the elected House of Burgesses, a contest that would be soon define itself as "national" struggle.

The monumental nature of the playhouse was also a bid for visibility designed to distance the American Company from the strollers of the previous decade. When the Hallam Company played in Williamsburg on their inaugural tour of 1752–1753, they occupied and refitted the old Murray–Kean playhouse, a space so far at the Eastern edge of town that Charles Durang succinctly described as "[i]t stood in the woods," and added that "the actors were wont to cater for their tables by shooting game" from the doors and windows of the playhouse.[17] In 1759 in Philadelphia, Douglass was obliged to build his first playhouse outside the city limits and the city's jurisdiction. The shift, the following year, to erect a permanent playhouse next to the capitol was a strategic choice to promote the idea of theatre from the peripheries of the culture to a permanent fixture in the civic and cultural landscape. "Art and architecture seeks visibility," writes Yi-Fu Tuan in his *Space and Place* (164), and Douglass appears to have had visibility in mind when he moved the playhouse to the site near the capitol. The choice was a statement of arrival. The playhouse at the heart of the city meant at one level that theatre in colonial America was repositioning itself in space and time in a bid for visibility, residency, legitimacy, and endurance. Indeed, the centrality of theatre to Virginia culture at least was remarked upon by one traveler with a fine eye for parsing out such distinctions. Noah Webster, the lexicographer, observed: "it seems to be the taste of the Virginians to fix their churches as far as possible from town and their playhouses in the center."[18]

The 1760 playhouse was not only of great importance for Douglass and his bid for legitimacy, but it was also important to the idea of theatre. Prior to 1760, theatre was a temporary institution in colonial America and players were strollers. The Hallam Company that arrived in 1752 and departed in 1755 played each major city once and departed the continent. They converted spaces into brief playhouses that were reconverted upon their departure because they did not conceive of theatre as a permanent fixture of American culture. It was certainly not real in the sense that real estate is real. Even Douglass, when he arrived in New York in 1758 and in Philadelphia the following year, used temporary buildings. The construction of the playhouse in Williamsburg marked not only the beginning of residency for the American Company, but also the point when theatre as a permanent cultural feature arrived. The 1760 playhouse in Williamsburg was the permanent property of the company. Douglass bought the lot and raised, possibly by subscription, the playhouse, and he retained the title to both. Even when the players were not in town, the playhouse—and the idea of theatre—remained a durable feature of the colonial cultural and civic landscape. Moreover it was one of many playhouses that Douglass retained title to, long after the American Company departed the continent.

The pattern holds true for Annapolis as well. Douglass's first theatre there was "inconveniently located" at the south end of Charles Street, by the water on Acton's Cove.[19] When he rebuilt, he chose a site at the heart of town, by the capitol and the church. Indeed the land on which he raised his playhouse originally belonged to St. Anne's Vestry. The new playhouse faced both the church and the state house in the concentrated urban hub of the hill. Again, in Kingston, Jamaica. When Douglass returned to the port city in 1775, he built a new theatre in the center of town, right off King's Street, the major street, at the north end of the parade.

The presence of such a substantial building on such an significant site is important to bear in mind because there has not been a playhouse there since the timbers were dismantled and the last bricks sold off in 1786. But the need to evoke the ghost of the playhouse remains vital to the narrative of colonial American theatre because its absence, like the absence of much genuine performance evidence from the period, has left a monumental void, filled instead—particularly in the early period—with an incommensurate amount of legal evidence—court records, antitheatrical prohibitions, and legislation—and there is something very disturbing about a performance history written from nonperformative evidence.

In this case the performance records of Douglass's 1760 season in Williamsburg are woefully scant. A few brief references alert us that players were in town, but neither playbills nor newspaper notices have survived from this season, and no record whatsoever is made of the new playhouse.[20] But the absence of evidence is not the same as no evidence. Of that season that left us little, left us postholes, and in this case, postholes may be enough.

THE LIMINAL, THE CRIMINAL, AND THE CITIZEN

The 1760 playhouse in Williamsburg was only one of many theatres that Douglass owned and maintained. He had only been on the continent for less than two years, and had already built three theatres and converted two others. Over the next decade he would build and retain eight more. I want to consider what ownership meant for the touring manager, particularly in the absence of a resident company.

David Mays, in his article "The Achievements of the Douglass Company in North America: 1758–1774," suggests that Douglass's greatest accomplishment was the overcoming of opposition to the theatre. Mays writes; "Reducing and neutralizing this opposition to the theatre is perhaps the Douglass Company's most impressive achievement."[21] Assuming the ontological position of theatre as intruder, Mays defines Douglass by his ability to mitigate the intrusion. At one level, Douglass indeed seemed to be quite adept at winning influential friends, negotiating with authorities, and overcoming both moral and economic opposition to the players. But Mays makes only a slight and passing reference in his final sentence about the permanent playhouses that Douglass built and owned, and yet it may well have been ownership of these playhouses that afforded Douglass the civic status to overcome opposition to the theatre, and allowed his company the degree of residence and success that eluded both his predecessors and his contemporaries. I would like to contrast Douglass's ownership with the practices of two other companies—Lewis Hallam's Company of Comedians from London eight years earlier and William Verling's Virginia Company, a contemporary—to expose Douglass's strategic, though burdensome, management choice that allowed for his success when the other two fared less well. What promoted the institution of theatre (a concept that struggled in the colonies since the first litigation surrounding the performance of *The Beare and the Cubb* in 1665) to a permanent position in colonial culture may have been partly or largely attributed to Douglass's ownership of playhouses. By retaining title and lease to the property, he kept theatre ontologically real—in the sense that real estate is real—insisting on the presence of theatre, even in the absence of a company.

The Liminal

Eight years before Douglass and the American Company built their playhouse in Williamsburg, Lewis Hallam and his company arrived in Williamsburg—early summer of 1752—and after a protracted contest to secure permission to play, Hallam bought the old Murray–Kean "playhouse" from Alexander Finnie for £150 on August 17, 1752, and converted it to a "regular theatre."[22] They opened their playhouse "in the woods" a month later and though advertisements were scarce, they probably enjoyed a healthy inaugural season. Quite early in the season (November) Williamsburg resident George Gilmer had noted: "Notwithstanding they take so much money never were debts worse paid." This was the same Gilmer who had cautioned the city council back in June that there was not ready money enough in the town to support a troupe of players. "The money," he continued in his November letter, "kept burning till they opened and then it flew among this Association of indigent wretches with a lavishness you would be surprised at."[23] It must have flown indeed. At the conclusion of the spring court session (mid-May 1753), Hallam's company was indebted to John Stretch, printer and postmaster, Edward Charlton, barber and peruke maker, as well as the unpaid balance on the playhouse. On May 19, 1753, Hallam mortgaged the playhouse to Stretch and Charlton for company debts—in spite of an outstanding bond of security to Finnie. A partial list of his actors' debts has been gleaned from the records of the *York County Judgement and Orders*: To John Stretch four company actors owed £46 and change, while to Edward Charlton four members owed £14. Thomas Clarkson, another actor in the company, owed Alexander Finnie, as did Charles Bell, both of whom defaulted on their debts on June 18, 1753.[24] The full extent of the debts may not be known but collectively it represented a sufficient amount that a lien was placed on the playhouse against the company's return to Williamsburg for the fall court in October. At the bottom of Charlton's *Day Book* is written, "If debts paid by 20 October 1753, this is void."[25] But the company did not return; they went to New York instead, where they encountered initial difficulties and could not or chose not to send back money. The Williamsburg debts went unpaid, the lien expired, the playhouse was forfeited, and claimants, Finnie, Charlton, and Stretch, immediately went to court over ownership. The names are bogus:

> Seth Seekright, plt. against Barnaby Badtitle, def. in ejectnt. for 2 lots of land contiguous together whereon the Playhouse now stands in the Parish of Bruton in the Co. of York at the demise of John Stretch and Edward Charlton.[26]

Hallam had washed his hands of the town, abandoned the playhouse, and did not return. Nor did the Hallam Company have permanent intentions in the colony of New York. Once permission was secured, Hallam raised a new playhouse—in a town that had seen at least three prior temporary playhouses—and his company played for a substantial season, performing three nights a week for six months. Yet at the conclusion, again he neither made plans to retain the building nor made plans to return to the city, though to their credit they did advertise to pay off their debts. Lewis Hallam sold his new theatre at Nassau Street to a congregation of German Calvinists and moved on to Philadelphia. This pattern established the Hallam Company as strollers, increasingly conscientious strollers, but strollers nonetheless with no intention of maintaining permanent property in or relations with the communities for whom they performed. They played each major city once, exhausted the thin markets, and then moved off the continent. The inaugural Hallam tour did little to alter the physical landscape of the colonial city: their playhouses were theatres of the day, and players were strollers, a rara avis on a flyway to elsewhere.

The Criminal

Eight years after Douglass built his 1760 playhouse, a rival company, William Verling's Virginia Company, played Williamsburg in late spring of 1768, and they too left a trail of debt, bad faith, at least two incarcerated actors, an absconded slave, and possibly an eloped wife—and no playhouse for bond or collateral. They were renters of Douglass's theatre, true strollers, the kind that gave players a bad reputation, what Cecil Price had aptly called "fugitive companies."[27] Only days after their departure, Williamsburg tavern-keeper Jane Vobe advertised on June 30, 1768 the runaway of her slave Nanny who, she intimated "has gone off with some of the comedians who have just left this town, with some of whom, as I have been informed, since she went off, she had connections, and was seen very busy talking privately with some of them."[28] The freewheeling and libertine lifestyle of the stroller may well have offered a release from the bonds of another kind of servitude. The Reverend Isaac Gilberne of Williamsburg, in a letter to Landon Carter, dated July 8, 1768, lamented the past elopement of his wife, who, he is "credibly informed," kept company "every night with some strolling players."[29]

In spite of its name, the Verling's Virginia Company had no residence and little allegiance to the colony of Virginia, and their brief sojourn in Williamsburg was marked by an alarming amount of legal and public grievances for a small company that had been in town for less than three months. George Walker (an actor in the company) sued for debt Richard Ferrell, Thomas Charlton, and James Godwin, all fellow actors in the company. James Godwin, in turn, was also sued for debt recovery by Williamsburg merchants Charles Miles and Samuel Hill.[30] On May 16, actor Christopher Bromage was sued for debt by Obediah Holt and forcibly detained. He remained in custody until a benefit performance was arranged for August 1, after which he left the colony.[31] Three other members of his company—William Burdett, Frederick Spencer, and David Jefferson—also had suits pending in York County.[32] William Verling, the manager, naturally took the brunt of legal assaults, all debt related. On May 16, Verling was sued for debt recovery in separate cases by Matthew Moody, Henry Tucker, and Jonathan Prosser.[33] On June 20, Thomas Younghusband and Joseph Scrivenor, in separate suits, added their claims against Verling for debt. When court closed, a writ of habeas corpus was issued against Verling, "returnable to the next court."[34] By that date Verling had left Williamsburg, failed to appear for his court appointment, and a judgment against his estate was issued for £21.[35] At the same time, Charles Parker, an actor, was arrested and detained for debt. Further recovery attempts against Verling dismissed him as "not an Inhabitant of the County."[36]

If litigation was heavy in Virginia, their stint in Williamsburg was just a rehearsal of the bad faith they would leave in Annapolis. In the Anne Arundel County Judgement and Order books for 1768–1769, William Verling occupies what must be a litigious record of continuous entries: a full 32 consecutive pages of suits. In the court records of Annapolis, Verling is a chapter to himself. Litigants came from as far away as Williamsburg for a piece of him. As manager, he was the default target of his company's debts, as well as his own, and the company's debts were legion. Charles Wallace, plaintiff, had a suit again Verling for £8.6.9 and damages; Francis Frazier sued Verling on behalf of his deceased brother at the same June court. Richard Charleton pressed his case from Williamsburg against Verling for outstanding debts as did Sarah Hallam—Lewis Hallam's estranged wife who had a boarding house in Williamsburg and had lodged both Verling and Charles Parker, while Annapolis tavern keeper Samuel Middleton sued the actor James Godwin. They were followed up in the same court by Edward Charleton for back wages. Robert Jones, actress Sarah Jones's husband, also sued Verling for £8.15 of his wife's back wages. Even his lawyer, Samuel Chase, the future signer of the Declaration, was obliged to carry Verling to suit to recover his own legal expenses. He inventoried Verling's "goods and chattells" and settled for an indentured servant, Oliver Anderson, "having 2 years and 5 months to serve." It would be all anyone got out of Verling. When the fall court reconvened, more suits were waiting. William Hardy added his name to the list of plaintiffs, but Verling had sailed off, carrying his company to the outer Caribbean where they renamed themselves The Leeward Island Company and opened in St. Croix.[37]

Statistically speaking, this is a rather high rate of litigation in the wake of one season's work. Such an attitude toward their markets characterized the Virginia Company as a sort of pirate raid on the economy of the colony: they came, they plundered, they absconded. Verling neither built theatres nor owned theatres, nor did he maintain buildings, leases, or residency in the colonies in which he worked. Like Lewis Hallam before him, Verling was ever a resident of elsewhere, legally, or so the court described him, "not an Inhabitant of the County."

The Citizen

In sharp contrast to the practices of his predecessors and contemporaries, David Douglass managed his American Company with an eye toward permanence, as a property holder and part-time citizen of the communities for which he played. To this end, Douglass developed a sustainable practice that included the building, maintaining, and leasing of permanent playhouses, like the 1760 playhouse in Williamsburg. Though the markets of colonial America were still too small to support a resident company, and touring was thus inevitable, Douglass nonetheless was careful to position his company not as strollers raking the frugal resources out of the small economies in a one-time raid, but as seasonal residents engaged in a sustainable relationship with the community, residing and returning to the capitals, sometimes biannually. Central to this new social positioning was the ownership of property.

Douglass built and maintained permanent playhouses in seven colonial cities, to which the American Company returned regularly, including Williamsburg. Though we do not have the original contract of the 1760 playhouse in Williamsburg, other surviving records suggest that Douglass built the theatre—as he would in many other colonial cities—by community subscription, on lots he had purchased, and retained the title to both property and playhouse long after the season had closed and the company moved on. This pattern afforded him a guaranteed place of residence when the company returned to each city, and no doubt mitigated against the need of securing and resecuring permission to play with each visit.

Records of many such contracts are preserved for the Annapolis Theatre; the Southwark Theatre in Philadelphia; the John Street Theatre in New York; Petersburg and Norfolk, Virginia; Kingston, Spanish Town, and Montego Bay, Jamaica; and the long-term lease of the Church Street theatre in Charleston. A look at the surviving subscription schemes, leases, and titles reveal much of the strategy that Douglass employed to establish his residency in the many communities for whom he played.

In Annapolis, Douglass built his new playhouse by a subscription scheme that provided the capital for both property and playhouse.

William Eddis, a surveyor, recorded a few of the details:

> Our governor . . . patronizes the American Company; and as their present place of exhibition is in a small scale, and inconveniently situated, a subscription by his example has been rapidly completed to erect a new theatre, on a commodious, if not an elegant plan. The manager is to deliver tickets for two seasons, to the amount of the respective subscriptions, and it is imagined, that the money which will be received at the doors from the non-subscribers will enable him to conduct the business without difficulty; and when the limited number of performances is completed, the entire property is to be vested in him.[38]

Such was the plan and, backed by the Governor, it was a successful one. Douglass built the new playhouse in 1771 on subscription funds and retained title to both it and the property. After he and the American Company left the city, Douglass contracted with the same prominent lawyer who sued Verling, Samuel Chase, to act as a rental agent for the property. Chase rented the building to St. Anne's Parish as a church:

> The Vestry agreed with Mr. Quynn on behalf of Mr. Douglass to allow him the Sum of Twenty pounds yearly for the use of the Playhouse for a Church for this Parish.[39]

This is all the more profitable when the terms of the original lease are revisited. Douglass leased the lot from William Reynolds, who ran what is still Reynold's Tavern and owned much of what is lot 60, off Church Circle bounded by West Street. Douglass took out a 38-year lease on the lot in 1772 for £6.6 per annum. For a man touching 50, he was thinking long term indeed. After his company departed the colony, Douglass sublet the property to the church, netting nearly £14 profit a year on the sublease.

Similarly in Philadelphia we learn quite late in Douglass's career that he had retained title to the Southwark Theatre he had built in that city in 1766 for nearly 20 years. On April 1, 1785, Douglass sold the playhouse to Philadelphia printer Thomas Bradford. Douglass's stepson, Lewis Hallam, Jr., was the agent of the sale, given what we would call power of attorney the previous year. The details read, "David Douglass, late of the city of Philadelphia, but now of the island of Jamaica, esquire, by Lewis Hallam, late of the said island of Jamaica but now of the said city of Philadelphia, for five hundred pounds Pennsylvania currency," transferred the property from Douglass to Bradford.[40] The American Company had used their Southwark Theatre intermittently between 1767 and the fall of 1773, and Douglass had rented it after their departure, but at the time of sale, 12 years and a revolution had passed since the company last visited Philadelphia; Douglass, now retired, finally let go of his theatre in the city in which he struggled so hard to establish it.[41]

In New York, Douglass's John Street Theatre was left in the proxy of Hugh Gaine, the printer. Gaine rented the space for Douglass to clients in his absence and thus maintained it as a playhouse. One of his clients was the British military, who rented the space intermittently from 1775 to 1782. Recorded in the published receipts and disbursements for the years 1780–1781 are two noteworthy items: "Cash paid to Mr. Hugh Gaine, on Account of Rent—£50. Cash Paid Towards liquidating a Debt incurred by the late Managers of the Philadelphia Theatre, £227-14-8."[42] Gaine was using the rental of the playhouse to settling old debts.

Douglass retained two additional theatres in Jamaica, in Kingston and in Spanish Town. After his death, his widow Mary Douglass remarried and sold the playhouse in Kingston. A decade later, his son-in-law, Hyacinth Daly, petitioned the city to recover back rent on the theatre in Spanish Town, being the only surviving heir.[43]

Rental notices also provide indirect evidence of Douglass's playhouses in the smaller hamlets of Norfolk and Petersburg, Virginia, of which we know little else. Permanent theatres at both of these sites have hitherto only been the subject of speculation, but diary entries of several itinerant Methodist preachers reveal rental arrangements for the playhouses in Norfolk, Williamsburg, and Petersburg.[44] Joseph Pilmore, traveling through Virginia in the summer of 1772, rented the playhouse in Norfolk. The curious thing is not that a preacher rented the playhouse—Pilmore rented the playhouse in Williamsburg as well, playhouses held more people than the courthouse—but that there is a permanent playhouse there at all. Norfolk does not seem to host a theatrical season, per se, but rather only an occasional visit from a company between court seasons in Williamsburg. Three or four weeks a year—December and January—were the only known performances there. Yet Douglass built a dedicated playhouse there and it is known as such, not the Pottery or a warehouse, where the Murray–Kean Company had played 20 years earlier, and has been traditionally recorded.[45] Douglass also built a permanent playhouse in Petersburg, up the James river, by the early 1770s, though it too boasted only an occasional visit from the professional companies. The playhouse was rented by Gresset Davis and Nathaniel Young, when they invited the Methodist Minister Robert Williams to preach in 1773. Davis and Young rented the Theatre on Old Street for many years, hosted many visiting preachers, and used the playhouse as a Methodist meeting hall.[46]

In Charleston, South Carolina, Douglass entered a slightly different arrangement with the printer and stationer Robert Wells, and three other "gentlemen of Charleston" in 1773 whereby he would lease lot 40 (on the west side of Church Street) for a term of 15 years, for £5 down, and a rent of £100 per annum, erect a playhouse at his own cost, and provide an annual benefit for the lessors.[47] To build his playhouse, Douglass raised a subscription and built the Church Street playhouse on a plan modeled on the 1760 Williamsburg theatre ("a brick foundation at least ten feet in height above the surface of the ground and thereupon a wooden frame of good and Substantial materials to be filled up with Bricks and also covered with brick on the outside with proper Necessary and convenient doors, windows, locks, hinges, bolts, and other materials").[48] Between residencies in the colony, Douglass retained the long-term lease and sublet the theatre, as one advertisement of June of 1774 announces:

> The new Play-house in Church Street, during the absence of the American Company from this province, is to be let for the benefit of the charity fund of the Union-Kilwinning Lodge; and as it is now entirely vacant, any person desiring to rent the same for one or two years may apply for further particulars to Robert Wells.[49]

Douglass chose printers as his agents (Robert Wells, Hugh Gaine, William Bradford, and Jonas Green), allying himself with one of the most central merchants in any colony. By retaining the playhouses in the agency of printers allowed the players to secure a sort of residency that extended even in their absence. The playhouse remained a playhouse, and theatre was an indelible institution; even in the absence of the players the building held the promise of their return.

A similar lease or title arrangement may have been in place for the 1760 Williamsburg playhouse. Evidence of Douglass's theatrical activity are scarce for the fall of 1760 when the playhouse was built and opened, but a few surviving later notices establish Douglass as indeed owner of the playhouse. From the receipt books of James Southall, printer and proprietor of the Raleigh Tavern, we learn that Southall rented the theatre from Douglass on at least two occasions and settled the debt when the company returned to town:

> Recvd. May 22 1772 of James Southall Sixteen Pounds Two Shillings in full for the yous [*sic*] of the play hous. P[ayment] R[eceived] D. B. Roberts.[50]

D. B. Roberts was an actor and business manager in the American Company. From the same receipt book we also learn that the previous year Roberts collected from Southall "seven pounds two shillings in full for the Company. D. Douglass PR. D. B. Roberts."

Southall may have acted as rental agent for the many occasional entertainments and services that demanded the playhouse. William Verling's New American Company, for example, rented the space for a spring season in 1768, and in the following year Joseph McAuslane rented the playhouse for a school, and later for a dance academy. Peter Gardiner, a puppeteer, also rented the building that same year (1769) to exhibit his "curious set of figures." Gardiner would return in 1772 with an expanded show. That summer, the itinerant preacher Joseph Pilmore also rented the playhouse, all of which provided income in the absence of the company.[51]

A clue to how the playhouse was originally raised might be culled from the diaries of George Washington who recorded on October 8, 1760 that he spent £7.10.3 on "Play tickets." This unusually large amount—7s.6d was the standard box price from 1751 to 1770—coincided with the opening of the fall court (usually assembled for 24 days beginning October 10). Unless he treated the entire west wing of the House of Burgesses, such a sum would have represented numerous nights in a box seat—not confirmed by diary entries—at a playhouse that had only opened on October 2. Rather, such a large expenditure might be a record of his subscription to the building of the playhouse itself—as in Annapolis cited above—an investment that entitled the subscriber to a share of tickets. There is no further entry in his diary for tickets for the remainder of the court session, which is highly unusual for Washington who was an avid playgoer. It appears that Douglass, as he had elsewhere, purchased the lots with cash, but raised the playhouse by a ticket subscription scheme. Colonel Washington was one subscriber, and he settled his debt when he arrived for court.[52] For his £7.10.3, Washington received 20 (slightly discounted) box tickets that he used the remainder of the season, and thus had no further need to record them in his memorandum book of expenses.

Even in the company's absence the empty playhouse kept the idea of theatre alive, like the publication of plays created audiences through readership. Between periods of residency the playhouse remained, reminding the inhabitants of its presence and the promise of return. Ebenezer Hazard visited Annapolis in 1777, five years after the American Company had departed, but Hazard noted the playhouse and the Assembly Room as discerning marks of culture, though the theatre was locked up at the time. The traveler Peter Kalm described a church without a pastor as "a waiting church"—North Carolina was full of them, churches that shared preachers and were obliged to wait for one service a month—and perhaps we have something similar in the playhouse between seasons.[53] It was an image of permanence, even in the absence of the players.

In each case, the above records remind us that—unlike his pre-decessors—in many colonial cities, it was the absence of the players that was temporary, not the playhouse. Theatre remained ontologically real on the landscape. Because Douglass retained his playhouses, his presence extended well beyond his departure. He was, for example, able to leave outstanding accounts, as he did with several of the Williamsburg merchants, and return to settle them. Edward Charlton, the same Hallam creditor, was shaving, cutting hair, and dressing wigs for David Douglass, Lewis Hallam Jr., Mrs. Douglass, and Sarah Hallam, Lewis's estranged wife, in August of 1770, and the bills were charged against the company's return in November of the same year. Other members of the company enjoyed the same security. Owen Morris and the formerly bad risk Charles Parker both left accounts on August 13, 1770 that were carried over to the spring of 1771 and then settled.[54] When disputes arose, Douglass was there to guarantee the cost of recovery, as when Matthew Moody sued company member Thomas Byerly to recover debts in a breach of promise, and Douglass left the security for £7.1.6 and costs.[55] Conversely, Douglass was able to collect outstanding debts owed to the company on his return as well, as when Southall rented the playhouse in the company's absence. Without making too much of actors paying their debts, owning property accorded a documentable degree of good faith to Douglass and his company that was not granted to either their predecessors or their rivals. One absence worth reading is that Douglass's name never appeared in the Ann Arundel County Judgement and Order books, in Annapolis, where his rival William Verling occupied so much of the court's time in 1769. And Maryland lawyer Samuel Chase, who was obliged to take Verling to court for his own unpaid legal fees, acted as Douglass's rental agent and collected fees for the playhouse in the manager's absence.

THE BLOOMERY OF BENJAMIN GRYMES

With the arrival of David Douglass in Williamsburg in 1760, theatre in colonial America became an architectural inscription on the landscape, and the playhouse—even one rented afterward as a lodge or a day school—was more than a deferred cipher. The presence of the playhouse was a landmark of high culture on the provincial skyline or forested map. It was, like an English garden, an ornament to a town. But the towns could not support a permanent company. Between seasons, it held out a promise of a homecoming, a waiting church, a church without a preacher, but still a church. Even vacant, the playhouse remained an indelible presence on the landscapes of colonial cities, familiar, in the many advertisements of land lots for sale "next to the playhouse." Between stints in the 1760 playhouse in Williamsburg, the landmark was a familiar sign in the newspapers. William Page advertised lodging "fronting the playhouse"; Thomas Brammer, merchant, advertised his goods "opposite the playhouse"; and William Willis, gunsmith, "lately opened a shop near the playhouse."[56] Even after the playhouse was dismantled sometime in the late 1770s, its presence was still felt. As late as June 6, 1780, Samuel Major would purchase a lot of land from John Draper, "whereon the Old Playhouse lately stood." And seven years later, though the playhouse was long gone, most of its materials cannibalized, and the land on which it once stood covered with a new building, Humphrey Harwood did record in his account book for January 27, 1787 a purchase to "By Old bricks in the Play House."[57]

I am intrigued by this marking of the landscape by the theatre, particularly in the absence of the company. It was being remembered far beyond its occupancy and there is something in the persistence of that memory that should alert us to the strength of the position the theatre occupied in the cultural imagination. I speak of this position later as "desire," and suggest it can (perhaps should) be read as one form of performance's potency.

I want to close with a final brief example from another riverside hamlet, Fredericksburg, Virginia, on the Rappahonock. Fredericksberg was like many tidewater Tobacco towns with landing warehouses and a river ferry built below the falls that necessitated river barges to stop and roads to start. Enterprising merchants, like William Allason, set up one-stop mercantiles, ferries, and wagoneer services, and the town gathered business from up and down the river. In 1760 it boasted a market square, a Long Ordinary, several taverns, churches, a Freemason's lodge, and somewhere visiting players played and had played as early as the 1750s.

The Murray–Kean Company passed through Fredericksburg in 1751 and the Hallam Company a year later. David Douglass and the American Company occasionally played Fredericksburg in the decade that followed (we have playbills printed in Williamsburg with dates and plays penciled in). A few preserved oblique notices also survive in account books and diaries. William Allason, the merchant of Falmouth, left his laconic entries of money paid for tickets in Fredericksburg and Williamsburg. As a merchant Allason was obliged occasionally to travel to the capital at court season for his debt recovery suits, and there he attended the theatre as well. After the opening 1760–1761 season, Allason added new inventory to his Falmouth mercantile: plays; "21 plays of different kinds," he ordered from his London distributor in February of 1761.[58] Plays had become a commodity, hamlets and capitals alike.

A more generous description comes from Jonathan Clark, a deputy clerk of the court in Fredericksburg, who left an unpublished diary that occasionally records scanty evidence of his playgoing. He had neither Jefferson's education nor Washington's ambition, spent his summers rather lazily, playing cards and fishing until called to court as a deputy clerk. Clark was either misremembering, misinformed, or satirizing when he recorded attending performances of "Venus Preserved" and "Romulus and Juliet." What he does evidence is that small as Fredericksburg was, it was nonetheless capable of supporting the American Company for three months in the summer of 1771. Though we have no playhouse, no newspapers, and only three preserved playbills for their summer season, Clark attended performances on a dozen occasions between late May and mid-August 1771.[59]

And here in 1770—not an English-raised governor, but a Virginia merchant and developer—Benjamin Grymes speculated on a playhouse. Grymes, whose holdings and plans for the development of Fredericksburg occasionally found him overextended and ultimately bankrupt, had purchased several lots and buildings in the new extension of lower Princess Anne Street, and in September of 1770, Grymes advertised a large framed building, formerly a "bloomery" (iron works), as available with three lots of ground for a potential playhouse site. It would make, wrote he, "a good theatre, which might be beneficial to the town in general, and country adjacent, if proper persons, and of good demeanor were to perform."[60] Even in rural hamlets like Fredericksburg, Halifax, and New Bern, theatre as real estate and a civic and civilizing institution was becoming desirable.

2. Mr. Sauthier's Maps ∾

"A DREARY WASTE" AND THE GOVERNOR'S GARDEN

At last America is in my view; a dreary Waste of white barren sand, and melancholy, nodding pines. In the course of many miles, no cheerful cottage has blest my eyes. All seems dreary, savage, and desert . . . My heart dies within me, while I view it, and I am glad of an interruption by the arrival of a pilot-boat, the master of which appears a worthy inhabitant of the woods before us. "Pray sir," I said to him, "does any body live hereabouts?" "Hereabouts," returned he in a surly tone, "don't you see how thick it is settled?"

Janet Schaw, *The Journal of a Lady of Quality*

So Janet Schaw described North Carolina when she regretfully arrived in that "dreary waste" in March of 1775. To the surly pioneer it was already settled, downright overpopulated; to the Scottish gentlewoman in the second wave of emigrants, it was a desert, devoid of any familiar civilizing effects. The expectations of the two residents—old and new—speak of the great reordering of colonial America that occurred between 1760 and 1775. Archeologists of Anglo-America, like James Deetz, Mark Leon, and Parker Potter, refer to it as the Georgian world view, as they have written extensively about this transition from survival culture to genteel culture that played across a broad sweep of colonial America: in dinnerware, architecture, the concentration of wealth and the concomitant consumption of imported goods, the creation of social clubs, finishing schools, and musical societies.[1] We recognize it as the rapid gentrification, sometimes bewilderingly so (as in the case study of Albany, New York discussed below, with the sudden arrival of British soldiers): new manners, new money, no goods, new moralities, new social sensibilities. The playhouse, as a spectacle space, had no small part in the social realignment as pioneer settlers of the 1740s accommodated, resisted, or aspired to the new Georgian urbanity of the 1760s. Ultimately, to consider what a playhouse might have meant in such a transitional culture we need to look at the most barren geographic landscape that ever supported a playhouse. And for that, we turn to the dreary land that Janet Schaw described: North Carolina, 1768, under the government of William Tryon.

In the feral, underdeveloped colony of North Carolina, a material amenity, like a playhouse, a book-seller, Josiah Wedgwood dinnerware, or even a proper English garden, was a thing to be proud of indeed. For despite the surly captain's boast of how thickly settled the land was, North Carolina was the poorest, least populated, and least developed of the southern colonies. The Scottish immigrant James Murray, writing in 1755, attributed the poverty and "thinness" of the colony to two practices, both peculiar to the colony: accepting no credit but paper money and "being able to hold a great quantity [of land] at a low rent without Cultivation."[2] Thin indeed. North Carolina was, after all, even in 1768, a colony without even a major city; it was so geographically disadvantaged by a lack of deep-water ports and lengthy navigable rivers, encumbered with barrier reefs and inland swamps, and surrounded by a foreboding seaboard ring of outer banks that severely restricted its trans-Atlantic commerce. It was, all in all, a colony that seemed to be overlooked or bypassed by many commercial venturers, beyond the staple river barge traffic of tobacco, hemp, and grain. Until 1766, North Carolina had neither a capital nor a capitol building; courts moved from county to county, and public records perished for want of a courthouse. It could not even support a newspaper. A printer, James Davis, had set up shop in New Bern in 1755 but did not find enough encouragement to support himself, and the *North Carolina Gazette* was discontinued by 1761—about the time Virginia and South Carolina were getting their second newspapers. In contrast to the governor's palace in Williamsburg, Virginia, the governor of North Carolina Arthur Dobbs had no official residence, but rather lived at his country seat outside Brunswick, which boasted in the late 1750s but 20 families. For the meeting of court and Assembly he groused of the poverty of renting a small town house "without either garden or field to keep either horse or cow."[3] The clergy were so few in North Carolina that at the death of Governor Dobbs none could be found to administer his funeral, and the former royal governor was buried by the justice of the peace.[4] When the new governor William Tryon arrived, to his shock, he observed that only one church in the town of New Bern was completed and the colony as a whole was so poorly equipped for religious service that he wrote back to London for a shipload of Bibles. Ten years later, itinerant preachers could still register surprise that churches in New Bern and Edenton could hold services no more than once every three weeks, obliged as they were to share ministers.[5]

Education, as an index of urbanity, was in an equally abysmal state. No public school could be found in the colony until 1767, and then raised only by private subscription. Private tutors were rare, public teachers nearly impossible to retain, and only a few North Carolinians ever arrived at any kind of higher education, even among the first families. Although Williamsburg was nearby, no North Carolinian attended the College of William and Mary before the Revolution. Only three students from the entire colony ever made it to Harvard before 1780, and of the legions of southerners who traveled to England for finishing, few to none hailed from North Carolina. Rogers Ekirch notes that of the 58 southerners who attended Cambridge or Oxford between 1720 and 1776, not one came from North Carolina.[6] All in all, the statistics do not promise a lot, and one feels for the want of an aspiring, educated, genteel community among the surly, the criminal, the undistinguished, and the uninterested. So concluded James Murray who settled there in the 1740s, "Bona terra, mala gens," and so concurred the anonymous French traveler who passed through in 1765 when he wrote of it in the worst of terms: "this province is the azilum [*sic*] of the Convicts that have served their time in Virginia and Maryland" (738).[7] A decade later Janet Schaw met a mathematician in North Carolina who complained of meeting no one in the entirety of the colony who knew enough math to understand him.

The general arrested state of cultural development was compounded by a lack of what we would call infrastructure. The scattered inns and ordinaries were notoriously discouraging to travel and travelers alike, with poor roads, scant victuals, and, worst of all, some complained, no liquor.[8] Even the actors avoided it. Both the Hallam Company and the American Company passed from Virginia to South Carolina, or Charleston to Philadelphia, with nary a layover in New Bern. Douglass would travel by overland road from Annapolis to Williamsburg, but by water to Charleston to avoid North Carolina's coach roads. Even by lean colonial standards, North Carolina was a backwater, and rightly did the anonymous French traveler conclude of it: "It's a fine country for poor people."[9]

And so when the 80-year-old Governor Dobbs finally died and William Tryon (1729–1788) was appointed to the post in late 1765, Tryon left England for the wilds of Carolina knowing enough about what he was getting into to carry with him a couple of good architects. John Hawkes would be America's first European-trained professional architect, and his appointment signals us to Tryon's project from the inception: the new governor went to build a colony in proper Georgian style. Hawkes was no carpenter, nor even an amateur master builder such as could be found occasionally in America, but a classically trained architect well versed in Palladio's four books and in the Renaissance aesthetic that would so inform the high Georgian order.[10] Hawkes's first major work would be the design and construction of the new governor's palace, a fitting official residence for a colonial governor, in New Bern. To find skilled craftsmen—masons, stonecutters—Hawkes was obliged to travel to Philadelphia. The governor's council levied a tax to underwrite the construction, and though there was grumbling—much grumbling—it was clear to the colony that Tryon's appointment would drag the colony into civility and impose upon it a determined Georgian order.[11]

Also in Tryon's entourage of new European professionals was Claude Joseph Sauthier, a 32-year-old French architect, draftsman, and surveyor. Sauthier's first commission from Governor Tryon was not to build, but to map the townships of the colony of North Carolina; it was a way of stocktaking of the province's resources before the building could even begin. If Tryon was ordering the land, he needed maps to do so.

Sauthier was not just a surveyor, such as Tryon could have found locally, but rather a trained architectural draftsman, whose *Architectura Civile* (Paris, 1763) was a manual for designing monumental and ornamental buildings: columns, porticos, pediments, landscape gardens for civic and private architecture. Sauthier represented the sort of civilizing force that characterized the second wave of many colonial emigrants and which many residents aspired to—including their governors—and sorely lacked when they found themselves transported to the wilds of America. He was one of the "Polite people" that Richard Bushman wrote of in his study of the refinement of early America, "[who] were bringing cities within the domain of genteel culture."[12] If one had a notion of mapping the Georgian order onto the wilds, Sauthier's book was exactly the sort of guide that would prove enormously useful for laying out towns and grounds on a proper European plan, for building up courthouses, English gardens, and provincial governor palaces on par with European residences. The problem was, of course, it was all too grand, too sudden, too Baroque to happen in the back-of-beyond. The carved capitals, pediments, and fluted columns that Sauthier proscribed and so longed to execute represented a European elegance that was beyond the resources of most of the colony. Though in the end little of it was realized, Sauthier's talent for the Baroque, and his appointment, should alert us to the shape of Tryon's dream. And in this case, it was the shape of the dream of the civilized that was important.

Governor Tryon seized on Sauthier and his gifts. Apart from his commission as draftsman, surveyor, and cartographer, Tryon also hired Sauthier to design the gardens at his new residency in New Bern. A proper English garden was the most urbane of marks on an otherwise wild landscape. Gardens—elegant, symmetrical, modeled after Versailles—were the stamp of the cultivated and a metaphorical mapping of Georgian culture onto the wilds of Carolina. Mark Leon has argued that emergence of landscape gardens in this period (1760–1775) reflects the rules of natural and social order, by which he means the ordering of the one naturalized the ordering of the other. Formal gardens, with perspective, prospects (constructed views), and balanced design, were thus "demonstrations" of the natural social order. But this reasoning could be applied to much of the layout of the new townscapes: a cultured imposition of natural, social, and geographic order mapped onto the vulgar spaces. Town plans, with their straight and symmetrical streets, intersecting at precise angles, hubbing around town centers, a governor's palace and gardens, or courthouse, were all part of the new constructed world of polite urbanity that men like Tryon and Sauthier were bringing to the wilderness towns of colonial America.

While palace and grounds were progressing, over the next 18 months (1768–1769) Sauthier functioned as designer, draftsman, and the governor's cartographer. In his capacity as the cartographer, he toured North Carolina and produced a series of maps of ten of the major hamlets of the colony, among them, New Bern, Halifax, Wilmington, Bath, Beaufort, Edenton.[13] The maps, when laid out, offer a poignant display of the magnitude of the civilizing project to come, displaying, as they do—as Janet Schaw described with a sigh—"the barren woods" of everything that was not there. The largest of North Carolina's towns had a population of less than 800 people, and the small geometric shapes of a few clustered houses on half-acre lots strain to claim endurance against the enormously overframed borders of forests. Some maps (like that of Halifax, the county seat, and Wilmington) were mostly trees, tracts and tracts of uncut woodlands, with three or four lean streets peeping out between the river and the one coach road to nowhere (figure 3). There is a curious compulsion at work in Sauthier's maps, an anxiety about the wilderness that situates the emerging towns, not with an eye toward their accomplishments (courthouses, capitols, churches), but within the vastness of the surrounding wilds, as if he were mapping everything that was not yet there. Overframed as they are with wilderness, the township itself occupies less than a eighth of the map; they are visual islands in the sea of woods, and their positioning as such seems to poignantly illustrate the magnitude of the governor's challenge. Sauthier's maps are a to-do list of everything that needs to get done.

Consider Sauthier's map of New Bern, the seat of the colonial governor: trees, woods, forests, one lone road, a hundred houses, and more trees, woods, and forests. How cultivated a space might seem a tidy English garden of the governor's palace against the woods that not border, but occupy and overwhelm most of the map of New Bern that Sauthier drew. How cultivated a space might seem a playhouse?

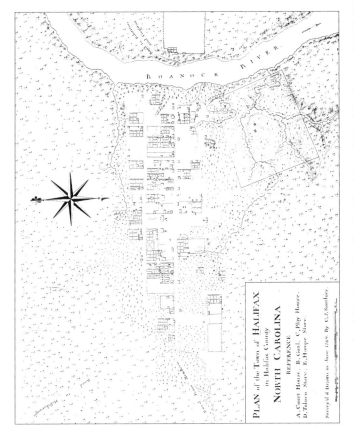

Figure 3 1769 Map of Halifax, North Carolina by Claude Joseph Sauthier. Courtesy British Library

"THE BEST ACTOR ON THE AMERICAN STAGE"

The new governor's influence was felt in many ways while his palace was in the building. Tryon encouraged the printer James Davis to reissue his newspaper. The *North Carolina Gazette* reemerged in May of 1768, enlarged to a crown sheet, with a new government contract. He encouraged the establishing of schools and to that end sought out capable scholars and recommended them for ordination in London. He proposed the establishment of a postal service, including funding and building a sorely needed post road through the province that would connect with the postal route that ran from Charleston up to Suffolk, Virginia. Under his new administration, the Freemasons were chartered in North Carolina (the last colony to secure a charter) and a network of lodges established. All the while the seat of the government, the palace, proceeded three years in the building—interrupted by a hurricane of 1769 that leveled two-thirds of the town.[14] It would be, on its completion, "the finest colonial house in the province," Richard Davis suggests, "if not in the American colonies, the culmination of Georgian building."[15]

And so it should not be surprising that under Tryon's civilizing project theatre would also find encouragement. In or before 1768, a provincial manager, one Mr. Mills, began to develop a circuit in North Carolina, following the courts, the fairs, and the races. Of this company we have little material evidence, no playbills, no newspaper notices, not even legal notices for debt recovery. But preserved are two character letters from Governor Tryon to document their stay in the colony, one perfunctory letter of introduction written by Tryon to Samuel Ward, governor of Rhode Island, and a second, personal letter written to the bishop of London on behalf of one of the actors.

From the first letter of June 1768 we can ascertain that Mills and company had been playing in North Carolina—in and around New Bern, Brunswick, and Halifax—at least since the beginning of 1768, and that they were leaving for Providence, Rhode Island, for the summer months and solicited a character letter from the governor. Tryon penned a mechanical and half-hearted letter to Governor Ward of that colony, dated June 15, 1768:

> Sir: Mr. Mills, who is the manager of a company of comedians, intends to solicit your permission to act in some parts of your Government. He has

therefore entreated me to mention their behaviour during their stay here of six months, which, as far as I have understood, has been decent, orderly, and proper. I am, sir, your most obedient servant, Wm. Tryon.[16]

As character letters go, it was not glowing and did not betray the least familiarity with the players, though they had been in the colony for half a year. Perhaps Tryon was rhetorically distancing himself from the bearer lest they proved undeserving of his high acquaintance. Though it was not the sort of letter the manager would publish, it did evidence the governor's patronage of Mill's Company—that the company had been playing with his license—and it might have proved useful in securing permission to play in the summer markets to the north.

The second letter, however, is less pro forma and may offer some insight into the governor's relationship with the players. Tryon wrote to the bishop of London on behalf of Mr. Giffard, one of the actors in Mill's Company, on June 11, 1768, with the idea of retaining him as a teacher in the colony. It is the only example of such a letter written by a colonial governor on behalf of a single actor, so I reprint it in full:

I was solicited a few days ago by Mr. Giffard a young man who is engaged with a company of comedians now in this province to recommend him to your Lordship for ordination orders, he having been invited by some principal gentlemen of the province, to be inducted into a parish, and to set up a school for the education of youth, He assured me it was no sudden caprice that induced him to make this application but the result of very mature deliberation, that he was most wearied of the vague life of his present profession and fully persuaded he could employ his talents to more benefit to society by going into holy orders and superintending the education of the youth in this province. I candidly told Mr. Giffard that his address to me was a matter of some surprise, that as to my own part I could have no reason to obstruct his present intentions, which might if steady and determined, be directed to the benefit of this country, but that I could not flatter him with success of your Lordship, as I was not assured how far your Lordship would choose to take a member of the theatre into the church, I however promised him I would give testimony to your Lordship that during his residence in this province, his behaviour has been decent, regular, and commendable, as such my Lord I beg leave to present him to you leaving the propriety of the ordination to your Lordships wisdom. He takes this letter by way of Providence being under obligation of contract to attend the company there. If your Lordship grants Mr. Giffard his petition you will take off the best player on the American stage. I am, &c. [William Tryon].[17]

This Giffard was Henry Giffard, Jr., son of the London theatrical manager of the same name, trained to the stage from early on, and by Tryon's estimation, "the best player on the American stage." How long he had been in America, or how long he was engaged in the "vague life" of his present profession is not known. He was married at the time, and his wife was also, and would remain, an actress. That Giffard was weary of the strolling life may suggest he had been at it for some time, longer than the company's residency in North Carolina.

One brief but tantalizing record of Giffard comes to us from the previous year. On March 24, 1767, the actor William Verling married Elizabeth Conner in Norfolk, Virginia. Verling, a Norfolk native, had been recruited to fill out a scratch company that David Douglass had formed in Charleston in 1765–1766 when the bulk of the American Company were detained in Barbados. When the Barbados corps returned, Verling either quit or was let go. He would shortly afterward form his own company—the Virginia Company, later, the New American Company—and compete with Douglass on his own southern circuit. But on March 24, 1767, William Verling got married in Norfolk, and the only recorded legal witnesses at the wedding were his wife's father and Henry Giffard, the lead actor in Mr. Mill's Company in North Carolina.[18] It is curious to speculate whether this relationship of actors (Giffard and Verling) developed while working together in a company of some nature sometime in the interim between the close of the 1766 season in Charleston and the spring of 1767 in Virginia, whether or not Verling had or had intended to assemble a company of his own in 1767, and whether Giffard and his wife were involved or already under contract with Mills, or whether Verling himself had played or was currently playing with Mr. Mills. What is clear is that Giffard was certainly present at Verling's wedding in Norfolk, but neither Giffard nor his wife signed on to Verling's Virginia Company when it did materialize later in 1767, though a pair of strong actors would have been a prize indeed. Mr. Giffard would spend 1768 playing in North Carolina, and follow Mr. Mills to Providence, and later to Nova Scotia, and later still to Jamaica. Why it was that after the wedding the two troopers split up and went to work with two separate companies is unclear—particularly when both companies were demonstratively understaffed.[19] I suspect Giffard was already under contract with Mills, which suggests the company was intact and playing early in 1767, a longer life span than the governor's character letter reveals.

Though Giffard was "wearied of the vague life of his present profession," it is not likely that the bishop of London paid much regard to the ambition of a stroller from Carolina. If he returned to New Bern as a school teacher, I have found no notice of it in the surviving press runs of the *North Carolina Gazette*. There are, however, intermittent references to him still on the boards, playing in Nova Scotia and Jamaica in 1768, and again in the Caribbean as late as 1783, and as many for his wife as well. He may not have achieved his ambition.

When Tryon characterized Giffard as the "best player on the American stage," against whom, exactly, was the governor comparing Giffard? Did he mean "the best in the company"? Or had Tryon experience with other companies? Tryon arrived in North Carolina in 1766, and did not leave the colony until he was transferred to New York in 1771. So if he is comparing Giffard, who else is in town? Or is he only repeating what was popularly known, a source of local pride, in a colony without so much, to be possessed of something of some value? An ornament in an otherwise unornamented province?

The governor's two letters—preserved in the minute books of state—represent most of the descriptive evidence we have of this company in Carolina. But the governor indirectly left a third imprint of the player's presence in a survey he commissioned on his colony. And for that we return to one of Mr. Sauthier's maps.

MR. SAUTHIER'S MAP

On one of the maps that Sauthier drafted, for the hamlet of Halifax, North Carolina, executed in June of 1769, five public buildings are noted in the legend. One hopes there were more than five notable buildings (e.g., there is no church in the legend, nor the Crown tavern), but Sauthier chose only five to letter and label. Halifax was a county seat, consequently it boasted a courthouse and a gaol, A and B, respectively, in the legend. Situated on the Roanoak river it brokered and inspected tobacco and hemp barged down from upriver plantations, hence inspection stations for both: D and E, the tobacco and hemp (Hampe) stores (storage or warehouses). Although the small town supported a population of well less than a 1,000 people, the fifth noted public building was a playhouse.

The playhouse in Halifax was located at the south end of the Palace green, or Market Green, where the public market was held and outlying farmers sold their produce and traded livestock and poultry. There were stalls and booths erected much of the year, and in June the green hosted the fair, the annual races, and when the courts met, the town swelled with visitors and litigants. The anonymous French traveler who passed through North Carolina in 1765 noted of Halifax at court season: "all the inhabitants of the adjacent Country come to deside [*sic*] their lawsuits and other differences" and the same writer estimated—perhaps on the high side—that there "might be 5,000 or 6,000 people here during the Courts."[20] Just south of both the courthouse and the market green was the playhouse (C on Sauthier's map), opening onto the public square. If five-building Halifax had a social center and aspired to any geometric Georgian order, this was it: the public green of the market square, between the courthouse at the north end and the playhouse on the south end.

Sauthier likely flattered the building to include it—it certainly was not stone or brick nor was it designed to last out the decade—but it was a playhouse, and in want of more Palladian structures, it was included. Why Sauthier chose to represent the theatre on the map may be linked to his anxiety about civilizing the province. To one classical architect involved in a project of reinventing the social landscape of the province, the playhouse was one of those forward-looking "polite spaces" of the town to come.

It was not the only playhouse in North Carolina under Tryon. Halifax is well over a 100 miles by coach road from New Bern, the governor's new residence, and more than twice that from Brunswick County (Wilmington) where the governor was temporarily residing in June of 1768 when he penned his support letters for actor and company. Not even coastal packets could make this distance convenient. As the governor had known the company, could speak personally and write personally of the actors, Tryon must have developed his acquaintance not in Halifax where the playhouse was recorded, but in New Bern or Wilmington where Mr. Mills may have erected or converted a space of some nature. The General Assembly of North Carolina met in New Bern from 1765 onward but the business of the government was so decentralized that Tryon was obliged to maintain four residences: a house at Wilmington to hold the semiannual Land Office; one at New Bern for the General Assembly and the courts of Chancery; his personal estate outside New Bern that was his permanent residence; and a fourth in Brunswick that had belonged to the late governor Dobbs. Though the governor, called from court to court, shuttled between residences, his itinerary did not include Halifax, and consequently his associations with the actors must have involved the actors in performance outside of Halifax. If there was a second playhouse in New Bern, it may not have survived to be mapped. A severe hurricane obliterated two-thirds of the town on September 8, 1769.[21] One survivor described New Bern then as "a spectacle, her streets full of the tops of houses, timber, shingles, dry goods, barrels and hogsheads, rubbish, etc. In so much that you can hardly pass along."[22] The solid brick construction of the new palace, however, remained and construction resumed.

There is another, less tangible, but nonetheless compelling, reason to suggest that a small circuit of playhouses was in seasonal operation. When theatrical records resume after the Revolution, we find a firmly established circuit in the state of North Carolina with documented performances in New Bern, Edenton, Fayetteville, Halifax, Wilmington, Cape Fear, and several companies all working it. This does not in itself suggest earlier activity, but if not, it would be an anomaly, as elsewhere in America the venues and circuits of the 1780s were built solidly on the venues and circuits of the 1760s. Indeed, I know of no theatrical venue in the 1780s that did not host theatre prior to the Revolution. In North Carolina, the 1780s was a rich decade for performance. The earliest accounts are from 1785 when an amateur theatrical society, the Thalian Association, was formed following a visit by a traveling company. Later that decade, Thomas Wall, formerly of the American Company, seeded a small company and played North Carolina. Several of his playbills are still preserved in the Rockefeller Library in Williamsburg. Mr. and Mrs. Hayden Edgar managed a company that also toured North Carolina in the 1790s; as did the Hendersons and the Kennas, who traveled up from Charleston. These were small companies operating below the threshold of newspaper notices. Indeed, Thomas Wall announced his performances by running a hired drummer through the town.[23] Yet they were traveling a traditional circuit that may have been established in the late 1760s by an equally unknown, equally overlooked company, and this company made the map and built the theatres that future strollers would follow and use. The touring companies, for their part, left in their wake the desire for theatre, the expectation of it, and amateur theatrical societies like the Thalian Association sprung up, in Halifax in 1785, in Edenton in 1787, in Wilmington and Fayetteville in 1788, after the visit of professional companies. Though the playhouses had not survived, somehow the circuit had.[24]

The theatre in Halifax that Mills occupied and Sauthier mapped are also no longer extant. It was doubtfully designed to last out the decade. Nor is there preserved any direct evidence of the playhouse in New Bern or Wilmington. Even the archeological excavation on the Halifax playhouse revealed no material artifacts that could be reliably dated and ascribed to the 1768 theatre. But some information about it can nonetheless be reconstructed. It was, for example, 60′ × 30′, based on the reliable dimensions recorded on the map, wood-framed and timbered, like most of the buildings of the town. The building itself was on a lot (lot 111) that was not owned by the players who performed there, but rather belonged to Joseph Montfort, a noted Halifax merchant and clerk of the County court. It is telling that the playhouse—at least to one merchant—was presumed to be a good investment.

Montfort was also a Freemason, indeed, soon to be Provisional Grand Master of the Free and Accepted Order of Masons, the highest rank in the order on the American continent. Under Tyron's tenure, Montfort had obtained a charter from the Grand Lodge of Masons in England on August 21, 1767 to found a lodge in North Carolina: the Royal White Hart Lodge. According to the archeological report on the excavation of lot 111—the playhouse—Montfort had intended to use the site for the erection of the Freemason lodge. The structure was never built. Instead, a playhouse was built and mapped as such.[25] A prominent merchant, the county clerk, a Master Mason, Montfort was as near the social center of Halifax as anyone. If he chose to sponsor a playhouse, theatre was not peripheral to this city. Perhaps Montfort speculated that a rented playhouse would be more profitable than a donated lodge. Or perhaps the two functions cohabited, in a concentrated social locus of playhouse and Freemason lodge? What is clear is that the building mapped as a playhouse insists on a very visible relationship to a certain civic and social power that came to North Carolina under the tenure of Governor Tryon, and that Tryon's project had spread, seeding the gentry, like Montfort, in a bid to gentility.

*   *   *

Governor Tryon, his architects, his surveyors, his palace and garden, his newspaper, his postal roads, and his Masonic lodges were all part of a civilizing force that one governor brought to a colony surrounded in forests, and began to carve out cities on decidedly European models. The playhouse was part of this project, conceived, like an English garden, as a *sine qua non* of polite English culture. It is a point of some irony that the Georgian taste imported by William Tryon, John Hawkes, Claude Sauthier, Joseph Montfort, and so many others, in goods and buildings in so many colonies, was so successful that by the eve of the Revolution, America was more culturally British than at any point in its colonial past. When Tryon left New Bern, the city was well on its way to becoming a homogenous English province. It is a second point of irony that Tryon never saw his project completed, or perhaps it was a testimony to the endurance of his mark on the landscape, felt as far away as Whitehall, London. Tryon moved into his new residence in 1770, and no sooner was he settled in than he was promoted and transferred to New York in 1771. So impressed was he with Sauthier that Tryon carried the draftsman/architect with him to New York.

The original Tryon palace, with its long facade of porticos, pediments, cornices, and landscaped gardens, has also not survived. It suffered severely during the Revolutionary war, when lead pipes and gutters were the first to be dismantled and melted down for armaments. Without gutters it leaked through the next decade. When Washington dined there in 1791, he described it as "a good brick building but now hastening to Ruins." Its final demise occurred in 1798 when it burned to the ground after hay piled in its basement caught fire.[26] If Tryon's palace was the image of Georgian order mapped onto the wilds of North Carolina, its disappearance may well have signaled the project's failure.

But as so often in this study, the grand palace's disappearance was not without a trace. The architect, Hawkes, preserved plans and a written description of the palace, complete with Sauthier's garden plans that he sent to a Venezuelan, Francisco de Miranda, in 1783. Included was an "exact plan of the edifice and gardens which gives a clear account of the whole." The plans were discovered in the early twentieth century and now reside in the British Library. From these copies the Tryon mansion was reconstructed, and so it stands again as it did in that dreary wasteland on the cusp of gentility, as Davis described it: "the culmination of Georgian building."

3. The Anatomy of Desire ❧

Being rich meant using candles after dark

Lorena Walsh, *Changing Lifestyles and Consumer Behavior in the Colonial Chesapeake*

October 30, 1771, Playhouse—2 boxes, 101 candles, £4.15.1
November 4, 1771, Playhouse—1 box, 53 candles, £2.9.10
November 6, 1771, Playhouse—1 box, 42 candles, £1.19.9

Galt-Pasteur Account Book, ms CW Rockefeller

DESIRE

In a study of material objects, desire leaves no footprint, but its immaterial presence is profound and occasionally very legible. A probated estate, for example, not only offers a complete inventory and worth of the material goods owned by the deceased at the time of death, but it can also offer an imprint of the social desire that drove the acquisition of goods. Because the estates are inventoried room by room, when the public rooms (parlours, dining rooms) of an estate of relatively modest value are lavishly, conspicuously furnished ("37 wine glasses," "16 red china dishes, 8 dishes blue china," "4 silver salt shakers," "two carriages") while the private rooms are (bedrooms) lean and impoverished ("1 hair mattress"), the profile of the deceased's spending patterns can betray a pronounced desire for social standing, an anxiety about class, an imitation of leisure, or a desperation for distinction that I think of as "the performance of gentility."[1] Why certain individuals chose to acquire certain goods at the expense of other goods can tell us as much about their desire—what they wanted to be (or to seem to be)—as what they owned. In this regard, the performance of gentility was a culture of contradictions. It was to appear leisurely—in public, in parlours, in playhouses—for those who in point of fact had little leisure, and to acquire what one could not practically afford. Surveying colonial American spending patterns for his seminal study, "The Consumer Revolution in Colonial America: Why Demand?" Cary Carson wrote succinctly of the contradictions of this desire: "For the privilege of taking tea in the parlour, more than a few families were content to continue pissing in the barn."[2] As with individuals and as with families, so too with cities that purchased and patronized theatres over other more pressing services, like paved roads or hospitals. Metaphorically speaking, cities too chose parlours over privies, and in this case, the parlour was the playhouse. Consider the desire that drove a town to choose to patronize a playhouse in the worst of times.

When David Douglass returned to Charleston from a London recruitment trip with five strong new actors to rendezvous with his company and open the theatre for a winter season, he landed at a most inauspicious occasion. He disembarked on Friday, October 27, 1765, four days before the Stamp Act was to take effect (November 1, 1765). Worse, he arrived on the same ship as the British appointed stamp distributor, George Saxby.[3] The entire week before the streets of Charleston were in a state of riot in defiance of the act and anticipation of Saxby's arrival. The newspaper had shut down. Mobs were prowling for supporters—like Henry Laurens whose house was broke open on the night of October 23, his household goods were rummaged while he was held at bay by a brace of pistols to his chest and his pregnant wife shrieked.[4] The same mob on October 25 threatened the local stamp distributor Caleb Lloyd who fled for his life to the protection of Fort Johnson. On October 27 when Douglass and Saxby arrived, the Sons of Liberty welcomed Saxby by burning his effigy at the wharf, and the mob, intent on destroying both stamps and agent, obliged Saxby to foot it to the Fort as well. Two days later the houses of both agents (Saxby and Lloyd) were pulled down and their household effects publicly burned. The stamps, meanwhile, were hidden, both agents resigned under duress, and when no one would take up the post, business quickly ground to a halt. Governor Bull insisted on following his British orders, but because no stamps were to be had, or anyone to distribute them, little could be done. No ship could be cleared without properly stamped papers, hence no trade; no jury empaneled without properly stamped writs, hence no trials. By the first week of November the courts and ports were both closed, the Assembly dissolved, trials were deferred, idle hulls choked the harbor, and merchants could neither clear cargo nor collect debts. Debtors, for their part, could not be prosecuted, consequently curtailing credit, resulting in shortages of goods and runaway prices until commerce came to a standstill.[5] Into such times stepped Douglass and his actors—or, rather, half his actors.

As if the political and subsequent economic troubles were not enough, Douglass had a major company crisis on his hands. Upon his arrival he was informed by letter that the core of his company—at least eight actors—was still engaged in Barbados and would not make the rendezvous in Charleston for the winter season. They remained in Bridgetown until the following May. So Douglass went public with the problem in a printed circular (the newspaper had temporarily ceased publication) dated November 4, 1765. The times, he acknowledged in a masterpiece of understatement, were unsettled, he was disappointed that more than half his company was unavailable, he had promised so much, had invested so much (new actors under contract, new scenery), and was now in a position to provide so little; and worse, without the promised payroll he stood to lose his new recruits. Nor could he board a ship and join his company on the islands, as no ships were clearing. In the midst of the uncertainty of it all, Douglass wrote that "some ladies and gentlemen insisted upon my opening the theatre with the little strength I have brought from London with me, and presenting such pieces as the thinness of my company will permit me to exhibit." Ten days into the Stamp Act, at the behest of "some ladies and gentlemen," David Douglass opened the playhouse, on November 11, with half a company and ticket prices reduced by 25 percent. Courts closed, ports closed, crop shortages, runaway prices, no circulating money, credit curtailed, but somehow he found encouragement enough to play through the winter with half a company. Such was the desire of Charleston in that winter of discontent.

The playhouses that were built in Charleston, Virginia, North Carolina, New York, Philadelphia, Halifax, Nova Scotia, and elsewhere were all built by such desire. They were part of the consumer revolution of the 1760s driven by a desire that reshaped the social landscape of colonial America.[6] Like the developing trade in tea equipage, porcelain, pewter ware, carriages, silk, or the Turkish carpets in country homes, theatre became an acquired, expensive, but necessary habit of the new Georgian taste that redefined "gentility" into material terms of consumption and display. Richard Bushman, writing of Wedgwood vases, remarked: "Genteel culture was not an inheritance; it could be acquired by purchase," and Bushman regarded the purchases of such as acts of "cultural usurpation."[7] Carpets were another small player in this game; their sudden appearance was noted by John Wayles who recalled in 1766: "In 1740 I don't remember to have seen such a thing as a turkey [Turkish] carpet in the Country except a small thing in a bed chamber, Now nothing are so common as Turkey or Wilton Carpets, the whole Furniture of the Roomes Elegant & every appearance of Opulence."[8] There is a wonderfully poignant image of the leanness of the time, of desire and material absence of the 1740s captured in the *Itinerarium* of Alexander Hamilton. Traveling through tidewater Maryland he met a tavern keeper at Treadways, who "professed music and would have tuned his crowd to us, but unfortunatly [sic] the two middle strings betwixt the bass and treble were broke." Later Hamilton visited Trinity church in New York where he saw the magnificent pipe organ "but had not the satisfaction of hearing it play, they having at this time no organist."[9] The fiddle with missing strings and the organ with no organist evoke the desire and absence that so troubled Hamilton most of his (too brief) American life. He who had known the fine assemblies, music, and theatre, who had lived through that impoverished generation of the 1740s and 1750s that wanted what it could not have. By the 1760s, however, material culture had caught up with desire and the "appearance of Opulence" was a sentiment expressed up and down the social ladder. Lieutenant Governor Francis Fauquier was dismayed at the unwillingness of Virginia "to quit any one article of luxury."[10] Like so many luxury items in a cash-strapped or unstable economy, a well-lit theatre was conspicuous to a fault, certainly, for both the consumer who patronized it and the town that hosted it. With few exceptions, neither could practically afford it. (After all, materially speaking, one acquired nothing by a trip to the theatre.) Nonetheless, after 1760 in colonial America, the playhouse became an increasingly desired ornament to any fashionable and aspiring society in which consumers were carving out, trying out, and wearing out their social positions. In the performance of gentility, the playhouse, like many objects of desire they would not be without, was often purchased and patronized against all sense beyond its singular driving desire. The anatomy of this desire is the subject that follows.

In the best of times no city or town in colonial America could boast enough population to support a permanent theatre and a residential company of actors, and certainly for smaller hamlets, such as Fredericksburg, Virginia, or Halifax, North Carolina, a permanent playhouse such as one Benjamin Grymes or Joseph Montfort promoted was lavishly extravagant. In this regard the economic objections that were raised against the theatre in every town were very real, and in some cases painfully apparent: in trading societies, the players, as de facto itinerants, threatened the fragile economies by carrying money out of the colony. Notwithstanding, we must recognize that the flourishing of a theatrical circuit and the rash of theatre building across the colonies in the years between 1760 and 1776 (nineteen theatres, seven colonies, and half a dozen islands, excluding the converted layovers and tobacco barns) was driven by a great desire—perhaps, like in Charleston during the Stamp Act, an irrational desire—but a desire worth understanding.[11] Playhouses were not imposed on the landscape by traveling actors and managers, but rather they were allowed by permission and their construction subsidized through private subscription schemes in which patrons advanced money in exchange for tickets, and once built, ownership defaulted to the manager, not the investors or the town. At a market level, subscribers like George Washington, who fronted £8 on the 1760 playhouse in Williamsburg, Governor Horatio Sharpe who headed the list of subscribers who raised £600 for the new theatre in Annapolis in 1771, or subscribers in Portsmouth, New Hampshire, who fronted $8 for "two tickets each, for twelve nights," or those "ladies and gentlemen" who encouraged Douglass in the thick of the Stamp Act crisis conceived of such spaces as desirable. So potent was this desire that even towns that did not want the theatre wanted the theatre. So what drove this desire?

"SUPPLIERS OF GENTEEL SERVICES"

Writing of the consumer signs and symbols employed by colonial townspeople of this generation to fix themselves in a social grid that was up for grabs, Cary Carson articulated something of this desire:

> Far more so than most countryfolk, urban dwellers needed a universal and portable system of social communications simply to signal to others who they were and to recognize birds of the same feather. Townspeople were therefore especially eager to learn the rules and acquire the goods that made the new system work. Where they settled densely, their patronage attracted and sustained communities of luxury craftsmen, traders and retailers, and suppliers of genteel services. Townspeople developed a distinctive lifestyle. At first it was not shared even with those nearby country gentlemen who were rich enough to join them, but having less occasion for polite intercourse among their all-too-familiar neighbors, had less need for fancy clothes, toiletries, tablewares, dining and seating furniture and later tea sets, gaming tables, and other pieces of specialized social equipment. Those were precisely the things that townspeople spent ever greater proportions of their non-capital wealth to acquire.[12]

Though Carson does not mention them, among those luxury craftsmen and "suppliers of genteel services" were managers and theatre builders like David Douglass. No single piece of "specialized social equipment" was nearly so spectacular as the playhouse that offered leisure and a monumental urban luxury for colonists a long way from London. Many towns, if they were indeed towns of any repute, would desire such services, whether they could afford it or not, even during the most unpropitious of times. What did it mean for a town to own a playhouse? We have seen something of what it meant for the promoters of Georgian culture, but what did it mean for the consumers?

There is a solid tradition of classic and recent scholarship from sociologists investigating the rapid expansion of consumption during the latter half of the eighteenth century. Thorstein Veblin's *Theory of the Leisure Class* that first introduced the notion of conspicuous consumption is still very applicable here, particularly in the plantation culture of the southern colonies: Virginia, Maryland, the Carolinas, Jamaica, where populations were less concentrated than in the urban centers of the northern and middle colonies. There public times—when the courts and the Assembly met—meant a trip to town, and a season of intense commercial, juridical, and social transactions. What followed was a frenzy of competitive display; relationships would be acquired or redefined, positions aspired to, appointments secured, preferments advanced, and a great deal of signaling from one to another would transpire, sometimes elaborately, sometimes with as commonplace a sign as the proverbial horse one rode in on.

Equally useful is Georg Simmel's study of the patterns of imitation (fashion) among the aspiring orders and the control of innovation by the hegemonic orders, as the playhouse would offer an ideal arena for both functions.[13] The printer's family, for example (including apprentices), might occupy a front box at the theatre only because they had bartered printing services (including newspaper advertisements) for play tickets; nonetheless, they were, for the evening, imitating gentility in a highly visible sphere, while those who sat near them would be very aware the gesture was exactly the kind of "usurpation" that Bushman spoke of.[14]

Woodruff Smith has more recently used both theorists to document how towns and their inhabitants in this period were consciously buying respectability through such purchase of genteel goods and pleasures.[15] Under Smith's model, respectability (gentility) is driven by a social competition that is marked by highly displayed patterns of consumption. Much of this is documented with regard to individual luxury commodities—wine sets, tea equipage, porcelain, carriages, even slaves—and those who could ill afford them, purchased nonetheless in imitation of those who could. The playhouse, however, has yet to be inserted into this model, as applied to either citizens or cities in which they lived.[16] As with individuals, so too did emerging cities participate in the consumption of luxury items often at the expense of necessary items (most colonial cities, for example, had playhouses long before they had hospitals). Williamsburg, Virginia, Bridgetown, Barbados, or Halifax, Nova Scotia may be a long way from London, but they were a little closer with a playhouse on the street. What we also see, particularly in the third quarter of the eighteenth century, is the street that boasted the new playhouse was not yet paved. Sewage was still thrown out the windows and a night watch was not yet funded, though the town councils recognized the need for both. The streets may be filthy, the poorhouse might be underfunded, the bridge may be out, but the playhouse would be open.[17]

When towns bought playhouses instead of bridges, schools, a town clock, or sanitation, when those many merchants and planters subscribed their £8, their £20 to a scheme of erecting a new playhouse in town, when laborers neglected their debts to attend the plays, and a young burgess like Thomas Jefferson was nightly purchasing tickets for four friends and punch in the pit, in short, when money is laid out when clearly there is little money circulating, what, exactly, were they buying? What is at the heart of desire?

Gentility for one thing. Visibility, for another, or rather visibly sporting (performing) one's gentility. Gordon Wood reminds us in his apt phrase that "consumption was a genteel prerogative," true enough, but we also need to recall that in no place could one become genteel faster than in colonial America. Here the desire for gentility was particularly rampant because it was particularly available. One of the running themes of Wood's work on the American Revolution was the blurring of traditional class boundaries in colonial America, accomplished, in part, by the absence of the uppermost social orders (there were no dukes in colonial America, for example, or earls, counts, king, court, nor true aristocracy; nor were there bishops in the church at the time, and thus all clergymen had to be ordained in England), and, in part, by the consumption of luxuries and titles by everyone below in the rush to fill the vacancy. "Everywhere wealthy commoners," writes Wood, "even those who still worked with their hands, sought to buy their way into gentlemanly status." In such a "truncated society" without the traditional English compass points of peerage, title, and hereditary fortune, the purchase of one's gentility was largely a game of goods and display, often self-display. It was, in essence, a performance. Wood documents this in terms of property, particularly "country estates" (usually valued below £50), but nonetheless allowed the owners to imitate their counterparts, the lesser gentry of England, while still wearing the leather in the shop.[18] The self-aggrandizement could be seen in a number of other ways, equally revealing: colonial Americans, for example, purchased portraits almost exclusively, over landscape painting.[19] Though portraiture offered a high display of status (or desired status), as Margaretta Lovell points out, individual and family portraiture was money poorly spent, as such goods—unlike, say, silverware—had almost no resale value. In terms of pure economy, portraiture, like playgoing, both belonged to the canon of what Veblin called "honorific waste."[20] But we are not speaking in market terms.

What is also clear is that it was not enough to purchase one's gentility (quietly on the country estate), one had to be seen at it. Portraiture marks an individual's or a family's upward movement, often fixes the moment of arrival (marriage or majority), but even in the parlours where they hung, these were not for general viewing. If one really wanted to be seen as having arrived, the playhouse was the place to do it. As the head-quote inventory of candles reminds us, the playhouse was very well lit, and hence, very visible. Royall Tyler's play *The Contrast* inserts a character, Jonathan, the proverbial Yank, into the playhouse unwittingly for a laugh at his naivete, but one of Jonathan's first remarks of the space was the "tarnal blaze of lights." In a culture of distinction, such visibility meant it was an ideal public arena to signal rank for those who had it, would seem to have it, or to signal a desire for rank for those who did not. For the lower gentry, the social aspirants, those mobile, unfixed members like the rising young lawyer Thomas Jefferson, the bachelor match-seeker Hudson Muse, or the newly arrived position-seeker William Hickey, the theatre offered a platform for the subtle spectacle of being seen as one who has already arrived. Sometimes performing gentility acquired gentility, sometimes it did not, but the sport was in the spectacle.

It did not work for William Hickey who traveled to Jamaica in 1775 in pursuit of a legal career. His training was solid with the requisite education, family connections, and character letters, but on presenting his credentials to the governor, Sir Basil Keith, he met with a sudden and peremptory disappointment. The island, he was told, was already overstocked with lawyers. Cast adrift and unemployed in the unfamiliar society he desperately desired to enter, Hickey fell into that huge category of would-be gentlemen who had desire, credentials, but no station. The raw desire for gentility without the purse to support it left him no way of signaling to others where in the social ordering he belonged but to *seem* what he could not *be*. He was, in essence, unmarked. So he did what any down-at-heels young man in his situation would do: he marked himself and went to the playhouse. His newfound companion was an island rake named "Young Bonynge," who offered Hickey the tout ensemble of dress, carriage, servants, and company to cut the requisite fine figure at the theatre:

> Young Bonynge told me that he kept a phaeton, a stylish Tim Whiskey, and half a dozen blood horses, all or any of which would always be at my service. "Apropos" he said, "we must go to town (Kingston) tomorrow, for there is a famous play performed in the evening at the theatre, being the first this season. They have a passable set of actors [the American Company], besides which all the beauties we boast of will be present, to some of whom I will introduce you."[21]

The evening was a tutorial in social broadcasting: the fancy phaeton carried them to the outskirts of town, where they were met with an entourage of four "Caffre servants" leading their pure-blood saddle horses. On their fashionable mounts they rode to their lodging where they dressed, thence to the tavern, where they dined in style and pronounced judgment on the host's champagne with impromptu panegyrics, thence to the playhouse where young Bonynge "collected five as pretty girls as a man would wish to look on," the seven finally retiring to a tavern and "passed a jovial night." That neither of the young men were employed did not seem to encumber their evening in the least. The strategy was to be seen in Woodruff Smith's phrase "sharing the symbols of the gentry's distinction" until they became gentry.[22] They were, of course, rank amateurs at it and earned little for the evening but a hangover and an empty purse. Still, Hickey continued his high life in Kingston, alternating between playhouse and tavern balls, all the while borrowing from his father in London and his father's friends in Jamaica, welching off Bonynge, who was himself welching off his father. Hickey was offered several clerical posts but living as a "gentleman" felt them beneath his station and so, preferring his sense of station to his sense of solvency, seemed what he could not be, until he depleted his credit and left the island destitute the following year. He used the genteel goods, services, and acquaintances—playhouse, phaeton, dinners, and dandies—to adopt a fashionable seeming to secure a social standing that the island could not, in the end, support.

A good dowry could have saved Hickey, and he allowed as much, but he met with disappointment there as well. The beauties he and

Bonynge collected at the playhouse were also part of the genteel goods and spectacle the theatre offered, and a part that caught the eye of more than the young rakes. Another bachelor Hudson Muse wrote to his brother of the social market he found available at the Williamsburg playhouse in 1771:

> In a few days after I got to Virginia, I set out to Wmsburg, where I was detained for 11 days, tho' I spent the time very agreeably, at the plays every night, and really must join Mr. Ennallis and Mr. Basset in thinking Miss Hallam super fine. But must confess her luster was much sullied by the number of Beauties that appeared at that court. The house was crowded every night, and the gentlemen who have generally attended that place agree there was treble the number of fine Ladies that was ever seen in town before—for my part I think it would be impossible for a man to have fixed upon a partner for life, the choice was too general to have fixed on one.[23]

As a civic space, the playhouse represented a social free zone, relatively unburdened by the formal protocols that governed most subdivided social spaces, where anyone with five shillings could sport in the panopticon of seeing and being seen. Muse thought of it as a kind of "court" where gentlemen and beauties assembled. Matches or liaisons could be made, partnerships brokered and broken. It was in this regard quite unlike other display arenas, churches for example, ordered by long-established protocols and marked geographies (arrangement and assignments of pews), or universities, whose students were sorted by their family's standing, or funerals, which could be lavish but equally ordered, or the governor's ball, which culled out such rising aspirants as William Hickey and courting beauties from the already arrived (they held their dances in taverns).[24] There is a wonderful example of such gatekeeping preserved in the National Library of Jamaica in a bound manuscript collection of the *Jamaica Mercury* belonging to William Archer, on the cover of which is a handwritten list of names of the disguised guests of a masquerade ball hosted by the governor of Jamaica. "Characters at the Masquerade in Kingston, the [ ] of March, 1788." "Miss Millwood, a Spanish Dancer, Mrs. Foote, A Beggarwoman, Col. Heath, a French Doctor, Mr. Thomas Harvey, A Scaramouche." It was a fashionable gathering, but the identities, even costumed, confounded none. Nor were they intended to. It was a display of the inner circle of the island, and no guest was unidentified or uninvited.

In contrast to which, the theatre was a relatively unordered space with no such ceremonies, no such restricted guest lists and few gatekeepers. Even the most basic and necessary internal separation of acting space and audience space could not be honored, as the hired stage-door keepers were bribed as often as not, in spite of the incessant admonitions on playbills that "no one will be admitted at the stage door."[25] Indeed, one of the biggest architectural differences between playhouses of the 1770s and those of the 1790s is that the latter sorted the classes on the street. The separate three-door system of discrete box, pit, and gallery entrances that builders like James Winston insisted on was a late century development.[26] Colonial American theatres, like most provincial theatres of the 1760s and 1770s, had one door and sorted everybody on the inside. This meant that at the point of entrance, the burgesses brushed elbows with the printer's family, the beauties and the gentlemen, the wife-shopper, the rake, and the governor.

Once inside, the social subdivisions were rudimentary and permeable— box, pit, gallery—and of those the only distinction that really mattered was the separation of boxes and gallery (in Philadelphia at least this was accomplished by the line of iron spikes). Boxes were clearly preferred (for seeing and being seen), but pit and boxes were sometimes "layed together" (and priced as boxes) and by the many remodels that occurred in which a second tier of boxes was added, apparently there were never enough boxes to accommodate demand.[27] Consequently, gentry spilled into the pit. Both Jefferson and Washington, for example, used box and pit as largely interchangeable spaces. Architecturally, at least, there were no essential comfort distinctions between box and pit. Both were—to our sensibilities—painfully crowded. Benches in the pit were a scant 9″ with 12″ of leg room and a seat and void (that cube of personal ownership) of 21″, while patrons of the boxes enjoyed a commodious 9 1/4 bench, with a leg room of 12″ and a seat and void of 21″.[28] If you could not choose your neighbor in the pit, nor could you entirely in the boxes, shy of purchasing the entire box. A sign-up sheet for boxes was kept at the theatre for the night of performance, and one could request a seat, or send a servant to secure a seat, but seldom were full boxes purchased. So what one bought for the addition 2s 6d was not physical comfort, but social distinction, visibility.

Within this spectatorial economy of seeing and being seen, in a culture where, in Lorena Walsh's phrase, "being rich meant using candles after dark," the playhouse was extravagantly visual. A well-lit playhouse would use half a box of candles a night, and with that one could buy a lot of visibility. I am not only speaking of consumers here—amateurs like William Hickey or the more studious social climbers like Thomas Jefferson whose spending habits are examined below—but also for the town itself, for which on playing nights it was the brightest place around. For the consumer the display potential that the theatre allowed was unmatched, and I suspect it was true for the town as well or a playhouse would not make its mark on a map like Sauthier's. Towns themselves confirmed their genteel status through acquired luxuries like the playhouse.

It was most apparent with consumers. One successful social aspirant in Williamsburg in the later 1760s and early 1770s was Thomas Jefferson. In 1770 he was only 26, single (he had yet to begin to pay his respects to Martha Skelton), and very keen to establish himself in law and politics. He was a promising young lawyer, but his practice was barely three years old, much of which had come to him from George Wythe, his mentor. Still, he was well connected (Peyton Randolph, the speaker of the house, was his mother's cousin), had just pulled off his first public position, and was sworn in May 8, 1769 as a newly elected burgess of Albemarle County. He was earning a reputation for a good pen, not much of a speaker, and clearly not the name he would be five years later when nominated deputy to succeed Peyton Randolph to the second Continental Congress, but he was, in May of 1770, one to watch. One superb place to be watched was the theatre.

"Avid" hardly does justice to Jefferson's playgoing habits. "Resident" might be closer. Though he left no written descriptions of his theatre-going, he did leave an account book of his daily expenditures, a memorandum book. Like the probate records that Walsh and Carr studied to determine what it was that consumers purchased, Jefferson's memorandum book reveals a good deal about what it meant to be a social aspirant on display at public times in the capital. Jefferson was called to Williamsburg for the meeting of the General Assembly from

May 21 until June 29, 1770. His evenings were enlivened enormously when the American Company arrived on June 13 and opened the theatre three nights later. Jefferson was in the house for the opening night on June 16, and most playing days afterward, until he left the capital on the morning of June 29: June 16 (17 was a Sunday), 18 (he purchased 3 box tickets and an additional pit ticket), 19, 20, 21 (5 pit tickets, punch and fruit), 23 (4 pit tickets and punch), 24 (Sunday), 25 (4 pit tickets and punch), 27 (3 box tickets), 28, his last night. Not only was he present in the playhouse five nights out of six, but he also had company and was usually the one entertaining the company.

In October of 1770, Jefferson returned to Williamsburg, but on this occasion, no sooner had the delegates arrived than the assemblies were postponed by the illness and untimely death of the governor, Lord Botetourt, on October 15. What a young burgess's role was in the public act of official mourning is not entirely known, but several entries from his memorandum book expose his awareness of being a new public figure. There were no frivolous expenditures for the week, no past-times; he absented himself from public displays of consumption. For the funeral he purchased only "mourning buckles" for 3s 9d and gave 5s to charity. He spent little that dull week and went nowhere.

But after a week of mourning, the late lord was decently interred and business as usual returned to the capital. The courts reconvened, the burgesses met, the theatre reopened, and spending resumed with a vengeance for lost time. By October 23 Jefferson had ceased his respectful frugality and his three first recorded purchases were play tickets (10s, or two pit seats), coffeehouse, and cakes. The week of October 29 to November 3, 1770 was spent at the courthouse by day, but his mornings and evenings were accounted for largely in two highly social spheres: the playhouse and the coffeehouse:

23—P[ai]d for play tickets 10 /

26—pd. at playhouse 5 /

27—pd. for play ticket 7/6.

29—pd. for play ticket 7/6.

30—pd. At Coffee H. 7 1/2d.

    pd. for play ticket 5/

31—pd. For d[itt]o. 7/6

    pd. for punch at playhouse 7 1/2d

1 [Nov]—Pd. for play ticket 7/6

2—pd. for d[itt]o. 7/6

3—pd. Anderson for dinner 10/

    pd. for play ticket 7/6

4—pd. at Davie's for dinner 5/

    pd. coach hire 1/3

    pd at play house 2/6

6—pd. Wm. Smith 20/

    pd. Greenhow fr. sundries 15 / 7 1/2

    pd. Mrs. Lightfoot for sendg. mare to Partner _3

    pd. for play ticket 7/6

    pd. at play house 1/3

7—pd. at coffee H. 7 1/2

    pd. for play ticket 7/6

8—pd. at Coffee H. 7 1/2

    pd. for Play ticket 7/6[29]

The week was a proper playhouse binge. The following morning, November 9, Jefferson left Williamsburg. While in town, between playhouse and coffeehouse, there was business to tend to: he appeared at court, at the Assembly, he arranged to have his mare bred, bought sundry goods at Greenhow's mercantile, settled debts, paid his taxes, and donated to charity. His trip to the capital was a business trip, but his leisure expenses—mornings in the coffeehouse, evenings in the playhouse—far exceeded his earnings for the period. As a burgess he was paid £16 per session, his legal work brought in additional fees, but debt and taxes aside, a cursory tally of Jefferson's expenditures for his October 1770 visit to the capital from the time of death of the governor until his departure on November 9, he spent over £40.

And money well spent. Coffeehouse and playhouse were public leisure spaces in which gentility assembled not to work but to, in part, demonstrate status. When the Scottish Dr. Alexander Hamilton first entered Philadelphia he went to the barber to be cleaned up and shaved first, and then directly to the coffeehouse to be introduced "to several gentlemen of the place, where the ceremony of shaking hands, an old custom peculiar to the English, was performed with great gravity and the usual compliments."[30] In the spacial currency of power, one can get a sense of how rich a site Charleton's coffeehouse in Williamsburg might have been at Assembly time and how much business was done on these steps by recalling that when George Mercer, the Virginia stamp agent, arrived in Williamsburg on October 30, 1765, just two days before the act was to take effect, he met a mob on the street before he could reach his lodgings who demanded his immediate resignation. Unfortunately for Mercer his arrival coincided with the meeting of the courts and the General Assembly and the town was full and the crowd was large. Declining to resign until he consulted the governor (Francis Fauquier), Mercer, followed by the mob, found Fauquier on the porch of the coffeehouse with most of the council. There on the porch the first conversation occurred over the wisdom of Mercer retaining or resigning his post, while the crowd watched and listened.[31] This was coffeehouse politics at its most public, most visible. Later the two men retired to the governor's palace, but the governor, council, and stamp agent in conversation on the porch of the coffeehouse goes a long way toward understanding the rich social potential of such a space.

Jefferson was not alone in his town sprees. Hudson Muse, who attended the following spring, reminds us that the playhouse was open six nights a week, and during the rush of court days, crowded every evening. Among the crowd of "gentlemen who generally attend" was George Washington, a frequent fixture in the pit and boxes that same spring of 1770. The company opened on June 16 and for the opening week Washington also recorded attendance for the evenings of 16, 18, 19, 20, and 22. In a playhouse that could hold nearly 300 spectators, this kind of nightly spending spree represented a substantial drain on a community, but a willing one. And we see it all across the culture, the toll of desire. When resources were scarce this pattern of consumption involved choices that often privileged the conspicuous over the necessary, to the theatre's great advantage. If their appetites outran their purses, it would not be the appetite that suffered. As Fauquier observed, the playhouse was one article of luxury that Virginians would not quit.

Like Jefferson who spent more than he earned, towns too would make the same consumer choices, ignoring pleas for buildings like a public hospital, paved streets, or a functional bridge, in favor of a playhouse. Lamented one op-ed in Baltimore of Dennis Ryan's company, "Many people who, at this time, would not give one penny towards paving the streets, &c. would give ninety times that sum, to see Cato well acted"[32] Or the editorial in New York that observed, "The money thrown away in one night at a play, would purchase wood, provisions and other necessaries, sufficient for a number of poor, to make them pass thro' the winter with tolerable comfort"[33] But the tolerable comfort of the poor was not a part of the anatomy of desire.

"THE INTENT OF DANCING"

Over and again, from early in the century to the beginning of the Revolution, throughout the records of the colonial American stage we find level-headed appeals against the playhouse not based in ontological or moral objections to the theatre, but rather that the small and frail economies simply cannot afford the extravagance of it all. On February 13, 1735, a letter was written to the London-based trustess of the colony of Georgia concerning a proposal to begin shipbuilding in Savannah. The postscript of the letter complained to the trustees of a fight with weapons ("dancing") that broke out in Savannah over the introduction of plays:

> Last Night a Quarrel happened between Mr. Bush the tythingman with his Guard and Some Gentlemen who were dancing many blows were given. Dr. Tailfer had like to have had his Arm Cut off by Bush with his Dagger . . . The Intent of Dancing was to Introduce Acting of Plays. I am humbly of [the] Opinion we have Scenes of Poverty Enough in reality without Inventing ways to Divert our thoughts from business & the Care of providing food for our Families. As to what I mention concerning the Play I beg my name be Concealed. I am no Enemy to the Gentlemen Conce[r]nd tho I am to their Indiscretion and to their way of thinking. In short we have too much of Publ. Entertainment.[34]

Just across the Savannah river, in nearby Charleston, South Carolina, Henry Holt's Company was currently performing that winter, including two performances on the week prior to the donnybrook.

When the Hallam Company first arrived in Williamsburg, Virginia, in June of 1752, contrary to their expectations and invitations, they were denied permission to play.[35] This was perhaps the most liberal colony on the continent and a town that had already encouraged William Levingston's company in the 1720s, an amateur company in 1736, a brief rival season of student theatricals also in 1736, and most recently the Murray–Kean–Woodham Company, 1751–1752. This was not a community with deep moral reservations against the theatre. Indeed, as Hallam informed his readers in a public letter printed in New York the following year, they had received encouragement to travel to Virginia. But when the company arrived, their solicitations were repulsed by the governor and his council. Dr. George Gilmer—the same "apothecary Gilmore" who had been a member of an amateur company back in 1736—in a letter of June 27, 1752, offered a telling reference to why a professional company was denied:

> I have nothing to trouble you with, only the arrival of Hallam and his company, and the quantity of slaves arrived and dayly expected, to the entire draining of this Country of what little cash was left. The Governor and Council, because you would not pass a bill for suppressing ordinaries and players, have made an order that no player should act here, which is likely to prove the utter ruin of a set of idle wretches arrived in Lee at about 1000 pounds expenses.[36]

The country was cash-strapped to the slave trade and drained of its capital. In an economic environment whose currency was tobacco, players threatened to siphon off "what little cash was left."

The fears of players draining ready money were not idle. Williamsburg was described as late as 1773 as lacking any manufacturing, having no substantial commerce, and relying on the court calendar to draw in support from surrounding counties.[37] It was true as well in 1752. Hallam, of course, opened his theatre, despite the bad economy, but in the end Dr. Gilmer proved to be the more correct in his assessment. In November of 1752 Gilmer wrote to Walter King about the fiscal imprint the players were making on the town:

> The money kept burning till they opened [the playhouse] and then it flew among this Association of indigent wretches with a lavishness you would be surprised at. Before Court they acted thrice a week at about 60 /2d [error

for £60 /2s?] a night. Since Court every night except two and received sometimes as much as £300 a night. Notwithstanding they take so much money never were debts worse paid.[38]

The initial flurry of commerce lubricated their appearance, after which debt and credit became the lingua franca of the company. In the end, the players took an economic toll on the town when they left Williamsburg, many of them with outstanding debts, including the playhouse itself, which was mortgaged and defaulted.[39]

The following year Hallam arrived in New York in June of 1753; he and his company were "unexpectedly repulsed," even though New York had recently supported the Murray–Kean Company for an 18-month run. Again, some indication of why they were opposed comes to us from a letter, dated July 17, just after Hallam wrung from the governor a slow leave to play:

> We are to have the diversions of the Stage the Season. There are Severall actors from some part of Europe who after much Solissitation [*sic*] have at last obtained leave of his Excellency to perform. They talk of building a house for that purpose and have offered themselves to Subscribe £100 for the Encouragement of it. This is a Melancholy Story among considerate persons that so Smale aplace [*sic*] as this Should Encourage the toleration of such publick diversions. People are dayly murmuring at the badness of the times as tho' they were actually concerned for their Interest but their conduct proves a contradiction to it. For men in every Profession are ever fond of some party of pleasure or other and as if they had not room enough to Spend their money that way they must for all put themselves under greater temptations in going to the play house. This I speak with regard to those who are Scarcely above want. These sort of people are the most fond of it which makes the Toleration of Publick Diversions the greater Nusance to a Place Especially as it Contains So few Inhabitants.[40]

It is pointed out over and over again, ubiquitously, that frugal economies cannot support the luxury of a playhouse, and they point to the indisputable fact that players, as itinerants, removed circulating money from the community. And over and over again we find permission granted and subscription schemes filled in spite of the financial burden that maintaining a playhouse entailed. Claims of financial extravagance from "anti-Thespis" so plagued David Douglass in

New York in 1761 that he was forced to publish an itemized account of his income and expenditures, documenting his numerous outlays in the community of printing costs, bill stickers, candles, hired musicians, and the like in the hopes of mollifying the claims of extravagance. But the bill also reveals that an average nightly audience was 350 people. At that time Douglass responded with a treatise he penned on the defense of the stage in which he first articulated and then countered the claim: "He ['Anti-Thespis'] says I spend my time and money foolishly, and perhaps can't afford it. I am firmly of the opinion that those imprudent people who spend what they can't afford this way, would do it in some other way; perhaps the worse."[41]

Further economic objections to the players plagued Douglass when he returned to Philadelphia in 1766. One op-ed penned an open letter that began

> To the Public. At a time when most Masters of Families are complaining of the great Scarcity of Money, and of the Stagnation of Trade, and are retrenching their Expenses, very great must their Infatuation be, who thus circumstanced, give Encouragement to a Sett of strolling Comedians[42]

"Strolling" is the damning word here. As no colonial American city was large enough to support a resident company, the players were, by necessity, obliged to be always temporary, always on the move elsewhere, while their small markets recharged. Against these claims Douglass would pen and publish a "Defense of the Stage," but it was something of a cheat, a rhetorical subterfuge, as the Quakers claimed extravagance but meant morality; Douglass, for his part, defended the morality and ignored the extravagance.

There were also trans-Atlantic and national perceptions at stake (if we can evoke such a phrase a decade early). Claims of extravagance were politically damaging to an economy roiling over taxation. During the hostilities of the Stamp Act, some in London intimated the presence of playhouses on the American landscape, like their indulgence in carriages and luxury townhomes, countered the American claim of poverty and hardship, and hence justified the imposed tax:

> The colonists plead their poverty, with what truth we may judge from private letters lately received from those parts, some of which give us to

understand, that the number of carriages kept in New York has, in about four years, increased from 5 to 70, some houses are let there for £200 per annum. At Philadelphia a play house is built, and as much frequented by the Quakers, as by those who have fewer external marks of religion. Cockfighting, fox hunting, horse racing, and every other expensive diversion, are in great vogue in the colonies, yet the colonists pretend they are not able to pay towards the support of their government.[43]

Even Bostonians like William Paine who had no moral objections to the theatres saw the economic disadvantage of it. Paine agreed with Isaac Smith when he wrote on April 16, 1769: "I am entirely of your Opinion with regard to Theatrical Performance (viz.) that this Country in its present Circumstances cannot Support a Playhouse without manifest Disadvantage to the Community."[44] Even during the thick of the war, when, for reasons of economy all public diversions were curtailed, a professional playhouse was reestablished in Baltimore and Annapolis, 1780–1781. Although many citizens complained in no uncertain terms to the governor and council that they had "cheerfully borne their Proportion of Taxes" toward the war effort, but their ability to continue was "destroyed or diminished by what we must take the Liberty of the thing, after every consideration is duly weighed, an unprofitable Extravagance." The address had little effect, as the company continued its venture, with permission.[45]

One could assemble a hefty portfolio of such examples, but the project at hand is not to document the economic opposition so much as to use the opposition to anatomize the desire that drove colonial cities to purchase when they could clearly so ill afford it, and to mark in some way the potency of that desire. What did the playhouse represent that it was worth so much when they had so little? In severe cases, the introduction of players into a cash-starved community, clearly below the population and financial threshold of supporting a strolling company, was little better than a pirate raid on a willing and over-committed community that could little afford the pleasures of a playhouse and bought one anyway. Such was the case in Halifax, Nova Scotia, in the late summer of 1768 when Mr. Mills and his company arrived. There was a lively debate that ran in the only newspaper of the region, the *Nova Scotia Gazette*, from which I cull the following case study.

MR. MILLS

In June of 1768 Mr. Mills solicited a character letter from Governor William Tryon of North Carolina to apply for permission to perform in Providence, Rhode Island. He was ultimately denied permission in Rhode Island and instead carried his company to Halifax, Nova Scotia. This was a newly developed settlement based around the central employer, Fort Anne, the northernmost British military outpost in North America, a post so far removed the English phrase "to go to Halifax" (like the Irish phrase "gone west") was slang for dying. Settling had been encouraged since early in the decade when the fort was active during the French-Indian wars, and by 1768 the hamlet was tottering on the cusp of becoming a proper town. For example, beyond the fort, Halifax had a court season, a provincial governor, and recently sported a newspaper. And so when the players arrived in August of 1768 and Mr. Mills announced his intentions of building a playhouse and opening a fall season in the emerging city his arrival occasioned no little flow of ink in the pages of the *Nova Scotia Gazette*. Detractions and defenses passed between "theatricus" and "anti-Thespis," commentaries, and inquiries. But the published objections were almost without exception fiscal objections. "Anti-Thespis," who opined in the August 11, 1768 *Nova Scotia Gazette* is representative:

> It has been likewise said that now the Players are here, it would be very hard on them not to be allowed to act: and that the Money they get will be spent in the Province. In answer to the spirt of these Assertions, I shall only say, that if it be a Hardship, they brought it on themselves; and I beg leave to remind those who are of so very compassionate a Disposition . . . that there is to be a collection for the Poor of this Town next Sunday; that they are ill provided for at present, and they will probably be still more numerous and miserable the ensueing Winter if the Players are suffered to proceed . . .
>
> Upon the whole, I am of opinion that on the present situation of this Province, the acting of plays will have many mischievous consequences; it will impoverish and give an idle Turn to the most useful part of the people; ruin our Servants, be a reflection on us among our Neighbors, and be of Disservice to us in England. Under these circumstances, though I myself am fond of plays, and frequented the Theatres when in London, more than most Men, I would vote against the Representations of them here, were they to be performed by a Roscius or a Garrick. "Anti-Thespis"

"Theatricus" (who was thought to be Mills himself) rebutted, denying players proved any addition "to the present Cry of Poverty; except the circulating of some Sleeping Cash can do it, since with their necessary expenses, it is very rare that any carry much Money from a Place, more than will see themselves to another." Again, in the following issue, "Theatricus" reminded the community that the Players "might play a Night for some public Charity: No uncommon Thing everywhere; a very easy Mode of raising a Sum, and where the Rich contribute the most to it, and carries the Produce directly to the Poor."[46]

Throughout the public forum of defenses and detractions, the building of the playhouse proceeded. But even this first gesture of economic contribution to the town was tainted. The carpenter who fitted up the stage in a "large and commodius house" had been hired away from one "B.G." and his former employer—to whom the house-carpenter was in debt and working off his bill—lamented publicly that such practices will ruin the town. Nonetheless, the carpenter completed the playhouse, Mr. Mills advertised his opening and attracted the attention of even the outlying populations. One farmer wrote to the paper from Windsor, Nova Scotia:

> Sir: I have heard with great pleasure of the Arrival of a Company of Comedians at Halifax. I am very sorry I cannot go down immediately, as our Hay-making is not quite over. Please to let us know what Stay the Players are like to make and what Pieces they propose to Act—I hope the Provok'd Wife is among the number. Sir John Brute is an amiable Character. Many of us will be with you when our Harvest is ended[47]

Others were more blunt with their cash shortages. One woman (signed "Doll Tearsheet") wrote to Mr. Fletcher, the editor, asking "if a poor Girl should be short of Money, will [the players] take things in pawn— We seldom have any *sleeping cash*. But I have a brand new Hat and Cloak."

The appearance of the players and a playhouse was generating a good deal of excitement and people were willing to give much for the chance to attend, but to pawn one's cloak in a northern latitude goes a long way to remind us that this town could ill afford the pleasure of it. The threat that itinerants posed to the microeconomics of the community were best expressed by a shopkeeper in Halifax, who introduced himself to the readership:

> This is the first time in my life that I attempted to write any thing to be printed, except an Advertisement now and then, on receiving a fresh Assortment of Goods, but the allowing of Players to get footing among us in our present Situation is really so alarming that I think a Man may be excused for giving his Sentiments upon it . . . We are a poor Province, and poor as Individuals—of the last of these Assertions, my Books furnish me with a melancholy Proof. Thou' I have a great many Debts due to me, I run frequently about Town for a whole Day without being able to collect a Shilling—And I have too much reason to fear, that many a laboring Man whom I have trusted with a check Shirt, a pair of Shoes, or some such little Article, instead of coming Saturday Evening to pay me Part of his Week's Earnings, will lay out his Money to buy a Ticket for the Play.[48]

Mills opened the playhouse on August 26 and commenced a short season playing at least twice a week, by the notice of his bills. A month into his run, Mr. and Mrs. Ferrel, formerly of Douglass's American Company, joined Mills in the leading roles, and the season continued with a strengthened cast. By the end of September, the haymaking was over and the rural population came to town. One enterprising merchant was offering ready money against the hay crop. The farmer from Windsor had postscripted an enquiry to trade his hay for play tickets. In response to the shortage of ready money, another enterprising speculator took out an advertisement in the same paper:

> If S.W. or any other of you Country Friends, who may be in want of Money to bring them to Town to see the Plays, can give good security for the Delivery at Halifax of a Quantity of Hay, not exceeding 50 tons, on or before the First Day of December next, I will pay for it now at Twenty Shillings a Ton—[49]

Goods were traded for cash, goods were left in hawk for cash, debts went unpaid for cash, and the cash went to the players. For his part, Mills paid out for a carpenter and the furnishings of a playhouse, probably to John Kirby the candlemaker who advertised his tallows for cash only, to Mr. Fletcher for his newspaper advertisements, and the company paid for its board and lodging. But in town, the laborers' paycheck went to the theatre, debts to the shopkeepers went uncollected, charities went ungathered, and the poor unprovided for. The farmers came to town flush with advances on their hay crop, the players played, the objections of merchants and anti-Thespis went unheeded. The players were traders with a unique set of goods that Halifax had not seen for many years. For a farmer who came to town after haymaking, *The Provoked Wife* was a rare commodity. For one night in the playhouse, after the work of summer and the prospect of a long northern winter in Windsor, Nova Scotia, for one night, Halifax was not that far from London and the memories of David Garrick and such a night were worth something to S.W. and Doll Tearsheet.

But all the while, almost weekly, the subscription notice for the poor pleaded in the pages of the *Nova Scotia Gazette*, and the poor went begging. Mr. Mills and his company increased their playing schedule to three nights a week for nine weeks, advertised a series of benefit nights (for themselves, not the town), offered double-cast versions of Shakespeare and Farquhar, afterpieces of Garrick and Bickerstaffe, and never even provided the customary benefit performance for the community's poor. Even William Verling—no philanthropist there—learned the goodwill earned by civic benefits. His struggling company on St. Croix would squeeze in a combined charity "For the benefit of the Church, the Hospital, and the Poor" all in one evening.[50] But Mills offered nothing in return for the good business Halifax showed him. By the first week of November, when the cold weather blew in the players closed the theatre and sailed south for the warm sun of Jamaica.

Mill's season in Halifax was a pirate raid on a small economy, exactly the thing that objectors to the theatre feared—even those who enjoyed the theatre. It was fine English goods, like the dinnerware advertised in the *Nova Scotia Gazette* "lately imported," beyond the reach of most but so very desirable.

THE POVERTY OF THOMAS PIKE

In the hierarchy of desire it is understandable that more pleasure is derived from supporting a playhouse than a poorhouse, or buying a play ticket instead of paying a debt. But in the highly competitive marketplace of delectable goods, the playhouse was preferred even over other genteel services, like a music room or a good dance academy. When David Douglass returned to Charleston, South Carolina, in 1773, after an absence of seven years, he found his old playhouse in poor condition, and he was once more obliged to initiate a subscription scheme to erect a new one. He had by this time met with great support in that city on his previous tours of 1763–1764, when he had raised a subscription and built the Queen Street Theatre, and when he returned after a recruitment trip to London and played Charleston again in 1765–1766, even with a partial company. By 1773, the economy was again struggling with a menu of nonimportation agreements, and this erstwhile friendly town for the first time saw public opposition to the project. It came in the person of the dancing master Thomas Pike.

Mr. Thomas Pike was also a competitor in this genteel service industry. He had introduced himself to the Charleston public back in 1764 when he opened his dancing school and Assembly Room on Church Street. There he taught dancing, fencing, was an able music master, sponsored the highly attended winter balls, and hosted the St. Cecilia Society concerts. For nine years he supported himself by the arts as a purveyor of "polite education." So marked was his success that he found his monopoly challenged by two other dancing masters, the Frenchman M. Valois and Andrew Rutledge, who also opened dancing schools. Pike dismissed them as pretenders to the art, but frauds or not, they cut into his market. The next we hear of Mr. Pike is in the summer of 1773 when his business was being sold to his creditors.

It was the same summer that David Douglass arrived in Charleston and made known his plans of raising a subscription to build a new playhouse. One "benevolus" (well-wisher) flatly urged that the citizens of Charleston support Mr. Thomas Pike instead of supporting a playhouse, as Pike was a resident of Charleston and the players were strollers.[51] The appeal found only shaky support and the first installment of Pike's estate was sold for the benefit of his creditors the following week.

The association was not an arbitrary one. The site that Douglass had chosen for his playhouse abutted Thomas Pike's Assembly Room. They were closer than neighbors; the two large buildings occupied two halves of the same lot, Lot #40, off Church Street. On the northern half, Thomas Pike had a Long Room, a space described by Bostonian Josiah Quincy, who heard a concert there, as a "large inelegant building . . . preposterously and out of all proportion large."[52] On the southern half, Douglass raised a theatre—one claimed to be "the most commodious on the continent."[53] At one end of the lot, a community had contributed a substantial subscription to erect a sizeable playhouse. On the other, Pike's Long Room, concert hall for the St. Cecilia Society, and personal holdings were all being auctioned off, and they were all happening at the same time:

> To be sold by public vendue [*sic*], at the usual place in CharlesTown, on Thursday next at 12 o'clock, the remaining part of the effects of Mr. Thomas Pike, consisting of a large pair of white framed glasses, one very handsome chimney glass, a large tent, a pidgeon house, his fine mare, horse and side-saddle.[54]

Mr. Pike continued to advertise his school (without his glasses), while every few months the remaining effects of his estate were sold off, piece by piece, by public auction. When the building itself was sold, Douglass's subscription was progressing nicely; carpenters were hired, the money was in the hands of his agent Robert Wells, the Scottish stationer, printer, and—incidentally—the auctioneer who sold off Pike's estate. Douglass had advertised his plan for a well-regulated theatre and kept his subscribers abreast of its progress via Wells's *South Carolina Gazette*. Below it, this rebuttal to Douglass's broadside on a Well-Regulated Theatre:

> Well regulated theatres may be proper objects of public encouragement, in very populous towns or cities, where the generality of the people are wealthy, have much leisure, and little employment, But surely it cannot be thought sound policy, or upon any account justifiable at this time, to encourage the establishing a permanent one here. Philo-patriae

Opponents to the plan went so far as to draft a petition for the last sessions for this district:

> We present as a grievance, the company of players, a playhouse in Charlestown being unfit for the present low estate of the Province; for although there is great want of money to procure the conveniences and even the necessaries of life, yet large sums are weekly laid out for amusements

there, by persons who cannot afford it; and is a means of promoting the frequent robberies that are committed, and of vice and obscenity. We recommend, that the legislature may suppress the same, tending to the corruption of youth, and the injury of many families.

This article was resoundingly quashed by the court.[55]

Philo-patriae was, of course, quite right, and he was also utterly wrongheaded. Of course the town could not afford it but that was not the point. No one was to tell Charleston they could not enjoy their pleasure. Charleston would have its theatre because it represented something to them, an idea of Georgian order, of a certain civilizing force, an arrival to that pretentious and potent culture of gentility. The imported goods that were its hallmarks were in high circulation and the fine folk would have them. The role of the fine arts in this civilizing generation was no small one. The brilliant assemblies that gathered for the St. Cecilia Society concerts and the playhouse astonished Josiah Quincy, the Boston traveler, who marveled at the numbered of fine ladies present. When the playhouse was ready the American Company opened its best and longest seasons. And poor Mr. Pike went bankrupt and moved to Philadelphia where he began again. But this time he prospered, carving out for himself a small part of that genteel appetite. Jacob Mordecai, the diarist, remembered him thus: "Before the war a man named Pike was all the fashion."[56]

THE FOUR HORSE PHAETON

In the world of material culture and immaterial desire, the study of the acquisition and consumption of such commodities is very revealing to the price of good standing, both individually and civically. For the cities that hosted the playhouse, the patrons who supported it, and the actors who worked there, genteel appearances promised to fix the "rootless" in the economy of appearances. Actors were also players in this game. In some regard—as we are speaking of role-playing and the performance of gentility—they excelled at it.

In this desire to fix oneself in a fluid social landscape of class and status, residents and newcomers alike employed highly visible markers. Fashion, display, ostentation, and conspicuous consumption—all the ingredients of Veblin's *Theory of the Leisure Class*—were pressed into pronounced service. In social terms this meant patronage, association, and membership in clubs, like the Masons, the St. Andrew's Society (discussed below). In material terms this meant the purchase and display of items like wigs, fine dresses, silver-handled canes, carriages: all props to the role of gentility. For in no population were such markers more essential than to a transient and socially ambiguous profession like acting. When Governor Tryon wrote to the bishop of London on behalf of the actor Henry Giffard, he betrayed his uncertainty whether a stage actor could even be admitted for ordination. Their social connections allowed them to mingle with the best society (governors, for example, from whom they derived patronage), but they were by profession, itinerants, never residents in any of the colonies in which they were patronized. They were at once both "strollers" and guests at the governor's table.[57] At no point was their ambiguous status more apparent than when one of the acting rank attempted to change professions as Giffard had done. Without an index of any sort to go by, lateral or upward movement was difficult, if not impossible, to secure.[58]

All the more reason to take control of the social instability of the profession and fix it with recognizable signs. Patronage was one method for the player to borrow status from his or her protector. To be acquainted with the best families was, no doubt, of good service. Consumption was another method to fix one's own place, independent of one's associations. Occasionally some insight comes from the goods the actors purchased.

A few account books have survived from Williamsburg's colonial past, and occasionally the actor's names are found in the merchant's books. Some are professional services—printing, a cartload of wood, candles, medicines, carting from the ferry—but some are luxury commodities privately purchased and with display in mind. Membership in social clubs, for example, or subscribing to a publication (as Douglass occasionally did) associated his name in a printed club of patrons. Or, at a more material level, wigs. A wig, wrote one Virginian, "was the distinguishing badge of gentle folk" (by which he meant *gentlemen*).[59] David Douglass, Owen Morris, and Lewis Hallam all wore wigs, and when in Williamsburg they paid dearly to have them serviced at Edward Charlton's, barber and peruke maker. That they were charged individually suggests these were not company wigs but personal ornaments, and only afforded by the first actors of the company. Mrs. Douglass, Mrs. Hallam, and Nancy Hallam also paid for "dressing" at the peruke makers.[60]

The grandest, most conspicuous display of an actor-manager aspiring to status through acquired goods occurred during a very successful season of the American Company in Williamsburg, 1770–1772. Sometime early in the season Douglass purchased a four-horse phaeton, a painted carriage like the one Young Bonynge had, and prior to leaving the capital he advertised it for sale. This was not a functional travel wagon for transporting the scenery and properties of the company—the proverbial stroller's cart—but a private carriage, for personal use, newly painted and smartly harnessed, for sporting about Williamsburg and the surrounding plantations. He advertised it thus: "A Genteel Pheton, not more than eighteen months old, in excellent order, very strong and newly lined and painted. There is a harness for four horses, made not above 9 months ago, genteelly ornamented with brass plates, etc."[61] Douglass was sufficiently well known in town at the time to leave only a name without an address. This is an impressive luxury item for an actor and a manager of an itinerant company in a small burg. William Dunlap made much of the aged John Henry, gout-struck, owning a carriage that carried him to and from the John Street Theatre after the Revolution. Dunlap (*History*, 150) noted what a presumption it was thought to be for a common player to be carried thus. Henry himself was so conscious of the critique of aspiring beyond one's class that he fashioned a faux coat of arms on the side of the carriage of two crutches with the logo "this or these." This was done to appease the New York public who thought such luxuries above the station of a player. That was after the Revolution when the French visitor Ferdinand Bayard called the upper tier of American society "the carriage class."[62] But two decades earlier when Londoners railed at American luxury they did so by quoting the rise of carriages in New York.[63]

Douglass purchased his phaeton sometime in 1770, used it, maintained it, and sold it in 1772 in the much smaller town of Williamsburg. Kevin Sweeny sees in the carriage a moving metaphor, "the genteel ideal of graceful, effortless movement through the landscape."[64] And there is something to it. The phaeton might move effortlessly over the flat tide-water geography, but would it be as graceful moving through (and up) the social landscape? Through such commodities as his carriage, could Douglass really purchase his position? Or was it all just a player's masquerade that spoke only of his desire to attain what occupationally he was not or could never be? Was it a spectacle of respect or ridicule? The man who built the carriage mistook the one for the other. Tradesman Elkanah Deane, Williamsburg's coach maker in 1772, flush with money like Douglass's, purchased a genteel house so close to the governor's palace that he was ridiculed for the presumption in the *Virginia Gazette*. "Palace Street Puffer" is what one fellow tradesman called him, where "puff" is used exactly like the theatrical term of self-aggrandizement.[65] Puff or no puff, maker and owner of the phaeton both alert us how potently genteel culture was associated with an appetite for display.

Dr. Alexander Hamilton betrayed the same appetite when he was once mistaken on the road for a person of quality. Hamilton confessed his swelling fluster when a "rustic" "frequently accosted me with *please your honour*, with which grand title, like some fools whom I know, I seemed highly pleased tho I was conscious it did not belong to me."[66] Douglass, like John Henry a decade later, must have been equally conscious of the transgression. Actor-managers—even successful ones—were not "carriage folk," any more than the carriage maker himself was. They were entrepreneurial tradesmen using luxury goods in a highly displayed manner to promote their own desire for gentility and purchase their way toward it. But it was not an empty game; others were successful at it. Apothecary George Gilmore—the same Gilmore who had complained of the Hallam Company's debts—was himself at the time spending a substantial chunk of change setting up shop in Williamsburg in his own pursuit of the same station. He ordered a set of china from England in 1752, but the real purchase price was the remodel he undertook to house it. Prior to the china's arrival he had built a fine cabinet to display it, and then wainscoted the whole dining room to display the cabinet. The remodeled room then required the installation of a "handsome marble chimney piece" to offset the cabinet, and finally capped the marble mantle with a looking glass. All this display for china. "It will," he concluded, "make a tolerable room for an

Apothecary."[67] Money well spent argued Ed Chappel who suggested Gilmore was able to parlay the investment of a genteel space into a series of appointments that ultimately promoted him from apothecary to Doctor Gilmore, and Doctor Gilmore to Councilman Gilmore: that is, by appearing genteel, he became so.[68] In the end, Douglass's carriage would also deliver, remaking the actor-manager into David Douglass, esquire, though he would give up the theatre to achieve it.

His insistence on gentility—even the advertisement ("genteel Phaeton" "genteely painted") betrays more of an anxiety of title than ownership—was part of a larger social strategy to display himself into a desired class that he initiated in his mid-career. From the late 1760s on, Douglass began to insist on a certain status (earned or unearned), with his wig, his carriage, his 37 wine glasses and two sets of china, and a title, esquire, evoking it whenever he could, though when and how he acquired it is very unclear. Early in his American career (1761) he wrote of himself as "of a good family" and having a "genteel and liberal education" but there were no claims of title. He is "Mr. Douglass" (as in "the proceeds of the house was on Wednesday paid by Mr. Douglass, the manager, into the hands of George Harrison, Esq.")[69] In the account books of Alexander Craig, Williamsburg merchant, for 1761–1763 he is referred to more commonly as "David Douglass, comedian." By 1770, however, in the account books of Williamsburg apothecaries, Galt and Pasteur where he purchased medicines, he signed himself "David Douglass, Esq." The same year he took out a subscription to William Bradford's *Pennsylvania Journal*, as esquire. Again the same when he announced his arrival in New York in 1774: "Yesterday arrived in town from Charleston, South Carolina, David Douglass, Esquire, manager of the American Company of Comedians."[70] The esquiring of Douglass brought with it his first post: Master of Revels. When Mrs. Douglass died in Spanish Town, Jamaica, she was listed in the parish records as an actress, "Comedian, wife to David Douglass, Master of Revels."[71] It was the first of what would be a series of appointments that allied him with the government (he would become "Royal Printer" of the *Royal Gazette*) and promised his desired arrival as "Gentleman." By the mid-1780s he had also been appointed a member of the council (1784), 1 of 24 Masters-in-Ordinary (1785), and 1 of the 22 Justices of the Quorum for St. Catherines (1785). When Douglass died, his profession was listed as "Gentleman," though at that point he had derived a fine livelihood from the printing trade.

That anxiety about his place never left him; with his fortune—his government contracts for publishing the Laws of Jamaica, editing and indexing the minutes of the Assembly were quite lucrative—his purchase patterns reveal that he accumulated not only the most visible social items, a house on the Parade, the stock of wine glasses, two sets of china, quoted above, but also a silver-handled cane and, at the time of death, two carriages. He had become "carriage folk."

If in 1772 David Douglass, comedian, was esquiring himself in an uncertain Virginia landscape with his coach and four, something else was also on display. Wealth, status, and desire, true enough, social over-reaching, possibly, but Douglass spending his way into gentility was also reminding the objectors to the playhouse that his profits were not leaving the city. He was countering the most severe claims of the objectors that the strolling player carried off the capital by displaying his ability to spend. Like his clients at the playhouse, his own purchase of the phaeton was a conspicuous display of fueling local economy with high-end goods and services. And by 1772, goods, particularly luxury goods (tea, silk, china, the "baubles of Britain"), were becoming increasingly politicized.

THE LAST ITEM ON THE LIST OF GOODS

I have been tracing the immaterial presence of desire through its material residue. At its best it represented a social hankering against all sense and discretion in times of bounty; at its worst, the desire ran amok amid financial struggle and political crisis. When the desire finally expired it did so under the most unwilling of terms: a forced boycott.

The call to boycott what Dr. Johnson called the "Baubles of Britain" had been in public circulation since the Stamp Act, when the flood of imported British goods became precisely politicized. Timothy Breen argues—convincingly—that it was in part due to the marketplace of imported British goods that generated the high degree of solidarity among the colonies, achieving through a shared market a common ideology beyond what most colonists thought possible.[72] What brought the "thirteen clocks" to "strike together" was the politicizing of material goods—tea is most recalled, but at the time the boycott of silk, imported china, suits, manufactured goods of all sorts coalesced the disparate colonists into associations of nonconsumption. From 1765 forward a growing list of contraband goods was accumulating great political weight. I say "precisely politicized" because choosing to wear imported silk or to drink tea had become a visible ideologic position after 1770 and by the first half of 1774, the colonies that responded to Boston's call were asked to publicly, consciously repudiate the entirety of British imports, in Breen's phrase the whole "empire of goods." Coffeehouses replaced East Indian tea and tea equipage, homespun replaced imported wool, local ceramic ware replaced the Wedgwood china. Yet in spite of these often public and sometimes elaborate rituals of nonconsumption, Douglass and the American Company of London-trained actors, performing a repertory of British plays (the only American play, Godfrey's *Prince of Parthia*, was a once-and-out production), enjoyed their best season of their entire career in their new theatre in Charleston. They played from December 1773 into June 1774, as close to a normal London season as they ever achieved in North America.

The colonist's appetite for the theatre was the last desire bridled by the boycott of British goods and the last desire curbed by the Continental Congress who drafted up and resolved a final nonimportation agreement in October of 1774. English-trained actors playing English tragedies, farces, and afterpieces had been exempt from the growing list of English goods and services under the earlier accords. When the first overture of revolution was played—the Stamp Act—delegates in Virginia gathered at the Raleigh Tavern and drafted the first association for nonimportation of British goods; theatre was not in the list. When the second overture occurred, the Townsend Acts, a second association was formed in Williamsburg. The burgesses were currently meeting for the June court and on June 22, 1770, members of the Second Association were elected and a resolution was drafted. It denounced Great Britain, followed by 14 resolutions calling for a boycott of a wide menu of British goods—including slaves, wine, beef, spirits, cheese, tallow candles, broadcloth, upholstery, watches, clocks, readymade furniture, and the like. It too made no mention of theatre, and though it also resolved to "promote and encourage industry and frugality, and discourage all manner of luxury and extravagance," Douglass and the American Company profited and bought a phaeton.[73] Indeed, so exempt was the playhouse, after the Bill of Association was signed by 164 burgesses and merchants—including Jefferson (who drafted it) and George Washington (who had prepared a similar draft in 1769)—many adjourned promptly to the theatre. Jefferson and Washington between them had purchased over 20 tickets in that week alone. When the burgesses drafted their Association to boycott British goods and frivolous spending they not only exempted the playhouse, but they also personally, consciously, and extravagantly supported it. By 1770, in Virginia at least, to the most respected and radical of citizens, the American Company of Comedians, and the desire for theatre itself, had somehow become an essential and American right.

When it was finally curtailed in the buildup to war, when the Continental Congress prohibited theatre in October of 1774, the oft-quoted moral objections of later historians were never cited. Rather, theatre, to the representatives at the first Continental Congress, was seen to be a unnecessary expenditure, like the ostentatious practice of handing out memorial gloves at funeral processions. It was discouraged in the interest of preserving capital. And it was the last thing to go:

> We will, in our several stations, encourage frugality, economy, and industry, and promote agriculture, arts, and the manufactures of this country, especially that of wool; and will discountenance and discourage every species of extravagance and dissipation, especially all horse-racing, and all kinds of gaming, cock-fighting, exhibitions of shews, plays, and other expensive diversions and entertainments.[74]

And so farewell to the pleasure of the races, the gaming, the show of funerals, and yes, even to the theatre. Douglass received the bad news in New York waiting to reopen the John Street Theatre. War was at hand, and the generation that grew up on theatre set their pleasure aside for the serious business of Revolution. The desire that embraced the theatre first, in the end parted last.

Except that during the first years of the Revolution, more theatre was going on than ever before, with soldier companies playing in New York, Boston, Philadelphia, Lancaster, Annapolis, and Valley Forge. It was perhaps this later site, under the command of Washington, that the Continental Congress had in mind when it reissued the prohibition in 1778:

> In Congress, October 16 1778, Whereas frequenting play houses and theatrical entertainments, has a fatal tendency to divert the minds of the people from a due attention to the means necessary for the defense of their country and preservation of their liberties. Resolved, that any person holding an office under the United States, who shall act, promote, encourage or attend such plays, shall be deemed unworthy to hold such office, and shall be accordingly dismissed. Order'd, that this resolved be published. A true copy of the journals, Moses Youngs, Secretary to the President of Congress.[75]

It will be noted, there was no further mention of cock-fighting or horse-racing.

4. The Countenance of Brother Douglass ~

"COUNTENANCE AND PROTECTION"

When the Continental Congress penned its eighth article that encouraged frugality and discouraged entertainments, David Douglass did not read about it in the New York newspapers. Rather, Peyton Randolph, the first president of the Congress, personally delivered the bad news to Douglass that informed him the desire had expired and war was likely.[1] Both men were in New York at the time—November 1774—one to open a theatre, the other to create a nation. Randolph was the head of that impressive delegate of Virginians who represented the colony in Philadelphia at the first Continental Congress (along with Patrick Henry, George Washington, and Richard Henry Lee); he was also Virginia's Speaker of the House of Burgesses (prorogued at the time), head of the Virginia militia (quite ready), and had been unanimously elected the first president of the Congress. He was, at the time, one of the most important and respected figures in that formidable assembly, and somehow he knew actor-manager David Douglass, knew him well enough and thought well enough of him to hand-deliver the news at the close of the Congress. Nor was he alone in his acquaintance. Dunlap informs us that the New York Committee of delegates—John Jay, James Duane, and Philip Livingston—also personally confirmed the resolution to Douglass. Unearthing the dense and intracolonial social network that connected these many unlikely acquaintances is the project that follows.

Peyton Randolph, Philip Livingston, and John Jay were not the only men of influence that Douglass supped with that month. When it became clear that the conflict was not going to blow over by Christmas, Douglass made arrangements to carry his company to Jamaica and sit out the storm. Prior to departing he secured one final important letter, also from an old acquaintance on the other side of the hostilities, the former New York governor Cadwallader Colden. Douglass had known the Colden family for more than a decade, and now waited on the former governor for a character letter addressed to the current governor of Jamaica, Sir Basil Keith, requesting the latter's support in advance. Colden dispatched it and Governor Keith replied: "Sir, a few days ago I received your favour of the 28th of January [1775], I am at present at a considerable distance from the Towns [Kingston and Spanish Town]; but on my return which will be in five or six weeks hence; I will with pleasure give all my countenance and protection to Mr. Douglass and his Company."[2] It was, in essence, a transfer of patronage. A few such documents survive, and they are very revealing about the ordered and immaterial world of power behind such letters, the textured and layered social hierarchies of patron and client in which the theatre lived and through which theatre managers like Douglass navigated. Gordon Wood has written of this network as a "delicate web of paternalistic obligation," which is a kind phrase for dependency. Sorting oneself amidst these kinds of dependencies—dense, complex, and pronounced—was the social grammar of colonial America and any advancement depended on how fluently one "spoke" this grammar. Wood identifies the paternalistic system as part of the old monarchical order that was dismantled by the new and radical republicanism—true enough in the Revolution—but in the third quarter of the century business was still being conducted the old fashion, vertical way. The new American notions of a democratic equality were a long way off from the *real politique* of a mid-century slave-holding southern colony like Virginia, or South Carolina, under the governance of a landed aristocrat, or Pennsylvania under the hereditary proprietorship of the Penn family. Here the sorting occurred through an elaborate grammar of highly stratified relationships that had been worked out for centuries and remained in place until the outbreak of the war: patronage, obligations, gratitude, reciprocity, all the beholding inequities of a classed society.[3] One may move within this structure of authority—vertically, laterally, fluidly—as the aspiration for gentility was all about movement within this structure, but the structure itself was never in doubt. Learning this grammar was a survival skill of the most essential kind. At no point was fluency so essential as the moment of introduction.

When William Hickey was first paying his respects in Jamaica, also in 1775, one of the men he was conducted to meet was a tavern owner Mr. Baggs. Their introduction is telling for the fluency in which both parties—whose positions were unknown to each other—rapidly sorted themselves and the other:

> Upon my being introduced, Mr. Baggs asked whether I was related to Mr. Hickey of St. Albans Street. Being told I was his son come to settle upon the Island in the profession of the Law, he expressed much pleasure at seeing me, saying how happy he should be to assist me and promote my views by every means within his power, and "give me leave to add, Sir," said he, "I possess some little interest and influence upon this Island.". . . Mr. Baggs told me he had for many years been acquainted with and highly respected my father, that he had been first introduced by his brother, the Major, who acknowledged himself under extraordinary obligations to him, both professional and pecuniary. After drinking half a dozen bumper toasts from enormous glasses we were permitted to depart, Mr. Baggs saying to me, "Believe me Mr. Hickey, I shall be happy to return to you some of those kindnesses my brother and self have received from your father. Let me request, whenever you are not otherwise engaged, that you will *sans ceremonie* consider this your home. Three times a week, at least, you will find a select little party, like this of today, always consisting of gentlemen of the first rank and on the island, with as good a dinner as Kingston affords, and there is no better in the universe. My wines will speak for themselves, and I promise you a cordial welcome. Here, Sir, I am *Squire Baggs*, upon a footing with the Governor or any other man—on the opposite side of the street [where he operated his tavern] the case is different. There I am *Jack Baggs*, the tavern keeper, where I know my distance and keep it, never using a freedom with any customers."[4]

Baggs was clear to sound out the young Hickey on his origins, and once confirmed, he was sorted according to the worth of his father (where Baggs stood indebted). That settled, he moved on to establish his own worth (brother of Major Baggs and a man of great influence on the island). He was clear to acknowledge the contractual reciprocity of a debt owed to Hickey senior, and paid in kindness to Hickey junior. But Baggs also made a spatial distinction that was probably more common than recorded: the tavern keeper was all merchant in the ordinary, keeping his distance and respecting his place as a servant to his customers. Across the street, however, at his own house, he was all Squire, on "footing with the Governor," and his wines and his company were the display of his geographically parsed gentility. Hickey sorted him accordingly, as a customer in his tavern but a guest at his house where the debt of past kindness of Hickey senior was repaid to the son.

Hickey, his father, Baggs the tavern keeper, and his brother the major were all known entities in the social mix of Kingston. A more complicated exchange involved the introduction of unknown actors seeking new patronage in a new society. When the American Company first opened in Charleston in 1763, Douglass carried a letter from David Colden, the son of the governor of New York to the (bed-ridden) Charleston naturalist Dr. Alexander Garden. Garden's brief reply articulates at least four levels of such dependency at work between the bearer of the first letter (Douglass), the addressee of the first letter and author of the second (Garden), the addressee of the second letter (David Colden), and his absent father (the governor):

> Sir—Your favor of Janry 26th 1763 was sent to me some time in November by Mr. Douglass. I was then confined to my room & had been for many weeks, as soon as I was able to see Company I begged Mr. Douglass to favour me with his & found him perfectly answer the Character which you drew of him. You may depend on this that I will not omit any opportunity to shew Every service in my power to him or any person whose acquaintance you are so obliging as to offer me.[5]

Douglass, given the honor of bearing the first letter, was beholden to the Coldens, who had troubled themselves to introduce the manager to Dr. Garden with a generous "character." Douglass, after his interview confirmed his worth, was now also indebted to Dr. Garden for his new favors and promised support. For his part, Dr. Garden was indebted to the Coldens (apologized for the delay, honored by the attention), and in the economy of power, promised to repay his debt by favoring their favorite. Garden, grateful to be of service as a friend of the Colden family, was clearly not a peer of either Douglass, who was beholden to Garden, or the Coldens to whom he was indebted. Garden, by honoring Douglass with his patronage, was paying his respects up the ladder to David Colden, and vis-à-vis (the next rung) to his father, Governor Colden. The Coldens (amateur naturalists, father and son), for their part, were acknowledging the respect accorded the doctor by requesting his support, while recognizing that a shared or superior scientific interest did not trump the Aristocratic privilege and position that separated the Coldens from the famous Dr. Garden. Douglass, as the vehicle in the exchange, both letter bearer and subject, was inserting himself into the company of learned Scotsmen (they were all Scottish), trading on the social stature of the Coldens to gain currency with Garden in the Scottish community of Charleston. Once in favor with Garden, the doctor would further broadcast his support of Douglass through his Charleston circles, like the St. Andrew's Society, and thereby increase his own social currency as an ally of the Colden family.

Patronage was this complex and invisible a system through which all social advancement occurred and most relationships were defined, and actors and actor-managers were clearly not exempt. They played, as the header of the bills remind us, "by permission," and consequently wherever there was performance, there was patronage of some nature. Most did not leave a trace—Colden's letter is unique—but it was this network that brought players into contact with the political elite—governors, congressmen, signers of the Declaration—and through which they found popular support. Popular support alone (the market) would go nowhere without patronage, as Hallam discovered when he arrived in Williamsburg in 1752. (Encouraged by "principal gentlemen" of Virginia he was nonetheless initially repulsed by the governor and council and lobbied for two months before securing the necessary permission; similarly with Douglass in New York in 1758.)

But as in any social system, the grammar of patronage came with rules and barriers, often unspoken, but never unobserved without a breach. Access to power through gates of decorum—like Garden's bedside—where lineage, character, deportment, association, education were all tested—and such letters of introduction like Colden wrote served to open the portals to power. Managers of traveling companies had exceptional need of such patrons, working as they did in a wide intracolonial network of allies, from local authorities to merchants, burgesses to colonial governors, in concert or occasionally playing one against the other until a leave could be wrung. Sometimes the negotiations were prolonged (Hallam, Virginia, 1752; Douglass, New York, 1758), sometimes perfunctory (Mills, Newport, 1768), and a rebuff of this kind would leave a company idle, while the manager made the rounds, paying his respects, establishing himself in that dense web of dependencies (what Tate Wilkinson called "seeding the rich," vol. I, 143). The success or failure of the company could ultimately depend upon how well one understood one's place in the unspoken social network. Hence it was vital to have developed a secure intracolonial system of patronage that allowed the itinerant company an expectation of license and a base of support in colonies far removed prior to packing the scenes and boarding the coastal packet. Public letters were of some use, such as the one Mr. Mills procured from Governor William Tryon or Douglass did when he left Virginia with a character letter "signed by the Governor, the Council, and near one hundred of the principal gentlemen of Virginia."[6] But colonial America in 1760 was a face culture (there were only three cities in 1760 that had more than 10,000 people, and one had no theatre); any success would ultimately be driven not by public advertisements, but by personal, face-to-face contracts of obligation and gratitude.

A circuit of theatres could not have been built without this kind of intensely personal social network, particularly buildings raised by community subscription. They were expensive investments for a manager like Douglass, utterly out of reach for fugitive managers like Mills and Verling; consequently managers found ways to share the burden of the building with the community and for this one's standing in the community needed to be clearly known. Occasionally it could be farmed out to a contractor on speculation, if one could be found willing to take the success of the project on faith. When David Ross built the Theatre Royal at Edinburgh, his contractor purchased all the materials himself and was reimbursed from the proceeds of the playhouse once it was opened.[7] The petition submitted by Alexander Alexander, who built the Society Hill Theatre in Philadelphia, 1759, reveals that Douglass also employed the practice of subcontracting the construction and cost to the builder early on, but once he was no longer a stranger, such practices gave way to subscription schemes (Williamsburg 1760, Annapolis 1770, Charleston 1773, Kingston 1775, and Spanish Town 1776). These subscriptions required a sizeable network of supporters and a local (trustworthy) broker in whose care the money (as much as £600) was deposited, and it was often done when the manager of the company was not even in residence.[8] Developing this social network could have been as much of a labor as erecting the building itself, particularly in the 1750s and 1760s, for managers like Walter Murray, Thomas Kean, David Douglass who were strangers in the colonies where they raised these theatres. To catch a glimpse of this social network at its thickest, I look to an unlikely source, the lodge records of the Ancient and Honorable Order of the Free and Accepted Masons. The association was suggested by an equally unlikely event: the theft of an actor's trunk. Once, in Philadelphia, Thomas Wall, an actor with the American Company, had his trunk broken into and among the items stolen were his tickets (actors were required to print off their own benefit tickets). With his benefit night approaching, he was obliged to lay out for a second run of tickets, but to distinguish them from the first, which would no longer be honored, he had them marked with a special sign: the Mason's symbol of the Grand Geometrician. It was not only a code to catch a thief, but Wall was also advertising his association with the fraternity. The choice of this sign began the inquiry into the Masonic associations of actors and managers, and a few small and very useful discoveries emerged.

THE ABSENCE OF WILLIAM QUELCH

For example, William Quelch, a young actor with the odd last name, also in the American Company, was not present for his own initiation into the fraternal order of Freemasons and was consequently fined for his absence when the fraternity next convened. He was, nonetheless, unanimously admitted to the order, in absentia. But because he was not there, we have a record of him.

Through a very odd chance we have preserved one page of minutes from the treasurer's account book of the Williamsburg Lodge of Freemasons for the two months of December 1762 and January 1763.

When Nathaniel Walthoe, treasurer of the Williamsburg Lodge, ran out of paper for his minutes one night in 1779, he ripped out a page from an earlier minute book and used the back of it.[9] The earlier treasury books are no longer extant. Only the one page has survived as an interleaf in the later manuscript minutes of the treasurer of this elite and secret society, an anachronistic hiccup in a calendar of 1779 that jumps for one page back to the winter of 1762–1763.

And so with delight and surprise we find two very familiar names in the Mason's treasurer's minutes for the night of December 21, 1762: "Mr. William Quelch paid his initiation of 4.6s." Mr. Quelch was, at the time, not present for the initiation in Williamsburg; he was engaged on the stage in Norfolk. Though the company resided in the capital for the court seasons of 1762, several weeks of the winter were spent in the surrounding towns of Norfolk, Petersburg, and Fredericksburg, and such work engagements obliged the Masonic members of the company to miss their monthly assembly. By the January meeting of the order, the company had returned to Williamsburg and it was on this occasion we learn that Quelch was fined for his previous absence. The treasurer recorded it duly as he received it: "By Mr. Quelch for last lodge being absent, 2s.6d." Below that, the second name from the company was also recorded: "Mr. Douglass, for being absent, 2s.6d."[10]

Records of absence. We do not have a lot else to go on—for example, we do not have a roster of all those who attended the Williamsburg Lodge, the treasurer's records note only those who were fined—but the fine marked the absence and the absence marked the presence of Mr. Quelch and Mr. Douglass, and that absence may be enough to tease out something of the complex relations between the players and the fertile network of patronage that Masonic membership offered them. What did it mean to be a Mason in 1760? More germane to our study, what did it mean to admit an itinerant player and manager into this society?

"ALL GOOD MEN AND TRUE"

A social history of Freemasonry in America has yet to be written, particularly for the eighteenth century when it enjoyed its great revival with a surge of new charters and lodges that spread to most of the American colonies. Some roster lists still survive from many of the older lodges and a study of how membership advanced and solidified positions within the small and often fractured communities would be enormously useful. The oldest lodges, like in Philadelphia (1731), Boston (1733), Charleston (1737), and New York (1739), were established during the same decade that saw the greatest statistical separation of wealth and the emergence of a controlling planter class and first families.[11] What did it mean to establish fraternities of universal equality by the very men who were rapidly concentrating the lion's share of the colony's capital? The Master Masons were nominated from this class, but this study is more interested in how the middling sort—who were also members—availed themselves of the fraternity. Printers, for example, are frequently deeply connected with masonry, often serving as the lodge's secretary (Jonas Green, Robert Wells, and Hugh Gaine), or actors like William Quelch.

By mid-century most of the colonies and the Anglophone West Indies had initiated lodges—in Virginia alone Masonic charters were granted to lodges in Williamsburg, Norfolk, Petersburg, Richmond, Port Royal, Hobb's Hole, Fredericksburg, Yorktown, and Dumfries.[12] Lodges were also established on the islands: Jamaica, Barbados, Antigua, St. Kitts, and St. Croix in the 1750s and 1760s.[13] Many lodge records are preserved and a cursory list reveals the membership was a who's who of the colonial elite: colonial governors, judges, councilmen, assembly men, prominent merchants, and burgesses. The Boston roster included the likes of John Adams, John Hancock, Joseph Warren, Paul Revere, and John Rowe. When William Quelch was admitted to the order in Virginia, Peyton Randolph was its Master Mason, and members included John Blair, Sir George Tucker, George Gilmore, and its secretary, Nathaniel Walthoe, was also the governor's secretary, as well as clerk to the General Assembly. George Washington's Masonic associations in his own Fredericksburg lodge has been the study of several works: he joined in November of 1752 and was Master Mason the following year.[14] The Virginia merchant and middling class was also represented by the likes of Peter Pelham, organist at Bruton Parish Church, William and Alexander Finney, Humphrey Harwood, builder, Edward and Richard Charlton, barber and peruke makers, later proprietor of Charleston's coffeehouse and quondam actor; John Galt, apothecary, and the printer and tavern

owner James Southall: merchants and gentry and players. It was a
well-stocked pond of the politically and commercially connected. In
Charleston, the Union Killwinning lodge could count upward of a 100
members in a town of a 5,000. The Masons were clearly the most
concentrated (male) social organization of the day.

It should not surprise us that an actor like Quelch would find
membership useful. What is surprising is how many actors were
Masons, and that we have any record of it at all. Being always visitors,
few found their names inscribed in the monthly rosters. I suspect that
many colonial American actors belonged to the fraternity without
leaving their names in the treasurer's books; certainly many had benefits
that were specifically supported by the Masons—William Verling,
Lewis Hallam, Jr., Thomas Wall, Walter Murray, Stephen Woolls,
David Douglass, Richard Goodman, William Moore, Mr. White—as
frequently in the benefits special prologues were written to court the
Masons. William Verling, as an actor in Douglass's company and later
as a manager of his own troupe, found great encouragement from his
fellow Masons. For his benefit night in Charleston, March 20, 1776, he
solicited and received the support of the fraternity:

> As the play to be acted on Thursday the 20th instant, is for the benefit of
> our brother Mr. William Verling, the members of Solomon's Lodge, with
> those of the several lodges in Charlestown, also all transient brethren, are
> requested to meet at the house of Mr. Robert Dillon, at half after four in the
> afternoon of said day, thence to proceed in procession to the theatre. By
> order of the Master, [signed] I. de Costa, Secry. March 18, 1766.[15]

Thomas Wall, whose reprinted tickets acknowledged his association
with the fraternity, was counting on their support for his benefit in
Philadelphia. His name appears in the minutes of the Fredericksburg
Lodge as a visiting brother. Stephen Woolls, recruited to the American
Company in 1765, often sang the Mason Anthem in the playhouse.
Was Woolls a Mason as well, or was he just lending his voice for the
company good?[16]

If actors found the fraternity beneficial, then the advantages for a
manager would be too large to overlook: not the least of which would
have been the introduction to a concentrated population of the social

and political elite in each city and town the company appeared. Setting aside both the spiritual attainment of the order and, as Hogarth reminds us, its conviviality, the Masons were one of the few meeting grounds that was not sorted by class—a model of that emerging radicalism that Wood writes of—and a manager like Douglass would be well placed to seek association in such a "universal Brotherhood." They were, for example, apolitical (at least until the Revolution), open "to all good men and true," not bound by party, indeed, "resolved against all politics, which never yet conducted to the welfare of the craft, nor ever will."[17] An association that aspired to transcend party, nation, denomination, colony of residence, and, to a striking extent, class, would have been enormously useful in times of increased nationalist tensions, like the Stamp Act or the Non-Importation Agreement. As a Mason in Williamsburg, a manager like Douglass could move among a select society of Virginia elite, including the governors (like Lord Botetourt who donated the Master Mason's chair to the lodge), his personal secretary (Nathaniel Walthoe) who also served as the order's secretary, the colony's printer, tavern owners, and merchants, soliciting patronage and support. Or consider the advantages of an association of smaller company managers like Mr. Mills in Halifax and the city's leading merchant, Master Mason Joseph Montfort. Or in Portsmouth, New Hampshire, where Mr. Morgan opened in October of 1772. Less than a month into his two-night-a-week run he played a "bespeak" ("By Desire of the Right Worshipful the Master, and Brethren of the New Hampshire Lodge of Free and Accepted Masons"). This was patronage at its most serviceable and accessible level.[18]

What did it mean to admit a player like William Quelch or a manager like David Douglass into such a society? Clearly they are not entirely the social outcasts of legend, if at some level, they were being accepted, initiated if you will, into a sort of residency. A kind of citizenship was being extended, a membership outside the ordered inequities of patronage, and the players used it to their great advantage in many ways. It simplified the grammar of patronage by allowing immediate access to the many tiers of society—merchants and artisans, mayors, councilmen, and governors. It allowed them lateral mobility as the Masons were a "universal association," and there was equal recognition accorded to the "visiting brothers" and "transient gentlemen" (e.g., ship captains) as to members.[19] Indeed, one mechanism allowed an easy passage and introduction from lodge to lodge for just such visiting brethren. A document called a Traveling Masonic Certificate was provided to members in good standing that allowed them to present their credentials to other lodges.[20] A list of lodges and their meeting schedules were available through guides that were published, like James Rivington's *A Pocket Companion and History of Free Masons.*[21] Membership also guaranteed a degree of social acceptability in a community where character, not coin, was currency, and in which colonial governors, judges, merchants, clergy, and dancing masters all brushed elbows. Most importantly, it allowed the managers a ready market of potential patrons that stretched across the social landscape.

But admission was not open. There were several barriers designed to keep out the undesirables. The complicated initiation process was one deterrent. In the first stage of admission, a candidate like Quelch or Douglass would have to be nominated by a current brother of the lodge in good standing. Then followed a waiting process until the next meeting (usually monthly) in which the applicant's character was reviewed. The third meeting advanced to a general vote. The vote had to be unanimous: "Each brother at the meeting dropped a ball into the ballot box passed around the room—a white ball for acceptance, a black for rejection. A single black ball excluded the candidate."[22] Once the vote was tallied, formal initiation was still deferred until the next meeting. As much as three or four months could pass from the start of the process to initiation. Once initiated, a member in good standing advanced by degrees within the order, culminating with the post of Master Mason.

Additionally there were financial barriers. Brother Quelch paid over £4 for admission to the first degree. This was on the low end. Boston lodge members paid out £10 for admission. Though restrictions on the basis of class was anathema, to encourage "men of eminence," the fees and fines were kept on the spendy side. And then there were uniforms and equipage: the gloves, the aprons, jewelry, the regalia and insignia, all had to be purchased. The initiated were also expected to host the lodge on the occasion, no small layout there. And there were dues— 18 shillings quarterly—and fines, like Quelch's for being absent, 2s 6d. And then, of course, the charities and these were not optional. The bylaws required donations "toward the Relief of the Poor."[23] All this would have been particularly taxing to the itinerant actor whose engagements frequently obliged them to be absent. Nonetheless, Quelch and Douglass bore the fines.

So what were they buying, exactly, with their membership? For an actor like Quelch, or Wall, association with the fraternity would have extended many social and practical advantages. The fraternal attendance on benefit nights alone would be worth the membership dues, as many actors discovered. For a manager like Walter Murray, or William Verling, or David Douglass, the rewards were far greater. Clearly the manager was buying access, for one. Many colonial governors and lieutenant governors—the very people from whom permission must be secured—were themselves Masons. William Denny, James Hamilton, Lord Botetourt, Henry Moore, Horatio Sharpe, and Thomas Balden were all Masons. As were many colonial mayors—William Plumstead of Philadelphia, William Prentice of Williamsburg. Status for another. Membership, like a wig, was a sign of certain social standing in spite of its altruistic aspirations of a classless assembly. Residency for a third. In practical terms, Masonic membership allowed a traveling manager like Douglass to enter a town not as a stranger or as a stroller, but as a "visiting brother," to present his certificate and find an instant community for all his needs: printers, merchants, building contractors, mayors, judges, men of influence, and occasionally governors. Many of the partners with whom Brother Douglass did business were Masons—certainly most of the printers—and one suspects that the Masonic connection lubricated and accelerated many transactions from securing permission to play to finding lots to lease, establishing accounts with the printers, initiating subscriptions, or acquiring a reputable rental agent to gather subscriptions in advance and look after and occasionally rent the property in the company's absence. The manager was looking for, in short, instant residency, and he did not have all summer to do it. What he found in the fraternity was the "countenance," the encouragement, permission, and privilege of a resident to set up shop and do business.

Upon entering a new colony, any manager would need four things in very short order: permission to play, a place to play, a subscription base, and a printer through whom to find his base. The single most concentrated place to find all of these under the same roof was the Masonic lodge.

When Douglass arrived as a stranger in Annapolis, for example, in early February of 1760, one essential contact would have been the treasurer of the Annapolis Lodge of Masons Jonas Green. As a fellow Mason, Douglass would have found in Green one-stop shopping. Green was the colonial printer who published *The Maryland Gazette*, the colony's only newspaper, with whom Douglass would do substantial business. Douglass would advertise in the *Gazette* weekly, Green would also run off the playbills, the handbills, strike off the tickets, and the printing office would outlet the tickets for a commission. Douglass was also able to lease a lot next to Green's printing shop, and there he built a playhouse rather hastily in February of 1760. For that he needed quick permission, encouragement, and an available builder. Green may have helped here as well. Beyond his duties as printer to the colony and Masonic treasurer, Green was also secretary to the governor, Horatio Sharpe (who was himself a Mason), and Green was also an alderman of the city and master of ceremonies for the famous Tuesday Club (when Dr. Alexander Hamilton was alive and the Master Mason of the Annapolis Lodge), and he was clerk for the Annapolis races—no mean post in this horsey town—and vestryman for St. Anne's Parish, in which capacity he arranged for builders and carpenters to make alterations to the church. If all these various positions did not thoroughly ensconce Green with the who's who of Annapolis, the printer was also, for many years, the postmaster of the city. As Lawrence Wroth summed up Green's social exertions, "there seems to have been no local activity of any importance in which 'the printer to the Province' was not concerned."[24] If Brother Douglass, armed with a Traveling Certificate, could introduce himself to the Grand Master or treasurer at the monthly assembly of the Masons in Annapolis, he could meet all his needs in one visit to one lodge: permission, place, printer, builder, base. And apparently he did. In an astonishingly brief period, Douglass was somehow able to introduce himself to the governor, the local authorities, secure permission to play, lease a lot of land next to Jonas Green, hire a contractor who would undertake to build a playhouse on faith, erect the building, and open it "to a polite and numerous audience" (which included the governor), with a special prologue and epilogue written for the occasion by the local rector James Sterling, and Douglass accomplished this level of support—building and all—in some six weeks start to finish in a town he had never set foot in before. In short, his Masonic membership allowed him to arrive as a resident.

Similarly, in New York, Douglass found in Hugh Gaine a Masonic point-person to facilitate his business. Gaine was not only a bookseller and the printer of the *New York Mercury* with whom Douglass did the usual printing business of the playhouse—printed the bills and weekly advertisements—but he was also the ticket seller and agent of the playhouse, through whom it was later leased, a lifelong associate of the actors (John Henry at his death would leave a legacy to Hugh Gaine), and Gaine was also for several years the secretary of the Grand Lodge of Masons.[25] Among the Masons Douglass would have met was the future master of the lodge in New York, Continental Congressmen William Livingston. In Charleston, the Masonic point-person was the Scottish bookseller Robert Wells, again, grand secretary of the Solomon Lodge. Wells was also the printer of the *South Carolina Gazette*, who leased a building site for the theatre and later collected and managed the £600 sub-scription to the building of it, and once opened, outlet tickets, printed the playbills, and who was also left as the agent of the playhouse when the company departed. Not surprisingly, Wells rented the playhouse to—who else?—Masons, the Union Kilwinning Lodge.[26] The Grand Master at the time was Sir Egerton Leigh, knight and a baron, a substantial landholder, judge of the Vice Admiralty, and attorney general for the colony of South Carolina. In station, Leigh was second only to the lieutenant governor. The Grand Master was also an amateur playwright and a public patron of the actors. Charleston merchant James Laurens, complaining to his brother on a business trip to London, wrote on March 3, 1774:

> I have nothing further to offer at Present on the affair of Mr. Leigh, whose Voyage to England it seems is Postponed & I have no doubt will be deferr'd till your return from thence. His Spirits have been lately Supported by a Company of Players who have been fleecing the town since November last, who when they do not entertain him at the Theatre (where by the by he has met with much disrespect), get drunk with him at his own house.[27]

Drinking (and one hopes dining) with the attorney general and Master Mason were the kinds of face alliances that would have opened, acceler-ated, and cemented so many necessary protocols so efficiently.

Even sounding out a new market, Douglass would use his Masonic connections. In Boston, in the summer of 1769, Douglass entered the city as a stranger on a reconnaissance of new markets. But he carried with him a traveling Masonic Certificate that he could present to the Grand Master of the St. Andrew's Lodge, John Rowe. Apparently he did just that, as Douglass secured the upper room of a tavern to perform his one-person "lectures"—Steven's *Lectures on Heads*—at the Bunch of Grapes. This tavern was owned and operated by Brother Joseph Ingersoll (a Mason) and the same upper room had been for many years the meeting house of the Masonic Lodge. Ingersoll's tavern still hosted the fraternity's dinners on St. John's Night. It was a Masonic space and a natural space for the brothers to assemble, and performance in such a space may have gone a long way in a town with prohibition against performance on the books. Grand Master Rowe, for his part, attended Douglass's "lectures" and recorded it, by name, in his diary: "31 July 1769—in the evening I went to hear Mr. Douglass lecture on heads; he performed well."[28] Douglass ultimately found no market in Boston, but his Masonic fellowship clearly facilitated his introduction.[29]

To test this, one needs only consider the introduction of two companies in Williamsburg. When Lewis Hallam, Sr. arrived in Williamsburg as a stranger in early June of 1752, it took him over three months to win the support of the town, secure permission of the governor and council, refit an existing playhouse and open by September 15.[30] When Douglass arrived as a stranger in the same capital sometime in August 1760, he made his introductions, bought or leased land, contracted a builder, raised a subscription (to which George Washington contributed £7.10.3 for 20 box tickets), erected a new playhouse from the ground up, and, as quickly as he did in Annapolis earlier, was open for business no later than by October 2: six or seven weeks start to finish.[31] What better place for Douglass to find support for building than a society of Masons? And once supported, what better place for Douglass to find a builder than a Masonic lodge? At the fundamental core, the Masonic image was the builder's rule, the Grand Geometrician. What better image for David Douglass, a theatre-builder?

THE CLEANSING OF PHILADELPHIA (PART I)

Consider a second case study in which the advantages of membership were equally protective, but less visible than Douglass's sterling opening evening in Annapolis. Throughout the late summer and fall of 1749, a company of low-profile actors were quietly performing a word-of-mouth season of plays in Philadelphia without the formal permission of the governor. Whether they neglected to secure permission, or, suspecting difficulties, opted not to, or simply, as Rankin (The Theatre in Colonial America, 30) suggests, could not afford to, we do not know. They also chose not to advertise in the newspapers, suggesting a clandestine operation. What little we know of their season—a passing diary entry for August 22, 1749, the recollections of the aged Robert Venable, and the town council meetings of January 8, 1750 when they were ultimately suppressed—nonetheless suggests a fully outfitted company with professional aspirations, certainly one with a solid repertory (under their belts or in the making) and a converted warehouse on Water Street for a theatre, within the city limits. We also know this company seemed to enjoy some degree of support from certain civic leaders, including their landlord, William Plumstead, former alderman, justice of the Peace, and soon to be mayor of Philadelphia, and a second "Great Personnage" who wrote and spoke the opening prologue of *Cato*, sometime that season, and as a guest undertook the role of Portius. We also learn from Robert Venable, one source interviewed for Watson's *Annals of Philadelphia*, that the company that gathered at the playhouse (the audience) was "genteel."[32] But something happened by January of 1750 and their season—such as it was—came to an abrupt end when the players were called before the city council by the Court Recorder William Allen and "bound over" on good behavior (i.e., "suppressed") but—tellingly—neither fined nor arrested. Shortly afterward the entire company, now known as the Murray–Kean Company, traveled to New York, where they were introduced as "lately arriv'd from Philadelphia" and where they secured permission, advertised and performed an 18-month season of plays—by far the longest sustained season of any colonial American company—with only a 6-week summer recess.

The story of their suppression in Philadelphia has been told many times in moral terms. The drift of the tale is Quaker hostility—more on that below.[33] But for now I want to explore the company's Masonic support, an association that may have allowed them to carry on a clandestine season of plays with the compliant toleration of the very authorities who would later suppress them. The story of their suppression is ultimately far more complicated than Quaker opposition to the theatre or neglecting to secure permission to perform, or when denied permission, performing anyway until they were caught. A company would not choose to play within the city limits if they had not some kind of authority to do so, or if playing itself were illegal. Twenty five years earlier a visiting company evaded the city's sanctions by setting up their stage outside the city in the southern liberties and enjoyed the patronage of the governor, to Mayor Logan's annoyance. That possibility was certainly still available to Walter Murray and Thomas Kean. But they did not need to resort to the margins because many of the councilmen who later suppressed them knew they were playing from the very beginning of their season, indeed, many of the councilmen were among the "genteel company" that attended the playhouse. They would not be tolerated for five months if there was not also substantial support, civic support, perhaps even gubernatorial support. And if they enjoyed such support, the question becomes not why the company was suppressed, or even why they were tolerated so long, but rather why was the support ultimately withdrawn?

Let me begin with a few important families. In the dense network of local power, many of the key players of the Common council, governor's council, and the Assembly—all the bodies that ultimately suppressed the players—were fully conversant with the plans of a playhouse within the city. Only one title of the Murray–Kean Company's initial Philadelphia season has been recorded, but how it was recorded may offer some insight into the mechanics of civic toleration.

In his diary for August 22, 1749, the Quaker John Smith noted with some distaste: "Jos: Morris & I happened in at Peacock Biggers, & drank Tea there & his daughter being one of the Company who were going to hear the Tragedy of *Cato* Acted it Occasioned some Conversation in w'ch I Expressed my sorrow that any thing of the kind was encouraged." John Smith, whose Quaker severity had little regard for the business of playing, was the son-in-law of the Quaker James Logan, who had even less opinion of the players. Logan will be remembered as the mayor of Philadelphia in 1723 who tried to discourage the company of players that had strolled thither and was unable to suppress them. In 1749 the long-standing patriarch of Philadelphia public office was now 75 years old, retired from public service to his country-seat at Stenton (some six miles from Philadelphia)—but was nonetheless still very involved in Pennsylvania politics, including Quaker politics. John Smith had married into the Logan family and counted his brother-in-law, Logan's eldest son, William Logan, amongst his closest correspondents. If Smith knew of the players and expressed his displeasure that Quaker families were encouraging them, it is not unlikely that the Logan family knew of them as well, and William Logan happened to currently sit on the governor's council, indeed, and was currently the president of the council. But the players continued to perform from at least August, when Smith first heard of them through the close of the year, until January of 1750 when the Court Recorder William Allen formally brought them to the council's attention.

But William Allen also knew of the productions long before he alerted the council through a separate social network that many of the councilmen also belonged to: the Ancient Order of the Free and Accepted Masons. The Freemasons were a significant political and social force in Philadelphia, establishing the earliest lodge in 1731.[34] By 1749 the Masonic lodge of Philadelphia met at the Tun Tavern (Sign of the One Tun, later the Royal Standard Tavern on Market Street near Second), operated by Brother Mullin, who also sold play tickets there. Its membership was a veritable who's who of Philadelphia's social elite, and no figure loomed larger in Masonic organization than William Allen, the court recorder. Allen was the Grand Master of the order as early as 1732, a position he occupied for 17 years, stepping aside only for the obligatory rotation of officers. Allen would remain an active and contributing member to the Masons until after his death when £50 was subscribed posthumously to erecting a new lodge. Councilman Benjamin Franklin was another long-standing member. Elected Masonic warden at the lodge's initiation, the printer quickly rose in rotation for the Grand Master's post. In 1749 Franklin was spelling Allen as provisional grand master (Allen would resume in March of

1750). The merchant William Plumstead, who rented the warehouse to the players, was another former Grand Master and in 1749 the Grand Treasurer of the Masons. The Lieutenant Governor James Hamilton, the ultimate arbiter of the player's plight, was another former and future Grand Master of the same lodge of Masons.[35] Also in the fraternity was Walter Murray, the manager of the acting company performing in Philadelphia in 1749 and early 1750, who was admitted, initiated, and promoted into the same Philadelphia St. John's Lodge during the summer and fall of 1749.[36] Did the Masonic brothers—Allen, Hamilton, Franklin, Shippen, Plumstead, and William Smith—know of their treasurer's playhouse? Of course they did, the manager was in their midst.

The Freemasons were a benevolent society, but they were not an open fraternity. As the charter makes clear, members were invited in with some discretion, strict inquiries were made into character, and if found credible, an initiate was raised into membership only after probation. Admission also required the unanimous vote of all Masonic members; one dissenting vote and the applicant was denied. As fortune would have it, there is still preserved a minute book of the Philadelphia St. John's Lodge of Masons, commencing June 28, 1749, on whose pages a roster of names has been left. Among the members provisionally admitted in the summer of 1749, is the name of Walter Murray, actor and manager of the company of players in Philadelphia. His name appears first in the June 28 meeting when he is considered for admission. At the next recorded meeting on August 16, we read "Brother Walter Murray passed." This refers to the first hurdle of admission—the inquiry into character—and on September 11, "Brother Murray passed and admitted" refers to the lodge's vote.[37] Once admitted, over the subsequent months of that fall, Brother Murray was active enough in the fraternity to be "raised" to the second degree, as we read on December 6, 1749.[38] With each elevation, the fee was collected by the treasurer (and landlord) William Plumstead. That Murray's activity in the lodge coincided with his activity on the boards is hardly coincidental, nor, I suspect, was it coincidental that Murray's name dropped from the Philadelphia Masonic records by the January 1750 meeting, when he was called before the city council. That Murray rented the warehouse-cum-playhouse from the Mason's treasurer and was voted into the order by Plumstead, William Allen, James Hamilton, Benjamin Franklin, and other prominent members of the governor's council troubles the account that this company was some six months later "called to the attention of the Governor Hamilton and the council by William Allen." That all parties involved belonged to the small but active lodge of Masons alerts us that the fraternity, at least, already knew something of the business of Walter Murray long before he was formally brought before the council.

Several other names on the list of provisional members from the same summer may also have been the actors in the same company but they are listed only by their surnames: Mr. Scott, Mr. Moore, Mr. Davis, Mr. Marks, all appear on the June roster with Walter Murray and may (I would say likely) refer to the actors of the same names in Murray's company.[39] Whatever else we do not know about the origins of the Murray–Kean Company—and speculations are legion—it is intriguing to consider a company of actors who, at one level, were citizens of Philadelphia, Freemasons, moving among other Masons, the governor, the council, aldermen, merchants, and the most powerful men of the city, initiating a clandestine season of plays in their midst, perhaps even for them, one of whom contributed a playhouse and another contributed a prologue and played Portius.

Why this network of power eventually failed the company and its manager Walter Murray was asked to discontinue is a tale that will be resumed later. Clearly the other side of partisan power is still power, and the hazards of evoking the patronage of one party (in this case the Anglicans) stands or falls with the fortunes of the party.

"SINGULAR SERVICE"

Some of the advantages to Masonic membership I have suggested; other privileges I have only begun to suspect. From the minute books of the Kilwinning Lodge, Port Royal, comes the case of Peter Corns, "a sea-faring man," who applied for a speedy initiation, obliged, as he was, to sail the next day. "They dispensed with many of the mysteries, and admitted him as an Apprentice when membership might be of singular services to him in case by the fortunes of war he should fall into the hands of the enemy."[40] What privilege or "singular service" might membership accorded to an English sailor in an Anglo-French war have? And what might have been socially useful to the players as well, to evoke membership to solicit influence or mollify any hostility?

But admission was steep and such barriers were designed to keep out exactly the sort of company that strollers represented. Though some Boston brothers prided themselves on excluding "improper persons," the fact that traveling actors, sailors, and ship captains, as well as prominent merchants, burgesses, and governors were among the order alerts us to the strength of Bullock's conclusion when he writes, "The vertical social range of the fraternity, however, did not constitute the primary focus of Masonic boasts of openness; rather, they were thinking of more pressing horizontal divisions of society."[41] It was a universal society, not bound by region or party, in which men of all orders would find a model for social intercourse. Freemasons, with their platform of universal love and acceptance, were the perfect social network for the actor or manager aspiring to residency.

So all those occasions when Douglass and his actors donned the Mason's Apron and did special prologues for the Masons, or played a bespeak for the fraternity on St. John's night, or donated a benefit to the Masonic lodge, they were not only performing for them, but they were also among them, they were them, giving back to a lodge that had given them something. When the Solomon's Lodge of Charleston celebrated its St. John's Day, "All the Brethren being properly cloathed with the Ensigns of their Order and their Flag carried before them," marching in public procession first to Church, then to dinner, they concluded their evening in the playhouse, where a "special prologue and Epilogue were given" and "Masons' songs between."[42]

Douglass would remain a Mason for his professional career. He would own Masonic regalia, aprons, gloves, deliver prologues and epilogues before the lodge members who had gathered at the playhouse dressed in his Mason's Apron, particularly on his own benefit night.[43] Masons would bespeak performance—sponsor the evening—and the bill would be sprinkled heavily with anthems:

At the New Theatre in Chapel Street, this present Monday, being the 28th of December, instant, by particular desire. And for the entertainment of the Master, Wardens, and the Rest of the Brethren of the Ancient and

Honourable Society of Free and Accepted Masons,—will be presented a tragedy, call'd, The Gamester. An occasional prologue to be spoken by Mr. Douglass, in the Character of a Master Mason. Between the acts, several Free-Mason's songs. After the play, the original epilogue; and after the farce, a Mason's epilogue, by Mrs. Douglass.[44]

For their part, the actors would dedicate charity benefits for the Masons. At the close of the Charleston season in May of 1774, Douglass and company donated an evening for the "Relief of All the Members of the Society of Free Masons, Their Wives, Widows, Children and Orphans, when in Distress."[45]

There is a further reciprocity between the players and the Masons that was mutually beneficial: playhouses and Masonic lodges were frequently shared buildings. The Masons found a builder in Douglass when they could not raise their own buildings, and acting companies found a landlord in the Masons when they could not raise a playhouse.

By the 1760s, even small hamlets like Port Royal boasted Masonic charters and growing memberships. But lodges, dedicated buildings themselves, were difficult to raise, and often the Masons hired taverns or long rooms for their monthly meetings. Erecting a dedicated lodge required a sizeable subscription, and as membership to the Masonic Order was limited, the pool of subscribers in the smaller hamlets were often too lean to conveniently raise the necessary funding for a building that had only occasional use.[46] But a playhouse, however—another building of occasional use—could be rented. The playhouse in Halifax, North Carolina, for example, was built on a lot owned by Joseph Montfort, Masonic grand master of North Carolina, and rented to both the players and Masons. When Douglass closed up his theatre in Charleston, South Carolina, to travel to the north for two years, he rented the building to the local chapter of Masons, the Kilwinning Lodge. In Norfolk, Virginia, after the fire of 1776 leveled the town, the playhouse was rebuilt and the foundations and cornerstones laid by the Masons in a formal and much publicized ceremony—largely because they shared the building.

The reverse was also true. In Philadelphia, Brother William Plumstead rented his warehouse to Brother Walter Murray for a theatre, and on the islands, in particular, players rented lodges from the Masons for playhouses. On the island of Antigua, an unidentified company of players had rented the Masonic lodge when the hurricane of August 31, 1772 hit and destroyed their stock of scenery.[47] The kindness for renting the lodge was returned some years later. In 1788 a company reopened in Antigua and the funds from the performance were dedicated to the erection of a new Freemason's lodge.[48] A short sail away, in the neighboring island of St. Kitts (St. Christopher), Janet Schaw, touring Basterre in early January of 1775, was shown a building she should not see ("I was shown that intended for my brother") and outside it she was presented with a playbill, "they are strollers of some spirit who strolled across the Atlantick."[49] Was this Verling's Leeward Island Company? And were they playing in a Freemason's lodge, the building, as a woman, she should not see? The buildings made very good theatres, and Masons made very good friends.

The Masons were also the sponsors of high culture and charities: musical concerts and theatricals to raise money for civic charities, an alliance the players would also have found useful. They represented the new gentrification of leisure, secular theology, and social politics. Even their public presence was itself a highly theatrical event: dressed in their uniforms, singing their anthems, accompanied by the regalia of rank, they attended public functions and holidays, funerals, St. John's day, groundbreakings, and cornerstone laying. The managers of the colonial theatre, like Douglass, Walter Murray, and William Verling, could exploit the Mason's attitudes toward universal culture by soliciting membership and support for their theatrical ventures. For the Mason's part, the theatre offered a practical public product for raising charity that they lacked. As early as 1737, Masons in Charleston were bespeaking performances. They sponsored civic benefits and charities in every city the players played and for every known company: Murray–Kean, the Hallam Company, David Douglass and the American Company, William Verling and his New American Company, even Henry Holt in Charleston in 1737.

Freemasonry provided a model of respectable, mobile citizenship that allowed the actors, not as "strollers" but as "transient gentlemen," to move horizontally in the culture from one community to another and be ever at home among their patron base at its highest and broadest levels. Douglass and his actors dined and drank with Master Mason

Egerton Leigh in Charleston. Grand Master William Allen initiated
Walter Murray in Philadelphia. Master Mason John Rowe facilitated
and attended Douglass's performances at the Masonic lodge in Boston;
Master Mason Joseph Montfort built a playhouse in North Carolina.
Douglass may also have earned the acquaintance of New York
Congressmen William Livingston through his Masonic membership—as
Livingston was Master Mason, as he certainly had acquaintance with
Sir Henry Moore, governor of New York and, earlier, Jamaica. And
when Douglass and Quelch were introduced to the Williamsburg
Lodge, it was Peyton Randolph who was Master Mason at the time.
Hence in December of 1774 when Randolph personally carried the
bad news to Douglass that theatricals had been discouraged, it was a
decade-old relationship that prompted the gesture. Randolph, Leigh,
Livingston, Rowe, Moore, and Sharpe were just a few of many
politically influential acquaintances that Douglass made through his
Masonic membership. As a "transient gentleman" with fraternal associations with major lodges in half a dozen colonies, Douglass may have
been one of the most well-connected Masons on the continent, on
familiar terms with many of the colonial governors, lieutenant governors, burgesses, aldermen, mayors, secretaries, merchants, and printers.

   Even when Douglass retired from the stage in Jamaica and returned
to printing, one of his most elegant publications was a Masonic guide-
book, *The Elements of Free-Masonry Delineated*, written by an actor in
the American Company, William Moore, whose name first appeared in
the Masonic records alongside Walter Murray's in Philadelphia in the
summer of 1749. Thirty-three years and a Revolution later, Moore
wrote *The Elements of Free-Masonry Delineated*, and it was published by
Douglass and Aikman in Kingston, 1782.[50]

5. Mrs. Warren's Profession ❧

Section 1: Be it enacted by the Lieutenant Governor, Council and House of Representatives, that from and after the publication of this act, no person or persons whosoever shall or may, for his or their gain, or for any valuable consideration, let or suffer to be used and improved, any house, room, or place whatsoever, for acting or carrying on any stage plays, interludes, or other theatrical entertainments, on pain of forfeiting and paying of reach and every day or time such house, room, or place shall be let, or improved, contrary to this act, twenty pounds.

Section 2: And be it further enacted, that if at any time or times whatsoever, from and after the publication of this act, any person or persons shall be present, as an actor or spectator of any stage play, interlude, of theatrical entertainment in any house, room or place where a greater number of persons than twenty shall be assembled together, every such person shall forfeit and pay, for every time he or they shall be present as aforesaid, five pounds. The forteitures and penalities aforesaid to be one half to his Majesty for the use of the Government, the other half to him or them that shall inform or sue for the same.

"An Act to Prevent Stage Plays," repr. *Boston Evening Post*, April 23, 1750

And that pretty well did it. Severe and early prohibitions guaranteed that professional companies avoided the Boston market for most of the eighteenth century, and so potent was the opposition of "puritanism" that the dyad of "puritan and player" became something of a trope of the field. Recognizing as we must that such a conflict does not, cannot, arise in absence, any exegesis of absence would be incomplete without a consideration into the nature and shape of the sizeable void of theatre in New England.

WHAT MUNGO SAID

Late in the colonial period, an anonymous writer to a Boston newspaper allegorized the vanity of the world in a sustained and detailed allegory borrowed directly from the playhouse:

> The Universal Farce Displayed. The world is a theatre; mankind are the comedians; chance composes the piece, and fortune distributes the parts; theologists and politicians govern the machines; and philosophers are the spectators. The rich take their places in the pit and upper boxes, the powerful in the front and sides, and the galleries are for the poor. The women distribute fruit and refreshments, and the unfortunate snuff the candles. Folly composes the overture, and time draws the curtain. The title of the piece is *Mundus vult Decipi, Ergo Decipiatur,* "If the World Will be Deceived, let it be so." The opening of the farce begins with sighs and tears: The first act abounds with the chimerical projects of men: The frantic testify their applause with re-echoed bravoes, whilst the sagacious bring their catcalls into play to damn the performance. At going in a sort of money is paid called trouble, and in exchange a ticket is given, subscribed uneasiness, in order to obtain a place. The variety of objects which appear, for a short time divert the spectators; but the unraveling of the plot and intrigues, well or ill-concerted, force the risible muscles of the philosophers . . . Such is the farce of this world, and he who would chuse [*sic*] to divert himself with it at his leisure, should take his place in some obscure corner, where he may unobserved be a spectator of the whole performance, and in safety laugh at it as it deserves. [signed] Honestus[1]

"Honestus" need not have been in a playhouse a time or two to so meticulously map out the correspondences of the world and the theatre, but to unpack his allegory the conventions of playgoing needed to be in the cultural imagination. To what extent did the readership know what theatregoing was without the lived experience, and how did they acquire that experience? This elaborately sustained allegory is but an extension of the traditional playhouse motto, found above the proscenium on colonial stages and Drury Lane that they imitated: *Totus Mundus agit Histrionem,* "all the world acts the player." The knowledge of such a motto, such a function, is the attraction of the allegory, and the circulation of that knowledge is best charted in Boston, where in 1771, when the above allegory was published, the city had no theatre. But the understanding of the experience of playgoing was not completely lost, as it would have been to, say, the first Albany, New York, audience who knew not what it meant to go to a play. There is the story told by Alexander Graydon of his aunt's visit to the Southwark Theatre in Philadelphia, accompanied by a dandy, who when asked what the Latin motto over the stage meant, *Totus Mundus agit Histrionem*, "wanting to pass himself off for a scholar" replied, "We act Mondays, Wednesdays and Fridays."[2] If there is any humor in the joke, it resides, like the allegories, within the confirmed playgoing experience. When the *Boston Gazette* of July 3, 1769 satirized Governor Bernard with a parody from the comic play *The Padlock* ("It must be true if Mungo said it"), how is it that Bostonians could get the joke without some theatre under their belt? What they knew, how much they knew, and how they knew it is the subject of what follows. If there is indeed as there was a pronounced and legislated attitude against the theatre, can this attitude be read at some level as immaterial evidence of theatre's potency within the cultural imagination?

It is a commonplace of the field that Puritan Boston disallowed performance; its moral pronouncements against the theatre were forceful enough to find severe—and largely unchallenged—legal penalties for acting, hosting actors, or indeed even attending the theatre. Douglass sounded out the town in the summer of 1769 with a solo performance of Steven's *Lecture on Heads*. He "lectured" for four weeks and was discouraged enough not to return. Yet in spite of the apparent absence of professional performance, I want to suggest that the idea of theatre was quite alive, was very much a part of the cultural imagination, and that New England's antitheatrical campaign might be read as one indication of the theatre's potency. This occasionally, as in the above allegory, the opposition to theatre—theatre's "other"—became so potent that it began to lend agency to theatre itself, to function as a surrogate for playgoing. It begins to look as if the opposition to the idea of theatre, the fantasies of suppression, became so compelling that it created a theatrical "space," even in the absence of a playhouse.

MALE ACTORS/MALE[F]ACTORS

This is almost certainly a misreading, but on May 3, 1736, the *Boston Gazette* carried this laconic note: "We are informed that Wednesday next is appointed for the execution of the three condemn'd male actors."[3] The news is reported secondhand from Philadelphia where the execution was to occur, and no further information is offered. Who the "actors" were and the particulars of their offense were points on which the paper was silent. The details, however, may very well have been immaterial: to the Puritan readership of the *Boston Gazette*, that they were actors, apparently, was crime enough.

More likely the note originally read: "We are informed that Wednesday next is appointed for the execution of the three condemn'd *malefactors*." The print is thin, wispy, and the "f" has likely evaporated. Reading even the legible early modern newspapers is often a sport of conjectural deciphering, and those in poor quality demand some kind of reconstruction. Intriguing as it is, the line probably does not refer to actors at all, but instead to some notorious trio of criminals terrorizing the Quakers. And indeed, as it turns out there were three accused currently awaiting execution in Philadelphia: John Watnell, Michael M'Dermot, and an unnamed woman accomplice, all charged with burglary. The two men were ultimately hung for their crime while their female associate was reprieved. So in one regard the first (mis)reading was not that far off: the male actors of the crime were indeed hung.[4]

Central to the following argument is the possibility that it was both: that to the Boston readership, actors and criminals could occupy the same semantic site, and the Boston newspapers played a large role in publicly cementing this association. The notion of male actors typographically cohabiting with male[f]actors may not be that unthinkable, given the local conditions of reading that encouraged such conflations. Worn print or an original slip of the typographer, perhaps, but hovering behind this highly packed portmanteau—signifying criminals but evoking players—is a campaign in which the ghosting images of executed actors may have functioned as a highly attractive cultural fantasy to its Boston readership. The notion is certainly far too intriguing to be left unexplored.

The colonial Boston newspapers platformed against many vices: players and playgoing being one of the minor sins in a canon that included gaming, dancing, drinking, and extravagance.[5] But the strategies employed against the theatre were unique. Through a complex set of allegories, the association of actors and malefactors was maintained with seldom the need for an outright attack on the institution. This subtle strategy stood in sharp contrast to the overt campaigns against other vices. Here is an extract against drunkenness, for example, from the same edition of the *Boston Gazette* that carried the note on the condemned male[f]actors, April 26–May 3, 1736. It is one of six narratives that opened the issue, all reprinted from a previous tract, *Of Drunkenness and What Hath Befallen Some Men in It*:

> When above thirty Years since, I was a Student in a famous University in the Upper Germany, some riotous Students were entertained by a Nobleman at his Chamber, who intending to treat them to the height of Intemperance, had so gorged himself with Wine, that he was fast asleep at the Table he sat by, in which Posture his Associates left him and departed. A great Wax Candle stood upon the Table, and in his sleep he had burned himself so inconveniently for it [?] burn his Breast, and the Parts about in such manner, that his Innards might be seen, which yet was not perceived by him that was burned in Wine. The Candle being burnt out, he yet remaining snoring and lying upon the Wax and Ashes. In the Morning he was awakened by his fellow Toss-pots, and invited by them to a Cup of Wormwood Wine, when he complained of insufferable Torments. The most skillful Physicians and professors of that Art were immediately sent for, but in vain did they endeavor to oppose so great a burning: so that in horrid Torments, upon the third Day following he concluded his miserable Life, having first warned his Companions with Tears to beware of Carousing.[6]

This patently moralistic tale—thirty years old at the reprinting—is followed by five other anecdotes culled from sources as old as Athenaeus, each offered to its Boston readership as illustrations in vivid details of the dangers of "Carousing."

The campaign against the theatre, however, was seldom so direct. Rather, through a sustained conflation of actors and malefactors, playgoing and providential disasters, the press assured its readers that theatre was presented in a uniquely ungodly light. This treatment persisted throughout the middle of the century (roughly 1736–1771), the same years theatre was establishing itself in the other colonies, and, as it turns out, in Boston itself. And yet in spite of such high-handed denunciations, theatre persisted, even here at the heart of the Puritan opposition.

A CATALOGUE OF CATASTROPHES

As one would expect from New England in the early colonial period, antitheatrical sentiments ran particularly high from most venues in the social sphere. From the pulpits, orators of the stature of Increase Mather sermonized on its dangers, and from the courts Judge Samuel Sewall denounced the offerings of the stage as "profane customs." Strong admonitions threw up a bulwark against entertainments and idleness in general, but the playhouse, in particular, seemed to Sewall a breeding ground for impiety. Although stage plays were not legally banned in Boston until 1750, legislature was largely unnecessary: the moral environment was so inclement that strolling players and amateurs alike found Boston a chilly market long before they were legally prohibited from testing the field. Against this harsh atmosphere, the struggles to establish professional theatre in New England have been well documented, as has the hostility from the pulpit.[7] What is less explored is the subtle but aggressive role that Boston newspapers played in furthering the campaign against theatre. Throughout the bulk of the eighteenth century, as playhouses and theatregoing were becoming established throughout the lower colonies and attempting inroads further north, Boston papers reprinted little of their victories, their seasons, charities, or significance, while generously reprinting every tragic accident that befell players, playhouses, and theatregoers in the American colonies, London, the provinces, the West Indies, and Europe, howsoever old or anecdotal. Indeed, press coverage for the theatre in Boston newspapers was little more than a catalogue of playhouse catastrophes, each more devastating than the last. Like Hollywood blockbusters, the Boston papers piled on the theatre one natural disaster upon another in hyperbolic doses—fires, earthquakes, hurricanes, volcanoes—that destroyed both player and audience alike. Catastrophe became the wages of attendance. Here is a very early example from New England's first newspaper, the *Boston News Letter*, February 18–25, 1706. The news, at the time, was hardly new:

> Bristol, August 4 [1703]. On Thursday last our players acted near this city: a comedy called the Metamorphoses, in which there's a song in praise of the devil, page 14, the first four lines are thus, "Hail powers beneath! whose

influence imparts / the knowledge of infernal arts, / By whose unerring gifts we move / to alter the decrees above." Near the end of the play the seats gave a great crack, and afterwards fell, so that the auditors were all rumbled together, and frighten'd as if there had been conjuration. The candles fell among the wood, and were like to have set all on fire. The crowd of the people stopt up the doors and made the passage very slow; some lost their swords, others their hats and wigs, and women their head-dresses and scarves; several persons were bruis'd but not killed; and the upper part of the gallery falling, several women tumbled down upon their heads, and were expos'd in the throng to great indecencies. The players run out at the back-door, and there was a report that something more than ordinary appear'd, but that is false, the devil was too sensible of his own interest to disturb those who invok'd him, and paid him such adoration. However several who were there look upon it as a judgement, and resolve never to go thither any more; but the players are so hardened, that they intend to act it again this evening.

There is no account of what disasters followed for the next evening, nor needed there be: the moral imperatives were clear enough. That the event is dated even by colonial standards reminds us that the value of such stories is not in its newsworthiness.[8] They function rather to confirm the grand Faustian narrative of all who presume to play at the Devil's house. This will be the hallmark of the colonial Boston press: its ability to recycle the topical into parable in the moral battle to preserve New England from the degeneration of plays and playgoing. In this battle, the Faust legend offered a particularly clear metaphor of the fall:

London Oct 4 [1736]: Yesterday morning Mr. James Todd, who represented the Miller's Man of Friday night last in the entertainment of *Dr. Faustus* at the theatre in Covent Garden, and fell in one of the flying machines from the very top of the stage by the breaking of the wires, by which accident his skull was fractur'd, died in a miserable manner. Susan Warwick, who represented the Miller's wife, lies at the point of death at the infirmary at Hyde Park Corner: the two other persons who fell in the same machine are like to recover.[9]

These details of play titles are not incidental to the mission. The Devil plays, the Faust plays, alert us that the readership need not a fine and familiar acquaintance with dramatic literature as a body, but were certainly acquainted with those notorious plays that offended—by title or subject—such as the play popularly known as *Dr. Faustus* (actually an afterpiece called *Harlequin Faustus; or, The Necromancer*). The accident that night at Covent Garden when the wire gave way and sent James Todd and Susan Warwick crashing to their deaths graphically literalized the play's theme, and the Boston readership was asked to regard the hellish fall of more than Faustus.

The tragic fall of actors like Todd and Warwick were offered as a lesson in divine vindication for a life misspent. But the indictment extended to the audience as well. During the catastrophe of Dr. Faustus cited above, the audience "was thrown into the greatest convulsion; a lady in the pit big with child fainted away, and was carried off very ill; Nothing was heard but shrieks and cries of the utmost surprize, agony and horror."[10] Theatres were of themselves the sites of God's wrath, a judgment that often made little distinction between player and auditor. From the *Boston Gazette* of December 1, 1741, we hear the following:

> Clonmell, Sept. 23. On Monday last was acted here the *Recruiting Officer* with the *Devil in the Wine Cellar*. As the actors began to play the devil (the farce) the lofts of the house not only fell down, but also the stage and front seats, with 200 persons that sate [*sic*] thereon, several of whom had their arms and legs broke, and others were so much bruised that their lives are despair'd of.

Playing the devil was not the only theme that invited destruction. Bostonians also read of the playhouse in Havre-de-Grace, Paris, that was destroyed by a "most violent hurricane" during a performance of *Samson* and "Upwards of 100 persons were buried in the ruins, which being set on fire by the candles and lamps, the whole was consumed."[11] Again, there is nothing incidental about the details revealed in the report. The production itself—*Samson*—indicts the audience as Philistines, who had gathered to watch an illicit spectacle, and the destruction of the theatre becomes in the analogy the destruction of the palace of the heathens. If the targeted providentially of the event were conclusive enough to dissuade the hardened playgoer, the account closed by noting the isolation of the havoc: "but happily, the flames were no communicated to any other building; had it so happen'd the whole town would probably have been destroy'd, as it consists chiefly of wooden houses."

The playhouse was the target of an isolated wrath. Further accounts included this Sabbath violation:

> Venice, Jan. 14. Last Sunday evening an Earthquake was felt in this city, by which some chimneys were thrown down, but no other damage was done: The shock was most felt at the opera and playhouses, where the performers and actors let fall the curtains and the company run out.[12]

The remarkable thing about playhouse casualties is not that they were seldom reprinted in any other colonial newspaper—which is generally the case—but that they are not printed as news at all, but rather as moralities. They are evoked, like texts in a sermon, not as topical events, but as points of instruction. This is best evidenced by the following tragic event that happened *37 years prior to its reportage*:

> The following tragical event happened in the county of Cambridgeshire, not many years since. Some strollers having brought down a puppet-show, it was exhibited in a large thatched barn, at Barnwell, a little village near Cambridge on the 8th of September, 1727. Just as the shew was about to begin an idle fellow attempted to thrust himself in without paying, which the people of the shew prevented; and a quarrel ensued; after some altercation, the fellow went away, and the door being made fast, all was quiet; but this execrable villain, to revenge the supposed incivility he had received by the shewmen, went to a heap of hay and straw which stood close to the barn, and secretly set it on fire.[13]

There were literally dozens of examples that were carried in the Boston papers between the 1730s and 1774 when the Congress discouraged all theatricals. The coverage ranges from recycling allegories of the past, "[Nero] threw off all care of public affairs, and the duty of an emperor, to attend the theatre, and gain the unpricely glory of singing and acting," to reprints of provincial touring accidents. It even extended to workmen employed by the theatre: "Yesterday a scaffold, erected for repairing the Opera House, on which were several workmen fell, down, some of whom were killed, and others wounded."[14] Or major theatre fires like the one that broke out in Petersburg, Russia, during a performance of *Tartuffe*.[15] All were pressed into a sustained smear campaign against players and playgoing that seemed to take a salacious delight in their catastrophes, seemed, at times, almost cruel. Take, for example, the reportage of the tragic death, by fire, of Mrs. Henry and her children off of Newport, Rhode Island. Mrs. Henry was an actress leaving Jamaica with her sisters (the Storers, Ann, Fanny, and Maria) and her mother, Mrs. Storer, to join the Douglass company when an overturned candle started a fire that set the ship ablaze. The young Mrs. Henry lost her two children and her own life. After the disaster is recounted, the paper notes (wrongly): "the woman that perished is said to be young Mrs. Hallam, an Actress."[16] It may be innocent coverage of a tragic accident, or it may be that her vocation is particularly noted to offer causality to the catastrophe.

Tempted by the coercion to local reading, even innocent texts become allegorized. Readers are reminded of the Lisbon earthquake of 1770 via the destruction of the opera house (*Boston Chronicle*, March 29, 1770), and the two earthquakes felt in London in March 1750 are reported as "warnings which God in his mercy affords to a sinful people." This is a familiar interpretive strategy but what followed in the issue is not. The bishop of London continues, "While I was writing this, I cast my eye upon the newspapers of the day, and counted no less than fifteen advertisements for plays, opera, musick and dancing."[17] Perhaps the most remarkable parable of God's judgment visited upon the theatre came from the very distant past. When the city of Pompeii was under excavation the story of the discovery was carried in several colonial papers (quoted above), but only in Boston was it pressed into parable. It was not the discovery of the ancient city as topical news that attracted the attention of the Boston editor John Draper but that the recovered theatre evidenced its own destruction: "that theatre which according to historians was buried by an earthquake in the reign of the emperor Titus."[18]

Taken together, such accounts offer a dense anthology of antitheatrical fables, a mythic framework in a sustained circulation against which the theatre was viewed. Collectively the death of an actress, workmen, audiences, the proximity of an opera house, the excavation of a Roman site, earthquakes, fires, hurricanes, and other catastrophes that target the playhouse created more than a running commentary against actors, playhouses, and playgoing; they formed a discourse of antitheatrical mythology in which natural and unnatural disasters of death and destruction evidenced God's judgment and conspired against the encroaching circuit of the professional player. But so forcefully did the campaign circulate that in its wake it guaranteed the idea of theatre in the cultural imagination. Against such a well-defined mythic body of evidence, the real theatre need only make an occasional appearance to reinscribe its fearful presence and generate an agency far beyond its material presence. And an occasional appearance it did make.

TALES OF A WAYSIDE INN

In spite of the saturated cultural campaign against theatre, clandestine theatricals found a foot-hold in Boston, indeed, as one might argue that they thrived, and for many years, quite regularly, Boston boasted competing amateur companies. Indeed, one might even suggest that the catalogue of playhouse catastrophes was in response to the rash of clandestine performance. Amateurs, visiting professionals, companies of soldiers, students, gentlemen companies, solo performers all produced plays in Boston and its environs in spite of the severity of laws and prohibitions.

When the bishop of London was reporting the earthquakes and lamenting 15 playbills in London in the spring of 1750, Bostonians read of the Murray–Kean Company advertising similar bills in New York. When word reached Boston of the Murray–Kean Company securing permission to perform in New York in February of 1750, its presence inspired both productions and prohibitions. In March of that year two young Englishmen and "some volunteer comrades" in Boston undertook to mount an amateur production of Otway's *The Orphan* at a coffeehouse on State Street, Boston. Although unadvertised, the eagerness of a large audience to witness the production was so great that it caused what the polite called a tumult at the door, and the detractors called a riot. George Willard offered a less partisan view of the disturbance: "the eagerness of the public to witness the performance occasioned a serious disturbance at the door."[19] As a result of the tumult, the General Court enacted legislation "to Prevent Stage-Plays and other Theatrical Entertainments," severely penalizing anyone mounting a production, acting in a production, hosting a production or attending a production, and published it in the papers in April of 1750. Among the possible members of this eager audience was one T. T. Jr, of Boston, who was inspired to write his own play, a farce in three acts, *The Suspicious Daughter*, and printed it in 1751.

And theatre begat theatre. Another round of amateur productions later in the decade inspired students at Harvard College to form their own amateur theatrical society. Students had an intermittent tradition of performing plays that dated back to 1690 when collegians at Harvard presented Benjamin Colman's *Gustavus Vasa*. Some colleges even boasted drama clubs, like the students at Yale whose Linonian Society mounted plays annually.[20] The students at Harvard, however, far surpassed their ivy league rivals in both the number of productions as well as in audacity, often taking their productions outside the college. The diary of Nathaniel Ames tracks his career from the point of his entering Harvard in 1758 at age 17. Among the more enthusiastic extracurricular activities of his freshman year was his attending plays and later involvement in the production of plays. His diary—omitted from most studies of the Boston stage—reveal a lively and somewhat subversive interest in theatre that spilled out beyond the halls of Cambridge. On June 22, 1758, *The Roman Father* (William Whitehead, 1750) was produced at the college, followed shortly afterward by *Cato* on July 3, 1758, and *Cato* again on July 6, acted "to perfection," added Ames, and once again on July 11 "more perfect than before."[21]

But the students had rivals; an amateur company of tradesmen in Boston also took to performing. This unknown company of artisans offered *The Revenge* on March 23, 1759, at a private house in Boston, *The Orphan* on April 13, 1759, and a week later Ames watched *The Drummer*, the last two performed at How's Tavern. That these were not student productions is made clear by Ames who notes when plays were "acted by ourselves," suggesting they were an amateur assembly availing themselves of the many wayside inns just outside Boston.[22] On May 18 this amateur company continued its season, mounting *The Brothers*, and the following month *The Recruiting Officer*. The students, for their part, carried on at Cambridge offering *The Revenge* and a remount of *Cato*, also in the summer of 1759.[23] If this all feels like an ambitious undertaking, the next season's efforts were even richer, both students and amateurs. It is unclear from Ames's diary whether it was the Harvard students who reprised *The Revenge* in November at Bowman's Tavern in Boston or it was the amateur group who assembled to perform *Cato* in December 1759. Their performances had by this time become public enough to warrant a reprint of the prohibition against theatricals, republished in The *Boston News Letter*: "At the desire of a number of the principal inhabitants of this town."[24] In spite of the reminder, both companies continued to perform in January, March, April, and June of 1760.[25] The students earned the rebuke of the college when it began to crack down on all extracurricular activities. A wave of discipline was meted out for various offenses, including "going upon the top of the college, or cutting off the lead, tumultuous noise . . . rudeness at meals, keeping guns, going skating, etc." One deduces that theatrical clubs fell under the same disfavor, as the last entry in Ames's dairy of acting in a student production occurred on June 12, 1760 of *Tancred and Sigismunda*—its third production—of which he appended "for which we are likely to be prosecuted."[26]

Yet in spite of the college crackdowns, and the republication of the prohibition, the interest and the production of clandestine drama continued, nearly unabated, as did Nathaniel Ames's participation in it. During the crackdown of the spring of 1760, Ames was still being roped into productions, "engag'd in a Play," he wrote on March 17, and lending plays to other students. Even after he graduated in 1761, Ames continued his theatrical associations in his native Dedham, Massachusetts, and at the many inns in the neighboring communities of Sudbury and Roxbury. How's Tavern in Sudbury, the original Wayside Inn of Longfellow fame, on the post road out of Boston was a particular favorite.[27] Nor was the Sudbury inn the only rural outlet for amateur drama in the Boston environs. Ames and his colleagues—now graduates beyond the censure of the college—acted a play at Battle's Inn, in Roxbury, in October of 1761, and was "rebuked for it by our parents." The rebukes, again, made little impact on him, as a month later the company was planning another production, this time in his native town, Dedham. Under the initiative of Ames and his colleagues, Dedham saw occasional productions between 1762 and 1772 at inns and taverns, presented in a "lecture" format. As he wrote in a concluding lines of one of his prologues, "Whatever people may conjecture / You'll safely call it but an Evening Lecture."[28] Meanwhile at Cambridge, after the departure of Ames, his under-classmen continued their theatrical activity, so much so as to cause the governors of Harvard to publish in 1762 a more severe prohibition, targeting plays:

> Whereas the attending upon Stage-Plays, Interludes, and Theatrical Entertainments, tends greatly to corrupt the Morals of a people, and particularly with respect to the College must needs (besides corrupting their Morals) be highly detrimental to their learning, by taking off their minds from their studies, drawing them into such Company, as may be very insnaring to them, expensive to their parents, and tending to many other disorders; Therefore Voted, that if any undergraduate shall be an Actor in, a Spectator at, or any Waies concern'd in any such Stage Plays, Interludes or Theatrical Entertainment, in the Town of Cambridge or elsewhere, He shall for the first Offence be degraded, according to the Discretion of the Pres[ident] and Tut[ors] and for any repeated offence, shall be rusticated or Expelled.[29]

The decree dampened activity at Cambridge, but the alumni outside its authority were unaffected. As late as 1772, Ames was still involved in amateur theatricals in Dedham, when his company mounted the farce of *The Toy Shop*, and Ames himself wrote the prologue for it, which is preserved:

> Here, though no Theatres our Land adorn,
> This work they left their children then unborn;
> We then, their offspring, diffident presume
> To make a present Theatre of this room.
> And tho' the piece we've chose fine thoughts displays,
> Tis not so striking as some other plays.
> Yet, if out undertaking you approve,
> Some leisure Night we'll all your passions move.
> We'll make you laugh or shed the generous tear,
> With plays yon virgins need not blush to hear;
> Or be as solemn, let it not alarm one,
> As the dull Priest who steals his weekly sermon.
> Of this, whatever People may conjecture,
> You'll safely call it but an Evening Lecture.[30]

Of that evening's production, Ames records in his diary that it was richly attended, performed "before a numerous audience of the most respectable inhabitants of the First Parish in Dedham both male and female. " Such a market encouraged Ames to consider a larger season (as intimated in the prologue), promising tragedies and discrete comedies for "some leisure night" at this makeshift theatre. That both the players and their patrons operated under the lecture format betrays their familiarity with another level of theatrical convention, evading authority.

In the mid-1760s another amateur company was also seeding audiences within Boston proper. From subsequent reactions, this was assumably a company of tradesmen who undertook clandestine performances in the city. On March 13, 1765, John Rowe attended one and recorded of it as follows: "Went in the evening over to Gardners to see The Orphan acted which was miserably performed. About 210 persons there."[31] This was a tavern performance, at Gideon's Tavern on Boston Neck, and in Rowe's recording of the event, there was nothing curious about well-attended plays in Boston taverns, only that this one was poorly done. Heather Nathans has observed of this entry that Rowe noted no attempt at all to prohibit the production, and was equally "undisturbed by the impropriety or illegality of witnessing" the production.[32]

Notices of the same or other amateur productions found their way into the Boston newspapers as well. The *Boston Evening Post* for March 9 and a rebuttal on April 13, 1767 in the *Boston Gazette* ask and answer: "Is it not surprising that such a number of lads should be encouraged to act in characters unbecoming their callings?" laments the first. "Does it not tend to take their minds off from their business, and instead of making them good taylors, shoemakers, &c. render them nothing more than strolling players?" The rebuttal defended the performers first before relating—in allegoric terms—the curious fate of the company:

> On the 30th of last month, "The Fair Penitent" made an appearance in Boston; she then look'd very beautiful, and with her attendants made a very brilliant figure (her Metamorphosis and all things considered); But as there was a great deal of nonsensical talk about her, and many impertinent things said of her, besides an inexplicable hypocritical fellow wrote such a [non sense] performance in the Evening Post, that she left the town immediately (dismissing her attendants at Boston) and went to Cambridge, where a number of grand young gentlemen (who had before entered into her service) immediately waited upon her, and invited her about a mile and a

half from town, where they most barbarously murder'd her before a number of grand spectators—Oh! cruel butchery—worse than "Cobblers and Bunglers."[33]

In the coded speak of the day, two productions are described. The first, the tradesmen (the Cobblers and Bunglers), were dismissed, and the "Fair Penitent" (either the play, the character, the "metamorphosed" boy-actor who played Lavinia, or loosely, theatre itself) transferred her talent to the students at Harvard, with whom she had played before, and who now produced a rival production at an inn some "mile and half" from Boston. According to the writer, the second production was far inferior to that of the tradesmen's. This, notwithstanding the severe published legislation, threats of expulsion, and parental rebuke.

Boston, though denied theatricals, nonetheless provided a base of support for both theatre producers and consumers, for amateurs and professionals alike. When David Douglass opened up a season in Rhode Island in 1761, he attracted Boston audiences, including Nathaniel Ames, who records a playgoing trip to Providence in August of 1761. B. W. Brown, writing of the American Company's visit to Newport in the same year also notes the Bostonians in the house: "News of the theatre spread to the hearth-stone of censorship—Boston; and wayward sons and daughters pleasure-bent braved a four hours drive in stage-coach to visit the world of make-believe and went away highly gratified."[34] Ames perhaps was not hyperbolic when he wrote this on September 9, 1761: "Boston people flock up to Newport to see the Plays by the English Actors."[35] Again, a week later: "Many people go from Boston to Newport to see the Plays." The following summer Douglass and the American Company returned to New England, this time Providence—suggesting some expectation of success—and again attracted a clientele from Boston. Samuel Arnold, in his *History of the State of Rhode Island*, tells us that in 1762 "Douglass had moved his company from Newport, built a theatre, and commenced playing in Providence, where large numbers of people came from Boston to attend the performances."[36] The same population that threatened it now supported it. Boston papers covered the players when they were playing in the area, as they were in 1761 in Newport and in 1762 in Providence.

After the amateur production of *The Fair Penitent* was performed, one worried op-ed rebutted:

> [The] acting of plays and tragedies in this town in now practiced with impunity . . . P.S. It is apprehended that when the American Company of Comedians, who are now at New York or Philadelphia, hear there is so great an inclination for such entertainments in this place, they will endeavor to introduce themselves.[37]

If the fear was that Boston knew too much of the American Company, the American Company would soon know of them, the fear was too late. Boston audiences knew all about the American Company from their summers in Rhode Island.

And clandestine performances continued. This time by a new population: soldiers. Soldiers from Fort Anne in Halifax, Nova Scotia—where a playhouse had recently been built, and Mr. Mill's Company just closed—arrived in Boston in November of 1768. England had responded to Boston's ongoing agitation by billeting troops. During their stay that winter (1768–1769) soldiers began to first rehearse and then openly perform plays, much to the chagrin of many who saw the troops openly flaunting the authority of the province. One writer to The *Boston Evening Post* wondered aloud:

> I am informed that next Tuesday night two plays are to be performed in this town by the soldiers now here. I should be much obliged to any one to inform me what right the commanding officers have to give leave to their men to perform any such entertainments here? Whether we are to be governed by the military law; or the military by the civil I hope the same spirit of piety reigns now as did in former times.[38]

One "SPECTATOR" rebutted the grievance with the reminder to the colonists that they lived under British law and theatricals were in no way violations of British law. "I would inform this writer," wrote the respondent, "and all other intermedlers, that there is an Act of Parliament licensing theatrical performances throughout the King's dominions, which I take upon me to say (and no one can contradict) entirely supercedes the Act of this province."[39]

The most level-headed critique came from William Paine, a Worcester physician, who wrote to Isaac Smith, Jr. in a letter of April 16, 1769:

> I am entirely of your Opinion with Regard to Theatrical Performances (viz.) That this Country in its present Circumstances cannot Support a Playhouse without manifest Disadvantage to the Community. But yet I think that the Stage affords the most rational Entertainment that I know of, and I look upon a well regulated Theatre to be of real Service, as it tends to promote Virtue and Discourage Vice . . . (But as you observe) I never should have Thought of Soldiers for Actors. Can it be supposed that a Person utterly unacquainted with The beauties of Language, can enter enough into the spirit of a Performance, which abounds with all the Flowers of Rhetoric, as to set up for an Actor? Certainly not. And I think they are a proper Subject for Ridicule for their attempting it.[40]

William Paine had already internalized both Douglass's argument and Douglass's language: "a well-regulated theatre" is "the most rational entertainment"—phrases that appear on the handbills circulated by Douglass when introducing himself to a new town. He used the same circular in the newspapers, and several versions of it are preserved.[41]

Students, amateurs, soldiers: such activity and audience base attracted the attention of the American Company, and indeed the fears were realized in the summer of 1769, when Douglass visited Boston on a reconnaissance for his company. In search of new markets, Douglass arrived in late July and undertook a series of solo performances of George Steven's *Lecture on Heads* at the Bunch of Grapes Tavern and found enough business to play three nights a week for nearly a month, while he sussed out the patronage. But Boston, in 1769, was a tense town, on the nervous edge of the great turmoil to come. The Sons of Liberty were active in August and early September. John Rowe writes of an affray between the British Commissioner and James Ottis that left the inhabitants "greatly alarmed." The times were not propitious for Douglass, and after a month he traveled down to Portsmouth. He may have, however, had an enduring, indirect, legacy nonetheless.

There may be no connection, but if Douglass visited the Masonic lodges to introduce himself as I have suggested earlier, he would have met both John Rowe and Joseph Warren, Master Mason of the Ancient and Modern lodges, respectively. We know he met Rowe, as Rowe attended his "Lecture on Heads" and may have had a hand in Douglass securing the Bunch of Grapes Tavern. But Joseph Warren, Grand Master of Masons in Boston, New England, and within one hundred miles of the same," raised to this the highest post in the colonies on May 30, 1769, would have been equally influential and a much more dynamic audience base.[42] Warren's attendance records in the St. Andrews Lodge confirm, as John Carey (*Joseph Warren*, 56) concludes, that "Warren was one of the most active masons in America." This was a lodge that listed among its brothers John Hancock, Paul Revere, Thomas Crafts, John Pulling, and many of the leaders of Boston's active revolutionaries. Warren was also deeply engaged in several other clubs with direct political connections. John Cary suggests that Warren attended the "Monday Night Club" in the company of Samuel Adams and James Otis, as well as Paul Revere's Sons of Liberty.[43] Though Rowe might guarantee a venue and an audience, Warren would have been ideally placed to assess the success or failure of repealing or bypassing legislation to allow exhibiting in that city. Douglass certainly would have been familiar with the promising audience base from the company's seasons in Rhode Island. One can only wonder whether Douglass, in his reconnaissance of patrons, made the acquaintance of young doctor Warren, Master Mason, who was a former student at Harvard, and a member of that amateur theatrical club that Nathaniel Ames wrote of. Indeed, as a student, at least one of the productions, a July 3, 1758 performance of *Cato*, was "acted at Warren's chamber."[44]

After Douglass left in September, he traveled to Portsmouth, New Hampshire, where he added the first act of *Love-a-la Mode* to his bill. But Douglass had no sooner vacated Boston than one Mr. Joan appeared, a solo performer who toured several New England towns reading plays and singing the roles. Mr. Joan introduced himself to the Boston public as "a person who has read and sung in most of the great towns in America." He performed John Gay's *Beggar's Opera*, "All the songs will be sung. He personates all the characters, and enters into the different humours, or passions, as they change from one to another throughout the opera."[45] Other pieces included many of the same fashionable repertory of the London stage: *Love in a Village, Damon and Phillida*, and *The Conscious Lovers*, all acted and sung in character.

Mr. Joan also carried his repertory of "recitations" to other Massachusetts townships, like Salem. In his recess from Boston, a second solo performer appeared. In December of 1769 Mr. M. A. Warwell also advertised and performed one-man versions of *Beggar's Opera* and other shows in Boston, Salem, and Portsmouth, New Hampshire. Joan returned to Boston in the spring of 1770. Additional pieces from Joan's spring season included one-man versions of Vanbrugh's *The Povok'd Husband, Beggar's Opera*, which John Rowe attended on March 23 and described as: "West in the evening to the Concert hall to hear Mr. Joan read the *Beggar's Opera* and sing the songs. He read but indifferently, but sung in taste. There were upwards of 100 people there."[46] Other titles in Joan's repertory included *The Reprisal, Damon and Phillida, Love in the City,* and *Lionel and Clarissa.* Though he was ostensibly evading the prohibition on performance, a one-man version of a play may have more than evoked the original for the audience.

So when one William Morgan—after a winter season of theatricals in Portsmouth, New Hampshire—traveled to Boston to commence a series of evening "entertainments" that included plays under the concert format, it was not an unthinkable violation. More than a decade of student, soldier, amateur, and solo performance had chipped away at the prohibition and created an audience.

In 1772 William Morgan opened a company in New England "after the manner of Saddler's Wells," playing in Portsmouth and advertising his theatrical project in Boston newspapers. The *Massachusetts Spy* of November 5, 1772 carried the notice of the company's activities: "Mr. Morgan has opened a theatre at Portsmouth, New-Hampshire. The exhibitions are on Tuesday and Friday evenings." He had solicited subscriptions during the summer and by early October the company was playing three nights a week.

In the spring of 1773, Morgan traveled to Boston and attempted to present his program of "oratorical exhibitions"—comic lectures and dramatic satires interspersed with music—at the British Coffee House. He had come off of a reasonably successful winter season in Portsmouth, New Hampshire, where he had assembled a small company of himself and four other known actors, converted an Assembly Room into a playhouse, and presented a series of comic sketches ("exhibitions") that included "A pantomimical entertainment in grotesque characters call'd *The Escape or Harlequin turn'd Doctor*," comic dances, and most germane to the current topic, local politic critique in the form of short and topical farces. *The Politicians, or What News? A Dramatic Satire* was the main feature of the bill in Portsmouth and remained on the boards throughout the winter.[47] Morgan had developed several Harlequin pieces and had provided for his equipage "scenes and machines." By spring 1773, when Morgan had played out his small audience base and moved on to Boston, he carried with him much of his repertory, including the political satires. In his wake, students at Dartmouth College initiated the first of a series of productions that would continue through the decade.[48]

But his Boston audience was perhaps not as tolerant of his political critiques:

> Various conjectures and reports having arisen concerning the comic-satiric lecture, intitled *The Times*, which was to have been deliver'd at Concert-Hall on Monday last, imagining it contains political reflections, and party invectives; Mr. Morgan begs leave to assure the public, that nothing political was ever meant or intended by the said lecture, he being desirous of not offending any party, and equally abhorring every measure that tends to create feuds and animosities, deface religion, disturb public tranquility, and destroy all order and government: The delivery of the lecture is therefore postponed for a few days, 'till the matter is set in a clear light, and the foundation of such reports invalidated by incontestible proof to the contrary.[49]

The "lecture" was not postponed but rather dropped from the bill entirely and no further mention of it was made in the press advertisements that followed. Instead, Morgan—a solid musician in his own right—substituted a concert of music with songs from popular plays, such as Mungo from the *Padlock*.

And there were the domestic readings, private households who gathered to read plays. John Rowe records one such event at his own home on January 29, 1770: "Mr. J. Lane read us the diverting farce, the Mayor of Garratt." This practice was clearly more widespread than noted, as the young Derbyshire traveler Nicholas Cresswell remarked: "After supper the company amused themselves with several diverting plays. This seems very strange to me, but I believe it is common in this country."[50]

With all the opportunities for performance in Boston, it should not surprise us that when the students at Princeton College, New Jersey, gave their final recitations in the form of a Latin play—in a class that included the sophomore Aaron Burr—the student who won the highest praise for his theatrical talents was from Boston:

> On Monday the 28th ult. the Grammar School at Nassau-Hall was examined, and the scholars acquitted themselves greatly to the satisfaction of the gentlemen who were pleased to attend . . . In the evening this class performed a dramatic piece in Latin, before a numerous and learned audience . . . [5 paragraphs describing competitions] In "pronouncing pieces from the stage," the highest premium was adjudged to Jonathan Mason, from Boston, New-England.[51]

MRS. WARREN'S PROFESSION

Two points emerge from this: that Boston conducted a lengthy campaign to prohibit theatre, and in spite of all the cultural and juridical prohibitions, theatre continued unabated. Both prohibition and practice conspired to assure the theatre's position in the cultural imagination of New England. It continued in the grammar schools, the colleges, at private homes, in companies of students, soldiers, and amateurs, all mounting plays, in Boston, Cambridge, and the surrounding villages; professional companies chipped away at the prohibitions with plays presented in "lecture" formats, solo performers offered abridgements of London stand-bys, and songs from popular afterpieces, while the more determined audiences slipped out of Boston across to New Hampshire and Rhode Island. Both points are helpful to bear in mind when we read, shortly afterward, an advertisement of Mercy Otis Warren's *The Defeat* "a dramatic performance lately exhibited":

> As many of your country readers have been out of the way of the theatrical amusements of the last season, it may perhaps be some entertainment to them to see a few extracts from The Defeat, a dramatic performance lately exhibited.[52]

What exactly does Warren have in mind? Is she being entirely satirical, facetiously referring to the Boston political landscape as the "theatrical amusements of last season"? Or is she situating herself within a tradition of clandestine performances, "lectures," amateur companies, or Mr. Morgan's rough season? In short, how theatrical is her concept of theatre?

Warren's career is a familiar story, and I need not rehearse her contributions to the American stage.[53] What I am interested in is the degree to which—in spite of the rigorous objections—theatre was for her and other Bostonians a very conceivable, culturally possible apparatus through which could be shaped critiques of contemporary politics. When Mercy Warren began to conceive of the growing conflict between Boston and Great Britain, why she chose to think of it in theatrical terms was not necessarily a rhetorical device, but clearly some index of the extent to which that theatre had become a material reality. A tradition of clandestine performances maintained the ideologic possibility of theatre, and a generation of theatregoers had made theatre ideologically thinkable. This was, after all, a woman who had, in corresponding to Mrs. John Adams, signed herself "Portia," a woman who was encouraged to use her pen to the political cause. *The Adulateur* (published 1773) to be performed in "Upper Servia" is chockablock with Shakespearean figures, Brutus, Cassius, and her own pseudonym, Portius. It was modeled on Addison's *Cato* and also uses passages from *Cato* for a head quote. *The Group*, probably written in the opening months of 1775,[54] enjoyed strong circulation. John Adams himself was responsible for much of it. On May 21, 1775, he wrote to James Warren from Philadelphia: "One half of The Group is printed here, from a Copy printed in Jamaica. Pray send me a printed copy of the whole and it will be greedily reprinted here" (quoted in Quinn, 39). Political studies far and wide have been made on the satire and policy of both plays. Quinn reprints a "key" to the figures of *The Group* (40–41), so it is beyond the present project to enter into interpretive discussions. Rather, questions such as whether or not the production actually occurred give way to the deeper notion of why was the problem conceived of in dramatic terms? I suggest that the language of rehearsing social problems in a dramatic medium was a fully developed discourse even in New England by both author and audience and that development has an antecedent in several decades of prohibiting theatre. Warren thinks theatrically because theatre had been a operational mode of thought even where it was most rigorously banned. The idea of theatrical performance informed the way writers like Warren thought about the national contest. Even the form of employing local political figures (Governor Hutchinson, General Gage, local judges, editors, etc.) harkens back to Mr. Morgan's satirical play, *The Times*, discouraged for its "political reflections."

We like to think of Mercy Warren as a unique contribution to the history of the stage, certainly the first woman playwright in America, all the more so being a Bostonian and one engaged in rehearsing the Revolution. There were, of course, a host of other plays on the conflict: Robert Munford's *The Candidates* and *The Patriots*, John Leacock's *The Fall of British Tyranny; or, American Liberty Triumphant* and *The Blockade of Boston*, and Warren's rebuttal, *The Blockade, the Blockheads, The Battle of Brooklyn, Battle of Bunker Hill*, and *The Death of General Montgomery*.[55] The sheer number of New England–composed dramatic pieces that conceived of the conflict with Great Britain in theatrical terms suggests the potency of theatre—ontologically if not materially. A long tradition of both performance and opposition to performance informs us that, at some level, Boston had already internalized theatre.

If Warren was not the only Bostonian who turned a dramatic pen to the cause, neither was she the only woman writer. She was not even— or nearly not even—the only Mercy Warren.

Joseph Warren, Grand Master of the Masons, doctor, and revolutionary, lost his first wife Elizabeth in 1773 and sometime afterward Dr. Warren met Mercy Scollay. The two were soon in love and marriage plans were laid. Mercy Scollay was to be Mercy Warren, and her fiancée was also persuading her to make use of her lively intelligence and—like the other Mrs. Warren—take up her pen. She did. The first fruit was a satire on ladies' fashion. It is intriguing to speculate whether the two— the once and future Mercy Warren—literary ladies of Boston in the country's cause might have met and if Scollay might have also modulated her satire to the stage? Scollay's literary career, however, was cut short by the untimely death of Joseph Warren.

"THE GREAT ASSIZE"

Reposing in the American Antiquarian Society, Worcester, Massachusetts, is a broadside first printed in England and reprinted in

several cities in America called *At the Theatre of the Universe*. It is laid
out typographically as a very dense playbill offering "By the Command
of the King of Kings" a great entertainment: "The Great Assize, or Day
of Judgement," with a topical addition: "Recommended to the
Inhabitants of Boston." What followed is a highly detailed, sustained
allegory of the Last Judgement conceived as a theatrical event, replete
with "The Principal Performers," "Solemn Processions," act divisions,
seating arrangements, ticket prices, orations, and—ominously—the
final curtain. The parody is particularly rich when describing the
interior of the playhouse:

> This Theatre will be laid out after a new plan, and will consist of Pit and
> Gallery only; and contrary to all others, the Gallery is fitted up for the
> reception of people of high (or heavenly) birth; and the Pit for those of low
> (or earthly) rank. N. B. The Gallery is very spacious, and the Pit without
> Bottom. To prevent inconvenience, there are separate Doors for admitting
> the company.[56]

I opened this chapter with a similar allegory of the world conceived in
theatrical terms and argued that the conceiving of theatre in Boston was
possible in part by the campaign against it. I want to close with an
actual theatrical performance of the final judgment, played out in
Boston.

In November of 1765, in the midst of the Stamp Act crisis that saw
Boston stamp agents and distributors hung in effigy, and a Boston mob
destroyed the lieutenant governor's house, Nathaniel Ames and a group
of amateurs were rehearsing *The Orphan*. But Otway's tragedy was not
the only clandestine production in Boston that month; it was not even
the most interesting. A more eventful farce was staged in Cambridge,
where several Harvard students—including Joshua Otis and Nathaniel
Rogers (both from the class of 1768)—were severely punished for
acting a play in disregard of the college's prohibitions again such. The play
the students presented was "The Great Assize." Nathaniel Ames,
though long graduated, kept one ear open for Harvard news and wrote
of their punishment for "acting over the great and last Day in a very
shocking manner personating the Jude clerical Devil, &c. Otis expell'd,
Rogers rusticated."[57] The Harvard College records offer a few more

details from the administrative voice: "whereas Otis hath been guilty of a great profaneness in representing the Proceedings of the General Judgement in a way of Farce, Himself personating the supreme Judge, in that awful Solemnity." The Final Judgement, circulated so often as an allegory against the theatre, had itself finally become a piece of theatre, and the students who tortured the metaphor into actuality were indeed "cast down" by the farce. Otis and Rogers, God and Devil, were both expelled from Harvard and never returned.

6. Assuming the Wall ✎

"AS EXPRESSED IN THE BILLS OF THE DAY"

The Speaker, by appointment of the House, applied to the Govr. to discourage a Player who had Strowled hither to act as a Comedian. The Govr. excused himself from prohibiting it, but assured them he would take care good ord'r should be kept, and so the man went on to publish his printed bills, as thou wilt see by one of them inclosed, and to act accordingly.

James Logan to Henry Goldney, February 9, 1723

Their bills they stuck on every nook They never did them spare.

From Hird's *Annals of Bedale*

In James Logan's 1723 letter,[1] the mayor of Philadelphia was first aware of the players when the manager posted his printed bills.[2] In New York in 1766, the Sons of Liberty who pulled down the Chapel Street playhouse were first aware of the players through their printed bills, which the mob burned, as if they were effigies of the players or the playhouse. In Richmond in 1774, the antitheatrical notice was itself posted on a wall next to the playbill. In Basterre, St. Kitts, Janet Schaw became aware of a company of actors on the small island, when one of them handed her a playbill. None of these playbills survives, though it was not their materiality that doomed them. Both Logan's letter and the antitheatrical notice that accompanied the bills were preserved. Material artifacts of the theatre are rare enough in any period and nearly absent in this one. The most common artifact should be a playbill, yet of the thousands that were produced, few indeed have survived. They were, when printed and posted, a highly visible metonym of theatre itself, standing in for the company on every wall and nook. What contributed to their wholesale disappearance and their occasional preservation had little to do with their materiality as it did the mentality.

The ghost of playbills past is what I evoke in this chapter, both materially and metonymically. Companies within range of a printer relied heavily on their "bills of the day," posted on walls about town, and smaller handbills dispersed to passersby, and were only occasionally published in newspapers. Most colonial newspapers were only published once a week—and the actor's circuit extended to many towns that had no newspaper, or were at such a distance that local advertisements were impractical, unnecessary, or designed to reach readers outside the cities. For the immediate attention of the residents and arrivals, playbills were the preferred medium.[3]

Of the most ephemeral nature, few colonial playbills have survived though thousands were printed each season. Nonetheless, the few preserved remind us how stridently they demanded visibility. For example, playbills have a unique typography, with each line centered, rather than the justified margins and borders, a typeset the printers replicated in newspaper advertisements for the playhouse as well. More strikingly, they are often printed in two-color type, with the play titles and benefit recipient offset in vibrant red letters—expensive and seldom used in commercial print—reminding us that they were designed to command attention. Three such playbills are preserved from William Verling's Virginia Company in Williamsburg in the spring of 1768, all benefit nights, for Mrs. Osborne (May 18), Mrs. Parker (June 3), and Mr. Charlton (June 8), all offset in red ink.[4] They could also be printed entirely in red, as Jacob Mordecai recalled from his youth at the Southwark, Philadelphia: "Playbills [were] always in red letters." So he remembered them; even as an old man (84) returning to the city of his youth, the impression remained.[5] And indeed two such playbills for the American Company in Philadelphia, March 30, 1770 and December 16, 1772, have been preserved, confirming Mordecai's memory, as both are printed entirely in red ink.[6]

Edwin Wolfe, who catalogued the surviving playbills, exposed the problem when he lamented "the major bibliographers of early American imprints have not been kind to playbills," and traces something of their haphazard arrival in print, archives, and the major catalogues of imprints (Evans and Shipton-Mooney). Most died a death of neglect, like the New York playbill Joseph Ireland quoted for November 26, 1761 once preserved at Windust's Restaurant in Ann Street (alas neither restaurant nor playbill remain), remained on walls in ragged layers of old seasons until the wall itself was pulled down, or were recycled into more pressing service. Such was the case of the anonymous gentleman in London who received from a stranger a wrapped package: "Upon opening the box, there were found a letter, written in a great variety of hands, to prevent a discovery, and two playhouse bills, in which something seemed to be wrapp'd: on opening the bundle, eight guineas were carefully concealed, and in the letter was wrote, Sir, the inclosed is yours, honestly yours, ask no questions, and you shall never know from whom this comes."[7] Returning found (or stolen?) money is a fine use for playbills too.

All told, less than two dozen playbills between 1751 and 1774 are still extant and copies exist of several more the originals of which are no longer preserved.[8] Nor is it likely that more will be discovered, but something of the original force of their visibility in the colonial American landscape might be evoked through the account books of the printers who printed them.

When the Hallam Company secured permission to perform a short season of 24 plays in Philadelphia in the spring of 1754, Lewis Hallam contracted with local printers, Benjamin Franklin and David Hall, to run his playbills and strike off his tickets. Although all but two of these playbills are lost, *The Account Book of Franklin and Hall* records payments for thirteen different playbills between April 12 and May 27, 1754. Each playbill received a sizeable press run of 200–600 copies, to be distributed about town, posted at the theatre, and carried off by patrons as they left the playhouse. For the first half of the season—April 12 to May 6—Franklin and Hall were running off 200–400 copies per evening. But after three weeks, the press runs increased to 600 copies of each playbill. When the season hit its stride with the actor benefits, the press run settled into a solid 400 copies per benefit. Copies of the bills for the company's general performances were charged to the manager, Hallam, but the actor's benefits were charged directly to the beneficiary, as were their tickets. In addition, 100 copies of a list of the company's general repertory was also printed as a catalogue to be distributed, sold, or offered to subscribers.[9] The same brace of printers struck off tickets for all of the performances, nearly 5,000 of them by the time the printers' receipts stopped on May 27. But the player's season continued until June 24, suggesting the printing of at least ten additional playbills and several thousand tickets that went unrecorded. One two-month season produced 6,000 or 7,000 playbills, of which two have survived.[10]

What does a company do with 600 copies of a playbill? Many were distributed inside the theatre (the young Tate Wilkinson routinely bought them to recall which plays he had seen), but the theatre itself could not seat more than 300. The remainder were published about town, stuck up on walls, dropped off in stacks in coffeehouses, several hundred of them, each night of performance. That is a lot of visibility. Knowing the sheer volume of these documents in circulation, at some level, should speak of a certain performative presence.

Such numbers could be extended for each of the colonial cities the many touring companies played—though the records are not as generous. The surviving account books of Philadelphia printer William Bradford also records the press runs of playbills for the American Company between June and August of 1759, as do occasional notices of Hugh Gaine in New York, William Hunter and Joseph Royle in Williamsburg.[11] We know the Hallam Company printed bills in Williamsburg because they left an unpaid debt for it. When the Murray–Kean Company played Williamsburg, the owner of the print shop, Joseph Royle, managed an account against which bills were deducted. "Pocket expenses dt. for Mr. Woodham for his Acct. settled with Mr. Murray, 12 s 7."[12] When David Douglass published an itemized list of his company's expenditures in New York in February of 1762, his expenses included £5.10s to the printer Hugh Gaine "for two sets of bills, advertisements, and commissions."[13] What Douglass refers to as "two sets of bills" is a large playbill for posting—such as is preserved—and a smaller handbill for distribution, as well as the advertisement in the *Gazette* for each night of playing. This represented a wide range of print visibility, and Gaine was paid handsomely for it. When the American Company returned to New York (winter 1767–1768), Gaine was still the printer of choice in spite of one mishap. One of his apprentices ran off a set of counterfeit play tickets for an actor's benefit night and was distributing them to other apprentices, much to the umbrage of the actor. A rival printer, James Parker, wrote of the shop news to a fellow printer, Benjamin Franklin, and noted that Gaine "did all their work."[14]

In the menu of material evidence, the 100 playbills posted on the stickered walls and "dispersed about town" is where performance found its first public. John Esten Cooke, the nineteenth-century novelist who wrote *The Virginian Comedians*, described the Hallam Company's playbill for Hamlet, "in letters half a foot long, and with a profusion of exclamation points."[15] Though Cooke's novel (and typography) is clearly in the realm of historical fiction, his insistence on the presence on the player's introduction to the town through the playbills strikes one as a very accurate approach to the period, particularly in Virginia in court season, when the capital was full of strangers.

Such a playbill stickered on a public wall would offer a good deal of information. The full cast of characters and the entire bill of the evening, with price structures, seating choices, the time the theatre opened, and when the curtain rose were all printed and circulated, beneath the banner that alerted the wary that these players were playing "by permission." Beyond the information, their topical value lay in the metonym they offered to the idea of theatre. Writing of the American Company in Philadelphia in 1773, one "Philalethes" noted the high visibility of the players—who could miss them?—"They publish their Bills; every one sees them."[16] The poet who wrote of Butler's company on the Yorkshire circuit could have been speaking of any provincial company: "Their bills they stuck on every nook / They never did them spare."[17] Surviving newspaper notices remind us of the hand circulation of the bills: "N.B. There will be an entertainment every evening this week, as will be expressed in the bills of the day."[18] For benefits, the practice extended to the custom of hand delivering playbills to ladies and gentlemen at their houses, a custom honored in the breaching as frequently as the observation. When actors themselves did not hand carry the bills, bill-stickers were employed. In the same published account of the finances of the American Company in New York cited above, bill-stickers were paid four shillings of each evening's proceeds to ensure the visibility of the company.[19] In terms of endurance, the stickered playbill is the antithesis of court records: what was once most public has disappeared, while what was recorded for the juridical few has endured.

A LONDON STREET SCENE

Walls of playbills are exactly what beg to be recalled. Dispersed about town, stuck up on the merchant's walls, private residences, 600 red-lettered playbills, "half-foot letters," carried to patrons, left in taverns, coffeehouses, and posted on playhouse walls in every colonial American city that hosted performance were the first point of contact between the players and the public, particularly in towns without newspapers. From Kingston, Jamaica, comes the account of the old theatre there, built by David Douglass after he left the continent, and described some years later, with just such a wall:

> Through an American lady belonging to literary circles, and who has just returned from a trip in the West Indies, we are enabled to give an excellent view of one of the oldest colonial theatres in the West India islands. The building is of red brick, the main entrance being at the side of the structure up a row of brick steps that skirt nearly the length of the building, terminating in a deep portico, supported by old-fashioned fluted columns of enormous size. The front wall is covered with the long-accumulated debris of old playbills, cuts, etc. that add a ragged, dismall [*sic*] appearance to the already crumbling, rat-beset structure.[20]

The wall of playbills seems such a vital point of contact between the public and the players, the public and the public. What news passed on the very walls of the city? Ephemeral as performance itself, evoking the wall of playbills is essential to reconstituting the visibility of the player in the social landscape. To evoke that image—that "front wall covered with the long-accumulated debris of old playbills"—I turn to the early nineteenth-century painter John Parry.

With remarkable attention to the commercial typography of his day, John Orlando Parry captured exactly this ephemeral nature of theatrical evidence in his painting *A London Street Scene* (1835; figure 4). A shop wall—not unlike the wall of the Jamaican theatre described

Figure 4 *A London Street Scene* by John Parry (1835)

above—plays host to layers of advertisements of London plays, from the freshly printed to the ragged scraps littering the streets. Below the wall a few pitiful vendors huddle selling chestnuts and old meat, a grenadier stands idle while a petty theft occurs. But the wall is not the setting of the scene, it is the very subject of it. In Parry's etude on typography, captured signifiers, authentically reproduced and stratified, compete for the attention of the passerby (and vis-à-vis, the viewer), each inscription extirpating the last, as poster is pasted over poster. Each layer emits its brief signal before receding into total erasure. The struggle for visibility is particularly poignant as a young chimney sweep attempts to read an advertisement even as the bill sticker buries it under the latest offering: Verdi's *Otello*. A few voices momentarily dominate the cluttered score: *The Destruction of Pompeii* every night at the Adelphi; somewhere a *Grand Concert* is offered, somewhere else a Jim Crow dance. Poster on poster, each competing inscription ensures the erasure of the last, reminding us that very little material evidence of theatrical performances is designed to be enduring. Most, like the show posters, are quite ephemeral, literally of the day.

I offer this unenduring image because such walls might be quietly assumed—perhaps even insisted upon–to resituate performance in the social landscape of colonial America, to command a certain temporal visibility against its more enduring detractors. A company of some nature was in Richmond, Virginia, in 1774, playing at a theatre, to— we must assume—an audience of some kind, who generated enough attention to provoke objectors. They built or leased or converted a playhouse there, which has not survived, but in prerevolutionary days this usually required an advance subscription of a sizeable audience base. We have no record of this playhouse, those subscribers, this season, or of that audience; we have no playbills, no records of the actors themselves, what company they were, or which plays they performed. But the company posted playbills—printed by the hundreds by William Hunter, Robert Wells, James Davis, Jonas Green, William Bradford, Hugh Gaine, and later Douglass himself—the purchase of those print runs was recorded in the printer's account books, and the players posted them on just such walls that Parry depicts, walls that also attracted antitheatrical notices, and for ideologic reasons the objection has survived when the playbill has not.

Fortunately, the reconstruction (or assumption) of absent evidence is not the same as having no evidence. We need not listen for the irretrievable tattoo of a hired drummer beating the town. The colonial American record is littered with all manner of oblique scraps of material and documentary records through which the ghostings of performance's immaterial self can still be seen. The few I have pressed into service—the account books of printers, Jefferson's memorandum books, Masonic records, postholes of a 1760 playhouse, the harsh tradition of antitheatrical broadsides—are only the beginning of a study that promises to yield a good deal more information about the dense social network in which theatre moved. Taken together, such a montage of ephemera can go a long way toward evoking the legitimacy, the visibility, and, to some extent, the permanence of performance and the importance of it in a field of enduring objectors.

Better still, walls of performance evidence, such as John Parry depicted, and I was assuming, can sometimes even be found. One such wall was, during a restoration of the Ludwell-Paradise House in Colonial Williamsburg. In the 1760s, the Paradise House was the Blue Bell Tavern, it stood on the Exchange, directly across from the playhouse. The details of the discovery are given in a history of the College of William and Mary in Williamsburg by the late librarian of the college E. G. Swem:

> In 1889 . . . [a] workman was engaged in knocking down the plaster on the walls of a room of the Old Paradise residence in Williamsburg (now owned by Mr. J. C. Stater) when it was discovered that on the original surface of the wall some papers had been pasted and subsequently concealed by successive coats of whitewash. The discovery came too late to save the papers intact. A small fragment of one of these proved to be part of a playbill of the "Virginia Company of Comedians," which, under Lewis Hallam, opened its first engagement in Williamsburg in 1752. Only enough of this remained to show, from the dramatis personae, that the play was Otway's *Venice Preserv'd.*[21]

It was not known, in 1889, when the workmen recovered the wall that it stood directly across the street from the theatre. Swem himself erred in attributing the company to Hallam in 1752, who titled his "The Company of Comedians from London." It more probably belonged to

William Verling's Virginia Company, which played in Douglass's playhouse in Williamsburg in 1768 and advertised its performances across the street on a wall of the Blue Bell Tavern. The excavation but briefly exposed a moment when playhouse and playbills occupied a large sphere of visibility on the Exchange, that east end of Williamsburg.

Other scraps of notices that survived on the wall of the Paradise House remind us how vital such places were. One announcement the workmen preserved in its entirety was a notice to the pallbearers of the deceased governor Lord Botetout to meet at the palace for the funeral procession, October 16, 1770. One would like to think the pallbearers all made it to the church on time, and did so, in part, on the strength of such walls. Also surviving was a broadside of the nonimportation agreement entered upon by the House of Burgesses on May 27, 1774, publicly signed, publicly posted. That such a wall was in use for the governor, the House of Burgesses, and the players, for a duration of many years, suggests that it was a space of some civic importance, certainly of some social visibility, and that is exactly what I am after. I am encouraged that old playbills, like Verling's production of *Venice Preserv'd*, remained on the wall long after the company itself had departed, indeed long after the playhouse itself had been dismantled, the *memento mori* of the theatre that was and would be again remained, speaking to passersby, past and present of a performance of a failed rebellion, along with the death notice of the English governor and the first public declaration of American resistance.

Part II. Caretakers of Memory ᦳ

PURITANS AND PLAYERS

An anonymous traveler, visiting Philadelphia in 1768 when David Douglass and the American Company were currently in town, found himself in an awkward dilemma one evening, the description of which he offered to the readers of the *Pennsylvania Gazette*:

> Gentlemen, please to give the following genuine relation a place in your paper, and you will oblige your humble servant and correspondent, J.R.: Having been introduced, a few evenings ago, into the company of some ladies and gentlemen (to most of whom I was an entire stranger) after the tea equipage was removed, one of the gentlemen produced some box tickets for the play, which he generously bestowed on the company; I as a stranger, being presented with one, which (having no taste for theatrical performances) a principle of complaisance prevailed on me to accept. What the unhappy consequence was, of their piece of generosity in the gentleman, follows. —Some of the company, who had before resolved to hear service at St. Paul's Church on that night, found themselves now much straitened to put their pious resolution in practice; in short, a division in sentiment took place, some being strenuously bent to see the play, and some to hear a sermon, and, in order to reduce their versatile inclinations to a general one, they agreed the matter should be determined by drawing cards, which was accordingly done, when giddy chance determined in favour of the theatre. Good God, Gentleman, what a degenerate age do we live in! Philad, December 19, 1768.[1]

In the social landscape of colonial Philadelphia, colonial America, the uneasy antagonism of playhouse and pulpit figured with great potency both in the period and later in its histories, but as in the narrative related above, the moral agon was more of a rhetorical posture than a practice. Members of J.R.'s company may have objected to the theatre, but by chance or desire, they supported it nonetheless.

Another anonymous voice, in Boston in 1772, echoed the same anxiety, when, in the satire *Another Sketch of the Times*, the writer reduced the troubles of the colonies to four words: "Empty Churches, Crammed Playhouses."[2] For the writer of the sketch, the contest was elegant in its simplicity: faith had fallen off to the licentiousness of the playhouse. That there were, at the time, no legitimate playhouses in Boston to cram was irrelevant to the writer for whom the players and playhouses offered an easy and fictive surrogate into which could be emptied all the time's troubles. As a rhetorical presence, this moral (and dramatic) impulse was a potent force that shaped contemporary attitudes and many early and enduring histories of the colonial American theatre. As I am tracing, to some degree, the redistribution of memory, the second half of this study concerns itself with how the history of the theatre in colonial America has been remembered, fashioned, consolidated, and emplotted into a storied contest of Puritan and Player.

Consolidation in any field is usually driven by a certain economy; in this case, an economy of memory, but in this field it was encouraged by a narrative tradition (it is not coincidental that so many of the early historians of the American theatre were themselves playwrights). The historical operation was not so much informed by a dramatic impulse as it was transformed by it. The second half of this study explores the force of this transformation. From the evidentiary inception, players struggling to gain legal and moral victories over the stern and joyless antitheaticalists, like Edward Martin in Pungoteague, Samuel Sewall in Boston, James Logan in Philadelphia (or Puritans, more generally, Quakers, Dutch Reformists, George Whitefield, Presbyterians), offered a wonderfully seductive narrative frame for patterning the history of colonial theatre into a contest, build, and final showdown of mighty opposites. The Accomac County "trial" of 1665–1666 functioned as the epitome in this narrative; like a rubric letter at the head of a medieval manuscript, it elegantly offers to contain the text to come with what Fredric Jameson has called "an organizational fiction."[3] Under such a fiction, the moments of highest interest are those that offered not the banality of a sustained and supported season of plays by a company invited to the town, playing with permission in a playhouse generously patronized, built by community subscription, or even the indifference of the patrons and citizens who moved about their business with no regard to the playhouse. Rather, what sustain such a fiction are the moments of greatest concentrated dramatic conflict of wills: moments such as J.R.'s described above and, I trace below, moments when playhouse and pulpit stare down the dusty western street or glower across the courtroom in uneasy antagonism. Such courthouse moments make rich drama, but as history they tend to overconsolidate memory with an excess of narrative, an excess of forgetting.

Such consolidation and excess is, in part, encouraged by a field marred by absence. We have, for example, no first-hand accounts of actors in the period, nothing like Tate Wilkenson's *Wandering Patentee*, Cibber's or Bellamy's *Apology*, no description of the theatres like James Winston left in his *Theatric Tourist*, not even a good collection of letters to go on. Consequently, the histories of both players and playhouses arrived through second- and third-hand intermediaries, recorded and passed on by those who were not there, who could speak for them in any authentic way. The second problem taken up in this half is one of such "flawed memories," and how the broken transmissions of the past arrived.

7. Spoiling Nice Stories ❧

Could we ever narrativize without moralizing?

Hayden White, *The Content of the Form: Narrative Discourse and Historical Representation*

CONQUISTA

Whereas Cornelius Watkinson, Phillip Howard, and William Darby were this Day arrested by Mr. John Fawsett his Majestie's Attorney for Accomack Country for acting a play by them called the Bare and the Cubb on the 27th of August last past, Upon examination of the same The Court have thought fitt to suspend the Cause till the next Court, and doe order the said Cornelius Watkinson, Philip Howard, and William Darby appear the next Court in those habliments that they then acted in, and gave a draught of such verses of other Speeches and passages, which were then acted by them, and that the Sheriff detaine Cornelius Watkinson, Philip Howard in his Custody untill they put in Security to perform this order. Its ordered that the Sheriff arrest the Body of William Darby for his appearance the next Court to answer at his Majestie's Suit for being artour [author] of a play commonly called The Beare and the Cubb.[1]

It was Arthur Hornblow who first brought attention to the performance and trial of *The Beare and the Cubb*, thus substantially antedating the colonial American field, in his seminal study *A History of the Theatre in America, from Its Beginnings to the Present Time* (1919).[2] Though colonial and early American theatre had several nineteenth-century historians, it was Hornblow who set out to chart the length and breadth of the field in his first (quasi)modern history of the growth of the American theatre.[3] And it was Hornblow who best articulated the dominant themes of contest/conquest that would become the master narrative of twentieth-century scholarship in the field, and replicated in so many subsequent works.

After dismissing the efforts of his predecessors—"For nearly two hundred years the theatre in America has been without a historian" (Hornblow, *A History of the Theatre in America*, 7)—Hornblow describes the task and scope of the American theatre historian working in a field who should

> start at the beginning and continue to the end . . . a complete chronologi-cal narrative of the growth and development of the theatre in this country, showing how the drama first took root in North America, how the players, then regarded as little better than social outcasts slowly overcame Puritanical intolerance, and a chain of theatres was gradually built, first along the Atlantic seaboard, and then through the great, sparsely settled West, the courageous thespians pressing their way through the still virgin forests, braving the perils of the great American desert, until they reached the Pacific Ocean. Surely a more fascinating story has never been told! (Hornblow, *A History*, 9)

Howsoever fascinating, the story strikes the modern reader with a very familiar feel having been enacted repeatedly. Hornblow's master narra-tive of American theatre is a conquista, as old as Cortez, and cut from the same bolt as William Prescott's *Conquest of Mexico* (1843): a meta-colonial project of westward imperialism in which (in Hornblow) the "courageous thespians" encounter, engage, and ultimately vanquish first the intolerant Puritans to establish the civilizing force of theatre, then overcome the anti-British sentiment of the rude and unlettered audi-ences, then press their way out into the virgin wilderness, metaphori-cally seeding, greening the desert, and finally by the act of cultural conquest, legitimate their own "outcast" status.[4] Modulating the mili-tary for a cultural conquest, Hornblow's victory of the theatre (culture mapped onto nonculture) fulfilled the same Euro-colonial myth of empire as Prescott's narrative of Meso-America, reminding us, in Inga Clendinnen's apt phrase, "Historians are the camp-followers of the imperialists." With Prescott in mind, Clendinnen continued: "[A]s always in this European-and-native kind of history, part of our problem is the disruption of 'normal' practice effected by the breach through which we have entered."[5] In our case, the historians of the early American theatre were themselves the beneficiaries of this practice. Consequently, in this theatre-as-empire narrative, there is a discernible tension operating between the conquerors and the conquered, informed by notions of boundaries and transgression, and a kind of gloating anxiety that marked the battles to celebrate the victories of a theatre that pressed its way onto the culturally resisting continent.

Narratives like Hornblow's whose historians have entered their own breach remind us that the cultures prior to the imposition of the Georgian order that the theatre represented—the Quakers, the Puritans, the poor, and the wild itself—became prior cultures that would have to be erased, ignored, conquered, or reclassified before theatre and all it stood for could happen. There is a beatific passage in Charles Durang's narrative of the arrival of the Hallam Company to America that prefigures the magnitude of Hornblow's colonial myth at its conceptive moment. Describing the actor's despair at seeing the nothingness that was Virginia in 1752 ("They saw nought but a vast expanse of wood stretching all along the horizon, and, while they admired the grandeur . . . each one whispered to himself, What is to support a theatre here?"), Durang relates how a rainbow suddenly appeared across the York river. "A few moments before this ever-animating sign of the heavens was seen, they were all despair; but this emblem of Providence and heavenly peace to man at once revived their spirits—for in that sign we will conquer."[6] Like Constantine on the eve of battle, the sign writ in the heavens providentially determined the outcome of the war that is on the wing.

By 1919, when Hornblow produced his study, the conquest was complete and the history that followed was a history told by the victors. Theatres were established from sea to sea, actors had achieved enormous wealth, celebrity, and the profession itself elevated in ways that would have been unthinkable a century earlier. But a chronicle that celebrated the triumphs of theatre also advanced a narrative frame that was inherently adversarial. Hayden White (*The Content of the Form*, 43) reminds us that "certain narrative discourses may have arguments embedded within them" and clearly we are in the presence of such an embedded narrative. For Hornblow—and, as we will see, many others subsequently—the history of the theatre in America from its evidentiary inception in Accomac County was emplotted as a series of conquests waged on a hostile landscape of "Puritanical intolerance." At its more pacific moments, it was characterized as a taming of the wilderness, a mapping of civilization onto raw nature, Georgian culture on nonculture. At its more antagonistic moments, a conquest of Columbian proportions. A glance at Hornblow's chapter headings, those husky all-cap headlines in the battle, announce the martial key of the contest: "BITTER PURITANICAL OPPOSITION TO PLAYS AND PLAY-ACTING"; "SEVERE LAWS PASSED PROHIBITING STAGE ENTERTAINMENT OF ANY KIND"; "DIFFICULTIES WITH THE AUTHORITIES"; "OPPOSITION OVERCOME IN THE QUAKER CITY"; "INVASION OF NEW ENGLAND"; "DEEP SEATED PREJUDICE AGAINST THE PLAYER"; "PLAYERS INVADE OTHER PARTS OF NEW ENGLAND."[7] "Invasion" and "Conquer" become the dominant verbs of the narrative that will circulate for the remainder of the century. Indeed, Hornblow extends this martial quality to the very characters of the principal players, emplotting managers like David Douglass with military prowess, whom Hornblow can claim "was the kind of man who is spurred by difficulties to greater exertions. He liked the excitement of the fray. Philadelphia, where the opposition was hottest, appealed to him particularly."[8]

The intent of the discussion that follows is not to correct, dismiss, or dismantle the narrative impulse that ordered the field, but to try to understand why it was ordered in such a way, why it survived, and what function such an ordering served to the subsequent tradition of historians who adopted it. Why, for example, performance in America could not arrive as dance did, or as music, a mark of gentility; or unemplotted as, say, a raw wall of playbills such as John Parry evokes. Such a model of history refuses to narrate in ways that Hornblow will have none of. Hornblow, writing at the end of Westward expansion (1919), saw the theatre as an allegory of the great and necessary civilizing agency of empire whose manifest destiny was to conquer the continent. Under such a governing allegory, the pioneering battles of conquest, like the performance of *The Bear and the Cubb*, or the contested introduction of the American Company into Philadelphia, the "invasion" of New England (footholds first, then "forts"), function as story points of hostile European–native contact: the border skirmishes in a theatre of war. Under such a frame, for Hornblow and subsequent historians, a quiet, sustained, and "warmly countenanced" season of supported productions in a prominent playhouse raised by a sizeable community subscription was not as historically interesting as a single contested performance when the form of the narrative was itself dramatic. Fashioning the history into a contest proved to provide such an attractive framework; it endured, far beyond its generation.

SPOILING NICE STORIES

The strength of such a governing narrative can be seen in many ways, and to be fair, Hornblow neither initiated the pattern nor trademarked it, but articulated it in its clearest form. Charles Daly, writing a generation before Hornblow, opened his lecture *The First Theatre in America . . . Including a Consideration of the Objections that Have Been Made to the Stage* (1896) with accounts of early opponents of American drama that so aggressively keyed the text that the author felt obliged to conclude the work with an entire and lengthy chapter—the titular addendum—summarizing and countering the moral objections to the theatre. Daly, like William Dunlap earlier, who frequently returned to the theme of legitimizing theatre with international and historic examples, was defending the institution that could not arrive in a state of cultural neutrality. Dunlap, in his *History of the American Theatre* (1832), had treated the theme repeatedly, offering examples of ancient Greece "where the arts attained a perfection yet unrivaled, plays were the organs of the public and the stimulants to heroism and patriotic self-devotion" and concluded his work with an appendix of a model supported national theatre: the Theatre Francais.

Hornblow's influence can be marked by the many twentieth-century historians of the colonial American stage who have fetishized this contest. William Dye's monograph, *Pennsylvania Vs. the Theatre* (1932), and a spate of similar studies, notably Robert Johnson's *The Struggle over the Theatre in Colonial Pennsylvania* (1950), Harold Shiffler's "Religious Opposition to the Eighteenth Century Theatre in Philadelphia" (1962), and Paul Little's *Reactions to the Theatre: Virginia, Massachusetts, and Pennsylvania* (1969), were all written singularly to chart the opposition to the theatre in that colony in spite of Thomas Pollock's calendar *The Philadelphia Theatre in the Eighteenth Century* (1933) that documented the success of theatre in the city. Edmund Morgan, in his work "Puritan Hostility to the Theatre" (1966), wrote of the introduction of theatre in America with Boston's Puritans more in mind than Virginia's planters when he claimed, "Our colonial ancestors did their best to keep it [the theatre] out of America, and when it arrived, they greeted it with the kind of demonstration they usually reserved for British tax collectors."[9] Arthur Quinn began to parse out a divided reception of northern opposition and southern encouragement in his *A History of the American Drama* (1923):

> It is the custom to attribute this hostility to the prevailing religious tone of the different colonies, and to point out that while Puritan New England, Huguenot New York, and Quaker Philadelphia were inhospitable to the playhouse and all it stood for, Episcopalian Virginia and South Carolina and Catholic Maryland welcomed the first traveling companies . . . It was to be expected also that the Puritan, who grouped the drama, together with the kindred arts of painting and music, with his dearest foe, Anti-Christ, should oppose the playhouse where it was performed.[10]

Southern theatre historians—I am thinking of Eola Willis (*The Charleston Stage*), Julia Curtis (*The Early Charleston Stage*), and Susanne Sherman (*Comedies Useful*)—are thankfully more relaxed, but lamentably exert little influence over the field against those who spoke for them. Rather, it was Hornblow's topoi of contest that was retained. Here is O. G. Sonneck, writing a generation later (1943) of Douglass's southern tour: "After this the American Company invaded Virginia and Maryland."[11] Harmless enough, but why not "invited," playing, as they were, at the request of the colonial governor who headed up the subscription list to the new theatre? Other samples:

> Ostracized by Philadelphia, Douglass experimented with Annapolis. He had no difficulty in obtaining permission to erect a theatre there, and while the building was in course of construction the company invaded Chester-town.
>
> From Newport the company returned to New York in the winter of 1761–1762, again visited Newport in 1762, proceeded to Providence, R.I., and then invaded Philadelphia for a second time.[12]

Sonneck's martial tones ring throughout the narrative, even where there is no contest, like a recruitment trip to another continent. Sonneck on

Douglass's return from London, 1765: "Not content with reorganizing his forces, Douglass was bent upon conquering Philadelphia to his cause in spite of Quakers, Lutherans, and Presbyterians" (34). Beyond the syntax ("invade," "forces," "conquer"), the weight of such an antagonism can be seen in the organization of the narrative as well, even in the work of the formidable archivist Hugh Rankin who opted to open his *The Theatre in Colonial America* (1960) with the Puritan settlers in New England and their pronounced opposition to the idea and practice of theatre, rather than the first productions in Virginia, a generation earlier. The opening chapter assumes resistance as the position against which theatre must struggle: "Opposition, even when tempered with ecclesiastical reasoning, cannot always stamp out the inner whimsie of man, for it was in Puritan Massachusetts that one of the first recorded plays written by an American was produced" (5). Rankin is citing Benjamin Coleman's *Gustavus Vasa*, acted at Harvard in 1690, though the first-known production, *The Beare and The Cubb*, was written and acted without offense some 25 years earlier. Why Rankin chose to begin his narrative in a state of contest and why we must arrive at our understanding of colonial theatre through the Puritan lens is central to the narrative's dysfunction and is potent enough to offer a governing organizing principle for the field. It makes a better tale to invoke, as Rankin does, the opposition to theatre in New York in 1765, strong enough "to convince Douglass that his company should remain in the West Indies until the fall . . . until tempers in that city had subsided."[13] It is less dramatic to note that the American Company remained in Barbados owing to its remarkable success there that extended its season by a solid year, not to any hostile attitudes in New York. One might see in the privileging of contentious anecdotes the seduction of a great agon at work: to foreground the one vaguely dated playbill of a "Moral Dialogues" in Newport, Rhode Island, as a subterfuge against authorities, over a less-discussed full season of plays offered in the same city the previous summer, or in Providence the same summer; or the op-eds of antitheatricalists in Philadelphia, over the amply documented calendar of productions; or the residents of Providence marching on the playhouse, John Brown turning the town canon on them and threatening to fire. Even the incidental notes that "Douglass had no sooner rid himself of his sea legs [debarking in Charleston] than he was contracting for a new theatre building and located it once again on Queen Street upon the very Spot where an established Church formerly stood" all remind us the uneasy and ubiquitous antagonism that hovers behind and below the history, perforating it in the absence of more complete explanations.[14]

Occasionally the opposition is so formidable that it becomes the study itself. Harold Shiffler, for example, in his work on *Religious Opposition to the Eighteenth Century Theatre in Philadelphia* catalogued the religious factions mustered against David Douglass in Philadelphia in 1759, whose petitions represented four major religious groups; together these objectors "numbered approximately 200,000."[15] With these numbers, Shiffler suggests, also came a commensurate political strength. Two hundred thousand would indeed represent an enormous political force, representing as it did in 1760, nearly double the total population of all the major cities of colonial America at the time. Against such formidable opponents Hornblow may justly celebrate. But in June of 1759 when Douglass opened the playhouse in Philadelphia, by permission, he found audiences enough for a supported six-month season in spite of the force of four congregations of objectors.

This is not to claim that there was no opposition—such would be absurd. In some colonies for some years legislation was demonstratively on the books prohibiting theatricals. The point is not that the opposition was insignificant compared to the support—which is arguable—but rather that that story has been told, redundantly told, and having been told it hardly accounts for the popularity of an extensive theatrical circuit from Nova Scotia to Barbados that grew and flourished in spite of whatever opposition it encountered.[16] Even in Philadelphia in the season that Shiffler cites, the petitions and their thousands or hundreds of thousands of signatures were rendered perfectly moot by a single private letter from the governor and a repeal in London. In the end, it simply did not matter that the Quakers opposed the playhouse, they did not go.

If Lewis Hallam's company was granted only 13 nights in New York in 1753, once opened, its season was extended and it enjoyed a six-month run. If Douglass was initially prohibited in Philadelphia in 1759, the law was repealed before it was even enacted. Debates may have played in the one newspaper in Halifax, Nova Scotia, when Mr. Mills brought his company to town, but in the end, the playhouse opened anyway, and the company sustained a three-month season in that small garrison and farmer town that had no ready money. The same was true when David Douglass first opened in Rhode Island in the summer of 1761. In writing of the introduction of theatre to Newport, George Willard (*History of the Providence Stage*, 6) reports that on the first day of August "a special town meeting was called at the request of a number of freemen, by warrant of the town council, and it being put to vote whether the freemen 'were for allowing plays to be acted in town or not, it was voted, not.' " That same day, August 1, 1761, the Boston diarist Nathaniel Ames recorded that he was in Providence, Rhode Island, to watch plays. He saw *Douglas* on August 1, "with Harlequin," and the following day saw *The Distress'd Mother*. In spite of Newport's opposition, Douglass was already in business and audiences were traveling from as far away as Boston to watch. Indeed, one letter, published in a Boston newspaper, described the brief uproar at the opening of the theatre in Newport:

> As to the opposition and clamour against the Play-House erected here, it was much too vehement to continue, and, like the snow or hail of midsummer, melted gradually away. The house was open'd on the second of the month with the Fair Penitent, and Aesop in the Shades: and I cannot think you ever saw the Royal houses of Drury and Covent Garden fuller (without being crowded) or any audience there more deeply attentive or better pleased.[17]

In the end, the opposition was never as potent as the playhouse itself (or there would never have been so many playhouses), but the contest, however, made for a far better story than the acquiescence. Consider B. W. Brown's account of the opposition of theatre in Providence, Rhode Island, in the summer of 1762:

> Rumor runs that one evening when the faithful had gathered within to see the show, the unenlightened gathered without with malice aforethought to stop the performance. Yes, with force if need be. Had not the town meeting voted no plays? Where were law and order? And who was better qualified to enforce the peace than the sober citizenry of Providence? Woe to you, ladies and gentlemen of quality! Woe to you players by candlelight! The voice of the people! And indeed the voice of the people might have prevailed had not young John Brown, twenty six and fearless, hauled out the militia cannon,

threatened the mob, sent them scattering to their homes-defeated . . . and the play *went* on!¹⁸

Large studies and small illustrate the influence of this pattern. What follows is one example traced through the entirety of colonial American scholarship, a rather small anecdote, all in all, but one with such a persistent history of retellings that it ably illustrates the strength of the gravitational pull of form on subject. The story concerns the providential death, on opening night, of the wife of William Allen, the judge who is said to have arbitrated a dispute to permit theatre in Philadelphia, against the better judgment of the Quakers. It occurred in 1759, for the inaugural season of David Douglass's company in that city. The source of the story is originally recorded in John Watson's *Annals of Philadelphia* (1830). The anecdote entered the tradition of theatre history with William Dunlap who reprinted it in 1832. Indeed Dunlap pressed the story into a clear moral parable:

> The Quakers and others arrayed themselves in opposition [to the theatre] and applied to Judge Allen . . . with denunciations of the players and petitions that his power might be exerted for the putting down of these intruders, these disturbers of the sleepy quiet of the formal city. The judge gave them an answer which must have been very unpalatable. Watson says he rejected the petition, and among other matter told the petitioners that "he had learned more moral virtue from plays than from sermons." What was the consequence? The playhouse was opened, and the wife of the judge fell sick and died. Such is the warning which tradition has handed down to us that wives may hereafter prevent their husbands giving them countenance to theatres.¹⁹

The Judge Allen episode became indeed, by the strength of its retelling, "the warning which tradition has handed down to us" and the force of that tradition far outlived the facticity of it. When Charles Durang, in 1848, wrote of the Judge Allen affair in his history of the Philadelphia theatre, he set the record straight. Durang recounted the apocryphal story and (with Watson and Dunlap in mind) dismantled its authority, one would think, with some finality:

> Mr. Watson, in his *Annals of Philadelphia* speaking of the opposition to the opening of the Society Hill Theatre, says: "The Friends [Quakers] made their application to Judge William Allen to repress them [the players]. His

reply was repulsive, saying he had got more moral virtue from plays than from sermons. As a sequel it will long be remembered that the night the theatre was opened and at which he intended to be a gratified spectator, he was called to mourn the death of his wife." This statement, which we shall presently show to be incorrect, has been followed by Mr. Dunlap in his *History of the American Stage*, without examination, and has been hitherto acquiesced in . . . At all events, he [Allen] was not punished for his repulse of the Quakers (if he did repulse them) by the death of his wife on the opening night. The Society Hill Theatre was opened June 25th, 1759, and closed on the 28th of December. On the 15th of May, 1760, nearly eleven months after the time fixed by Watson, and nearly five months after the theatrical company had left the city, the *Pennsylvania Gazette* announced the death of Mrs. Margaret Allen, wife to William Allen Esq. Chief Justice of the Province, on Monday evening last.[20]

So the story turned out to be nothing more than a story, a Quaker antitheatrical "puff" with its own self-generating tradition ("it will long be remembered"). Yet as a story it carried great historical weight in establishing (or confirming) the essential antagonist of the narrative and the strength of the opposition in Philadelphia, as well as the status of actors as moral pariahs. In 1888 George Seilhamer also reprinted it in his work on the American stage (vol. i, 100) before reluctantly dismantling it: "It's a pity to spoil such a nice story," and his reluctance is apparent by reprinting it in the first place. But spoil it he does, "as Mrs. Allen died May 12th, 1760, when there were not only no players in the province, but when plays were prohibited by law, her death cannot be looked upon as so clearly a judgement." This was 1888, and one would have thought the tale was decisively laid to rest. Yet even twice rectified, a generation later, Arthur Hornblow, who billed himself as a corrective to Dunlap's unexamined anecdotal approach, nonetheless found the story of Allen's providential loss too seductive to omit:

> In spite of this official support, the hostility continued, the Quakers going so far as to apply to Judge Allen for an injunction against the players. The story goes that the judge not only dismissed the application, but retorted with a quiet chuckle that he had always got more moral virtue from plays than from sermons. Shortly after this, the judge's wife died and the "antis" were prompt to pronounce this domestic misfortune Heaven's judgement for having given encouragement to profane stage plays. (Hornblow, *A History*, 104)

Having acknowledged the "story" as suspect, Hornblow nonetheless resuscitates its authority, prompting the curious to ask, what is at stake in such a retelling? Why is it important that the drama be contested? Why was resistance imperative to the narrative? Is it merely anecdotal interest to spice a dull meal, or is there something more invested in perpetuating these battles?

Following Hornblow, sober thinking returned with Thomas Pollock's local history, *The Philadelphia Theatre in the Eighteenth Century* (1933), and Glenn Hughes's *A History of the American Theatre* (1951) neither of whom felt the theologic compulsion to evoke "Heaven's judgement" and the higher court appeared to have been again laid to rest in the shallow graveyard of spurious anecdotes. Nonetheless—in spite of its debunking, resuscitation, and re-debunking—at least three more contemporary theatre historians, solid scholars all, exhumed the indefatigable anecdote yet again and pressed it into a moral campaign. The first was Robert Johnson, in his monograph *The Struggle over the Theatre in Colonial Pennsylvania* (1950), who could not resist rehashing the Watson account:

> A group of Quakers appealed to Judge William Allen to suppress plays. His answer, that he got more moral virtue from plays than from sermons, served only to make religious heads nod when on the day on which the judge was to attend the play opening he was called upon to mourn for the sudden death of his wife. (Johnson, 36)

He was followed by Hugh Rankin, perhaps the most rigorous historian of colonial America theatre, in his seminal work *The Theatre in Colonial America* (1960). Rankin was a first-rate scholar and archivist who combed the holdings at Colonial Williamsburg for deed records, judgment orders, day books, letter books, and carefully compiled his findings into what is still the standard text on colonial theatre. Rankin knew his sources; he had read Durang; he was familiar with the passage in which Durang discredits the tale; indeed he quotes from the passage. But like Johnson and Hornblow before him, and Dunlap before him, and Watson before him, Rankin "acquiesced" and again printed the story of Judge Allen and the providential death of his wife on opening night:

> Once this was determined, [to allow the theatre] the religious factions closed ranks and rose up against this evil in their midst. Their first move was

to appear before Judge William Allen, requesting an injunction against the players. In rejecting their suit, the judge observed "that plays brought him more moral virtue than sermons." Yet on the night the theatre opened, Judge Allen was unable to attend; he was mourning the death of his wife. No doubt many of those subjects of his rebuke secretly rejoiced in this manifestation of the wrath of a jealous God. (Rankin, 81)

Nor did this persistent tradition end with Hugh Rankin. The *coup de theatre* belongs to William Young, who, in his *Documents of American Theatre History* (1973, i, 16–17), designed and intended as a source book of primary material, reprinted the anecdote twice, once from Dunlap, followed by Hornblow's account, with only half a line donated to the successful six-month season—with permission—that also characterized the Douglass company's first entrance to Philadelphia.

"Can we ever narrativize without moralizing?" asks Hayden White. These are not omissions or historical errors. Watson, Dunlap, Hornblow, Johnson, Rankin, Young were all, at some level, attracted to the telling of a tale of mighty opposites, a tale in which the contest of Puritans and Players if not sustained, certainly figured heavily in the driving narrative that legitimized the final triumph of the playhouse. The compelling assumption of such a contest pits the ontology of theatre against the harsh moral codes of a community that is ultimately defeated by the civilizing force of theatre. Under such a narrative, theatre in colonial America arrived with an "other," an antitheatre, and the struggle of this hostile pair became so potent that it ghosts the most rigorous of studies. Hornblow's conquista represented the culminating moment when theatre defeated its other.

The trouble with telling such tales of cannons and contests is exactly the fine tales they make. What they do not account for is the evidence of the support for the theatre, for example, in Williamsburg, a rather large playhouse in the center of town, right next to the capitol on one side and the Presbyterian meeting house on the other; or in Annapolis, next to St. Anne's Parish Church, on ground owned by the church, built by a community subscription that included the governor and the parish rector, supported by the gentry, merchants, and the House of Burgesses. What they do not account for are six or eight months of sustained and supported seasons in places like Philadelphia, where Douglass built his largest playhouse on the continent. What they do not account for is the support of the players at the highest levels of government, British and burgess, Tory and emerging American; nor do they account for the admission of strolling players into the elite social clubs of high society, like the Freemasons and St. Andrews Society. Nor do such tales account for the range and depth of a circuit of playhouses from Halifax, Nova Scotia, to Christiansted, St. Croix. Once we begin to recognize playhouses, seasons, and the breadth of support the players enjoyed, the potency of such tales begins to evaporate back into the rhetoric gestures of the anonymous Boston writer who complained of "empty churches, crammed playhouses."

*   *   *

This positioning appears all the more curious, all the more unique to colonial America, when contrasted with comparable emerging touring circuits in other Anglophone countries. Histories of eighteenth-century Ireland, for example, carried none of the stigma that characterizes colonial American studies. William Clark inaugurated his seminal study *The Irish Stage in the Country Towns 1720–1800* by noting "A sociable [*sic*], beneficent attitude in a majority of the upper classes, and a remarkable sense of humour in the lower orders, made the eighteenth-century Irish towns an alluring 'Ultima Thule' for English as well as native performers." Clark recorded the social objections to the profession of acting had all but "disappeared" from the minds of the Irish audiences, and illustrated it with an opening anecdote of a Dublin clergyman's son who joined a troupe of actors at Cork because their "dress, manners, and education [assumed] the character of gentlemen and [were] accepted in the city as such."[21]

In market terms, for English-speaking actors driven from London by the Licensing Act, colonial America differed little from its Irish counterpart: they were both developing provincial venues, as was Scotland, Wales, and the Anglophone Caribbean. But in attitudes toward such development, the north American colonies were far behind. They seem to contain the same cultural prohibitions—clergy, political, and economic—that traveling English players had faced when Fletcher's company went to Edinburgh in 1599. In that case the clergy directed that "no one was to visit the playhouse, or if they did, it would be under the kirk's severest displeasure."[22] But the players, in that case, had arrived at King James's behest, and James graciously let his will be known with a public proclamation, and neither players not audience suffered the kirk's displeasure. Indeed, the players were handsomely rewarded, including a conference of citizenship bestowed on the company. Ultimately, opposition should not diminish the accomplishments of the provincial players in establishing professional theatre, nor, would I argue, that the ultimate accomplishments be characterized against such opposition.

It should be remembered—particularly in colonial America—that the theatre lived in a wide network of culture, of players straddling nationalities, emerging economies, multireligious, multicultural, with degrees of toleration that ranged from overindulgent support (Thomas Jefferson attending 11 nights in a row) to students who organized amateur companies in Boston in spite of severe legislation (£500 fine for performing): and all were part of the colonial American social landscape. Maryland, whose governor personally donated to the building of a playhouse and attended opening night, should be no less American than Boston that prohibited theatre. It should also be remembered that in most cases and certainly that inaugural Philadelphia season of 1759, David Douglass secured permission from Governor Denny, and he and his American Company raised a subscription from supporters for their project, substantial contributions on which to build a playhouse on the strength of that support, ran off playbills, posted them on the walls of shops, private residences, coffeehouses, and taverns, and performed three nights a week for six months. The Quakers petitioned against them, as did the Baptists and the German Lutherans, and their petition came to nothing; the Quaker-controlled Assembly passed a law forbidding plays with a daunting penalty of £500 for violation, and the law and its penalty came to nothing. The governor deferred the commencement of the law until the following year with the understanding that the law would be nullified in London, as it was on September 6, 1759. William Allen, whom so many claimed lost his wife for allowing the players, in point of fact chaired the committee that prohibited them. That Allen supported the project and his committee banned it should alert us to the complexity of the tale. Three weeks after the law was passed, the playhouse opened for a successful six-month run. The law was indeed voided in London—as each prohibition against the theatre had been since 1705. Judge Allen was an audience member and would later subscribe to the publication of Philadelphia's first native playwright, Thomas Godfrey's *Prince of Parthia*, and chaired the committee that prohibited the players. Allen's wife survived the opening season, the company earned enough profits on the season to purchase lots and build two new playhouses in the next eight months—one in Annapolis, and one in Williamsburg. At their departure from Philadelphia, they also raised two civic benefits for the city, one toward purchasing an organ for the College, and a second for the benefit of the Pennsylvania Hospital. And the objectors from both the college and the hospital, in spite of their moral reservations, nonetheless collected the considerable donations from the players. In that season of opposition, as many as 80 plays were performed for one of the best seasons that Douglass and his company would enjoy in their colonial tenure.

Douglass and the American Company would return many times for many other successful seasons in Philadelphia—from 1767 to 1773 they played five seasons in Philadelphia. They would meet opposition and they would meet encouragement, and they would build playhouses and they would return. They would always return.

THE DROPP'D PERFORMANCE OF *THE MINOR*

Two weeks after Lewis Hallam's Company of Comedians from London opened in New York, mid-September 1753, a curious story found interest with the nearby Philadelphia readership. From the *Pennsylvania Gazette* of October 4, 1753:

> By a letter from Edinburgh, we are informed, that on the 2d instant Mr. Whitefield, being at Glasgow, and preaching to a numerous audience near the Play-house lately built, he inflamed the men so much against it, that they ran directly from before him, and pulled it down to the ground. Several of the rioters are since taken up, and committed to goal.[23]

George Whitefield, the charismatic and indefatigable preacher who learned his rhetorical postures from David Garrick, was a potent force against the theatre and the players on both sides of the Atlantic. Whitefield toured the American colonies extensively from 1739 to 1770, exactly the time professional theatre was establishing itself. The Swedish traveler Peter Kalm described the preacher in his early tours: "His delivery, his extraordinary zeal, and other talents so well adapted to the intellects of his hearers, made him so popular that he frequently, especially in the two first years, got from eight thousand to twenty thousand hearers in the fields."[24] Among the many vices Whitefield railed against was the playhouse, in America as he had against those in Scotland. Why such a story would be reported at just such a time would not be lost on the readers. The Hallam Company had just opened in New York and the account of Whitefield's inflammatory preaching in Edinburgh was offered as a clear moral parable for the New York readership of the *Pennsylvania Gazette*.

But if there was a moral to the reportage of the Edinburgh incident, I am not sure whether it functioned as an incentive or a deterrent. To the followers of Whitefield in Philadelphia (and the followers in Philadelphia were legion), it may have incited the citizens to disallow the playhouse, but it might just as well have reminded the readership that there is nothing illegal about theatre, and the willful destruction of playhouses constituted a criminal act for which the rioters would be taken up.[25] But ultimately, the account offers only a fantasy of destruction, a surrogation of suppression and violent eviction that was not to be. The playhouse in New York was not pulled down. The Hallam Company enjoyed a six-month season and then moved directly over to Philadelphia, and the behest of "several gentlemen," where it opened, with permission, in spite of Whitefield and his admonitions.

Over the years, Whitefield returned to Philadelphia on eight occasions, preaching in the commons when the churches were closed to him. Once in 1770, Whitefield and the American Company were both in Philadelphia at the same time, Whitefield fulminating against the players, but this time we have a record of how the players responded. Philadelphia-resident Alexander Mackaby frequented the playhouse, and wrote to his brother:

> I believe I have never told you that we have got Whitefield among us. He preaches like a dragon, curses and blesses us all in a breath, and tells us he hopes to die in the pulpit. He abused the players, who in turn advertised to perform *The Minor*. The parsons petitioned the Governor against it, and the performance was dropt.[26]

The Minor was a satirical piece penned and made famous by Samuel Foote, who played his caricature of the squinty-eyed stigmatic

Whitefield (Dr. Squintum) to the delight of London. The piece was nearly as well known as Whitefield himself, and the threat to play it was enough to illicit the governor's intervention. Hugh Rankin might describe the event as "the only time the players ever stood up against the redoubtable Whitefield, and certainly the first time they had gained a victory," but it was an agon without an antagonist.[27] *The Minor* was pulled from the bill, and the contest never happened. Whitefield railed and denounced the players, Quakers drafted petitions, AB and YZ debated the usefulness of the stage in the pages of the *Gazette*, and the players played on anyway, for nine months that year—their longest sustained run of their colonial career.

If it begins to look like the antitheatrical contest is a trope whose time has expired, several things sustain it still. Material evidence for one, and the memory consolidated around it. In 1759 when Douglass arrived in Philadelphia and the Quakers et al. petitioned against their establishing a playhouse, their petitions found permanent repository in the published minutes of the meeting of the Assembly, wherein the various petitions (Baptists, Presbyterian, Quaker) are lodged, along with the committee's motions, drafts, and recommendations in response: all preserved. What has not survived is the unofficial and private letter that Governor William Denny wrote to David Douglass guaranteeing him the governor's personal permission to play. That was private correspondence and outside public memory. There is, however, some residue of its existence in a roundabout way.

When Douglass met with the governor in early April of 1759, he secured his letter granting him permission to play, and on the strength of the governor's written promise, Douglass hired a contractor, Alexander Alexander, to build his playhouse. Douglass presented Denny's letter to Alexander, who, assured of its authority, undertook to erect the building at his own cost. When Alexander heard rumors of the Quakers' attempts to prohibit the project, he became worried and petitioned the governor to exempt Douglass from the prohibition. His petition has survived from which we learn, indirectly, of the private letter that has not:

> To the Hon. William Denny, Esq., Gov. of the Province of Pennsylvania, &c. The Petition of Alexander Alexander, Smith, and Wm. Williams,

painter, Humbly Sheweth:

That Mr. Douglass having been favoured with your Honours "p'mission of the 5th of April last, to build a Theatre and Act without the bounds of this City," he applied to your Petitioner, Alexander, to erect a large building for the purpose afores[ai]d, and to your Pet. Williams to provide and paint a new set of Scenes for the said Theatre; at the same time producing to your Petiti[one]rs your Honours p'mission of the purport aforesaid in your own Handwriting.[28]

The governor's handwritten letter to Douglass ultimately trumped all the petitions and Assembly motions. It was, in the end, the absent document that proved the most reliable. What it also tells us is that there were two codes at work: a legal system of petition and redress, council and committee, that allowed or prohibited, and a second system of private patronage and Royal repeal that overrode the local and vocal concerns.

"EMPTY CHURCHES AND CRAMM'D PLAYHOUSES"

The coercion of such a structure of opposing puritan and player was potent, tempting to employ, and found no end of modulations in the period and in the histories that followed. J. R.'s account of his party in Philadelphia split between hearing a sermon or a play, giddy chance put them in the playhouse. The Boston writer of *Another Sketch of the Times* was another. Nonetheless the players seemed a fitting target and the fantasies of their suppression played out far more frequently than the realities. In Boston in April of 1750, in the wake of an amateur production that was so well attended it caused disturbances at the door, one anonymous writer with the unfortunate initials V. D., submitted to the newspaper a verse of a dream he had:

As many people now-a-days
Seem pleas'd with nothing more than plays,
I lately dream'd I saw a new one;
Tho' tis a dream, it may be a true one;
Therefore to them that love such stuff
I'll point it out to 'em plain enough.

What follows is a catalogue of farcical characters who strut and fret and so weary the auditor—unaccountably also present at the production—that he starts up in a great rage and gives o'er the play:

> Good sirs, go home, leave off your brawling
> And each one mind his proper calling![29]

The verses of V. D. and the *Act to Prevent Theatricals* that shared the same issue of the *Boston Evening Post* offer a moment of great clarity in the cultural fantasy of suppression. But the spring of 1750 was also a great moment for the inception of professional theatre in America. On March 5 at the Nassau Street playhouse in New York, the Murray–Kean Company opened a remarkable season that would carry them, with only a brief summer recess, for 18 months. In spite of Boston's campaign, the players had already arrived.

Ultimately, the opposition to the theatre—and there was certainly opposition of many kinds—was far more complicated than agonistic structures of "empty churches and cramm'd playhouses," or puritans battling players. Every company of players that played in most colonial cities secured permission far more often than it was denied it, most, like Lewis Hallam, Sr. and David Douglass, were repulsed initially and gained permission ultimately in all but a few cities. Why they were initially denied may never wholly be known, as well as why permission was finally secured, or the nature of the negotiations in between. Often permission or denial to perform had more to do with the predilections of the current governor or lieutenant governor and honoring the protocols of patronage than representing any community will, as communities then and now rarely achieve any consensus. To illustrate the complexity I turn next to three case studies: the first example, from Philadelphia, 1750, explores the expulsion of the Murray–Kean Company caught in a complex cross-fire between Quakers and Anglicans, Proprietarians and anti-Proprietarians, during a divisive mayoral election, one candidate of which owned the playhouse. The second is from Albany, New York, where soldiers stationed at Fort George during the French-Indian Wars introduced a new social landscape of urbane habits that included balls, concerts, and plays, against the protestations of the Dutch pastor who committed suicide over the affair. They were the new gentrified demographic, transported to the wilds, and their presence occasioned a sharp cultural and generational rift in the town against which the clergy remonstrated, fruitlessly, and, in the end, tragically, pointing up the very ineffectiveness of the clerical opposition in one rural community at least. The last case study is the only example of violence against the playhouse in colonial America. In the midst of the Stamp Act riots in New York, John Tomlinson's Company made the mistake of posting playbills on stamped paper and the Sons of Liberty took the liberty of dismantling the playhouse.

8. Case Studies ᙂ

THE CLEANSING OF PHILADELPHIA (PART II)

Throughout the late summer and fall of 1749, a company of low-profile actors were quietly performing a word-of-mouth season of plays in Philadelphia without formal permission of the governor. Freemasons, moving among other Masons, the governor, the council, aldermen, merchants, and the most powerful men of the city, initiating a season of plays in their midst, perhaps even for them, one of whom contributed a playhouse, another contributed a prologue and played Portius.

There may be more story still to evoke for this company and their clientele, first mentioned above. In Watson's *Annals of Philadelphia*, speaking of the first theatre in that city, is an interview of an aged black man Robert Venable who recalled Philadelphia in mid-century as dirty and unpaved, "Filthydelphia." Venable claimed he went to the "first play at Plumstead's store to light home Master and Mistress. The company there was genteel."[1] Venable's statement has sometimes been understood to refer to the Hallam Company, which later converted the Plumstead warehouse into the Water Street Playhouse in 1754. But Venable's next recollection was that of one Philadelphia resident, Nancy Gorge (George) who earned the town's displeasure by taking to the stage. Nancy George never played with the Hallam Company, but, rather, with the Murray–Kean Company. Her name is preserved in the cast rosters from New York, when the company moved out of Philadelphia. It may very well be that when Venable recalled the first play at Plumstead's it was in 1749, not 1754, and it was the Murray–Kean Company that Nancy George had joined, that Venable's

Master and Mistress went there, and the company (the audience) was "genteel."

Who was this genteel company that Venable recalled? In the dense network of local power, there were many family connections that guaranteed a certain degree of shared information. If the Quaker John Smith could share his displeasure with his in-laws the Logans, William Allen might share his support with his in-laws as well, related, as he was, by marriage to Lieutenant Governor James Hamilton (Allen was married to the governor's sister, Margaret Hamilton).[2] Providing there was any conversation among families of the town, opponents and supporters alike would all be in the know from the summer of 1749, and the supporters included the governor, the president of the governor's council, the court recorder, the alderman and soon to be mayor, and several key assemblymen (Edward Shippen, Benjamin Franklin), and William Smith, chaplain to the Masons. Recalling the events of the first company that journeyed to Philadelphia in 1723 to which James Logan objected and could do nothing as the governor himself patronized the players, one suspects that a similar civic dynamic was at work. Though no notice of the players and their patronage has survived beyond John Smith's comment, in the nepotistic network of local power, it is unlikely that the players, once known to the civic elite, escaped the attention of many. So to the question why they were allowed to perform without permission, one could suggest they found encouragement among enough of the civic leaders to undertake a season with the understanding that it was "unofficial" but tolerated, and likely supported (particularly among the Masonic membership). They had, in short, a private arrangement as David Douglass would have, later in 1759. Allen and Hamilton, as well as Provost Smith, were all known to be principal patrons of the arts. All were, for example, contributing members to the Philadelphia Academy: Smith, a vocal advocate of student theatricals at his College of Philadelphia, and Allen and Hamilton, generous supporters of the portrait painters Benjamin West and Charles Peale, and the publication by subscription of Philadelphia playwright, Thomas Godfrey's *Prince of Parthia*.[3]

So why was this fledgling company of players initially supported by the cultural and political elite of Philadelphia, and what happened to cause this support to be withdrawn? Why were they ultimately expelled from the city? If it has less to do with the illegality of playing, or the lack of licensed support, or a moral fallout from the Quaker community, we must look elsewhere. I suspect why they were finally suppressed, like why they were allowed was a far more complicated tale, and this tale begins in the fall of 1749 when the mayor and the town council had a serious problem of nightly disturbances of unregulated streets and unchecked growth.

Evening Disorders

Throughout the minutes of both the Assembly of Pennsylvania and the council of the mayor of Philadelphia for the end of the year of 1749, there is a documented imperative to clean up the town. Literally and figuratively, "Filthydelphia" had become disorderly. Peter Kalm, the Swedish traveler who visited Philadelphia in 1748–1749, noted the increase of population and the city's struggle to keep abreast of its own growth. The south end of town particularly suffered from an influx of new populations. Benjamin Franklin, as well, noted in 1750 "the rapid building-up of the south end of town and the fact that many of the principal merchants were moving thither to live."[4] Complaints had also begun to surface about the unregulated growth of taverns and "places of entertainments" that contributed to the evening disorders of the streets of Philadelphia. In September of 1749—a month after John Smith's notice of the players—a petition was delivered to the Assembly from "sundry inhabitants of the County of Philadelphia" complaining of the

> number of publick houses of entertainment [that] hath been excessively augmented within these few years, far beyond any Necessity or Use . . . Most of these Houses are Nurseries of Vice and Immorality, such as promote Drinking, Gaming, Idleness and many gross Evils, enticing Youth and others to the lavish Spending of their Money, wasting their Time in Tippling and corrupt Company, and by this Means neglecting their proper Business.[5]

The petition was read and set aside ("tabled," we would say). When the General Assembly reconvened on October 18, 1749, the petition was resubmitted—and again the Assembly set it aside. When the body reconvened on November 20, the petition was again submitted.

Three times the Assembly acknowledged the petition and three times set it aside. On the fourth submission, the Assembly was finally prodded into action. They requested a list of the new taverns and ordinaries for the last 15 years and a committee was appointed to produce a report on the matter. It was a bureaucratic solution to a problem nobody wanted to confront. The process occupied two months during the late fall of 1749. A report was at last produced on the nagging petition, confirming the complaints. "The Committee on the Affairs of Publick Houses reports that it appears by the list referred to them, that within 10 years past the Publick Houses in Buck's County have increased from eleven to forty eight; in Chester county from thirty eight to fifty six."[6] Though they only reluctantly took on the problem, their solution was equally impotent. A toothless resolution was drafted and moved up to Lieutenant Governor Hamilton, prohibiting nothing, merely reminding the justices to ensure proper order.[7] This was a solution for people to whom public houses and places of entertainment were not a pressing problem. And rightly so, there was too good a living to be made in the licensing of ordinaries. It was an expected perquisite of the governor's position to collect fees for issuing licenses. Governor Tryon, in North Carolina, discovered to his surprise and delight, that his annual salary of £1,000 was handsomely supplemented by the £4,400 he made in "proclamation money"[8] There was little incentive on the lieutenant governor's part to curtail their growth, and hence the delay of any serious action.

If the petition looks like a Quaker strategy for indirect suppression, it is not unthinkable. The strategy was frequently used not to attack institutions directly but to attack their funding sources. Peter Davis has argued that the complaints of economic threats the players presented were a disguise for the moral concerns that attracted broader support. For example, the Quaker petition against lotteries was an indirect attack on Provost Smith, who supported the playhouse and who funded his college by public lotteries. But in this case a bill against ordinaries would not impact the playhouse materially, as they were not classed as such.[9]

Immediately following the consideration of the petition on that November meeting, the Assembly took up a related issue: the complaint of nightly disturbances and the need for regulating the watch. This was a problem toward whose solution all branches of government were employed.

In addition to the Assembly, on November 6, 1749 the mayor had called his city council on the same complaint. There was no regular watch being kept up in the city at night and disturbances were being reported. In short, the Assembly had moved the problem to the mayor's office. The constables were called in and examined one by one, "in Relation to the manner of keeping the Watch at present, and how many and what sort of people commonly attended that service." What emerged from the ad hoc enquiry was a report on the dismal state of civic security. The housekeepers, the constables reported, had been refusing to pay their Watch Money, "pretending they will attend the Watch duiy [sic] when they are warned, but frequently neglect to do it." The board unanimously agreed that the most effective way to amend the oversight would be to levy a tax and hire a proper force, "as is done in London and other great towns in England." But that was a time- and money-intensive venture, which the city could not afford, and the great complaints of nocturnal disorders were immediate. For the short-term crisis, the constables were to be held in strict account by writing a daily report—any bureaucrat's solution: "the Mayor [gave] directions to the several Constables, that each in his Turn, the Morning following his Watch-Night, do return in Writing to the Mayor, the Names of the persons, by him warned, and likewise of such of them as appeared on the watch in order that such Measures may be taken with the Delinquents as may be thought proper and necessary to oblige them to the performance of their Duty." Citizens were suborned to patrol citizens and it is likely that the players' names appeared on this list, engaged as they are in an evening business.

When next the council met, January 8, 1750, they returned to the matter of the negligent night watch. "The matter," the mayor was told, "since that time was grown rather worse than better"—this in spite of the new legislation passed by the Assembly—"and that the Grand Jury of this City had again presented the Weakness and Insufficiency of the Watch at the last City Sessions." This session carried an urgency about it that was lacking in the fall meeting, and one senses, even in the minutes, the impatience of all parties. The overtaxed watch, in their defense, laid the blame on the general conditions of the streets themselves. The merchants, they countered, were prevented from carrying out their watch duty by the extreme filth of the city, the next item on the council's agenda:

> [T]hey had likewise taken notice, in their Presentment, of some other Matters, which he would recommend to the Consideration of this Board, namely the extreme dirtyness of the streets, not only for want of Pavement in some places, but through the disorderly Practice of throwing out all manner of Dirt and Filth, without any Care taken to remove the same, whereby the Streets that have been regulated at a Public expense are render'd exceeding deep and miry in wet weather.

The mayor and council appointed a committee to pursue the compound problem of the night watch and the filth; their mandate was the backdoor route of the original petitioners to the Assembly: to cleanse the city—literally and metaphorically. And this time they got serious and appointed a bi-partisan blue ribbon panel including Benjamin Franklin, Alderman Edward Shippen, William Logan, among others. Their twin directives were to solve the problem of the watch and "likewise desir'd to consider of what has been observed relating to the bad Condition of the Streets, and by what means the People may be induced or obliged to pave and keep them clean for the Future."

Immediately following this resolution of ordering and cleaning the city, William Allen, the court recorder, offered his report:

> The recorder [Allen] then acquainted the Board that certain Persons had lately taken upon them to act Plays in this city, and as he was informed, intended to make a frequent Practice thereof, which it was to be feared, would be attended with very mischievous Effects, such as the encouraging of Idleness and drawing great sums of Money from weak and inconsiderate People, who are apt to be fond of such kinds of Entertainments tho the Performance be ever so mean and contemptible. Whereupon the Board unanimously requested the magistrates to take the most effectual Measures for suppressing this Disorder, by sending for the Actors and binding them to their good Behavior, or by such other Means as they should judge most proper.[10]

And send for them he could, knowing right where to find them. The players offered an easy solution to a complicated series of unsolvable problems: the unchecked growth, the derelict night watch, the evening disturbances. If the taverns could not be closed, the playhouse could.

That the players were "bound over" "to their own good behavior" and not fined alerts us that circumstances were being mitigated.

For example, in London in April 1752, Justice Fielding issued a warrant to suppress "a set of barber apprentices, young men, staymakers maid servants, &c. [who] had taken a large room at the Black Horse in the Strand to act the tragedy of the Orphan." They were arrested, paraded through the streets in costume, and Fielding "out of compassion to their youth only bound them over to their good behavior."[11] But this company in Philadelphia did not consist of apprentices and they were not unknown. They were not fined, were not arrested, but "bound over." Mild as it was, one might still ask, what prompted William Allen to take the action when he did?

The nature and language of the grievance was borrowed from the original petition to the Assembly; Allen claimed the actors were "encouraging of Idleness and drawing great sums of Money." The timing of the two issues suggests that the magistrates found a scapegoat for the disorder in the streets in the actors, and in suppressing the actors they found a solution for the Assembly's persistent and unresolved problem of the unchecked houses of vice. The players provided an easy compromise to the difficult problems of the growing entertainment industry, the lack of a night watch, and the evening disturbances. The company was flushed out of the city, figuratively accomplishing what the council and Assembly physically could not do. Expelling the players did little, of course, to halt the growth of the taverns and nothing to provide for a night watch, nor did it do anything toward solving the vexing problem of the filth on the streets. What it did offer was a bureaucratic gesture, and that, in the end, proved to be enough.

Five years went by and nothing further was done about the night watch, the dirty streets, or the spread of taverns. Neither action was revisited by the council or the Assembly. What was so pressing in the fall of 1749 had disappeared by the winter. Expelling the players seemed to be order enough. Ten years went by. No further civic action was taken. Finally, an act for paving the streets was passed in October of 1763, to be funded with a lottery; in the same session, an act for regulating the nightly watch was also passed.[12]

* * *

One could parse the suppression even further, and probably should, had I not labored it enough. But in January of 1750 when the council finally suppressed the players, William Plumstead had just been elected mayor of Philadelphia, against the vocal opposition of many of the council. The notion of local politicians using the players would not be unprecedented. Rip Van Dam, mayor of a deeply divided New York in 1732, sponsored a company and lodged it in his own warehouse. When David Douglass first arrived in New York in the fall of 1758, he arranged to play in the warehouse of Mayor John Cruger. And the council, falling out with Cruger, banned his players. A company that attached itself to a mayor enjoyed the patronage and permission, but stood or fell with the mayor's political fate.

The civic conversation of cleansing Philadelphia and the ultimate expulsion of the players straddled the mayoral elections, and there may have been nothing incidental about the two events. The players were, in essence, one of Plumstead's businesses, and he and his interests had many detractors. The Logan-Smith family, for one; the Quakers in the council, for another. Both Plumstead's politics and religion made him a polarized candidate for Philadelphia's mayor. For one thing, Plumstead had been "read out" of the Quaker meeting, departed the faith of the friends on the unkindest of terms and had become an Anglican. This stinging betrayal put him on the wrong side of the politically powerful Quaker church, the equally potent Logan family, and the majority of the council. The Anglicans embraced Plumstead as a rising star in the city. He was a successful merchant who was elected to the Common council in 1739, an alderman in 1747, and now mayor, 1750–1751. He shared their social sensibilities, their appetite to the arts and assemblies; Plumstead was one of the founding subscribers to the first Dance Assembly in Philadelphia in 1748. Anglicans, to their credit, were also more encouraging of the theatre. James Burd and Edward Shippen were both Anglicans, and indeed Burd himself had taken to the stage in an amateur production in the winter of 1748–1749.[13] The Anglicans, in short, were the fashionably social sort.

But in his rise Plumstead had also crossed the Proprietary party, the old Quaker following of the original Penn charter. He sided rather with the movement toward Royal Government. The Proprietary system derived its legitimacy from the original charter given to William Penn, which still remained in the Penn family. Currently the nominal head of state was Thomas Penn, who, while in London, had undertaken a campaign to decrease the authority of the Pennsylvania Assembly by withholding their funding. Against the proprietary party sat the campaign for establishing a royal government, such as existed in the other colonies. This was the formidable body that constituted much of the Assembly, including the new mayor.

That Plumstead was elected mayor meant that the Anglicans and the royalists were gaining the ascendant. But the council was still largely the domain of the old Quakers and Proprietary party men. William Allen was the party chieftain who was involved in a political contest with the Assembly over the balance ("reform") of power, and it will be remembered that it was Allen who broke the news of players.

Seen in this light, the suppression of the players may have been a covert and politically blunted attack on the part of the council against the new mayor, against the Anglicans, against the Royalists, or all of the above, under the pretext of cleansing the disorders of the streets. Ultimately, all of the involved parties were deeply, perhaps even inextricably, implicated in the affairs of each other, bound up in a dense network of social, religious, political, and commercial relations that may never be wholly penetrated. Dense as it is, it is exactly within such a web of culture that the players must be read.

Colonial companies fought many battles, moral, legal, economic, few of them as simple as a moral agon of Puritan versus Player. Even in the above-cited contest in Philadelphia with Judge Allen, the opposition never found the focus of a single driving antagonist. The same Judge William Allen who allegedly lost his wife for allowing theatre in 1759, who supported and then expelled the Murray–Kean Company when they began playing in Philadelphia in 1749, was a member of the young and elite social club of Philadelphia, the Philadelphia Academy, headed by James Burd, a club that sponsored dances and mounted, yes, amateur theatricals. Allen was one of few subscribers to support the Philadelphia playwright Thomas Godfrey with the publication of his play, *The Prince of Parthia* (1765). And it was the same Allen, though a Proprietary party chief, who repulsed the petition of the Quakers, claiming he learned more morality in the playhouse than in the pulpit. This is a complex relationship to the institution of theatre and may very well have more to do with the shifting demographics of power and local politics than any moral or ontological objections to theatre.

A STICK, A PAIR OF SHOES, BREAD, AND A DOLLAR

We do sometimes find a single antagonist engaged in a moral campaign against the theatre, and in the following case, it tells us next to nothing.

As part of the buildup at the start of the French-Indian Wars, 300 recruits arrived at Fort George, Albany, New York, in the winter of 1757–1758 under General Shirley. To the insular village of not quite 2,000—mostly Dutch—this represented a sudden influx of a substantial new population, a young male population, and worse, they were English.[14] As this new population was not engaged immediately in military action, they took to diverting themselves through their first winter with balls and concerts, and later with amateur theatricals. This urbane and social young regiment was part of a larger sea change in the society of the satellite, infecting the young Dutch of this closed community with an infusion of "anglomania." One detailed account— Mrs. Anne Grant's—described it as a clash of cultures, generational and moral:

> A regiment came to town about this time, the superior officers of which were younger, more gay, and less amenable to good counsel than those who used to command the troops . . . By this time the Anglomania was beginning to spread. A sect arose among the young people, who seemed resolved to assume a lighter style of dress and manners, and to borrow their taste in those respects from their new friends [the soldiers] . . . balls began to be concerted, and a degree of flutter and frivolity to take place, which was as far from elegance as it was from the honest, artless, cheerfulness of the meetings usual among them . . . Now the very ultimatum of degeneracy, in the opinion of these simple good people, was approaching; for now the officers, encouraged by the success of all their former projects for amusement, resolved to new fashion and enlighten those amiable novices whom their former schemes had attracted within the sphere of their influence; and for this purpose, a private theatre was fitted up, and preparations made for acting a play; except for the Schuylers and their adopted family, there was not perhaps one of the natives who understood what was meant by a play.[15]

The account forcefully reminds us of the extent of the provincialism and the fragility of cultural institutions like theatre that require generational contact or the very notion itself becomes culturally inaccessible.

In Albany in the late 1750s, like many of the smaller hamlets and frontier towns of colonial America, a generation had passed between the arrival of the first emigrants from cultural centers, and a second generation had now grown up far from even the major cities of New York, Boston, and Philadelphia.

Such a sea change as the soldier's wrought in Albany could only attract its dissenters, none more than the pastor of the reformed Dutch church, the Reverend Theodorus Frielinghuysen: the "domine." The domine raged from the pulpit against the levity of the soldier-players and the rift in the town that the manners and social expectations the gay new regiment caused:

> And by this time, the town, once so closely united by intermarriages and numberless other ties, which could not exist in any other state of society, were divided into two factions; one consisting almost entirely of such of the younger class, as having a smattering of New York education, and a little more of dress and vivacity, or perhaps levity, than the rest, were eager to mingle in the society, and adopt the manner of those strangers.[16]

As noted, the faction was largely generational, the older, more established members shied away from the new frivolity that threatened the sobriety of business and good religion, while the younger generation sought the occasion of new society. The height of the division occurred when this new regiment and their young followers furnished a playhouse and announced their production, against the protestations of domine Frielinghuysen. Mrs. Grant resumes:

> The play, however, was acted in a barn, and pretty well attended, notwithstanding the good domine's earnest charges to the contrary. It was *The Beaux Stratagem*; no favorable specimen of the delicacy or morality of the British theatre; and as for the wit it contains, very little of that was level to the comprehension of the novices who were there first initiated into a knowledge of the magic of the scene, yet they "laughed consumedly" as Scrub says, and actually did so, "because they were talking of him". They laughed at Scrub's gestures and appearance, and they laughed very heartily at seeing the gay young ensigns, whom they had been used to dance with, flirting fans, displaying great hoops, and with painted cheeks and colored eye-brows, sailing about in female habiliments . . . The fame of these

exhibitions went abroad, and opinions were formed of them no way favorable to the actors or to the audience.[17]

But in spite of the patristic objections, further plays were offered. The satire of one production, *The Recruiting Officer*, in which the soldiers tailored their performances to caricature their own major, was over-shadowed by a greater rift in the town. The domine viewed the diversion as the height of frivolity, a great assault on his moral authority, and fulminated against the practice. "Mr. Frelinghuysen, who invoked heaven and earth to witness and avenge this contempt, not only of his authority, but, as he expressed it, of the source from whence it was derived." Finally, the soldier-players had heard enough.

> Early one Monday morning, after the domine had, on the preceding day, been peculiarly eloquent on the subject of theatrical amusements, and pernicious innovations, some unknown person left within his door a club, a pair of old shoes, a crust of black bread, and a dollar. The worthy pastor was puzzled to think what this could mean; but had it too soon explained to him. It was an emblematic message, to signify the desire entertained of his departure. The stick was to push him away, the shoes to wear on the road, and the bread and money a provision for his journey.[18]

The gesture wounded the domine to the quick; the pastor fell into some consternation, "night and day he mused on the imagined insult," languished, thence to depression, and at length resolved to indeed depart the province. Determined to sail back to Holland, the domine promised to write, and later, when he had recovered his spirit, to return. He did neither. Rather, his ending was as morose as his life: "this victim of lost popularity had appeared silent and melancholy to his shipmates, and walked constantly on deck. At length he suddenly disappeared, leaving it doubtful whether he had fallen overboard by accident, or was prompted by despair to plunge into eternity."[19]

One could, I suppose, press the above anecdote into an agon of clergy and players in which the church suffered a humiliating defeat, but the good domine and his constituency were wrestling with powers in more temporal places. It was the theatre of war that brought the English soldiers—and English culture—to Albany, and when the war moved on to other fronts, the English soldiers left, and with them the balls, the concerts, the dress, the vivacity, and the theatricals.

But the damage had already been done. The Dutch inhabitants who had before the war never seen theatre, never known the fashionable high life of balls and concerts, had been introduced to it, now "understood what was meant by a play." And so it is not surprising that an appetite was left in the mouths of the younger sort. Before the decade was out (1769), David Douglass would carry his American Company to Albany for a summer layover. The soldiers were long gone by then; the desire they had created, however, was not. Douglass secured the permission of the governor, and played a brief summer run, but the market of the postwar provincial town was small, out of the way, and there were better towns to the south. As the railings of the domine did nothing to discourage the introduction of theatre, so also the triumph of the theatre over the Dutch domine did nothing to open the market for the players. Douglass never returned to Albany.[20]

THE HANDIWORK OF THE SONS
OF LIBERTY

For all the riots that troubled the London stage in the middle decades of the eighteenth century—the half-price riots, the Artaxerxes riots, the Chinese Festival, the Bottle Hoax—the only physical assault on a playhouse in colonial America happened on May 5, 1766 in New York, when a mob destroyed the Chapel Street playhouse from inside the theatre. The riot commenced in the second act of *The Twin Rivals* "by the usual English Signal of one candle," and when it was over, only the shell of the playhouse was left standing. Several preserved accounts all concur that severe damage was done, both to persons and to property. One boy had his skull fractured in the fray and many others were hurt. The havoc wreaked on the interior of the playhouse, coupled with the loss of scenery, costumes, and properties, effectively put the scratch company out of business. Where several accounts differ is in the motivation of the mob that targeted the playhouse.

The company has traditionally been attributed to Mr. John Tomlinson, who had been an actor with David Douglass since his arrival in New York in 1758, but his roles were gradually demoted over the subsequent years, and by 1764 he and his wife Anna dropped out of the company roster. Rankin (*The Theatre in Colonial America*, 108) suggested that Tomlinson was sent as an advance agent to New York "to await the return of the remainder of the company from the islands. Rather than mark time, Tomlinson and his wife Anna gathered a group of young theatrical aspirants and opened the playhouse." Perhaps. But, as noted above, Douglass was struggling in Charleston for want of actors in the winter of 1764–1765, so it is unlikely that he dispatched a useful, though unremarkable, pair. Perhaps Tomlinson left the company to seed one of his own. Whatever the cause of the separation, 1765 finds the Tomlinsons residents of New York city where John had assembled a small corps of actors ("young gentlemen") and mounted productions. Two newspaper advertisements survive for March 4 and April 10, 1765 (Odell, *Annals of the New York Stage*, 92–93). Nothing more is heard from the company until the actors reappeared in New York the following spring, leading Rankin (108–109) et al. to suggest that the interim was spent strolling, as they were indeed noted as "strollers" when they returned to New York in the fateful spring of 1766. On April 3 a production was announced for the following week and immediately their presence captured the attention of the Sons of Liberty. The next day Captain John Montresor, a British officer and engineer stationed in New York at the time, noted in his journal the reaction of the players from that organization:

> A Grand meeting of the Sons of Liberty to settle matters of moment, amongst the many whether they shall admit the strollers, arrived here to act, tho the General [General Gage, military governor of the colony] has given them permission . . . Some stamps as tis said found in the streets were publickly burned at the Coffeehouse together with some playbills, all to prevent their spirits to flag.[21]

The issue behind the hostility was the Stamp Act, and the indignant incendiaries were the Sons of Liberty, an association of working class new American radicals that Montresor at least felt woefully out of station to undertake the affairs of state. But they were the ones who suffered most directly from the policies. The New York labor class particularly felt the economic pinch at the close of the war with France, as the shipbuilding and maritime industries were left in the havoc of a postwar depression. By August of 1765, opposition of the workers to the Stamp Act was so virulent that the first stamp distributor, James McEvers, a wealthy merchant, resigned his post before the stamps even arrived for fear his house would be pillaged. When the stamps did arrive a month later, they were initially prevented from being unloaded by dockside mobs. The stamps had to be escorted ashore by a military regiment in the dead of the night.[22] New York's Lieutenant Governor Cadwallader Colden beefed up the fortifications and the crowd responded by rampaging the houses of suspected British sympathizers. On the night of October 31—a few hours before the act was to take effect—the mob made a bonfire of the governor's coach and threw his effigy on top of the flames. Colden's family was obliged to seek protection aboard a British Man of War in the harbor.

After the first skirmish, Lieutenant Governor Colden was removed from office over his handling of the Act. Chief Justice William Smith, a British aristocrat in New York at the time, described the lieutenant governor's "obnoxious character" to have "added Fuel to the general Discontent."[23] Turning the Battery's canons onto the city and threatening to reduce New York to ashes may also have contributed to his unpopularity. Merchants who relied heavily on paper products—targets of the Stamp Act—had the greatest difficulty negotiating the ordinance. New York printer Hugh Gaine evaded the order by first ceasing publication, and after the stamped paper had been seized, by reissuing his newspaper with the header "No Stamped Paper to be Had."[24]

The British responded to the local resistance by sending Governor Henry Moore, General Gage, and more troops to oversee the execution of the Stamp Act, by force if necessary. Moore's mandate was very clear: enforce the distribution of the stamps. For instance, when the judicial Assembly appeared to disregard the act, Moore buttonhooked the chief justice and threatened to unseat any judge who presided over cases that were not properly stamped; he could, implied Moore, expect to lose his seat in the council as well as the bench. The stratagem worked, as Moore related: "had the proper effect on him [the chief justice] as well as on his brethren."[25] Moore was the enforcer, and any company of actors that expected to play at his license would have had to honor his policy.

Into such a contest did the players arrive in the opening days of April 1766. They secured their introductions, Governor Moore granted them permission to perform, and on April 3 posted their first playbills, advertising their opening production. Of that day William Smith wrote: "the whole town in an uproar all the 2d: and 3d instant."[26] The opening, originally announced for April 9, was postponed. And rightly so, the Sons of Liberty were busy making daily resolutions against British trade, British Admiralty Courts, boarding ships, seizing cargo, and threatening to pull down the house of anyone not publicly and vehemently opposed to the Stamp Act.[27] Indeed, the day before the players secured permission, Montresor records, "Forty ruffians, calling themselves Sons of Liberty pillaged and Ransacked a Gentleman's house and family in Connecticut for being a neutral person and not declaring his sentiments."[28] Despite the violence on the streets, the American resistance to the Stamp Act had found enough support in London to warrant serious conversation concerning its repeal, rumors of which were in the air as early as February of 1766. By April 9, Tomlinson reposted his playbills with a nota bene begging the indulgence of the town, claiming (prematurely) that the Stamp Act had been repealed. We hear nothing else of the players for the rest of the month while New York awaited confirmation.[29] On May 5 when news of the repeal of the Stamp Act were already in circulation, a new playbill went up: "As the Packet is arrived, and has been the Messenger of good News relative to the Repeal, it is hoped the Public has no objections to the above Performance." That night Tomlinson and his company finally opened, and that night their long-delayed season got no further than the first two acts, as the "Public" did indeed have objections to the above performance.

The various accounts agree to the general destruction that followed. The signal was given, rioters commenced the damage from within and without the playhouse. There was a tumult for the door and in the confusion several injuries occurred, including one fatality. The players were harassed off the stage, and one boy, cross-dressed, was whipped in his skirts for the sport of it. Why the players were targeted—and they were the only casualties of that night's riots—is worth investigating.

The account of the destruction was carried in several colonial newspapers. Weyman's *New York Gazette* of May 12 offers no motivation for the destruction; Holt's *Post-Boy*—more frequently reprinted—laid the cause of the riot on "having given offence to many of the inhabitants of this city, who thought it highly improper that such entertainments should be exhibited at this time of public distress, when great numbers of poor people can scarce find means of subsistence."[30] And quite likely a troop of players did give offense. The claims of great distress hovered throughout the postwar period. The church wardens alerted the Common council of the city the previous winter that the monies raised for the relief of the poor "have been long since Expended" and the "distresses of the Poor" were so pressing that unless new monies were found many would perish for want of food and firewood.[31]

Joseph Ireland, in his history of the New York theatre (*Records of the New York Stage*, 40), lays the blame with the player's association with the unpopular governor, as does Odell (*Annals of the New York Stage*, 95). The playhouse "whose tenants were not popular with the republican portion of the community, and were looked upon as special adherents of the crown, and *proteges* of the governor."[32] Their association with the governor, Henry Moore, marked the players as "British goods" at a time when New York merchants were drafting associations against the importation of all British goods.

Capt. Montresor, however, never generous to the unruly colonists, found the whole occasion a diversion for the picking of pockets and a coarse example of populism. Montresor records it thus:

> This evening a play was acted by permission of our Governor, to be performed by a company of comedians or Strollers, notwithstanding the Sons of Liberty without any Reason given pulled down the Playhouse the beginning of the 2nd act, put out all the lights, then began picking of pockets, stealing watches, throwing Bats, sticks and bottles and glasses, crying out Liberty, Liberty, then proceeded to the Fields of Common and burnt the materials. One boy Killed and Many people hurt in this Licentious affair.[33]

But as this assault on the playhouse was the only occasion of such violence on the colonial American stage, occurring in the thick of the Stamp Act, it may have had as much to do with the playbills as the players.

The first notice of hostility occurred when the players posted their bills, back in April, when they were burned outside a coffeehouse, with some stamps that had been found "to prevent their spirits to flag."

Were they separate anxieties, loose stamps and playbills? Or were the bills themselves stamped? These bills would have been printed locally and, in April of 1766 before the repeal was official, it would have been difficult if not inconceivable that the players indebted to the British governor and general both assigned to enforce the Stamp Act for permission to play should not have been in the uncomfortable position of accepting stamped paper—just as the court had been forced to comply. This put the players in the uncomfortable position of either courting the loyalists or risking the displeasure of the resistance. The sight of a playbill printed on stamped paper would have been enough to inflame the Sons of Liberty and to position the players—lamentably so—as soundly in the camp of the British officers trespassing on American liberties. The destruction of the playhouse was a target of British imperialism, like the vandalized coach of Major James. One clue is a surviving placard, handwritten when the stamps first arrived. It warned: "the first man that either distributes or makes use of Stampt Paper let him take Care of his House, Person, and Effects. We dare. Vox Populi."[34] "Vox populi" may have indeed been good to their word, and Tomlinson, who was obliged by his license to use the stamped paper, lost his house and effects. His person survived their patriot's wrath, but he gave up managing a company, and he and his wife returned as actors to Douglass's American Company. The Chapel Street playhouse was never rebuilt.

Three tales, three antagonists, one America.

9. The Burning of the Lena Edwin ⌒⃫

The most persistent mode of forgetting is memory imperfectly deferred.

Joseph Roach, *Cities of the Dead*

CARETAKERS OF MEMORY

In 1751 when the Murray–Kean Company was winding down its New York season, readers there were entertained with news of the discovery of Pompeii and Herculanuem, including an account of the discovery of the theatre in Herculaneum. "The theatre must have been a fine one, as it is all encrusted with marble, which is carried off as fast as they removed the earth before it."[1] Having laid buried for 700 years, once recovered it immediately disappeared again. It did not have to be. It was the misfortune of the theatre to be discovered in an age that preferred piracy to preservation, private acquisition over public monuments, in short, a poor age for caretaking memory. The loss is particularly great as the theatre was, at the time, in a state of remarkable preservation:

> faced with the finest marble enriched with columns and statues, the greater part yet standing in their proper places, and the others so well preserved that the whole might have been easily restored to its original order and perfection; but they contented themselves with despoiling this theatre of its ornaments, leaving only the shell of it, of which they took the dimensions.[2]

In the mid-eighteenth century the culture of the past in toto had less currency than its individual relics. Had the building survived into the following century, Guiseppe Fiorelli would have proved a far better caretaker.

Relics of the past are always being disappeared, carried off, destroyed, and though I have argued that performance's disappearance is never wholly without a trace, its trace is frequently marred by imperfect remembering. The contest of Puritan and Player is one such "imperfect remembering," but consider others. Brooks McNamara has demonstrated that the widely published images of the interior of the John Street Theatre in New York (images that would be our only surviving images of the interior of a colonial American playhouse) are utterly spurious, produced in the 1870s and more accurately reflect Westminster school plays.[3] Though they were doctored, the spurious images betray a genuine and authentic desire for memory. I am deeply intrigued by this desire for memory passed on through these imperfect transmissions, these shells of broken mementos in the care of bad caretakers for the longing they betray. Under the poor guardianship of pillagers (Herculaneum), frauds (John Street), and occasional poor scholarship, the memory of the past limps and stutters feebly across the centuries, dragging its fractured, eviscerated mementos with an astonishing persistence that far outlives its accuracy. It is this persistence that I turn to next.

One of the earliest companies playing in New York—indeed it preceded the Murray–Kean Company's arrival by 20 years—is one such subject whose memory was left in the hands of one such most imperfect steward. Little indeed remains of the company—we do not even have a name for it anymore—and only one actor's name can still be corroborated: Thomas Heady, barber and peruke maker to his honorable Rip Van Dam. No evidence survives to document the other members of this company, legal or otherwise. As far as we know they were never prohibited, never sued, never run out of town; indeed, to the contrary, they enjoyed the protection of the mayor, Rip Van Dam, and as he was involved in a complicated schism of local power, players associated with him would not likely have remained culturally neutral. But we know very little of the company and what they might have meant to New Yorkers in the first years of the 1730s because what little evidence had survived into the nineteenth century, when the first New York theatre histories were assembled, did not survive into the twentieth.

The nineteenth-century New York theatre critic and historian T. Allston Brown had (had) the most information on this elusive company; it was he who first discovered them, introduced them, and documented them in ways no historian since has been able to corroborate.

For his work on the early American theatre, Brown traveled extensively collecting theatre ephemera, newspaper clippings, advertisements, playbills, letters, any notice of performance, particularly early performances. He recounted his Odyssean journey that he commenced in 1853, interrupted by the civil war, and resumed in 1869:

> In 1853 I commenced to compile "A History of the American Stage" and for five years thereafter devoted my entire time to it. I traveled over the United States from Maine to California, visiting the libraries of the different cities and towns in search of possible information relating to the drama in America . . . During the winter of 1869 I continued my research for any dramatic performances in America prior to 1749. For weeks I had access to many private and valuable libraries, as well as to all the early newspaper publication. At last I discovered an advertisement in an old weekly paper of a dramatic performance to be given in September, 1732.

Brown's diligent quest was at last rewarded with the discovery of a company performing in New York beginning in 1732: performances, personnel, and playhouse. Of this company he wrote:

> In September, 1732, a company of professionals arrived [in New York] from London and secured a large room in the upper part of a building near the junction of Pearl Street and Maiden Lane, which was fitted up with a platform stage and raised seats, capable of seating about four hundred people. They continued their performances for one month, acting three times each week. Early in December of the same year they resumed, having made several additions to their party.[4]

Brown offered quite a lot of information about the playhouse, audience, and, particularly, the personnel. Working from sources (playbills? newspapers?) that he collected, Brown offered the following names of actors in the company: Mr. R. Bessel, Miss Brennan, Mrs. Centour, Mrs. Chase, Mr. Cone, Mr. Drown, Mrs. Drown, Mr. Eastlake, and

Thomas Heady. Brown further claims that this company continued playing in New York until February 1734. From other issues of the *New York Gazette*, Brown cites the notices of more plays:

> This evening will be performed the tragedy of "Cato," and for three evenings next week the following comedies will be acted Viz: "The Recruiting Officer", "The Beaux' Stratagem", and "The Busybody."[5]

Brown's discovery might have been a remarkable find, one of the earliest known full companies playing in America, and certainly the earliest New York company. Unfortunately, whatever information Brown had collected in his travels about company, venue, and repertory is now and has been largely unverifiable. No subsequent record has been found of Mr. Bessel, Mrs. Chase, Mr. Drown, Mr. Eastlake. Nor can any information about the theatre on Maiden Street be corroborated. So even if the company that played at Maiden Street did indeed sustain several successive seasons, little of their accomplishments will ever be recovered, as the playbills and whatever other sources Brown was working from are no longer extant. Only one notice remains, for a December 6, 1732 production of *The Recruiting Officer*, reprinted in the *New England and Boston Gazette*, January 1, 1733. The only name that is still preserved is that of Thomas Heady, a barber and peruke maker. All else has been lost for reasons that are very germane to the present project.

THE BURNING OF THE LENA EDWIN

Brown produced two pieces of scholarship on the American stage: his aforementioned collection of biographies, *History of the American Stage: 1733–1870* (1870/1969) and *A History of the New York Stage* (1903), both published initially as serials in the *New York Clipper*. In the process of researching his history of New York theatre, Brown was struck by the frequency of nineteenth-century New York theatre fires—for good reasons to anyone familiar with the alarming regularity with which nineteenth-century theatres burned—and Brown appended to his second volume a short list of such catastrophes—not the thousand-entry compendium that E. O. Sachs would assemble on the subject, but a solid list in its own right. Brown's appendix of theatre fires is of interest only in so far as it documents the historian's first-hand acquaintance with the regularity of nineteenth-century playhouse conflagrations, and consequently the hazards of storing precious ephemera above wooden theatres. Given his personal and scholarly attention to that gruesome side of theatre history, one would suppose that the meticulous Colonel Brown—as a caretaker of memory—would have had the care to reside, work, write, and store his valuable archives collected from Maine to California anywhere but above a wooden nineteenth-century theatre. Not so. Brown lived, worked, stored his research, and wrote his histories above the Lena Edwin theatre. And yes the Lena Edwin Theatre did indeed burn to the ground on the night of November 28, 1872, taking with it Brown's extensive collection of ephemera painstakingly collected from the libraries, cities, and towns through which he had traveled since 1853, and whatever playbills he had found for his 1869 publication of the material relating to the company in New York, 1732–1734. "Among the first awakened and made aware of the danger," reported the *New York Times*, "was Col. T. Allston Brown, dramatic agent, who was hurried into the street in his night clothes."[6] The Lena Edwin burned completely and too quickly to salvage anything.

So we can confirm next to nothing of Brown's claims of a company of actors performing in New York in 1732–1734. George Odell, whose multivolume *Annals of the New York Stage* is still the standard text, cautiously set the whole business aside for exactly this reason. Of the players—Mr. R. Bessel, Miss Brenan, Mr. Centour, Mrs. Centour, Mr. Chase, Mrs. Chase, Mr. Cone, Mr. Drown, Mrs. Drown, Eastlake, and Thomas Heady—nothing further has been heard. They were like Hamlet's ghost: "tis here, tis here, tis gone," and gone they remain.

What are we to do with this? A company of some nature—Brown thought them professional and from London—was playing in New York 20 years before Lewis Hallam arrived. They built a playhouse in a building owned by the mayor and that playhouse was included in a map of New York city drafted in 1735.[7] Just enough reliable residue has remained to suggest its presence, and not enough to document it. Whatever performance evidence Brown had assembled of the company, the cast, their repertory, their support was lost in a fire, his history of the company was published with reconstructed evidence, most of which still cannot be corroborated. Brown, as the result of some imprecise scholarship elsewhere, has been dismissed in most subsequent studies, most notably George Odell's, cited above.[8] Odell (writing in the 1920s) further erased Brown by reassigning the discovery of the company to Judge Charles Daly, who published the item in 1885 in the *New York Herald*. To the later charge, Brown responded (via the *Clipper*): "Judge Daly's discovery (?) that the first theatre in this country was opened in 1732 is not news to old *Clipper* readers, for T. Allston Brown published that 'item' in this paper just seventeen years ago."[9] But to the larger claim of poor scholarship, Odell was quite right, in his kind and killing way: "Colonel T. Allston Brown gives the names of several players in the company of 1732, but fails to cite his authority therefore; I have, likewise, been less fortunate than he in finding in the Gazette a list of plays given in 1732–1733. Nor do I know whence he derived the information that the season continued to December 31, 1734."[10] So Brown as a caretaker of the lost company was himself also disappeared.

Historiographically, these frustrating, bittersweet dilemmas present themselves from time to time, when one is asked to either accept the unverifiable claims on faith or dismiss them outright and consign the original to the irrecoverable void. In 1825 the Medievalist Thomas Sharp published a dissertation on the Coventry pageant plays. He printed extensive records for many of the pageants—back when some records were more available—and transcribed the entire text of the Shearmen and Tailors's play. Sharp was working from Guildhall texts that went back to the sixteenth century, but a subsequent fire (1879) and air-raids (1940) destroyed many of the original documents and Sharp's transcriptions remain the only surviving source for much of the information about the Coventry cycle. His transcribed pageant is a two-part Nativity scene that includes one of the most-quoted stage directions in Medieval theatre: "here Herod rages in the pageant [wagon] and in the street also." Herod's hyperbolic style was a performance trope well into Shakespeare's time, but the evidence of it comes to us through a text whose originals survived into the nineteenth century but not beyond.[11]

FLAWED MEMORIES

In the quest for recovery we listen for voices in the rubble and when we do finally hear something, it proves to be only the slipping of the wreckage. In a field plagued with second and third generation transcriptions of lost originals, broken transmissions, notes of sons of actors who knew actors who worked with the original actors when they were young, small voices struggle to ghost up through the ruins and wreckage of flawed memories. The absence of many first-hand accounts of theatre culture from the period encourage an excess of historic imagination that makes certain formations (Puritan and Player) more understandable. Among the other absences, we have, for example, no first-hand actor memoirs from colonial America. Neither David Douglass nor his wife Sarah Hallam-Douglass, her son Lewis Hallam, nor his cousin, Nancy Hallam, nor comanager John Henry, nor William Verling left any personal written account of their lives and travels. It was not their fate to be the guardians of their own memory. Tate Wilkinson, Colley Cibber, George Ann Bellamy had no autobiographical equivalents in colonial America. Instead, what memoirs survive come to us orally from the nineteenth century, from actors and managers like John Bernard, John Durang, William Dunlap, who knew actors from the original American Company in their retiring years, and sometimes not very well, and passed that memory on to their sons and daughters-in-law, who knew them not at all.

John Bernard was a popular comic actor on the British stage who arrived in America in mid-career, in 1797, and continued his trade here until his retirement in 1819. He returned to England and began his memoirs, but he died before he saw them into publication. His notes, *Retrospections of the Stage*, were edited by his son Bayle Bernard and published in England in 1830. These memoirs are concerned with the early part of John Bernard's life and career in England. In his subsequent volume, *Retrospections of America, 1797–1811*—from which we are obliged to derive the ur-narrative of the theatre in colonial America—Bernard relates how he learnt from "Old Mr. Morris"— [Owen Morris]—"the history of the establishment of the drama in America."[12] Morris was, when he and Bernard shared a company in 1809, "far advanced in years," indeed, he was over 90. At that precarious age he passed his recollections onto his fellow actor, John Bernard, who died and passed them onto his son, Bayle Bernard, who in turn died before he could see them into print. Owen Morris's memory of the theatre in colonial America was not published by either Morris or

John Bernard, or even John Bernard's son, Bayle, in any of their lifetimes. It remained a manuscript of notes, to be gathered up from the posthumous papers of the widow of Bayle Bernard in 1887, some 75 years after John Bernard left America, and a hundred and a quarter years from the historic moment itself.

A similar distance spans the memoirs of John Durang who acted with the American Company after the Revolution, and derived his history of the early stage in America in the early years of the nineteenth century from the few older actors still alive—Old Hallam, "Old Man Morris." John Durang also passed on his narrative—late in his life—to his son, Charles Durang, also an actor. But John Durang (the father), like John Bernard, had no first-hand experience with the theatre before the Revolution, and when his son Charles (born 1794) chaperoned the memory into print many years later, both his father and the grand old figures of the age when his father was a boy had long since been dead and buried. In editing his father's text (published in serial in 1854), he supplemented his father's notes with the notes of one John North, whom Durang styled as the "caretaker" of the Southwark Theatre for many years in the early nineteenth century, where some earlier records were still kept.[13] But North was another poor custodian of memory, holding the reposited history of lives he did not know, and because he did not know them, he could do but a yeoman's service to their reputation. Working from the notes of Mr. North, Durang recounted the death of Mrs. Douglass in Philadelphia:

> Mrs. Douglass died in this city [Philadelphia], Mr. North said, after the close of the season of 1773. She died at a large frame house which then stood nearly opposite the South street theatre. All the ladies in the neighborhood, North said, attended her funeral . . . She was buried in the Presbyterian ground corner of Fourth and Arch streets.[14]

North was only a boy during the Revolution and never saw Mrs. Douglass, never knew her, and certainly was not at her funeral. There is something embarrassing and slightly unfair about him being the caretaker of the memory of her passing, speaking as if he were attending the funeral of a friend, when he was far more comfortable remembering the frame house in which Mrs. Douglass died (still standing in his day), than the deceased actress herself. North:

> The house in which she died was a tavern, and kept in 1807 by one Hanna, an Irishman. The sign was "The Convention of 1787," which was the body that formed the Federal Constitution. I remember the sign well: Benjamin Franklin appeared on it, with a large fur cap and spectacles on nose. This figure took my fancy. My father told me that the sign was a good representation of the Convention. Many of the members had red coats with very large buttons, and powdered heads. The following lines were underwritten, which I remember well: "These thirty eight great men having signed a powerful deed, / That better times, to us, shall very soon succeed."[15]

That "which I remember well" was not the actress at all, but the subscript of an image on the sign of a tavern North knew in his youth and where Mrs. Douglass once lived. The *momento mori* of her passing is replaced by the sign of the Convention—the birthing of America—as the strongest image of North's memory of her death. That Mrs. Douglass died there was a footnote to his recollection of the building, Franklin and his fellow Conventioneers, while Sarah Smythies Hallam Douglass, wife of Lewis Hallam, Sr. and David Douglass, mother of Lewis Hallam, Jr. and Mrs. Mattocks, aunt to Nancy Hallam, actress and first lady of the colonial American stage, remains largely unknown. It was her fate, like the fate of most of her generation, to be remembered most imperfectly, by strangers, and unreliable ones at that. Even her image, the crude sketch "said to be of Mrs. Douglass" in the Harvard Theatre collection, is as frequently attributed to be Mrs. Osborne.

As it turns out, North even got his own memory of her death wrong, which was not in the famous frame house in Philadelphia at all, nor at the close of the season in 1773, nor was she buried there in the Presbyterian cemetery and mourned by all the ladies. Nor was North alone in mis-reporting her death. In September of 1773, premature notices of Mrs. Douglass's death were published in the *New York Mercury* and a month later in the *Virginia Gazette*. Both lamented her demise in Philadelphia on September 23.[16] In Philadelphia, the same month, the *Pennsylvania Chronicle* reported her death in Annapolis. She was, however, demonstratively still very alive and wrote a notice correcting the obituary:

> The Account in this week's gazette, under the New York Head, of the Death of Mrs. Douglass (taken from Mr. Rivington's paper) we find to be erroneous, for by late Advices from Annapolis in Maryland, where the American Company of Comedians is now performing, that Lady was in very good health, and acting on the Stage with her usual Applause.[17]

Nor was it even the first time in her life that the death of Mrs. Douglass had been mis-recorded. When the actress of Mrs. Storer died in the shipboard fire just offshore of Newport, Rhode Island, in August of 1767, she was misidentified in several newspapers. They were thinking of the former Mrs. Hallam, now Mrs. Douglass, when they wrote: "One of the women that perished is said to be young Mrs. Hallam, an actress, who with other comedians were returning from Jamaica."[18]

But Mrs. Sarah Douglass survived Philadelphia in November 1773, survived the season in Annapolis, the winter season in Charleston, and returned to New York. Our last American notice of her comes from the shipping news of June 21, 1774, when she and her husband sailed from Charleston, and on June 30 they arrived in New York, both in good health. She left New York and traveled to Jamaica with her husband and the rest of the American Company, and one surviving playbill from Kingston for July 1, 1775 records her in the role of Lady Capulet.[19] Her death is definitively recorded in the St. Catherine Parish records of Spanish Town, Jamaica. April 22, 1777, Mrs. Douglass, wife of David Douglass, Master of Revels, died of what was described as "gout of the stomach." One assumes that this is the more accurate, as her husband remarried in April of 1778.[20]

So Mrs. Douglass did not die in Philadelphia in 1773 at the well-remembered tavern, with the well-remembered sign, nor was she buried in the Presbyterian cemetery, as North recalled and Durang related, nor apparently did all the ladies in the neighborhood attend her funeral. As it turns out, it was worse than being a stranger at the funeral: North was a stranger who made up the funeral, and that purloined memory of her death, like those exaggerated rumors earlier, were transmitted to other, equally dedicated but occasionally unreliable caretakers of memory.[21] Durang reprinted North's memory for one, but more notably, it was

George Seilhamer who improved upon the demise of Mrs. Douglass with an embellishment designed to bypass the necessity of confirmation: "the [Presbyterian] burial-ground unfortunately has been dug up and the ashes of the dead scattered, so it is impossible to identify the spot where her remains reposed."[22]

Seilhamer preserved the story from Charles Durang who published the story from his father who got it from the notes of Mr. North who got it from the notes of the Southwark playhouse itself, where someone preserved the amusing newspaper story of her first false death from Rivington's *Gazette* that got it all wrong. T. Allston Brown, George Seilhamer, Joseph Ireland all reprinted the story from Durang, as did Thomas Pollock, who wrote the history of the Philadelphia stage (1933). Hugh Rankin (*The Theatre in Colonial America*, 1960) reprinted it from Pollock, and Weldon Durham (*American Theatrical Companies*, 1986) reprinted it from Rankin, until her well-circulated obituary found its final monumental consolidation in the *Oxford Dictionary of National Biography*. With each flawed repository and each broken transmission, the authority of the narrative increases while the subject hopelessly recedes. That her death should be in Philadelphia, the stronghold Douglass fought so hard to conquer, is part of the mythic framework of the great agon, a casualty in the fantasy of a conquista.

When Charles Durang published his father's memoirs, he employed yet a third generation of Durangs, his son, Edwin Forrest Durang, an architect named after an actor, to reconstruct an image of the Southwark Theatre. Edwin Durang had not known the playhouse that Douglass built in 1767, having burned down in 1821, and Alexander Young's distillery erected on the shell. Edwin Durang provided a sketch of the distillery copied from an advertisement, with the handwritten note "The old South Street Theatre as it appeared in 1860. The building on the left is raised up on the old walls of the theatre."[23] Hornblow claimed that the original walls were still standing in his day (1919), but the "walls" were nothing more than "a portion of the brick basement on which the framework rested"—essentially part of a foundation of part of a wall.[24] As a *lieu de memoir* as little of the old playhouse ghosts through a distillery's foundations, as did the death of Mrs. Douglass through the notes of Mr. North. Yet memory persists, even for all the wrong reasons. Nothing of the old Southwark Theatre remained longer or more persistently than its memory. When Durang published his illustrations of the building, they were rendered by his grandson as a conjectural reconstruction, although he had no first-hand contact with the space that burned down before he was born. It is a point of some irony that in spite of its imperfect transmission (rendered as it was in 1884, some 60 years after its destruction by the actor's grandson), Edwin Durang's conjectural reconstruction of the old Southwark Theatre may still be our most reliable image of a colonial American playhouse.

The colonial American record is full of such broken vessels of memory, voices in the rubble, most of which remain utterly unrecoverable, or at best, so damaged—like North's notes—or so distant—like Edwin Durang's rendering—as to be unverifiable. What is most interesting in all this is not the refutation, is not getting the past wrong, or the righting of it, but the persistence of memory itself. That Mrs. Douglass's memory should survive in spite of, not because of, her caretakers. That all the ladies of the neighborhood should have gathered at a funeral that never happened may alert us to the desire for her memory, rather than its facticity.

One of the more persistent, transmitted memories that made of itself a small and bungled monument was the "First Prologue Delivered in America" reprinted in many early histories of the American stage. This piece was originally composed by John Singleton, the poet in the Hallam Company, for the September 15, 1752 opening of the theatre in Williamsburg. How it survived in the cultural memory was an exceptionally circuitous, fragile, and ultimately botched route, memorized and recalled from actor to actor until it was set down on paper. Singleton composed it but it was Mr. Rigby who memorized it and delivered it that opening night. Somewhere in his career, the young Lewis Hallam, Jr., 15 in 1752 (Dunlap says 12) and, by his own admission, subject to stage fright, also memorized it. And many, many years later—55 years later—the prologue still lived in the memory of young Hallam, now Old Hallam, who recalled and recited it to one Mr. Bailey, a member of the Chestnut Street theatre company in 1807. "Bailey," wrote Durang (*The Philadelphia Stage*, 5), "took it down from old Lewis

Hallam's lips, in 1807, at the back of the old South Street theatre stage, during a rehearsal, and he afterwards gave it to my father." John Durang then left his notes for his son, Charles, who published the first prologue in America in 1858, 106 years after its delivery. It is a remarkable journey and a testament to the powers of memory and the endurance of the oral tradition.

The accuracy of this tradition was confirmed by William Dunlap—our third ur-source of colonial American theatre—who was also a beneficiary of this recitation. He too got it from the "lips of Old Mr. Hallam," and Dunlap also published the "First Prologue," securing the transmission by duplication. For Dunlap, the preserved prologue represented an inaugural moment, marked with a ceremony that elevated the composition above the rank and file of house-greeting prologues and rendered the dawn of American theatre "the more memorable." "It gave occasion," wrote he (*History of the American Stage*, 17) "for the first composition connected with the drama which was written for, or addressed particularly to, an American audience." That Old Hallam could still recall the lines *verbatim* after so many years on the boards confirmed the prologue's importance. And indeed, subsequent historians of the American stage (Ireland, Seilhamer) relying on Dunlap, have reprinted the poem, cementing its transition from Old Hallam's memory into the public memory.

It was Arthur Hornblow who noticed the trouble: the version that Durang and Dunlap had published, the version that Ireland and Seilhamer republished, the version that Old Hallam recalled and recited to Mr. Bailey and to William Dunlap, was not the same prologue that John Singleton wrote for the occasion of the opening of the theatre. Singleton's prologue, Hornblow discovered, was also printed in the *Virginia Gazette*, September 22, 1752, a week after the opening of the theatre.[25] That edition of the newspaper has fortunately survived, and in this case, the printed version from the opening week trumped the oral tradition printed everywhere else.

There are some telling differences between the printed prologue and Hallam's recollection that may signal why one was preferred over the other. For that inaugural event, Singleton derived his model of theatre as didaskolos διδασκγλγϛ (teacher of the state) from ancient

Athens that represented the high watermark of culture:

> For this the bard, on Athen's infant stage,
> At first produc'd the drama's artful page;
> At once to please and satyrize he knew,
> And all his characters from nature drew,
> Without restriction then, as nature taught
> The player acted, and the poet wrote;
> The tragic muse did honour to the state,
> And in a mirrour taught them to be great;[26]

Hallam's version of the evening, however, was decidedly more imperial. The "Muse" may stand in for Athens, but there is no question Great Britain becomes the cultural model, that kindly sent its servants to please and instruct the rude and the ignorant:

> To this New World, from famed Britannia's shore
> Through boist'rous seas where foaming billows roar,
> The Muse, who Britons charm'd for many an age,
> Now sends her servants forth to tread your stage;
> Britain's own race, though far removed, to shew
> Patterns of every virtue they should know.
> Though gloomy minds through ignorance may rail
> Yet bold examples strike where languid precepts fail.

In Hallam's version, the players become necessary emissaries of high culture arriving to deliver the bold examples of virtue these Virginians sorely want, a memory less applicable in the postrevolutionary war when it was recalled.

It is an odd moment, the misremembering, and likely an innocent moment. But the mistaken prologue troubles the authority of memory as the source of history (in particular, Old Hallam's memory and Dunlap's use of it). When Dunlap introduced the prologue in his seminal work, he pressed the moment into an example of high authenticity and a pointed testament to the abilities of Old Hallam (and vis-à-vis his own narrative, derived as it was from his subject's memory). Hallam, wrote Dunlap, "seemed to remember every transaction of that period, every circumstance attending those first histrionic adventures, as though they were of yesterday" (17). What does it do the very narrative of the field, derived as it is from that same troubled source of history, if its highest moment was mis-remembered? To what extent was Dunlap working, as he claimed, from Old Hallam's memory, if Dunlap too, as he did (63), also misreported Mrs. Douglass's death in Philadelphia in 1773? could Lewis Hallam, whose powers of recall were such that he recalled "every transaction of the period," recite verbatim a 60-year old prologue but not remember when his own mother died?[27]

UNLIKELY CONFIRMATIONS

Occasionally, thankfully—as it turns out in the case of the Singleton's prologue, and, as we shall see, in the case of Colonel T. Allston Brown— we are not left with the choice of accepting bad memories, broken reconstructions, or dismissing the evidence outright. Occasionally something turns up that does indeed confirm the conjecture and re-authorizes the caretakers of memory. The ground plan of the 1760 playhouse in Williamsburg goes a long way to confirm Edward Durang's posthumous rendering of the Southwark Theatre, with its brick foundation and clapboard walls, its stage door, ventilator, and shed to the side. In the case of T. Allston Brown, one very good piece of additional information has since come to light that does at least solidly corroborate the presence of a company of players in New York city sometime between 1732 and 1735, and that quite possibly they were a touring company that may have wintered in New York and traveled to other locations. In her manuscript autobiography, *Some Account of the Fore Part of the Life of Elizabeth Ashbridge*, the subject, the young Elizabeth Ashbridge, was indentured in New York for a term of four years, beginning in the summer of 1732, to a very religious and tyrannical master who at one point nearly drove the poor girl to suicide. She had concluded to end her miserable existence with a rope in the garret when a religious vision forestalled her plans. She resigned herself to live awhile longer, but she was not out of despair yet:

> But alas! I did not give up nor Comply with the heavenly Vision, as I think I may Call it, for after this I had like to have been caught in another Snare, which if I had would Probably have been my Ruin, from which I was also

preserved. I was Counted a fine Singer and Dancer, in which I took great Delight, and once falling in with some of the Play house company then at New York, they took a Great fancy to me, as they said, & Perswaded [*sic*] me to become an Actress amongst them, & they would find means to get me from my cruel Servitude, & I should live Like a Lady—the Proposal took with me & I used no small Pains to Qualify my Self for it in Reading their Play Books, even when I should have Slept, yet was put to the Demur when I came to Consider what my Father would say who had forgiven my Disobedience in marrying and earnestly desiring to see me again had sent for me home, but my proud heart would not Consent to return in so mean a Condition; therefore I chose Bondage rather.[28]

Elizabeth arrived in New York on July 15, 1732, and her indenture commenced two weeks later. When, exactly, her encounter with the players began she does not tell us, but she does relate that upon arrival at her new master's "for a while at first I was Pretty well used, but in a little time the Scale turned" (Andrews, *Journeys in New World*, 152). It is difficult to establish a timeline for her encounter with the players, but the paragraph that follows the quoted description of the players begins: "When I had served near three years" (i.e., summer 1735), which may follow immediately after her flirtation with the playhouse or indicate only the next eventful moment in her narrative. Lacking any clearer indication, Ashbridge's brush with the players could have occurred anytime from the winter of 1732–1733 until the close of 1734.

Though the journal of Elizabeth Ashbridge offers no names or details about this company of players, she does describe an active company in a resident playhouse that she had some first-hand acquaintance with, and if this is 1733 or 1734, then they have been in town for up to two years. She also characterizes them as "then at New York," suggesting that the company traveled, and was often or occasionally elsewhere. Though Brown's original evidence may be lost, his conclusions may be vindicated in part, as he had claimed a professional company played in New York through December 31, 1734, some duration of which could be confirmed by the Ashbridge journal. The poor girl in her despair to avoid becoming a player may have proved unwittingly the player's best caretaker.

10. Silent Travelers, Silent Journals ✺

4 July 1776: "Pd. Sparhawk for a thermometer—£3-15."

Thomas Jefferson, *Memorandum Book*

When Fiorelli was waiting for his plaster to set at the excavations of Herculaneum, the thought no doubt crossed his mind that maybe the hole he just filled was only just a hole. Sometimes they were not all the casts of lost bodies; some holes yielded absolutely nothing. Like the fine marble theatre in Herculaneum that was "carried off as fast as they removed the earth before it," the history of performance is marred by its own absence. It is to absence— irretrievable, unreconstructable absence that has not even benefit of a broken transmission—that I turn to next.

And that absence abounds. How little notice was taken by most of the culture of the theatre in its midst–even a new playhouse—is a deafening record in itself. How, for example, could a company of players introduce themselves to a small shipping town like Norfolk, Virginia, seek and secure permission from the town council and his lordship the mayor, and with a fully documented collection of the preserved *Minutes of the City Council* find not a single mention in the public record? Yet every major company played Norfolk (Murray–Kean, Hallam, Douglass, Verling) and not a word of the civic response to the players grace the minutes.[1] This from a town that regulated everything, down to the size of its streets and the diameters of its wells. This chapter acknowledges the depth of absence, not in the hopes of imaginatively reconstructing anything, but to listen a moment to the size of the silence and to situate the contested narrative of divided loyalties against the sound of silence that surrounded it.

DIVIDED LOYALTIES

It has been my running insistence that the theatre in colonial America lived in many cultures, in networks of patronage and organized opposition. Where supported, warmly countenanced; where opposed, it found ways to negotiate the opposition. Resistance and support were often found in the same city, and more than once, in the same person. The oft-quoted Bostonian, Josiah Quincy, visiting New York in May of 1773, recorded his deeply conflicted sentiment when he wrote in his diary:

> Went to the playhouse in the evening, saw The Gamester and The Padlock performed . . . I was much gratified upon the whole, and I believe if I had staid in town a month, I should go to the theatre every acting night. But, as citizen and friend to the morals and happiness of society, I should strive hard against the admission, and much more the establishment, of a playhouse in any state of which I was a member.[2]

Quincy remained deeply conflicted about the theatre, attending and objecting, objecting and attending, whenever he could. Beyond his visits to the playhouses in New York and Charleston, Quincy spent time in London, where he sampled the talents of Drury Lane, Covent Garden, and the Opera. He admired Garrick at the close of his career but was most susceptible to the "wanton" roles. Of one visit to a production of *The Beggar's Opera* (November 18, 1774), he wrote, "I am still further satisfied in my opinion that the stage is the nursery of vice and disseminates the seeds of vice far and wide [in the] powers of eloquence." But, lest his mind waver, he returned on November 29, December 12, December 21, and January 21, 1775. The seeds of vice were particularly appealing on the December 21 production of Milton's *Comus.* "Comus was altered much for the worse, and no part was performed well but the part of Miss Catley, which, being wanton, was done admirably by her."[3]

Another ambivalent patron was Benjamin Franklin's wife, Deborah Franklin. She and her sister (both Quakers) slipped away to the playhouse one night, when her husband was abroad, to cheer her failing spirits. She mitigated her transgression by visiting the Presbyterians. In her poignantly illiterate style she wrote to her husband of her poor health, before confessing, "I had taken up a resey lusion [resolution] never to make aney complainte to you or give you any disquiet to you." And so on to good news: "I have to tell you sum thing of my self what I believe you wold not beleve of me oney I tell you my selve. I have bin to a play with Sister. I expeckte that sumbodey to speek to me but I have bin to twise to the prispatreiny [Presbyterian] metin which will be worse to sume folkes. I did no more on that side."[4]

There is no question that the theatre in colonial America was opposed by some populations for a host of reasons, moral and economic, and in some cities these opponents organized petitions and occasionally succeeded in enacting legislation that prohibited or retarded its introduction. But it should also be remembered that such legislation was often rendered moot, repealed, or evaded by those who patronized and encouraged its introduction, and seldom deterred playgoing. Those who supported the theatre were often the socially privileged and politically influential who had exactly the power to shield, protect, and countenance. The New York that initially refused Douglass permission also hosted two of his playhouses and many seasons were spent there. In 1773 when Quincy attended the playhouse in New York nightly, the American Company had found audience and encouragement enough to play straight through the heat of the summer in a building with such poor ventilation that Douglass was obliged to open the roof. They had done the same in Baltimore, playing through the hot August nights, yet, wrote one, "notwithstanding the disadvantages of an inconvenient playhouse, and hot nights, have been universally well received and encouraged."[5] The same Philadelphia that gathered so many signatures to oppose him also boasted the largest playhouse Douglass ever built. When court was in session in Williamsburg, the company could play six nights a week, and on several documentable occasions, played both afternoons and evenings and profited enough to purchase his phaeton and four. If the Quakers boycotted the playhouse, Franklin and her sister might nonetheless steal a visit, while devotees like Thomas Jefferson would be in it nine nights out of ten, and Washington would ride half a day to see a play. When the burgesses and merchants of Virginia signed the nonimportation agreement, they exempted the playhouse. Several successions of colonial governors of Virginia, Maryland, Pennsylvania, New York, and the West Indies were personal acquaintances of Douglass, patronized his theatres, recommended him, with whom he dined on occasion, carried letters, and supported his business. By 1767 the new Pennsylvania governor, John Penn, was so fond of the players that Thomas Warton complained to Benjamin Franklin that he was constantly in the theatre and invited the players to dine with him.[6] When the (premature) obituary of Mrs. Douglass appeared in the *New York Gazetteer*, she was noted as "recommended to the friendship and affection of many principal families on the Continent and in the West Indies."[7] And if one parsed the loyalties further, among the Americans in his camp were burgesses, Continental Congressmen, and signers of the Declaration of Independence (including Peyton Randolph, Samuel Chase, and William Paca, the last two signers from Maryland, who acted as subscribing and rental agents for Douglass and managed his property in Annapolis).

It should also be remembered that such opponents also counted people like Mrs. Franklin and Josiah Quincy among their members. That, for Mrs. Franklin writing to her husband, many Quakers felt the Presbyterians were far more threatening. The Virginians thought as much of the Methodists, who in Petersburg and Richmond were far more threatening than the playhouse they occupied.

Far from a hostile combatant, the pulpit and the playhouse cohabited in the culture of many colonial cities. In Annapolis, Douglass would build his new playhouse on a lot directly across from St. Anne's Parish Church, on Church Circle, and the rector of the parish Jonathan Boucher composed prologues for the plays and an encomium for the actress Nancy Hallam. After the company left Annapolis, Douglass rented the theatre to the Parish, who fitted it up for a church. In Williamsburg, the 1760 playhouse stood on a lot next door to the Presbyterian meeting house. Itinerant preachers like Joseph Pilmore and Robert Williams rented the playhouses in Norfolk, Petersburg, and Williamsburg. Recall Noah Webster, who noted wryly and rightly that "it seems to be the taste of the Virginians to fix their churches as far as possible from town and their play houses in the center."[8]

But beyond the strident supporters, detractors, dabblers, and back-sliders, who have played so large a role in this study, was the population we do not often speak of: the bulk of the populace for whom the theatre was inconsequential. They neither opposed it nor patronized it, but ignored it entirely. This population was legion, and they, too, are part of the same America and their attitudes might also be recovered and included in our understanding of how theatre functioned in early America. Historiographically, this narrative is the most challenging, built as it, from absence, but if this project is, at some level, an exegesis of silence, their silence must also be vetted.

SILENT TRAVELERS

For many in the colonies, the toils were tremendous and the luxuries few, and playgoing was clearly a frivolity out of reach, out of pocket, out of interest, and out of memory. The year 1768, for example, is an enormously rich year for theatre in colonial America. Five professional companies played in ten cities throughout the colonies and the Caribbean, including Annapolis, Williamsburg, Charleston, Philadelphia, and New York. In Philadelphia, the Quaker Elizabeth Drinker left a poignant record of her life in a daily diary. For the Drinker family, 1768, was a year that began, ended, and was marked by illness, miscarriage, deaths, and departures, without a single trip to the playhouse:

> Charles Jones dyed, Janry I: 1768. Hannah came to live with us towards the end of the Month:—she went to Duck Creek, to live with her Father, April 1768.
>
> Phebe Morris, Widdow to A Morris dyed. March, 1768.
>
> H[enry] D[rinker] was let blood March 23, 1768.
>
> May 26. 1768 ED. Miscarried.
>
> B Swett Senr. Went to live at New Castle June the I, 1768.
>
> June the 3. 1768. Becky James miscarried.[9]

Drinker's diary is a sorrowful account of a struggling life. Yet she was not among the lowly; her's was not, in Thomas Gray's phrase, "the short and simple annals of the poor." Her husband, Henry Drinker, was a merchant, in time a prosperous merchant, who could rent a fine house for £90 per annum, travel, engage in the politics of Philadelphia and of the Quaker church, yet his life in the wider world remained largely opaque and inaccessible to his wife's diary. When the Quakers of Philadelphia initiated their campaign against the playhouse in 1766, her husband was signatory to the letters penned to the governor. They also circulated petitions, published antitheatrical diatribes in the papers; if her husband was involved in this campaign, his wife Elizabeth recorded not a jot of it. Her sphere was the domicile, its ordering, its caregiving, and her interests of the wider world wander seldom in her record of it. When the American Company opened in Philadelphia in October of 1768, Elizabeth was nursing sick children. The company played through the close of the year, at least three nights a week for three months. Here is Drinker's diary for this period:

October 17: Jammy Smith has been confind with a fever for a week past. Docr. Evans tends him.—continues poorly.
Sally Drinker began to shed her teeth befor she was 7 years old.

Novr. 4: Jammy Smith continues ill—he has been 3 times let Blood, and Blister'd: Grace, his father's Housekeeper, came here to tend him Octor. 31—

Novr. 13. Went to the Burial of Danl. Drinkers little daughter Betsy.

Novr. The 17. Our good Friend Sarah Sansom, departed this life.

Novr 20. Sarah Sansom's corps was taken to the Bank Meeting House this afternoon, from thence to the [Buring] Ground: snow all day: HD. And Sister were at the funeral.

1768 Novr. 25. Jammy Smith after 6 Weeks illness, is so far recover'd as to go to Burlington; Grace Bauchanan, with him, his Head is still very week.

My dear little Nancy very unwell with a Fever &c, Evans tends her— Novr. 25, 1768.

Decr. 21. Nancy much better, she has had a tedious fever of the kind of Jammys.[10]

Elizabeth Drinker lived through the same period that saw professional theatre established in America (1735–1807), and never in the least participated in it. It was among the many things simply outside her interests. She mothered nine children, tended them through illness and buried many of them. She lived on Water Street (near Plumstead's warehouse, where the Murray–Kean Company played, and later the Hallam Theatre), and within a few block's walk of the new Society Hill Theatre that Douglass built, and later the Southwark Theatre, and never went to the playhouse, never bothered with actors, nor ever left a word about her unruly neighbors.

But if her eye noted little of the luxury of life, noting mostly the high occasions of birth, death, burials, and the incessant illnesses that plagued a large family, she was not alone. Indeed, it is a rare colonial diary that ever records a visit to the playhouse. Most lived out their lives far from the capitals, where entertainment meant no more than a gathering for tea. I am thinking of young Elizabeth Porter, the only daughter to a widow who lived in rural Massachusetts and saw a city—Boston—for the first time when she was 21. She complained sometimes of her "solitary situation" when company was rare and high times were no more than "a singing lecture," quilting, and blackberrying in the summer. Her diary reminds us that most households in colonial America were like young Elizabeth Porter's, rural, quiet, solitary, sometimes distressingly remote, where theatres were as distant as London itself, and a trip to town could be the event of a young lifetime.[11]

The few family memoirs I have pressed into service for this study—Jonathan Boucher, Jacob Mordecai, Josiah Quincy, Elizabeth Ashbridge, and William Hickey—are a thin percentage of the extant diaries and travel journals available from the period. Of these, few residents and fewer travelers—whose eyes are open to the novelty of the new world—describe or even mention the colonies' attempts at theatre. Europeans, of various denominations and faiths, may be impressed by the new flora and fauna and make meticulous hand-colored illustrations of opossums, warblers, rattlesnakes, and Florida alligators, or note the strange practices of the Quakers, the frugality of the Dutch, the square layout of Philadelphia, Indian wigwams, or offer often elaborate descriptions of the social landscape of this new country, but few bother to note American efforts at drama. The Swedish traveler Peter Kalm, the German Gottlieb Mittelberger, and the French traveler who published his narrative anonymously, all toured through the colonies between 1749 and 1766, noting the remarkable features and making no mention whatsoever of the emerging theatre in their midst. Nor did the unfortunate indentured servant William Moraley, who lived in New York at the time of the first playhouse and company there, but pursued by debtors, ever attend or wrote of it. Nor did the socially privileged William Smith, Jr., who could afford it and wrote an extensive early history of New York, who was more concerned with the government than the amusements of the colony. Nor Nicholas Cresswell, who toured Maryland and Virginia just prior to the Revolution. Nor did the Charleston resident Eliza Pinckney, or the Annapolis resident William Gregory, or Lord Adam Gordon who wandered the streets of Williamsburg, stood on the steps of the capitol and failed to note the playhouse 50 yards away. (He also overlooked the church, recording only the "very handsome Statehouse [capitol] commodious for all the Courts," "a very handsome College," and the Governor's house.) Patrick McRobert not only toured the northern cities, registering many of the public buildings, but also found the theatres below notice.[12] The Quaker John Woolman roamed the eastern seaboard for nearly 30 years in mid-century, from New Jersey, south to the Carolinas and north to Cape Cod, including Philadelphia, but his eye was directed to the evils of slavery, and was as uninterested in the theatre as he was in the flora and fauna. The Philadelphia farmer Jacob Hiltzheimer came to town to hear Whitefield preach but not to the playhouse. William Mylne, repairing a ruined estate, disembarked in Charleston the very week the new Church Street playhouse opened with great publicity and wrote not a word about it.[13] Neither did James Murray, 35 years earlier, when he tarried a month in Charleston while Henry Holt and Charles Shepherd opened the first theatre that winter.[14] The naturalist William Bartham lived much of his adult life in Philadelphia (1750s–1770s) and wrote extensively on the botany of North America, but as far as we know, he never entered a playhouse or weighed in on the debates and campaigns against it. Benjamin Mifflin toured Philadelphia and Maryland and likewise overlooked the theatres in his civic descriptions, though he must have walked past the playhouse in Annapolis in the company of Jonas Green.[15] Certainly the Italian Count Francesco dal Verme was in Baltimore and Annapolis when Dennis Ryan and

Thomas Wall opened up their first theatre during the waning years of the Revolution, and overlooked it.[16]

Occasionally one encounters a curious traveler who might have left a memorable account of a performance or a theatre, but caught the playhouse at an inopportune time, or whose journal has been imperfectly preserved, or who arrived too early, or too late. Dr. Alexander Hamilton would have been very interested in the theatre in Philadelphia—as he was in the nascent Masonic lodge—had he traveled there a few years later.[17] On his travels he kept up his remarkable journal, he caught Philadelphia between companies, and when the companies visited Annapolis, Hamilton kept no journal. Joseph Harrower also just missed the actors, who arrived in Fredericksburg, Virginia, at fair time. In past years the players were regular features there, but not this year, 1773, when the town had only puppet shows to entertain the race crowd.[18] Elizabeth Nugent kept a careful account of entertainments in Jamaica during her tenure there, but it happened, again, in the hiatus between resident companies. Colonel James Montresor (father of Captain John Montresor above) was a military engineer stationed in New York whose detailed journal has a large and untimely gap for the Winter of 1758–1759, exactly the months when Douglass and the American Company arrived, played, and departed that city. Andrew Burnaby spent nearly a year in and around Williamsburg in 1759 and 1760, but left just weeks before the American Company arrived. He likewise missed them in Fredericksburg, Annapolis, and Philadelphia, arriving in each city just before or after. When Burnaby did finally meet the company they were playing in a barn in Marlborough, Maryland, and he was on his way elsewhere. He paid a cursory visit to the building ("a neat, convenient tobacco-house, well fitted-up for the purpose") but not the play.[19] Ebenezer Hazzard who arrived in Annapolis after the same company departed noted that "There is a playhouse and an Assembly Room here: the former being locked up I could not view the inside of it."[20] All the more of a loss when one reads the elaborate interior description Hazzard lavished on the Assembly Room that was opened. One hundred words on the arrangement of the space, the gallery for musicians, with private stairs, the fireplace, retiring rooms, even the full-length portrait of Pitt painted by Peale, down to its Latin inscription. But the playhouse was locked, and consequently we have no description. The most detailed description of an interior of an American playhouse comes to us from a French traveler from well beyond our period. Moreau de Sainte-Mery offered a wonderfully descriptive account of the auditorium of the Chestnut Street Theatre, but that was in 1794, when memory left greater monuments. Twenty years earlier French travelers wrote not a word about the theatre.

Nor can that absence be made legible or intelligible. It was not the knowing omission of the politically discrete subject, the prohibition speakeasy noted with a nod before turning away, such as the illegal theatricals that James Wright wrote of during the interregnum in England. Of those, Wright recited a host of fines for performing plays during Cromwell's time before noting slyly, "But I suppose nobody pretends these things to be Laws. I could say more of this subject, but I must break off here."[21]

Or again, Narcissus Luttrell writing of the birth of the Pretender (the "bed pan baby") that precipitated the Glorious Revolution: "[there was] great liberty in discoursing about the young prince, with strange reflections upon him, not fit to insert here."[22] Such silences partner with the reader to invite collusion and supply the absence with an unspoken, undocumented, but understandably active tradition. For the omissions above and the many other travelers and residents who passed through and wrote nothing, the theatre was not a subject discretely avoided, it was simply invisible.

Worse were the travelers who most certainly knew about the theatres, used them, hired them, preached in them, for example, and still left not a word about it. The itinerant preachers—and there were many, Methodists particularly—Robert Williams, Devereux Jarratt, Archibald McRoberts, and Joseph Pilmore, for example, all traveled through the southern colonies introducing Methodism, all rented playhouses to preach in, all left solid travel journals and memoirs of their tours, yet none squandered any words on the theatres he preached in. Evangelists, botanists, travelers, all visited or lived in colonial capitals where theatre was currently available, all curious enough to keep a travel journal, and most had the wherewithal to publish it, but none took the slightest notice of the theatre, either by description or by rumor. Two frustrating non-records belong to Mrs. Janet Schaw, a "woman of quality," who left an exquisitely detailed account of her voyage from Scotland to the

West Indies and on to North Carolina, and Alice Lee of Annapolis. Schaw laid over on the small Leeward islands of Antigua and St. Kitts (St. Christopher) in January of 1775. On both islands she was royally received, feted, and offered the best entertainment the island afforded. While touring the town of Basterre, St. Kitts, she was shown all the public buildings, including one she should not see ("I was shown that intended for my brother"—a Freemason lodge?). Outside, she was presented with a playbill. Of the company she only noted "they are strollers of some spirit who strolled across the Atlantick." On account of the great heat, she was unable to tolerate a confined space and so did not attend the play, and she made no further mention of the players, nor betrayed the slightest curiosity about them, who patronized them, what their productions looked like, or how they were received. She went to the dances instead.[23] Who this company was, handing out playbills in Basterre in 1775, we can guess, but that it was below the curiosity of a supremely curious woman tells us a good deal about the status of theatre to many in the culture.

Alice Lee might also have told us a great deal about the social conventions of playgoing, who had a fine eye for the protocols of genteel society and a passion for the plays. "The American Company of Players are here," wrote she in September of 1772, "and are said to be amazingly improved. I should like to see them, as I think theatricals exhibitions a rational amusement—but I shall not be there."[24] And there she was not.

That the theatres themselves were routinely overlooked is understandable. For the most part, colonial American playhouses—like most commercial buildings—were uninteresting structures, hastily built and featureless, certainly not the notable stone architecture that would arrest the eye of the traveler like Lord Gordon or Burnaby for whom notable architecture meant handsome stone or brick with Palladian symmetry.[25] The 1760 playhouse in Williamsburg that Gordon overlooked or the 1760 playhouse in Annapolis that Mifflin overlooked were both erected in eight weeks and, by colonial standards, they would have looked like another barn, another clapboard tobacco warehouse, with a "rugged appearance" as one wrote of the first Annapolis Theatre, interesting only on the inside. And these were the purpose-built theatres. The temporary buildings (the converted tobacco houses that

Burnaby saw) were even less interesting. Such is the case with William Plumstead's "playhouse," the warehouse in a row of warehouses recorded in the "prospect of the City of Philadelphia" of 1754. But being uninteresting or overlooked is not the same as being opposed or resisted. That few travelers note the playhouses or American efforts at theatre should not compel us to conclude of their absence, as William Young has concluded, "Because of the antipathy of many people to the theatre, little documentation is available concerning it."[26] Even monumental events get overlooked as, case in point, Thomas Jefferson's entry in his *Memorandum Book* for July 4, 1776: "Pd. Sparhawk for a thermometer—£3-15." I think rather the theatre was overlooked because for much of colonial America it was unimportant. When Burnaby surveys the arts and amusements of cities like Philadelphia (where the American Company that he had just met had just left), Burnaby spoke for more than himself when he omitted theatre from the list of musical gatherings, dance assemblies, and sleighing parties that constituted the entertainment of the city. When Burnaby described the summer "fishing parties" (16 couples of young men and women) with their own Assembly Room built on "a romantic situation on the banks of the Schuilkill," but registered no effect of the theatre among the same crowd, a theatre that was recently built there with some controversy, and the company of actors that had only recently departed, he was describing the world of Elizabeth Drinker, a world in which theatre did not matter, and that world was large.

COACHMEN AND GROOMS

If the fortunate traveler of quality was uninterested in it, many others had not even the option of experiencing a genteel evening of entertainment. A city like Philadelphia or New York in 1760 may have hosted a population of 15,000 people but most had not the resources to attend its amusements, and many more had not the inclination. Alonzo May noted of Baltimore in 1773, of the nearly 5,000 inhabitants, "2/3 of whom were menials, and less than one tenth enjoyed the privilege of franchise."[27] Patrick McRobert, touring America in 1774, noted of these many "menials" that a tradesman at that time could make but six shillings a day, and a laborer, three or four shillings.[28] The cheapest seat in the upper gallery of the playhouse (3s. 9d) would require nearly their full day's wages. When James Smith of Cape Fear, North Carolina, was seeking a sober indentured coachman and groom in 1760, he offered what he considered the generous sum of £15 for the first year, and a good suit of livery. Generous wages, perhaps, but break it down and it would require a full day's labor to purchase a single gallery ticket. And no punch.[29] The percentage of wages to prices never improved throughout the century. When William Moraley arrived in New York while Thomas Heady's company played (early 1730s), Moraly's last job in a blacksmith's shop had netted him no more than eight shillings a week, which he saved up to buy a fine shirt ("the first I wore since my Departure from England").[30] Sixty years later the sentiments of his class were summed up when one "mechanic" lamented in a Boston newspaper: "From my situation in life, I am virtually debared [*sic*] from any of the common amusements of this town."[31] No wonder apprentices were accused of resorting to criminal ways to acquire their tickets, a claim not unfounded.[32] One large class of residents—the indentures, the apprentices, the bondsmen, the laborers, and most of the minor tradesmen—were largely priced out of the playhouse.

DROMO AND MUNGO

Or consider another sizeable population of colonial America that the theatre excluded: slaves and free blacks whose voice seldom or never perforates the narrative. When Dr. Alexander Hamilton traveled on his "itinerarium" he was accompanied by his servant ("my boy," "my man," "my negro Dromo") who is noticed but in the briefest of moments. For four months and 1,600 miles Dromo and Doctor shared the roads, ferries, byways, and inns of colonial America. He too saw Philadelphia, Delaware, New York, Albany, Boston, and Newport, but his thoughts and impressions of their travels went unrecorded and unenquired. At no point in the travelogue did Dr. Alexander ask Dromo what he made of it all. The reader enters Dromo's world (literally his room) only when the doctor's portmanteau went missing. Dromo and the many like him that accompanied the mobile tourist and merchant were among the most silent of silent travelers. Few accounts—particularly those for the southern cities and the islands—even acknowledge that the servants in the theatre (as in "Ladies and gentlemen will please to send their servants at four o'clock") are really slaves, and having saved the seats till their masters and mistresses came, were free to leave. Dunlap (*History*, 56), writing of the John Street Theatre, recalls how, between four and six in the afternoon, "the front seats of the boxes were occupied by blacks of every age, waiting until their masters and mistresses made their appearance." But after six, when the house filled and the play began, they disappeared from both playhouse and its history. The only notice I have seen of a slave presented with a ticket to attend, never went. He sold it.[33] What those servants might have thought of Lewis Hallam in black-face capering about as Mungo in *The Padlock* has also yet to be retrieved. When John Watson was assembling his *Annals of Philadelphia*, he interviewed Robert Venable, "an aged black man"— 94 at the time of interview—who remembered attending "the first play at Plumstead's store" only "to light home Master and Mistress."[34] He too saw the playhouse, if only to light home the master, but he and his class were clearly outside the patron base of the playhouse, outside its brief and urban range of drawing room representation, and they were equally outside the range of recovery. They were, in short, historically unavailable.

The "Charming Sally" that brought the first London company of actors to America was also a trading vessel that trafficked in slaves. The actors were supercargo. When apothecary Gilmore complained of those same actors, arrival, he noted in the same line the batch of new slaves. On another trip, destination New York, the Charming Sally had "A parcel of likely slaves, Men, Women, and Children . . . N.B. Among the slaves there is a boy that may properly be call'd a Tubler [tumbler], putting himself into all kinds of postures; and is truly admirable in gesture."[35] That performer was sold into another line of work and his life remained unknown, uncelebrated, and unrecoverable.

The most pronounced notice of slaves in the theatre was published in a proclamation to rid the theatre of them. William Verling, advertising for the Bass-End playhouse in St. Croix, affixed the following nota bene: "No person can be admitted behind the scenes; nor any Negroe whatever in the House. It has been disagreeable to several Ladies; therefore the Manager hopes no person will be offended, as it will render the Theatre more comfortable to the Ladies and Gentlemen who honour it with their appearance."[36] These were the islands whose black populations outnumbered the whites ten to one and the theatre, as a commercial European venture, was clearly uninterested in nine-tenths of the population. When the *Cornwall Chronicle* wrote of the deceased Mrs. Douglass as "a humane mistress" in Jamaican culture they were referring to her treatment of her slaves, of which we have no other record. When were they acquired? When did she become "mistress"? When Douglass was sporting around Virginia in his phaeton, was a slave driving it? When Dunlap (150) remarked of John Henry's gout that necessitated a coach, he was keen to point out the coach was "driven by a black boy." Was the boy a slave of the manager? Did Douglass also keep a driver, and was "his boy" also an acquired ornament in his bid for gentility? When Douglass died a decade later, among the "property" in the inventory of his estate were eight slaves, including two named "Apollo" and "Bacchus."[37] Most he had acquired once he left the theatre—pressmen for his print shop in Kingston—but Mrs. Douglass's eulogy suggests slaves were in the manager's household earlier, when she and her husband were both still on the stage. Were Apollo and Bacchus, those two great gods of theatre, backstage, dressing the actors, shifting scenery, or were they given the sooty job of keeping the fires and trimming the candles while a blacked-up Mungo and Othello pranked and raved? Would Apollo the candle-trimmer on the forestage of Othello even be seen?

WHAT ATTAKULLAKULLA SAW

At the close of the French-Indian wars (the Seven Years War, 1756–1763) the map of the eastern colonies and what is now northeastern Canada was re-drafted reflecting the terms of the Treaty of Paris (February 10, 1763). France had given up all claims in North America, including the towns and forts down the St. Lawrence and the upper Ohio river valley. Spain had ceded Florida and the Bermudas in the same treaty, expanding the British holdings on the continent from the delta of the Mississippi on the gulf of Mexico, along the eastern seaboard, to the Fishing Banks off Nova Scotia as the unified and uncontested territory called British North America. The Seven Years War was a decisive victory for the British that guaranteed their monopoly on the continent. To ensure that victory, the British had promised extensive land treaties with many of the Indian tribes (the Ottawas, Cherokees, Shawnees, and Six Nation Iroquois who were largely inclined to side with the French, who were trappers and traders, but not settlers like the English). They promised before the war and the map and treaties after the war guaranteed the Indians their traditional lands against the encroachment of further settlements. On the new map, along the ridge line of the Appalachian mountains from Maine to the Savannah River in Georgia was marked a bold boundary for all to read: "Land reserved for the Indians."[38] Before the ink was dried inroads of English settlers and land speculators compromised the treaty, including, most notably, Daniel Boone and Samuel Calloway who opened the Cumberland Gap in 1764. Great Britain may have promised the Indians a reserve, but the colonists seeking fortunes on the land saw the sealing off of the west as another imposition on the nascent but growing list of British tyrannies.

The first serious and organized offensive from the tribes came less than a year after the treaty. Pontiac, chief of the Ottawas, led a series of attacks in 1764 to drive the white settlers back across the mountains, and though he and his coalition raised havoc for the summer, the campaign's failure ultimately resulted in a built-up of English troops, a network of forts, and the further encouragement of settlers. Frontier skirmishes against the back settlers continued through the decade, as did land speculation, punctuated by efforts to secure a more lasting peace. In 1767 a general council of northern and southern tribes was called to meet with British agents in Albany for the following spring, and in December of that year (1767), a party of Cherokees from what had become South Carolina passed through New York en route to the gathering. Led by Attakullakulla (Little Carpenter), the Cherokee chiefs were entertained in New York by the governor, Henry Moore, and General Thomas Gage, commander in chief of North America. Hearing there was a theatre in town, Attakullakulla expressed a desire to see it. And so on the evening of December 14, 1767, the nine Cherokees and their interpreter were gifted a side box at the John Street Theatre.

Attakullakulla had some experience in theatres long before he arrived in New York, and he knew quite well what it meant to be on display. As a young man he was one of a small delegation of Cherokees who traveled to London in 1730 with Sir Alexander Cuming to meet "the great King" (George II) and was deeply shaped by his London experience. He knew first hand the extent of the power, technologies, population, splendor, and degeneracy of this English race. Upon his arrival in England so great were the throngs of sightseers at the quay that his disembarking was delayed. Everywhere the visitors appeared in public, they were objects of intense observation. They sat for portraits ("The Trustees of Georgia") and engravings, walked with the king in St. James Gardens, visited the theatre, and the opera.

Anticipation was high on the night the Cherokees went to the theatre; the house was sold out and many turned away. The chiefs saw Richard III and a Harlequin afterpiece, and the rest of the house watched the Indians watching the play. Even Attakullakulla who had some experience with the whites spoke little English, and a translator would be hard-pressed to narrate a Shakespearean play on the wing. What they thought of it all is recorded only in the English language newspapers by those who watched them watching:

New-York, December 17 . . . The expectation of seeing the Indian Chiefs at the play on Monday night, occasioned a great concourse of people; the house was crowded, and it is said great numbers were obliged to go away for want of room. The Indians regarded the play, (which was King Richard the III.) with seriousness and attention, but as it cannot be supposed that they were sufficiently acquainted with the language to understand the plot and design, and enter into the spirit of the author, their countenances and behaviour were rather expressive of surprise and curiosity, than any other passions. — Some of them were much surprised and diverted at the tricks of Harlequin.

The story of an English King who lied and murdered his way into power and holdings may not have been all that incomprehensible to the Cherokees. They had some experience at this—there on their way to yet another council to secure yet another treaty and watch it broken by squatters on their land. King Richard may have offered a perfectly comprehensible model of English power. Or perhaps the plot of the play itself suggested a remedy, like Richmond to take up arms and put down the usurper, "till poor England weep in streams of blood"?

What exactly Attakullakulla saw and how much they understood is not clear and certainly was not recorded. The Cherokees published no travel journals. They left New York for the council at Albany, where British agents—including General Thomas Gage—schemed to foment the tribes in war against each other. Faced with the prospect of Indian-Anglo wars or inter-tribal wars, the agents chose the latter without reservation.[39] In spite of the council—and the many councils that followed—and in spite of policies that ranged from benign neglect to active extirpation, the claims of encroachment and prior ownership never went away until the Indians themselves were forcibly removed.

Nor did the ponderous "Indian Problem" ever find representation on the colonial American stage, though five generations of white settlers had lived with the uneasy anxiety of sharing space, claiming, surveying land, warring for it, and ultimately removing the native Americans to carve out a nation that no longer included them. Patriots like Patrick Henry might find an apt and timely political metaphor expressed in rebellion plays like *Cato* or *Julius Caesar*, never in the repertory did any-thing vaguely approach the contest of Anglo appropriation of native lands, or the threat of Indian retaliation. The spate of Indian plays that appeared on the London stage in the first decade of the eighteenth century in response to a visit of the "Indian Kings" (Dryden's *Indian Emperor*, Southern's *Oroonoko*, the Mohawk *Macbeth* that Joseph Roach examines) never appeared on the colonial American stage.[40] The first American play to treat native Americans, James Barker's *The Indian Princess*, belonged to the early nineteenth century. When Richard Cumberland wrote and Douglass staged *The West Indian* in 1771, its subject was the Jamaican planter class, not the Caribs before them. Not even a comic version of the Indian (like "Attakullakulla in London") ever found representation on the colonial American stage. Though they were the subject of all the gaze of London, in the British theatre of colonial America, the American Indian was literally inconceivable, impossibly beyond and below the threshold of representation. Except on two occasions, and neither of them by actors.[41]

When Attakullakulla and the Cherokee warriors returned through New York after the council the following April (1768), they desired to return to the theatre. This time, however, it was not to watch a play, but rather to offer a performance of their own. It was, we would call today, a performance exchange. Douglass advertised it as such: "The Cherokee Chiefs and Warriors, being desirous of making some Return for the friendly Reception and Civilities they have received in this City, have offered to entertain the Public with, the WAR DANCE, which they will exhibit on the stage, after the Pantomime."[42] Douglass was careful to remind the audience of it's manners on the occasion. "It is humbly presumed, that no Part of the Audience will forget the proper Decorum so essential to all Public Assemblies, particularly on this Occasion, as the Persons who have condescend to contribute to their Entertainment are of Rank and Consequence in their own Country."

And there on the stage of the John Street Theatre, Attakullakulla and his warriors danced a war dance. The gathering in Albany had not gone well. They were returning to South Carolina empty-handed. There were no guarantees of peace. No guarantees that their traditional hunting grounds would remain unmolested. No borders that could be sealed off from the droves of American settlers. And what's more, a series of forts were being established and manned (heavily manned) to ensure the protection of the settlers already there. Attakullakulla was going home with the heavy choice of losing the land and their traditional way of life, adopting the white life, or taking up arms, as Pontiac had done, resisting, and finding defeat, as Pontiac had done.[43] When they took the stage at the close of the farce, did the performance of a war dance mark the moment when the Cherokee tradition capitulated from the active imagining of war to a formalized but impotent ritual? Or were they intimating their own response to the "Indian problem?" Was it, in short, a war dance, or a representation of a war dance? Was it an act of a past ceremony, or a promise for a solution to come?

The Treaty of Paris that reserved their lands was violated so repeatedly that it was given over as unbinding. Two generations later, the Shawnee chief Tecumseh was still advocating Pontiac's strategy of resistance. He organized a league of tribes in 1811: "the way, and the only way, to check and to stop this evil, is for all the Redmen to unite in claiming a common and equal right in the land, as it was at first and should be yet; for it was never divided, but belongs to all for the use of each." Tecumseh's campaign made a national hero out of another Cumberland Gap land-speculator, Andrew Jackson, when, in a decisive battle at Horseshoe Bend, Jackson's allies slaughtered 800 Creeks. The allies in the battle that saw the final resistance broken were the Cherokees.

The only other occasion the character of the Indian was performed in colonial America was on shipboard of the trading vessel *Dartmouth* in Boston harbor on the night of December 16, 1773. Fifty men "dressed in the Indian manner" boarded the ships in which lay stored chests of East Indian tea and jettisoned 90,000 pounds of the cargo into Boston Bay. The act of savagery that finally pushed the momentum of resistance beyond a critical point to open rebellion could only belong to the savage imagination of those who were never seen, and were already beyond.

The contest of Anglo and Indian, American and British, were battles that never appeared on the stage that fought and re-fought Bosworth field. The theatre in colonial America was eastward looking, transatlantic. There was little that was American about the American Company and the backyard, backwoods battles to the west never made it to the stage. Rather, it promised the urbanity of the London drawing room, the comfortable associations of Drury Lane, of Garrick, of theatre gossip, clubs, and periodicals. Jean Christophe Agnew has written of it, "What reflections its spectators found on this stage were of a world some three thousand miles away, and at times, a century removed from their own."[44] It did not, and was largely constitutionally unequipped to, look to itself. Not the poor of Philadelphia, not the emerging Americans, not the Dutch merchants, nor the African slaves, nor the native Indians, not the Quakers, not the new gentry, the backwoods frontiersmen setting up trade on new lands, or Jonathan the Yank. That would all belong to the next century. And so among everything else one cannot look to, one cannot look to the plays.

*   *   *

The colonial record abounds with such absences. It is always tempting—very tempting for performance historians—to inflate the role of theatre in the emerging nationalism of any country, to tease out representations and circulations of identity, and colonial America is no exception. Insightful studies could and have been made on General Washington's use of *Cato*, of David Douglass straddling nationalities as he transformed his London-trained actors into the American Company, of the civilizing imposition of theatre on the landscape.

But such none-records as Elizabeth Drinker's, Robert Venable's, Janet Schaw's, Dromo's, and Little Carpenter's remind us that performance was also situated within a culture that was largely uninterested in it or of whom the theatre was uninterested; whose lives were ideologically and materially utterly unchanged by each other's presence. And that, too, was part of America that needs to be recovered.

11. The Perfect Storm

My young gentlewomen like everything in their own country, except the retirement, they can't get the plays, the operas, & the masquerades out of their heads.

William Byrd II writing from Virginia to John Boyle,
February 2, 1727

The persistence of memory is what created theatre in the colonies and memory is what carried it through the Revolution when it was "discouraged" and into the new Republic. The same longing that Byrd's gentlewomen could not get out of their heads saw it through the years of absence. Even before it had been professionally established, its memory was in circulation, among the lettered, the traveled, in the emerging capitals and in places one would not expect it. When Dr. Alexander Hamilton, traveling in 1744, cleared the dense woods on the road out of Albany and was rewarded with a majestic vista of the village of Schenectady, he compared it immediately to the experience in the playhouse: "all at once the village strikes surprisingly your eye, which I can compare to nothing but the curtain rising in a play and displaying a beautiful scene."[1] This was, of course, years before he would enter a playhouse in America. Earlier on the same trip he met a ferry man at Elk Ferry, Pennsylvania ("who plied his tongue much faster than his oar"). When their conversation turned to books, the ferryman "told me of a clever fellow of his name who had composed a book for which he would give all the money he was master of to have the pleasure of reading it. I asked him who this name sake of his was. He replied it was one Terence."[2] It is recognizing that memory that I close this study with.

THOMAS WALL'S TRUNK

Hugh Rankin concluded his seminal work on the theatre in colonial America with an epilogue that dismantled the playhouses. In Rankin's crepuscular final chord, the playhouses, one by one were converted, receded back into precolonial oblivion. Douglass's playhouse in Annapolis became a church for St. Anne's Parish; the Church Street theatre in Charleston burned down in 1782; the 1760 Williamsburg playhouse was sold to a Mason, James Moir, who carted off the bricks. Rankin brought the curtain down on his study with a falling light: "With the playhouse gone, Virginians could only manifest their interest in the drama by reading plays to one another—just as they had done a hundred years before."[3]

But like Byrd's gentlewomen earlier, they could not get it out of their heads. And so they read plays, and through such vehicles did memory—in part—survive. Alexander Graydon recalls the arrival of the American Company in Philadelphia, while he was a student, "induced me to open books which had hitherto lain neglected on the shelf . . . I became a regular reader of plays, and particularly of those of Shakespeare, of which I was an ardent and unaffected admirer. From these I passed to those of Otway, and Rowe, and the other writers of tragedy, and thence to the English poets of every description."[4] In 1781 the idea of reading drama was still so marketable that two Charleston merchants, Nathaniel Mills and John Hicks, could request from their London purveyor: "that you will Ship by the first runner for Charleston 500 Plays well chosen and sorted, including all the New ones, and half the Number for New York."[5] If the amount seems excessive, it is. The brace of merchants noted in the same letter to their supplier the phenomenal success of the new publication, *The Political Magazine*, because it sold 100 copies. More than one young woman sighed when they realized, as the poor young British woman realized in New Jersey in 1780, and versified to her sister: "This morning, quoth Bet, as she lac'd on my stays, / It enters my head, we shall have no more plays."[6]

But performance was not entirely on hold for the Revolution; Bet and her playgoing companions need not read their way through the dreary times to come, and to frame the idea of theatre as a temporary institution that struggled, flourished, and vanished, leaving not a brick behind, belies the history early American stage, founded as it was on the same circuit by the same managers and supported by the same audiences.

Before the bricks were cleared from the Old Theatre in Williamsburg players had already returned upriver to Richmond. Before that boatload of plays arrived in New York and Charleston, audiences had already returned to the theatre. Dr. William Smith, attending a production of *Gustavus Vasa* in Philadelphia in 1781 was so impressed by the "vast crowds that resort to such places" that he suggested that a state-sponsored company of actors would "afford [the] Government a great revenue."[7] The military in New York assembled a near-professional company, refitted and re-opened the John Street Theatre as early as 1777.[8] When the Church Street playhouse burned down in Charleston in 1782, it was rebuilt almost immediately. The theatre itself had been rented to the Freemasons since the departure of the American Company, and John Troup, secretary of the order, advertised:

> The Members of the Union Kilwinning Lodge, since the burning of the Play House and the adjacent dancing Assembly Room, having been solicited to build upon their lot where the play house stood a suit of Public Rooms; give notice that, in consequence of such request, they intend erecting upon the foundation of the late theatre such a suit of rooms properly calculated for the reception and accommodation of Ladies and Gentlemen, as well as for the use of any public societies that may think proper to frequent them.

The "suit of Public Rooms" built on the ruins of the playhouse was back in play as a theatre four years later by the company of Dennis Ryan and Thomas Wall, with permission. Its four year hiatus was less than the time between the two sustained visits of Douglass and the American Company who departed in 1766 and returned in 1773. When Ryan and Wall abandoned the space, John Sollie opened it first as a concert hall and later as a theatre for his company.

Dennis Ryan had been the prompter with the American Company in New York in 1773, and Thomas Wall, who comanaged with Ryan, was a former actor with the same company. Neither had left the continent when Douglass and his actors departed for Jamaica in early 1775. Wall had played throughout the Revolution, throughout the colonies, almost continuously; he played solo, with his wife, with scratch companies, and he joined Bourgogne's company of British officers, and when they were captured, marched with them down to Charlottesville, Virginia. Here, as a prisoner of war, Wall and his company of interred actors built a playhouse with the permission of the governor, Thomas Jefferson, and continued to play right through the Revolution. He was brought to military court once for claiming more food for himself and his family than he was allotted, and the commander wrote to the governor on his behalf:

> If anything further is required to gain this poor Devil his liberty or ease the minds of those that are alarmed on the subject, I will do it with pleasure, not only from the principles of justice and humanity, but from gratitude, for the tiresome hours this man help'd us to pass over in the wilds of Virginia, by acting on a little Theatre the officers erected at the Barracks.[9]

Wall was released sometime shortly thereafter and began immediately assembling a professional company, secured permission, and opened a playhouse in Baltimore first and later in Annapolis. On June 8, 1781, the State Council of Maryland voted that "Thomas Wall is hereby permitted to exhibit Theatrical performances."[10] It was one of several companies back in operation by the early 1780s; indeed, four years before the Continental Congress's prohibition was lifted, Thomas Wall and Dennis Ryan were playing in Baltimore with an entire company, scenes and machines.[11] Later Wall toured North Carolina, returning to a circuit in the 1780s and 1790s that Mr. Mills had established before the war, with preserved playbills for Edenton, New Bern, Bath, and Wilmington.

In one regard Mr. Wall's career is a perfect image of both the persistence of memory and the endurance of theatre in colonial America, carving out markets, straddling nationalism. And all the better for us that it was him because Mr. Wall—during his lifetime at least—preserved a good deal of his own career. A surviving playbill in the Harvard Theatre Collection for March 27, 1773 (*Earl of Essex*) has this tantalizing acquisition note attached to it, an auction description,

Item 886: "Southwark Theatre, Phila. Playbill of performance for the benefit of Mr. Woolls and Mr. Wall . . . Neatly repaired on the folds. Of extreme rarity. From Mr. Wall's collection."[12] Edwin Wolfe concluded his introduction of the catalogue of American playbills by asking (facetiously), "The large-scale disappearance of early American playbills is a phenomenon easily understood. Who but possibly the printer or the manager of a theatrical company would have saved them?"[13] In England many theatres would save playbills, usually binding them into books, marked by the year. But in America where companies were by nature itinerant, who indeed would save playbills?

Thomas Wall would. Over the duration of his career, Wall preserved his own collection of ephemeral material artifacts of his life in performance: newspapers notices, letters from fellow actors, notes from patrons, copies of playbills, many of them with handwritten notes about casting changes, date changes, and the income that the plays earned. Though much of his original collection is now lost, broken up, or sold off, enough of it has survived to get a sense of what all was once there in Thomas Wall's collection. We learn, for example, from an acquisition note in the New York Historical Society's collection of playbills, "from Thomas Wall's trunk," that the ubiquitous Wall carried his collection around with him over the course of his long career in a mahogany trunk. It was, during its time, a mobile museum of theatrical ephemera. Even the trunk itself had a history.

Alonzo May, who wrote but never published a history of the American stage (*Men and Women of the American Stage*), and left his annotated proofs of the work in the Maryland Historical Society, related a small part of that trunk's history:

> In 1902 there was found in Baltimore in an old trunk a collection of programs, bound and printed on thick paper. On the cover were the words "Playbills of the year 1784, performed at Annapolis in Maryland." Thomas Llewellyn Sechemere Wall.[14]

The trunk itself has not since survived. But in its day, it had its own precarious career, contents aside. It was broken into once in Philadelphia, and stolen at least twice. On one occasion it was described as "a mahogany chest full of player's cloathes" stolen from a tavern-keeper's house where two actors of the company were lodging.[15] Wall advertised a handsome reward for its return. On another occasion, also in Philadelphia, costumes were pilfered, and on the next occasion, a run of tickets were stolen. Seilhamer (*History of the American Theatre*, vol. I, 356–357) mistook the value of the contents when he dismissed Thomas Wall as "first among these theatrical fops" because he advertised for his missing trunk "indicating the value the owner placed upon the wearing apparel it contained." The value of the trunk was not in the clothing—foppish or not—but in the personal collection of playbills, letters, and notices that documented Wall's American career. He was, in this regard, his memory's own caretaker, and the cargo was the single most concentrated source of theatrical material preserved from the period.

The bundle of 1784 playbills found in the trunk that Alonzo May noted was only one part of Wall's collection of playbills acquired by Charles N. Mann, a Philadelphia barrister with an interest in drama and an exquisite drama library. The Mann collection was catalogued at his death in 1907, and though the collection was dispersed, the catalogue remains. Most of our preserved colonial American playbills—at the Harvard Theatre Collection, the Rockefeller Library, New York Historical Society, and the Maryland Historical Society—are all derived from Mann's collection. Mann's early American playbills relating to the Baltimore theatre (1781–1783) were acquired by George Loeb of Philadelphia, who sold them to the Maryland Historical Society in 1954 for $150.00. The bills relating to Virginia were acquired by the Colonial Williamsburg Foundation. And so the surviving contents of Thomas Wall's trunk found a resting place among the many libraries and historical societies.

Much of the collection, however, had already been broken up before Mann acquired the trunk in 1902. How large was it, originally? Who knows. In the Mann collection one can find playbills from several venues in Virginia, Alexandria, Suffolk, Fredericksburg, and Williamsburg, for 1769, 1770, 1773, a whole season from Fell's Point, Maryland, 1781, another season from Baltimore and Annapolis, 1782–1783, the New York collection (probably not Mann's) that dates from 1784, and several playbills from 1790s when Wall was seeding a company in North Carolina. Altogether the separate holdings represent only a fraction of what was once assembled. Still, enough fragments remain to begin to sense the magnitude of what was lost. Between the many repositories one can still find from the collection of Thomas Wall handwritten prologues to plays; a manuscript list of all the plays given at the John Street Theatre in New York, 1773; letters between actors; newspaper advertisements; playbills. Below the casting corrections, Wall often penciled in the gross takes for the night, postponements, notes on attendance, including the governor's ("At this play his Excellency Governor Lee honoured us with his presence," February 15, 1782), even a list of the songs that accompanied the productions, and who sang them. One of the more interesting items was a handwritten sheet containing the rules of the company, including an index of fines for missing rehearsals, performances, or showing up drunk, and so on. A second sheet spells out the rules regulating benefits. What we have, in essence, is the remains of an operational manual for a provincial company.[16] A few letters have also been preserved, one to Wall from several patrons of the playhouse threatening disapprobation in the house over roles.

One of the more poignant items in the collection is a letter between two actors—two old troopers who crossed paths on occasion, one now down on his luck and soliciting the assistance of the other. Dr. C. Bayly, who ran a small company in New York and Charleston in 1767–1768 and performed with puppets when he could not assemble actors, wrote to Thomas Wall quite late in his career, soliciting permission to use Wall's playhouse in Baltimore. I print the urgent, scrawled, and unpunctuated letter in full:

Mr Wall:

Sir—your poor old friend Doctor Bayly whom you may remember many years ago in Phila [delphia] and in Lancaster, arrived in town last night very lame and infirm—being by a long [series?] of illness prevented many years from exhibiting his former Entertainments and now on crutches—though yet willing is not so able as formerly—having in this course of the war and by his unhappy marriage lost all his scenery, most of his cloathes, and puppets, yet proposes if not disadvantageous to your theatre to perform twice a week during a short time, on the Evenings of your vacation and would be proud and thankful for your assistance in some trifling matters, relative to the proper appearance, of a performer

Would be glad of a private interview but am not able to walk in such weather

I am sir yours Dr. C. Bayley

Saturday noon[17]

These two troopers clearly had some passing acquaintance, but curiously not from the known venues of New York or Charleston where Bayly operated his theatres—the Orange Tree and Bacchus on the Bay—but rather from Philadelphia and Lancaster—the later site has yet left no documented theatre or performance evidence. Nonetheless, somewhere in their Pennsylvania travels, the two developed a nodding acquaintance and now the old and infirm Bayly was banking on Wall's assistance.

Wall kindly assisted. Bayly secured permission and soon his advertisements were in the *Baltimore Advertiser*, putting the best face on his infirm condition: "The noted Doctor Bayly, being now so well recovered of his illness and Lunacy, as to be able to exhibit, as usual, well perform by permission of the Mayor his most amazing dexterity of hand, etc, etc, his grand and well-known puppet shew."[18] Additional notices followed announcing performances by the noted "Old Artist" of lectures, sleight-of-hand, tooth-pulling, and a play and a farce by "his artificial company of comedians." Over the playbill, Wall—who saved them—has written "Baily's Advertisement." Bayly, whose health was not nearly so mended as his bills suggest, advertised for a young man to assist him while he continued to perform in Baltimore, Annapolis, and Alexandria. It is with some sadness that we read in May of 1783 that not only his collection of figures were inventoried and auctioned at his death, but also note that Bayly's passing also occasioned a full description of his act, published in the *Maryland Journal* of May 6, 1783:

Baltimore Town. May 1 1783. For sale, for cash only. All that incomparable apparatus, lately belonging to the inimitable Doctor Bailey deceased; consisting of his Artificial Company of Comedians near four feet high, properly dressed—a play and farce, with a variety of drolls and interludes. The complete machinery of the amazing table tricks of slight of hand and deception. Also fifty figures, representing the various nations of the earth in their proper colours and dresses, from four to eight feet high, with moral lectures on each figure. For terms apply to Jacob Henninger.

Jacob Henniger was the young man Bayly had employed to help him. By the end of May 1783, Henninger had found no buyers and so he himself carried on Bayly's entertainments: "The noted Jacob Henninger," reads the ad, "Will exhibit his grand Medley of Entertainments." The bill was Bayly's: sleight-of-hand, moral lectures, and "the whimsical humours of Seignior Punchinello and his artificial Company of Comedians, four feet high, richly dressed, by whom will be performed a play and farce, with sundry drolls."[19] And through such means as the poor legacy of Dr. Bayly like the battered trunk of Thomas Wall, the memory of theatre stumbled on.

Through the scraps of Wall's collection we glimpse something of the rich professional circuit of theatre that endures only in scraps and pieces. That Wall should know the old Doctor, fraternal in their strolling vocation, should stay in touch over their travels, perhaps should not surprise us, though we have no prior evidence of it. It was, after all, a small profession, even if it stretched over an immense geography. Acting families like the Storers could leave Jamaica in 1767 to rendezvous with the American Company in Philadelphia with some unrecorded prior arrangement. Or, without arrangements, disgruntled actors like the Parkers or Henrietta Osborne could shuttle between companies, guaranteed of work elsewhere. Once in Baltimore another name from the past reappeared in Thomas Wall's company with the introductory note on the playbill, "his first appearance on this stage": Robert Upton. Robert Upton, it will be remembered, was the advance agent for the Hallam Company who absconded way back in 1751 and was not heard from again. He finally turned up on the stage in Baltimore; somehow he knew Mr. Wall, and thirty years after absconding with the Hallams's advances, he reappeared, and it was preserved in a handwritten note.

Only a fraction of Mr. Wall's collection has survived, but enough of it remains to remind us that by saving the ephemera, one actor, at least, conceived of himself and his vocation as endurable, memorable, and battered as that memory is, the surviving artifacts should alert us to the vastness of what was once there. It should also remind us, for example, that—like the appearance of Giffard's name at Verling's wedding, Upton's name in Wall's company, Bayly's letter to Wall—these troopers all knew each other, bound up in a wide circuit of professional markets, and just below the surface of the historic record moved a network of professional players and that there were far more of both than what has been preserved.

1768

To recall a glimpse of the size and scope of this network, I want to evoke some the ephemera of one rich year over the range of the colonial American circuit: 1768. When the Philadelphia traveler J. R. found himself in an awkward dilemma one evening in 1768 of either hearing a sermon or a play and ended up in the playhouse, the odds were not so long against finding a good play. In the season of 1768, six known companies played the colonial American circuit, playing nearly every major city at some point in the year. Theatre was available in Boston, New York, Philadelphia, Annapolis, Charleston, Williamsburg, Fredericksburg, Norfolk, New Bern, Halifax, North Carolina, Halifax, Nova Scotia, and Kingston, Jamaica.

David Douglass and his American Company—the most visible of the professional companies—split the year of 1768 between the John Street Theatre in New York and the Southwark Theatre in Philadelphia. They offered a winter season in New York that carried them into June. They advertised "positively the last night" for June 2, but were still playing on June 28 of the month.[20] The company either recessed for the summer or, more likely, played smaller venues, below the threshold of the press, like Perth Amboy, New Jersey, before reconvening in Philadelphia in late September for an October opening. They advertised for one month only, but their season continued until mid-January, when they returned to New York.

In Boston, English troops were billeted in the winter of 1768–1769, where they began to rehearse and then openly perform plays the Following spring, much to the chagrin of many who saw the troops openly flaunting the authority of the province.

To the south, in North Carolina, Mr. Mills operated a company that boasted "the best actor on the American stage," Henry Giffard. They had played several venues in the colony—New Bern and Halifax—for at least six months before moving on to Halifax, Nova Scotia. As rehearsed above, there they opened in September and played for eight weeks. Before the year was out they had opened in Jamaica.

In Virginia, William Verling's New American Company began the year in Norfolk. Our notices slice into their season at the close of it, with actor benefits. By the end of March they were installed in the theatre in Williamsburg and played the spring court season well into June. Their summer whereabouts are unknown—they were playing small hamlets along the Virginia river routes and beyond the arm of the law. George Washington attended several of their performances in September in Alexandria, after which they opened in Annapolis for the winter.

While Charleston, South Carolina, saw the opening of the younger, healthier Dr. Bayly's new theatre, the Bacchus on the Bay. Bayley offered both large puppets (his "artificial company of commedians") and a small company of full-size actors playing farces and Harlequinades. He had moved to Charleston from New York, where he had operated a similar establishment, the Orange Tree, the previous year.

Even further south, in Savannah, Georgia, an unknown company is scratching for an audience at Mr. Lyon's Long Room, where they will read Garrick's *Lethe*, with permission. What became of the venture is not known.[21]

And in Jamaica, enough oblique evidence remains to suggest an active and ongoing company. After the death of Mr. Storer in 1767, his wife, four daughters, and the young John Henry all departed the island, as did Mrs. and Mr. Charles Parker. The Parkers would join William Verling's company, where they were introduced as "recently from Jamaica," but a shipboard fire took the lives of the elder Mrs. Storer, one of her daughters, and her two children. John Henry and the three surviving Storer sisters joined David Douglass and his American Company in Philadelphia. Yet even this major evacuation (at least nine actors left Jamaica in the summer of 1767), a company was still in operation. Many years later, in 1783, Mr. and Mrs. Giffard would return to Jamaica with the exiled American Company, and introduce themselves after an absence of "fifteen years." Among other members of that 1768 company was a young sailor disgusted at the slave trade. John Paul Jones loitered on the island waiting a ship back to Scotland and picked up a job as an actor. He debuted as young Bevil in *The Conscious Lovers*.[22] Both Richardson Wright and Errol Hill have assembled the material evidence of this Jamaican company: Master of the Revels, Tax roles, two playhouses, Kingston, Spanish Town.

Beyond the professional companies, there were the amateur and student productions, like Ames in Boston, as well as the solo performers touring Steven's *Lecture on Heads*. No doubt others were in operation, though they have left no record behind. If one expanded the survey to include the previous and following years, professional theatre could be found in Georgia, South Carolina, North Carolina, Virginia, Maryland, Pennsylvania, New York, Rhode Island, New Hampshire, Massachusetts, Nova Scotia, and several islands of the West Indies. All of which should deter us from hastily concluding, as Silverman (*A Cultural History*, 60) has, that "Theatre in British America meant one troupe."

THE STORM

To reveal the extent of the missing but indefatigable circuit, I want to conclude with a final "plaster cast" of a company that had disappeared, not once, but twice. In 1769, after a string of debts in Annapolis, William Verling and his New American Company cautiously dropped out of sight, and off the record. Hugh Rankin (*The Theatre in Colonial America*, 151) assumed they had disbanded, an assumption replicated frequently enough to develop an agency of its own. Done in by debts and the "vagaries" of the strolling life, the Verling Company was assumed to be extinct, and a cursory glance at Verling's court record would have suggested extinction was a good career move.[23]

But neither Verling nor his Company were finished just yet. Their story, like that of Pompeii, began with a storm.

On the evening of August 31, 1772, an exceptionally violent hurricane hit the Leeward Islands in the Caribbean, those small but lucrative cane and rum-producing English colonies of St. Croix, St. Thomas, Antigua, Nevis, St. Kitts, Anguilla, Montserrat, and Tortola. In a season of storms, this one was particularly brutal for its force and its odd trajectory that hit, stalled, recycled itself, and struck again. We have several preserved accounts of the hurricane, from the first rains on August 27 to the demolition of whole towns by the early morning of September 1. Hyperbole aside, all of the accounts describe the storm as the most catastrophic in living memory. The death count was ultimately unknown; what scanty news service there was trickled out a woeful tale of lost ships, lost cargos of slaves, flattened townships, a trail of injured whose lives were soon despaired of, untold property damage, and the aftermath of ruin: homelessness, brackish water, diseases. Here is one account of the hurricane as it hit the town of Christianstead, St. Croix, written by a young and promising counting clerk—the 17-year old Alexander Hamilton, to his father—later published in *The Royal Danish-American Gazette*:

> Dear Sir: I take up my pen just to give you an imperfect account of one of the most dreadful Hurricanes that memory or any records whatever can trace, which happened here on the 31st ultimo at night. It began about dusk, at North, and raged very violently till ten o'clock. Then ensued a sudden and unexpected interval, which lasted about an hour. Meanwhile the wind was shifting round to the South West point, from whence it returned with redoubled fury and continued so till near three o'clock in the morning. Good God! What horror and destruction—it is impossible for me to describe—or you to form any idea of it. It seemed as if a total dissolution of nature was taking place. The roaring of the sea and wind—fiery meteors flying about in the air—the portentous glare of almost perpetual lighting—the crash of the falling houses—and the ear-piercing shrieks of the distressed, were sufficient to strike astonishment into Angels. A great part of the buildings throughout the island are leveled to the ground—almost all the rest very much shattered—several persons killed and numbers utterly ruined—whole families running about the streets, unknowing where to find a place of shelter.

Other narratives of the great storm were carried in colonial American newspapers, as the sloops and scows limped back to the ports of Boston, New York, and Charleston. *The New York Mercury* of October 12 reported the storm "the most violent Hurricane that has ever been known here [St. Croix] or perhaps on any island in the memory of man."[24] In Frederickstead, it continued, "but three houses [were] left standing." Other accounts concur: "On the 31st August came on the most dreadful Hurricane known here in the memory of Man." And from St. Eustastius: "On the 31st we had a violent gale of wind here, such a one as the oldest man amongst these islands has never seen the like. Our houses are leveled with the ground, all our vessels drove out, many known to be lost . . . Capt. Moore's schooner of your island [St. Croix] is lost and

Moore with all his crew are drowned."[25] The royal governor of St. Croix declared his island what we would call today a state of emergency, or a disaster area. Drinking water was rationed, field hospitals were set up, looting laws and curfews were stridently enforced, surviving residents met to clear the rubble and consider "the melancholy situation of this island from the late Hurricane." Among the more poignant details of the storm was the description of His Majesty's Hospital in Antigua that collapsed and of the many sick who were buried in the ruin.[26]

One of the few buildings on St. Croix that did survive, though shattered, was Daniel Thibou's printing office, in Christianstead. It took him a full nine days to resume publishing *The Royal Danish-American Gazette*, the first newspaper of the Leeward Islands. Caribbean newspapers were few and far between outside Jamaica, and preserved issues of those presses are even more rare. So how very fortunate we are to have a substantial press run of *The Royal Danish-American Gazette*, the paper that printed young Hamilton's letter.[27] Because, as it turns out—and here is the destination of this calamitous prologue—on the same night of the great storm, August 31, 1772, there was a company of actors on St. Croix, advertising a play for that evening: "By Permission, at the Theatre in Bass-End, By the Leeward Islands Company of Comedians, *Douglas* and *Catherine and Petruchio*, the doors will be open Half after Five, and begin Half after Six o'clock." That evening was to be the debut, on the Bass-End stage at least, of Frederick Spencer, the only actor singled out in the press notice. He was robbed of his debut, as it was about curtain time when a troubling wind from the north began and persisted with an unabated violence. One hopes the play, at some point, was given o'er—as the playhouse did not survive the storm. An account later published in a Boston paper confirmed the destruction of that part of the island: "Bass-End is a heap of confusion."[28] Though the St. Croix newspaper continued for several years more, no further notice of the company is advertised again, on St. Croix or any other island. For all we know, the company perished in the storm, among the many casualties of this deadly but unchristened hurricane. Nor is there any further reference to the Bass-End theatre being rebuilt or reopened. I think it would be safe to assume that it was among the "heap of confusion" left in the wake of the great storm that ended the island's flush times.

The one name preserved for the evening provides a clue to the company's identity: Frederick Spencer was a small but recognized name in the calendar of colonial American theatre. He was a minor actor who joined William Verling's Virginia Company sometime in late 1768 or early 1769. Verling's company—the only serious competition David Douglass and the American Company ever endured—retitled itself the New American Company when it traveled from Virginia to Annapolis and with it Spencer played through the spring of 1769, after which, troubled by debts, the company plunged out of sight, and Spencer had dropped from the record.[29]

The identity of the remainder of this unknown company can be traced through the pages of the *Gazette* prior to the great storm.[30] Exciting as it is to find evidence of a new and previously unknown company playing at what turns out to be a rich and long-standing circuit in an established playhouse on this small island, the Bass-End theatre at Christianstead was not the only playhouse on St. Croix. A second theatre, the West-End theatre in Frederickstead, across the island, was also destroyed by the storm. It was empty on that fateful night, but not empty 22 months earlier when a rivalry played out between two competing companies on this small but vibrant island: the Leeward Islands Company and the West-End Company. William Verling was involved in both. In the fall and winter of 1770 the tiny island of St. Croix boasted more theatrical activity per capita than any colonial American city. Verling and his Leeward Islands Company arrived, joined an existing company (Mr. Hill's), played a combined fall season, squabbled over the ordering of the benefits, broke up, and formed two competing companies that played a second season across the island. Many of these actors were known from the American circuit (the Parkers, William Verling, James Godwin), some of whom had traveled over with Lewis Hallam, Sr., on the inaugural tour in 1752 (Patrick Malone and his wife), some of whom had later played with David Douglass (George Hughes), some were remnants of Verling's Virginia Company, some from Mill's Company (the Giffards), and there is evidence that they had been playing on the island for many years, in a minor, independent circuit, a sort of AA league, one notch removed from the major stops of the provincial American touring circuit.

It gets stranger still. As it turns out, this disastrous hurricane left evidence of yet another company also playing the Leeward Islands the same evening. The storm that ravaged St. Croix also struck the islands of St. Christopher, Montserrat, and Antigua. The account was carried on shipboard from the island of Antigua, back to Philadelphia. According to this account, the town of St. John in Antigua was severely devastated, including the Freemason lodge, lately rented:

> Sep 2. On Monday morning late, about one o'clock, arose here, the most terrible hurricane of wind and rain that ever was known in the memory of the oldest man living. This dreadful tornado seemed destined by providence to complete what the storm on Thursday last only threatened us with.

In a moment of bathos, the author interrupts his catalogue of casualties to footnote another inconvenience of the storm:

> The wind found entrance into the Free Mason's lodge, which is lett to a company of Comedians, who had obtained his Excellency's permission to play here, and destroyed all their scenery, &c., so that it will take them up a fortnight before they can put it in statu quo, and open it.[31]

So who are all these players? Not the two companies on St. Croix. Nor were they the company currently playing in Jamaica, nor were they the company currently playing on Barbados.[32] What it reveals is a circuit far larger than the material evidence has preserved, including a dense network of actors and competing companies in the smallest of venues. Yet the islands—particularly the Leeward Islands—had a sustained history of hosting performance. These islands were the provinces of companies that hubbed out of Jamaica and moved along the trade routes between islands and the continent. When David Douglass first arrived in New York in 1758, he carried with him a character letter from the governor of St. Croix. John Singleton, actor with the Hallam Company, had left a poetic description of many of the smaller islands of the Caribbean, one assumes from his travels there as a player. Prior to the first notice of Verling's arrival on the island in 1770, one Mr. Hill already hosted a company in Frederickstead. There is enough intermittent evidence to suggest that the Leeward Island Company was roaming the lower Caribbean during the Revolutionary war.

The first good source of first-hand evidence of performance on the Leeward Islands is the press run of *The Royal Danish-American Gazette*, Daniel Thibou's newspaper. From the pages of the *Gazette* we read a thriving rivalry between two companies—The Leeward Islands Company of comedians (William Verling's) and the West-End Company. They trade productions, barbs, and actors in the fall of 1770, until the death of Patrick Malone (formerly of Hallam's company) united the jarring camps into a single company. The island could not support even a single permanent company, so they island hopped: St. John, St. Croix, Antigua, and St. Kitts. In their absence, seed companies sprung up. Mr. Warwell, a traveling solo performer "who has read and sung in all the great towns in North America" (including performing ballad operas in Boston), arrived in St. Croix in March of 1771. He initially performed solo, "he personates all the characters, and enters into the different humours," but quickly gathered the local talent, including Mrs. Giffard (of Mill's Company), now apparently in residence on St. Croix. Together they commenced a short season, filling out the cast as best they could: "the rest of the Characters will be disposed of to the best advantage."[33]

Also in the company was James Verling Godwin, who played with Douglass and later Verling (his uncle? Godfather?), and would survive the storm, return to North America and open a company of his own in Savannah, Georgia, and later, Charleston. The fluid exchange of actors from company to company over a circuit that ran from Nova Scotia to Barbados reminds us that at times it seems the colonial Anglophone world of the eighteenth century must have been awash in actors. Students, soldiers, gentlemen companies, touring professionals and solo acts from Savannah, Georgia, to Halifax, Nova Scotia, and the Anglophone West Indies of Jamaica, Barbados, St. Croix, where permanent playhouses were built, St. Kitts, where they played in the Freemason lodge, Antigua, where the storm destroyed the scenery, Tortola, where William Hallam died, Cuba, where a playhouse opened in 1762 and was still in business 20 years later when Count dal Verme visited it, in Montserat, Martinique, in Providence, Bahamas. Indeed, almost everywhere there was a colonial governor, there was a colonial theatre.

The great hurricane, devastating as it was, put a temporary end to the playhouses in St. Croix, but not to the Leeward Islands Company or to its manager William Verling's career. On the small island of St. Kitts (St. Christopher), Janet Schaw, the Scottish traveler, found a company of strollers playing in Basterre at the Freemason's lodge in January 1775. Was it Verling, still strolling the islands? If so, he had competition from several other companies: The American Company was shuttling between Kingston, Spanish Town, and Montego Bay, Jamaica; another company opened and operated the Patagonia Theatre in Bridgetown, Bardados, in the 1770s, while yet another unnamed company from Glasgow had also introduced themselves to the islands. A few years after Schaw's visit to St. Kitt, another Scottish lady, Elizabeth Mackenzie, writing to Lady Pitcalnie, October 8, 1781, copies a letter from Mackenzie's sister in one of the English Caribbean islands and it is not Jamaica. The cited letter is undated, but events related inside it reliably fix it sometime late 1780/early 1781 (she refers to the French, English, and American privateers, and the devastating hurricane of last October 11, 1780, "a dismal subject so will give it up"). Moving on to the local news, she writes: "We have gote the Glasgow Players here they have made up a wooden playhouse which three times a Week is full of all [size?] and ranks or people in town and country, even the Clergy. They have gote non of my money yet nor do I think they will as many have got severe Colds by going to the Plays."[34]

Indeed, the period of the Revolutionary war concentrated the companies of American actors into a dense island circuit, crossing and crisscrossing the dangerous waters while the times swirled around them. When the war on the American continent lurched toward a treatied peace, companies began to return. Hallam and Henry had both pressed their claims in 1782 and the American Company followed en masse in 1783. James Godwin was not far behind. So by 1785—a decade after the theatre was prohibited—professional companies were up and playing again in Charleston, South Carolina, Savannah, Georgia, Richmond, and Alexandria, Virginia, Baltimore, Annapolis, Maryland, Philadelphia, New York, and Albany.

And when they all returned—all the flotsam displaced by the great storm—one old veteran appeared among the list. William Verling apparently also survived the hurricane. Our last notice of him comes from Petersburg, Virginia, still in the business, still in circulation.

From the *Virginia Gazette* of October 10, 1787, we read the following notice:

> We hear from Petersburg that the new commissioned Company of Comedians, under the old veteran V———, shortly intend to show new and old faces in a new stile, at the Old Theatre in the city. And however strange it many appear, tis said that they are chiefly from Old and New England, and even part of the Old and New American Company.

"Strange as it may appear," the old veteran V——— and the New American Company were still at it, in spite of debts, hurricanes, loss of scenery, flattened playhouses, attrition of actors, prohibitions, competition, and a Revolution, reopening the Old Theatre as they had for 20 years, as Douglass had before him, and the Hallams before him. It is a wonderful image of the indefatigable veteran of a perdurable profession, enduring, and ultimately irrepressible field that played out right through the storm.

MEMORY AND HISTORY

Does there not exist an intermediate level of reference between the poles of individual memory and collective memory, where concrete exchanges operate between the living memory of individual persons and the public memory of the communities to which we belong? Paul Ricoeur, Memory, History, Forgetting, *131.*

Ricoeur is speaking of close relations, situated somewhere between ourselves and our culture at large who can speak for us ("people who count for us and for whom we count"), and in whose care our memories lie. I am thinking of other kinds of intermediaries. The waiting playhouse that William Smith saw in Philadelphia during the Revolution and suggested be reopened held the memories of the company that once played and would return, standing against the vicissitudes of those troubled times; or the repositories of memory like the Thomas Wall's trunk of playbills and letters, or the antitheatrical campaign conducted in the most theatrical of terms, or the memory of

Bryd's gentlewomen, or Dr. Alexander Hamilton, standing outside Schenectady, reminded most potently of nothing so much as well-made scenery: all such were intermediaries who sustained the idea of theatre in its material absence. If individually the memory of colonial American theatre was marred by a kind of "incomplete remembering" at many levels, collectively the culture somehow did much better.

Among the memoranda Thomas Wall carried in his trunk was a list of rules relating to the ordering of benefits. For actors, this was the most important and potentially profitable evening of the season and regulations governing the company's participation in these events were essential to the profession. Wall, as a manager, had copied the list from his days as an actor in the American Company, where Douglass used the same protocols with his own company. It is likely that Douglass borrowed it from Lewis Hallam, Sr., in their joint company touring the islands in the late 1750s; Hallam, in turn, had brought it from his own theatre in Lincolns Inn Fields, London. The company protocols of ordering this night were passed down, one manager to the next from London in the 1740s to Wall's company in Baltimore in the 1780s, in the same way lines of business, or costumes and properties were passed down, one actor to the next, like John Henry's silver stage foil that was bequeathed at his death to Lewis Hallam, Jr. Much of Henry's estate (gathered through three marriages with three Storer sisters, all actresses) came to rest with his last wife, and at her passing, she in her turn left it to fellow actor Stephen Woolls, who at his death bequeathed it to yet another actress Ann Allyn. The material legacies, like the protocols of performance, passed from actor to actor, generation to generation, company to company in a profession that materially changed little during the eighteenth century.[35]

When the *Virginia Gazette* announcement of the returning actors in 1787 abbreviated the old veteran's name to "V———," both writer and readership were expected to have remembered the manager from the 1760s, though we have no record of Verling in Virginia since his departure 19 years earlier. Both writer and readership were expected to have remembered the Old and New American Companies—equally absent—and, more broadly, Richmond itself was expected to have remembered what it meant to do theatre. It was the enduring memory that ultimately sustained the theatre through the sparse colonial period, into and through the Revolution, and beyond, into the new Republic of the next century. The theatre in early America (1780s) was a product of the memory of colonial theatre—the circuits, the actors, the managers, the audiences, the brokers and agents, the conventions and protocols of performance, even the company names, preserved in often immaterial ways, through periods of material absence.[36]

American theatre after the Revolution happened because it had happened in the 1760s and its memory was prompted back into currency. The managers of the 1780s and 1790s—Verling, Hallam, Henry, Wignell, Wall, Ryan, Godwin—were all earlier members of the American Company, and were remembered as such. Jacob Mordecai: "After the war of the Revolution I saw the same managers with the addition of Wignell and Harper; Old Morris and his wife still among them—the interval near 25 years."[37] Their circuits—New York, Philadelphia, Charleston, Baltimore, Richmond, even North Carolina—were the circuits established two decades earlier. But the colonial theatre of 1750s–1760s also carried a memory of its London origins, indeed, it traded on it. When the Hallam Company first arrived in Virginia (and later New York, Philadelphia, and Charleston) it announced itself as the Company of Comedians from London. The actors were advertised as from the stages of London ("[Mr. Douglass] collected some very eminent performers from both the theatres in London," "Thomas Wall, from the Theatre-Royal, Drury Lane"). The audiences, like Byrd's gentlewomen who patronized the first playhouses, were remembering London, as was Alexander Hamilton, as was the farmer outside of Halifax, Nova Scotia, who remembered Garrick's performances, read of them in the American newspapers, and carried that memory to the fields of Windsor. The design of the theatre remembered the provincial playhouses of England, as the provincial theatres aspired to the principal theatres of London.[38] The repertory, the authors whose works were recalled on stage ("the new comedy of The Fashionable Lover, now acting at the Theatre Royal, Drury Lane, and Edinburgh with the utmost applause, will shortly appears on our theatre"); the diction of the actors, the music in the orchestra, the rhetoric of both objectors ("strollers") and defenders ("a well-regulated theatre," a "rational entertainment") were all borrowed from a larger discourse circulated by London periodicals (*Tattler, Spectator,*

Gentleman's Magazine); the size and ordering of the evening bill, the typography of the playbill, the painted scenery ("done by Mr. Dall, principal scene painter to Covent-Garden House"), the iron spikes that line the stage, even the Latin motto above the proscenium at the Southwark Theatre borrowed from Drury Lane, all served to evoke the memory of London playgoing and all that it stood for.[39] It was in this regard a memory far larger than the experience itself, nor did it require the conversance and participation of all, or even many, to ensure that memory's survival. A single prologue from the pen of one who had known professional theatre was enough to remind its American auditors who had not known of its London antecedence. James Sterling was one such, a one-time playwright turned Maryland rector, who spoke to this memorial gulf when he enjoined his fellow Annapolis auditors:

> Let no nice sparks despise our humble Scenes
> Half-buskin'd Monarchs, and itin'rant Queens!
> Triflers! Who boast, they once in Tragic Fury
> Heard Garrick thund'ring on the Stage of Drury!
> Or view'd, exulting, o'er each gay machine,
> The Feats of Covent-Garden's Harlequin![40]

Garrick, Rich, the scenes, machines, and thundering rhetoric of London theatregoing and the sparks who attended are all deliberately evoked to introduce the theatre in Annapolis as a site of memory recalled. These were not rhetorical gestures, but spoke to a certain repository of cultural memory. When "YZ," the author who published the review of the August 30, 1770 production of *Cymbeline* rhapsodized on Miss Hallam's performance ("methought I heard once more the warbling of Cibber in my ear!"), he was recalling Susannah Cibber, and his own experiences in the London playhouse a decade or more before. When the loyalist Alexander Mackaby complained of the poor spirit for celebrating St. George's Day in Philadelphia in 1770, he was lamenting the strained politics at the time, not the amnesia of the colonists. If he collected a poor company for Roast Beef and toasting George III, he found memory enough when he entered the playhouse: "where we made the people all chorous 'God Save the King,' and 'Rule Britannia' and 'Britons Strike Home' &c, and such like nonsense; and in short, conducted ourselves with all the decency and confusion usual on such occasions."[41] Musicians and audience alike already knew music and words and the protocol of "such like nonsense." Chorusing insists on a continuum of culture, of collective, lived, relived, acted, and re-acted memory. Not to have forgotten the songs, the sparkish behavior, the voice of Cibber, the thundering of Garrick, the character of Sir John Brute, the antics of Rich, not to have been novice to the conventions and protocols expected in a theatre, was to return to the theatre, not to have entered it for the first time. It was the culture's ability to return, to always return, that kept the theatre alive in its absence. It was a sentiment best expressed by Thomas Wall, who penned a prologue on the opening of the theatre in Baltimore in 1782, which may stand as a testament to both his own and his profession's indefatigable spirit: "we theatric merchants never quit."[42]

Notes ✑

INTRODUCTION: IN THE CELLARS OF THE VATICAN

1. For the Kelly riots, see George Ann Bellamy, *An Apology for the Life of George Anne Bellamy* (London: J. Bell, 1785), vol. I, 154f. In the National Archives of Scotland is an account book of the builder of the Theatre Royal Edinburgh, 1767, 1768. The theatre was built on speculation by one Mr. Williams, who kept a meticulous list of all the building materials. Among the square-headed screws, pine frames for flats, and yards of linen that furnished the interior is an entry for 9″ spikes.
2. Paul Ricoeur, *Memory, History, Forgetting* (Chicago: University of Chicago Press, 2004), xv.
3. Peter Davis, e.g., "Puritan Mercantilism and the Politics of Anti-Theatrical Legislation in Colonial America," in *The American Stage: Social and Economic Issues from the Colonial Period to the Present*, Dan Wilmeth and Christopher Bigsby, eds. (Cambridge: Cambridge University Press, 1993). Jean-Christophe Agnew, *Worlds Apart: The Market and the Theatre in Anglo-American Thought 1550–1750* (Cambridge, UK: Cambridge University Press, 1986); Heather Nathans, *Early American Theatre from the Revolution to Thomas Jefferson: Into the Hands of the People* (Cambridge, UK: Cambridge University Press, 2003).
4. *Accomac County Records*, vol. 1663–1666, fol. 102; cf. Henry Alexander Wise, *Ye Kingdome of Accawmacke or the Eastern Shore of Virginia in the Seventeenth Century* (1911; repr. Baltimore: Regional, 1967), 325–326.
5. William Dye, "Pennsylvania Vs. the Theatre," *Pennsylvania Magazine of History and Biography*, 55 (1931): 333–371 at 350.
6. John B. Linn and William H. Egle, eds., *Pennsylvania Archives*, 2nd series (Harrisburg, PA: Lane S. Hart, 1878), vol. VII, 71–72.

7. See, e.g., *Minutes of the Executive Council,* June 13, 1752; Dr. George Gilmer's letter to Thomas Walker, June 30, 1752 (Odai Johnson and William Burling, *The Colonial American Stage, A Documentary Calendar* [London: Associated University Presses, 2001], 156–157); and November 3, 1752.
8. Douglass remained in South Carolina; Lewis Hallam, John Henry, Miss Storer, and Stephen Woolls had just embarked on a recruitment trip to London. Owen and Mary Morris, Miss Wainwright, "and others" had traveled to Philadelphia. Eola Willis, *The Charleston Stage* (Columbia, SC: The State Company, 1924), 75.
9. Alexander Quesnay would open his academy in 1786, allegedly the first playhouse built in that city.
10. At the time of writing, from colonial Williamsburg, there is still to be seen posted on the wall, outside the printing office of the historic area, a single antitheatrical broadside, Edward Martin's voice still speaking across the centuries against a theatre that is no longer there.
11. One early example of an unrecovered voice of support was Lieutenant Governor Nanfan of New York, who granted a petition for one Richard Hunter to perform in New York in either 1699 or 1700. See *Calendar of Historic Manuscripts in the Office of the Secretary of State,* Edmund B. O'Callighan, ed. (Albany, NY: Weed Parsons, and Co., 1866), 284.
12. William Byrd II, writing from Virginia, to John Boyle, February 2, 1727, in *The Correspondence of the Three William Byrds of Westover, Virginia, 1684–1776,* Marion Tinling, ed. (Charlottesville, VA: University Press of Virginia, 1977), vol. I, 361.

PART I   (IM)MATERIAL WITNESSES

1. *New York Evening Post,* February 4, 1751.

1   WORKING UP FROM POSTHOLES

1. Brooks McNamara in his study of American playhouses of the eighteenth century (figure 17, p. 53) reprints an image of the Southwark Theatre in 1766 but notes that it is a reconstruction based on the research of Charles Durang. The image is discussed below.
2. *Virginia Gazette* (Purdie and Dixon), September 22, 1763.
3. William Young, *Documents of American Theatre History* (Chicago: American Library Association, 1973) vol i; Brooks McNamara, *The American Playhouse in the Eighteenth Century* (Cambridge, MA: Harvard University Press, 1969).

4. Because of lack of records on his methods, the present archeological team assumed that he had dug out the entire theatre pit because he drew a full profile drawing. However, he started by only putting perpendicular trenches through it. He appears to have dug out much of the eastern half based on a photograph of the dig, although the western half remains untouched.

5. For the archeological report I am indebted to Lisa Fischer, archeologist at the Colonial Williamsburg Foundation, and Tom Goyens, research assistant, also of the Colonial Williamsburg Foundation.

6. *South Carolina Gazette*, November 5, 1763: "The company of Comedians arrived here last Monday from Virginia who are called the American Company . . . A theatre is already contracted for 75 feet by 35, to be erected near where that of Messrs. Holliday and Comp. formerly stood and intended to be opened the 5th of December next." For full citation, see Johnson and Burling, *The Colonial American Stage, A Documentary Calendar* (London: Associated University Presses, 2001), 231–232.

7. Mark Howell, in his article "The 'Regular Theatre' at Jacob's Well, Bristol 1729–65," offers an appendix in which he documents the dimensions of many provincial Long Rooms, Theatres, and Theatres Royal, from which we learn that Bath in 1750 was 60×30, Plymouth in 1758 was 68×32, Colchester in 1764 was 64×38, Margate in 1779 was 66×36, Penzance in 1787 was 67×30, Worcester in 1781 was 66×36, Ipswich in 1788 was 81×40, and Richmond in 1788 was 67×28. *Scenes from Provincial Stages: Essays in Honour of Kathleen Barker*, Richard Foulkes, ed. (London: Society for Theatre Research, 1994). For a more detailed blueprint, the CWF has been relying on James Winston's material in the Harvard Theatre Collection, Folger Library, and particularly the Winston architectural drawings in the Theatre Museum, Covent Garden.

8. *Humphrey Harwood Account Book*, Ledger B, fol. 88. John Rockefeller Library, Special Collections, Colonial Williamsburg Foundation, Williamsburg, VA.

9. Arthur Hornblow, *A History of the Theatre in America*, 2 vols (Philadelphia: Lippincott, 1919), vol. I, 120–121.

10. *Charleston County Land Records*, Misc. Pt. 64, Book C5, 1779–1781, 47.

11. McNamara, *The American Playhouse*, 47; William Young, *Documents of American Theatre History: Famous American Playhouses* (Chicago: American Library Association, 1973), vol. i, 26; George O. Seilhamer, *History of the American Theatre*, 3 vols (Philadelphia: Globe Printing House, 1889–1891), vol. I, 329–330.

12. Toward the early 1770s, Douglass would rely more heavily on spectacle, importing, commissioning, and touring with elaborate "scenes and

machines" for such operas as *The Tempest* (Dryden), *Comus*, and *Cymon*. The first two pieces premiered in Philadelphia in January and March of 1770, respectively, and were carried down to Williamsburg for the spring and fall court seasons that year. The sub-pit may have been carved out to accommodate the needs of the machinery at this later time.

13. According to William Dunlap's description (*History of the American Theatre* [New York: J. Harper, 1832], 51), the John Street Theatre in New York as well had small side rooms to accommodate actors prior to going on. Originally under the stage, they were later moved to the west side. We know actors occasionally lived in the theatre as Patrick Malone, of the Hallam Company, was surprised one night by burglars. The pattern of equipping buildings with sleeping sheds is evidenced in the *Virginia Gazette*'s description of Market Square Tavern, a building that included "at one end of it a place for people to sleep in" (Purdie and Dixon), August 30, 1770.

14. Whitfeld J. Bell, Jr., "Addenda to Watson's Annals of Philadelphia," *The Pennsylvania Magazine of History and Biography* (Philadelphia: Historic Society of Pennsylvania, 1974), vol. 98, 157.

15. The wall surrounding the current capitol impeding visibility was a later addition.

16. Presumably to match the color of the brick. Descriptions of the painted Southwark Theatre in Philadelphia and the John Street Theatre in New York are found in both William Young's, *Documents*, vol. i, 18, 21 and William Dunlap's *History*, 41, 51.

17. Charles Durang's *The Philadelphia Stage from 1749 to 1821* was run as a serial in the *Philadelphia Sunday Dispatch*, vol. iii, May 21, 1854.

18. James Scott and Edward Wyatt IV, *Petersburg's Story* (Petersburg, VA: Titmus Optical Company, 1960), 40.

19. In 1772 William Buckland applied to the Annapolis Mayor's Court for "two lots of ground, each 40 feet square, to begin at the end of the lots of Mrs. Ann Beall on which the old Playhouse now stands and bounded by the lands of Mrs. Tasker on the waters of Acton's Cove." Ann Beall was the widow of Benjamin Beall, who owned a stocking factory, a warehouse, and "other pieces of land" at the lower end of Charles Street. I am indebted to Jane McWilliams of the Annapolis Heritage Association for calling the lease records to my attention.

20. George Washington made two account book entries for money spent for "play tickets" while in Williamsburg, October 1760 and March 1761, respectively, and a brief note by Maria Byrd whose niece was carried to town to see the plays (Johnson and Burling, *The Colonial American Stage*,

209, 211). There is an unfortunate lacuna in the preserved press run of the *Virginia Gazette*, and no playbills from the opening season survive.

21. David Mays, "The Achievements of the Douglass Company in North America: 1758–1774," in *Theatre Survey*, xxiii:2 (November 1982): 141–150 at 142.

22. In a notice published in the *Virginia Gazette* of August 21, 1752, Hallam advertised the expensive remodel of the building used by the Murray–Kean Company the previous season.

23. *George Gilmer Letterbook*, ms copy, Colonial Williamsburg.

24. All debt figures are culled from the *York County Records, Judgement and Orders*, vol. ii, 537–538.

25. *Edward Charlton Day Book*, ms. Colonial Williamsburg Foundation.

26. *York County Records*, November 19, 1753, vol. ii, 537–538. Here the "demise" is not the death, but "the transfer of an estate by lease or will" OED.

27. Cecil Price, *The English Theatre in Wales* (Cardiff: University of Wales, 1948), passim.

28. *Virginia Gazette*, June 30, 1768.

29. Walter R. Wineman, *The Landon Carter Papers in the University of Virginia Library. A Calendar and Biographical Sketch* (Charlottesville, VA: University of Virginia Press, 1962), 20.

30. *York County Records, Judgements and Orders*, 1768–1770, 43.

31. *York County Records, Judgements and Orders*, 1768–1770, 24; *Virginia Gazette*, August 11, 1768.

32. *York County Records, Judgements and Orders*, 1768–1770, 16, 483, 484, 503.

33. Ibid., 24, 10, 43.

34. Ibid., 67, 50.

35. Ibid., 67.

36. Verling and Parker were both sued by Richard Charlton. See *York County Records Judgements and Orders*, 1768–1770, 74.

37. *Anne Arundel County Judgement Records*, State Archives, Annapolis, EB-2, 95–127, 426–427; ibid., EB-1, 163.

38. Aubrey C. Land, *Letters from America*. William Eddis, ed. (Cambridge, MA: Harvard University Press, 1969), 48–49. Douglass had began advertising for the subscription during the court season of 1770 and originally published it in the *Maryland Gazette*, October 4, 1770.

39. *St. Anne's Parish Vestry Book*, 1767–1818, 89, for September 5, 1775. The lease renewal for the following year is recorded on September 3, 1776 in ibid., 94.

40. *William Bradford ms.* (Legal catalogue), Historical Society of Pennsylvania.

41. The Southwark Theatre was still known and occasionally used as a theatre after the departure of the American Company. For example, a slack wire artist offered a benefit for the poor of that city that was advertised for February 11, 1780 "at the theatre in Southwark" in the *Pennsylvania Packet-Philadelphia.*

42. *The Treasury Book of the Theatre Royal, New York,* 1780–1781, New York Historical Society.

43. *Journal of the Assembly,* November 1793.

44. Frederick Maser and Howard Maag, eds., *The Journal of Joseph Pilmore, Methodist Itinerant for the Years August 1 1769 to January 2 1774* (Philadelphia: n.p., 1969), 149, 151.

45. "Long prior to the Revolution theatrical performances were held in a wooden building that had been used as a pottery on the South side of Main Street near the river shore." The origin of the often-quoted line is Colonel William Steurt, *History of Norfolk County, Virginia* (Chicago: Biographical Publishing Co., 1902), 359.

46. A more detailed account of the history of the playhouse as a Methodist Assembly is found in William Bennett, *Memorials of Methodism* (Richmond: n.p., 1871), 56–59.

47. Robert Wells—a Scotsman like Douglass—published the *South Carolina Gazette* in which Douglass advertised his productions. He also printed and sold tickets while the American Company was in town. The lease is recorded in *Charleston County Land Records,* Misc. Pt. 64, Book C5, 1779–1781, 47. The details of the lease are printed in Johnson and Burling, *The Colonial American Stage,* 452–453. See also Julia Curtis, "Charlestown's Church Street Theatre," *The South Carolina Historical Magazine,* 70:3 (Charleston, SC, July 1969): 149–154.

48. *Charleston County Land Records,* Misc. Pt. 64, Book C5, 1779–1781, 47. The terms of the subscription scheme were published in the *South Carolina Gazette* of August 9, 1773.

49. *South Carolina and American General Gazette,* July 8–15, 1774. It may have been that the lease in South Carolina was secured earlier by John Henry in 1769. Julia Curtis argues that Henry, acting as a company representative, selected a site that Douglass would build upon in 1773. See Julia Curtis, "Charlestown's Church Street Theatre," 150.

50. *Robert Southall Receipt Book,* Colonial Williamsburg Foundation Library, May 16, 1771; May 22, 1772.

51. *Virginia Gazette,* April 13, 1769; November 19, 1772; "Upon being acquainted that a school-master, to teach reading, writing, and arithmatick,

was much wanted in this city, and that a proper person for that charge would meet with good encouragement, I was induced to make a trial, and accordingly opened school, about six weeks ago, at the playhouse (the only tolerable convenient place I could procure at that time)," September 7, 1769. Maser and Maag, *The Journal of Joseph Pilmore*, 151.

52. One surviving subscription scheme proposed by Lewis Hallam, Jr. in Kingston, Jamaica, for 1780, solicits 200 subscribers at £8 each, which would be ticket prices for 24 plays (Jamaican currency), which may correspond roughly to the Williamsburg scheme. The scheme was published in the *Kingston Mercury* of January 24, 1780. Douglass himself publicized a scheme in Charleston in 1773 soliciting subscribers to purchase 20 box tickets in advance to raise the capital on the new playhouse. See below.

53. The Methodist Joseph Pilmore was able to use a church in Edenton, North Carolina, "where they only saw preaching once in three weeks" (Maser and Maag, *The Journal of Joseph Pilmore*, 171).

54. From *Edward Charlton Day Book*, ms copy in Charlton's Peruke shop, Duke of Gloucester Street, Colonial Williamsburg. I am grateful to Charles Bush for introducing me to this and other merchant account books.

55. *York County Records, Judgement and Orders*, 1771, 2.

56. *Virginia Gazette* (Rind), March 17, 1768; July 23, 1768; *Virginia Gazette* (Purdie and Dixon), September 22, 1763.

57. *York County Judgements and Records*, Book VI, Deeds, 94; *Humphrey Harwood Account Book*, Ledger B, fol. 88, ms in Colonial Williamsburg.

58. *William Allason Daybook*, ms. February 1761, Virginia State Library.

59. *Diary of Jonathan Clark*, unpublished manuscript held by the Filson Club. Reprinted with permission.

60. *Virginia Gazette-Williamsburg*, September 20, 1770.

2   MR. SAUTHIER'S MAPS

1. See, e.g., James Deetz, "Material Culture and Worldview in Colonial Anglo-America," and Mark Leon, "The Georgian Order as the Order of Merchant Capitalism in Annapolis, Maryland" both in *The Recovery of Meaning, Historical Archaeology in the Eastern United States*, Mark Leon and Parker Potter, eds. (Washington: Smithsonian Institute Press, 1988); and James Deetz, *In Small Things Forgotten, the Archaeology of Early American Life* (Garden City, NY: Anchor Books, 1977).

2. The full passage reads as follows:

> The poverty of this Province appears to me (but to few in the Province besides me) to be owing in a great measure to our dabling in a paper currency and dispensing with all special Contracts, under pretince of supporting the Credit of that Currency, but in truth to answer the ill designs of the Champions for it to enable them to pay their Creditors on their own terms. Another causes of our Poverty, idleness and uselessness to our Mother Country, and likewise of the thinness of our Settlements, [is] a Single person being able to hold a great quantity at a low rent without Cultivation. All instructions restraining this are continually broke through. (Nina Tiffany, ed., *Letters of James Murray, Loyalist* [Boston: Gregg Press, 1972], 79)

3. Alonzo Dill, *Governor Tryon and His Palace* (Chapel Hill, NC: University of North Carolina, Press, 1955), 108.
4. Paul Nelson, *William Tryon and the Course of Empire* (Chapel Hill, NC: University of North Carolina Press, 1990), 18–23.
5. Frederick Maser and Howard Maag, eds., *The Journal of Joseph Pilmore, Methodist Itinerant for the Years August 1 1769 to January 2 1774* (Philadelphia: n.p., 1969), 171.
6. Roger Ekirch, *Poor Carolina: Politics and Society in Colonial North Carolina* (Chapel Hill, NC: University of North Carolina, 1981), 42–44.
7. Tiffany, *Letters of James Murray*, 23.
8. For a classic description of unfortunate and unfriendly traveling through North Carolina, see Elizabeth Cometti, ed., *The Journal and Letters of Count Francesco dal Verme, 1783–1784* (Charlottesville, VA: University Press of Virginia, 1969), 48–52.
9. "Journal of a French Traveler," *American Historical Review*, xxvi (1921): 726–747 at 738.
10. Andrea Palladio and his aesthetic arrived in England with Inigo Jones in the seventeenth century, but found its greatest circulation in the eighteenth century via the many pattern books, such as William Adam's *Vitruvius Scoticus* (1750), William Salmon's *Palladio Londoniensis* (1734), and Isaac Ware's *A Complete Body of Architecture* (1756). For a full description of the influence of Palladio on the Georgian style in America, see Richard Davis's *Intellectual Life in the Colonial South* (Knoxville, TN: University of Tennessee, 1978), vol. iii, 1149–1195.
11. The Regulator Uprising of 1768–1771 has been seen as an early American revolt against taxation, in this case taxation to erect the governor's palace. Eight leaders were executed before Tryon quashed the rebellion. It might also be seen as a resistance to the urbanization of the colony.

12. Richard Bushman, *The Refinement of America, Persons, Houses, Cities* (New York: Alfred Knopf, 1992), 139.

13. The originals of Sauthier's maps of the colony of North Carolina are all housed in the British Museum's George III Topographical Collection.

14. For a description of the damage, see *Colonial Records of North Carolina*, vol. viii: 71, 22–25, and below.

15. Richard Davis, *Intellectual Life*, vol. iii, 1169.

16. William Tryon to Samuel Ward, June 15, 1768, William L. Saunders, ed., *Colonial Records of North Carolina* (Raleigh, NC: Trustees of the Public Library, 1886–1890), vol. viii, 786–789.

17. Ibid.

18. "Abstracts from Norfolk Co. Marriage Bonds," na, in *Lower Norfolk County Virginia Antiquary*, Edward Wilson James, ed. (Baltimore: The Friedenwalk Co., 1902), vol. iv, 56.

19. A prologue for Mr. Mill's company was published in the *Nova Scotia Gazette*, September 8, 1768, one stanza of which concedes, "Or should our ladies, as they will appear / (for the best Wives some times the Breeches wear) / a little diff'rent from the Sex they claim / You'll on our Scanty numbers lay the blame."

20. *J. Franklin Jameson, ed.*, "Journal of a French Traveler in the Colonies, 1765," *American Historical Review* (July 1921) xxv, 739, 742.

21. Sauthier surveyed New Bern sometime in 1769: before or after the hurricane is unclear, but no mention is made of a playhouse.

22. *North Carolina Colonial Records*, vol. viii: 71, 22–25.

23. The Edgars and Hendersons were both overlooked in Weldon Durham's collection, *American Theatre Companies 1749–1887* (New York: Greenwood Press, 1986), who mentions them only as an unknown "rival troupe" who supplied actors to John Sollee's French Company in Charleston (ibid., 223–224); playbill in the Rockefeller Library, Colonial Williamsburg.

24. Archibald Henderson, "Strolling Players in Eighteenth Century North Carolina," *The Carolina Play-Book* (Chapel Hill, NC: University of North Carolina Press, 1942), 43–47.

25. Deed book 9, 523; John S. Duvall and Stuart Schwartz, *Research and Archeology, Halifax, North Carolina, the Playhouse Site* (Raleigh, NC: State Department of Archives and History, 1970), 5.

26. James D. Kornwolf, *Architecture and Town Planning in Colonial North America* (Baltimore: Johns Hopkins University Press, 2002), vol. 2, 835.

3   THE ANATOMY OF DESIRE

1. The list of goods is extracted from the inventory of the estate of David Douglass, *Inventories*, Liber 76, fol. 81r, Jamaica Archives, Spanish Town.
2. Cary Carson, "The Consumer Revolution in Colonial America: Why Demand?" in *Of Consuming Interests, the Style of Life in the Eighteenth Century*, Cary Carson, Ronald Hoffman, and Peter J. Albert, eds. (Charlottesville, VA: University Press of Virginia, 1994), 505.
3. A vivid portrait of his arrival is painted in Kenneth Silverman, *A Cultural History of the American Revolution* (New York: Thomas Cromwell, 1976), 91–92.
4. For a full description of the affair, see Philip M. Hamer, *The Papers of Henry Laurens* (Columbia, SC: South Carolina Historical Society, 1968), vol. v, 29–32.
5. The port was closed until February 1766; the courts were closed until April 1, 1766; as for merchants, Henry Drinker was speaking for his class when he recognized what the closing courts meant to merchants: "we shall not be able to commence Actions against Persons who are indebted to us not proceed legally in many other Respects, until it is some way Settled. In Short, we know not whose Lot it may be ruin'd." Quoted in Edmund Morgan and Helen Morgan, *The Stamp Act Crisis: Prologue to Revolution* (Chapel Hill, NC: University of North Carolina Press, 1995), 177.
6. For a general discussion on the consumer revolution, I am indebted to the following texts: Woodruff Smith, *Consumption and the Making of Respectability, 1600–1800* (New York: Routledge, 2002); Lorna Weatherill, *Consumer Behavior and Material Culture in Britain, 1660–1760* (London: Routledge, 1988); Richard Bushman, *The Refinement of America Persons, Houses, Cities* (New York: Alfred Knopf, 1992); Cary Carson et al., *Of Consuming Interests, the Style of Life in the Eighteenth Century* (Charlottesville, VA: University Press of Virginia, 1994).
7. Bushman, *The Refinement of America*, 410.
8. John Wayles to Farrell and Jones, August 30, 1766. T. H. Breen notes the same in New York advertisements, *The Marketplace of the Revolution: How Consumer Politics Shaped American Independence* (Oxford: Oxford University Press, 1965), 57.
9. Carl Bridenbaugh, *Gentleman's Progress: The Itinerarium of Dr. Alexander Hamilton* (Chapel Hill, NC: University of North Carolina Press, 1948), 7, 45.
10. Quoted in Wood, *The Radicalism of the American Revolution* (New York: Vintage Books, 1991), 117.

11. Dedicated playhouses were erected in at least the following known sites: Philadelphia (Society Hill), 1759, Annapolis, 1760; Williamsburg, 1760; Newport, 1761; New York (Chapel Street), 1761; Norfolk (?), 1762; Charleston (Queen Street), 1763; Petersburg (?), 1763; Philadelphia (Southwark), 1766; New York (John Street), 1767; Halifax, North Carolina, 1768; Halifax, Nova Scotia, 1768; Christiansted, St. Croix, 1770; Fredericksted, St. Croix, 1770; Annapolis, 1771; Baltimore, 1773; Charleston (Church Street), 1773; Kingston, Jamaica, 1775; Spanish Town, Jamaica, 1776.

12. Cary Carson, "The Consumer Revolution," 608–609.

13. Georg Simmel, "Fashion," *International Quarterly*, 10 (1904): 130–155.

14. A lamentable irony, but we know of the printer's attendance at the theatre in Bridgetown, Barbados, because the beam that supported the gallery above the front boxes broke and shattered the leg of the printer, broke his elder son's ankle, his younger son's ribs, bruised the shop foreman, and the collective damages to the staff closed the newspaper. The accident was reported in the paper's final edition, *Barbados Mercury*, December 4, 1784.

15. Woodruff Smith, *Consumption*.

16. Lois Green Carr and Lorena Walsh, "Changing Lifestyles and Consumer Behavior in the Colonial Chesapeake," in Carson et al., *Of Consuming Interests*. Jean-Christophe Agnew approached the subject of the theatre in the marketplace ("The Spectacle of the Market," in *Worlds Apart: The Market and the Theatre in Anglo-American Thought, 1550–1750* [Cambridge: Cambridge University Press, 1986]) but was primarily concerned with Samuel Pepys and the English theatre in the seventeenth century.

17. Two examples: the titular bridge of Bridgetown, Barbados, that collapsed during its inauguration and waited ten years for repair, and the bridge and streets of Baltimore that Dennis Ryan helped pave through a series of benefit performances in 1783. Both are discussed below.

18. Wood, *The Radicalism*, 35, 112–119.

19. Margaretta M. Lovell, "Painters and Their Customers: Aspects of Art and Money in Eighteenth Century America," in *Of Consuming Interests*, 285–286.

20. Thorstein Veblin, *Theory of the Leisure Class* (New York: Penguin, 1979), 116.

21. Alfred Spencer, ed., *Memoirs of William Hickey* (London: Knopf, 1923), vol. ii, 32.

22. Smith, *Consumption*, 32.

23. Hudson Muse, to his brother, *Original Letters*, 240–241.

24. One account of the detailed ordering of a governor's ball is found in Lady Nugent's journal. She is describing a fete in Jamaica, 1801:

    > The ball they are to give me occupies every one. What hour shall the ball begin? What door that I enter? &c . . . Start for the ball at 8, with a grand cavalcade. Received at the door with great ceremony; led in by two stewards, and followed by a large party of gentlemen, the music playing God Save the King. Immediately on my being seated on the state sopha, all the company came up and paid their compliments. I then opened the ball with Mr. Henry, one of the Members of the Parish, and really a gentleman-like man. After dancing a little, the carriages were ordered; but first I walked about the room with my suite, and after curtseying and making fine speeches, took my leave, with the same ceremonies with which I entered. (81)

25. On the back of an insert leaf into the account book of a New York leather merchant William Alexander Livingston can be found a page of theatre receipts, including an entry for May 17, 1773: "Paid for a box to the stage man 2 shillings and sixpence." *William Livingston Account Book*, ms. New York Historical Society. A nota bene to a 1778 playbill reads, "Gentlemen are earnestly requested not to attempt to bribe the Door-keeper." A facsimile is reproduced in Alonzo May's manuscript, Men and Women of the American Stage (Unpublished ms, Maryland Historical Society), 57.

26. See the many illustrations in Woodfall, T., *James Winston—The Theatric Tourist* (London: Harvard Theatre Collection, 1805).

27. Both the Williamsburg and Annapolis playhouses were remodeled to add a second tier of boxes. For the shortage, see Douglass's note in the *New York Mercury*, April 10, 1769: "The reasons why the pit is made box price, this evening, are first, in compliment to the gentlemen who are to perform; next, on account of a new set of scenes, which were painted at a great expense, for the occasion; and, because the demand for boxes has been so great, that the director of the theatre, could not, otherwise accommodate one half of the ladies and gentlemen who have applied for places."

28. These figures are culled from the unpublished collection of architectural drawings of James Winston, provincial theatre manager and amateur architect. His drawings are held in many archives, primarily the Theatre Museum at Covent Garden and the Harvard Theatre Collection.

29. James A. Bear, Jr. and Lucia C. Stanton, eds., *Jefferson's Memorandum Books* (Princeton, NJ: Princeton University Press, 1997), vol. I, 210–211. See also Odai Johnson, "Thomas Jefferson and the Colonial American Stage," *The Virginia Magazine of History and Biography*, 108:2 (2000): 139–154.

30. Bridenbaugh, *Itinerarium*, 19.
31. Morgan and Morgan, *The Stamp Act Crisis*, 161.
32. *Maryland Journal*, February 11, 1783.
33. *New York Journal*, January 7, 1768.
34. "Letter to the Board of Trustees of Georgia," in *The Colonial Records of the State of Georgia*, Kenneth Coleman, ed. (Athens, GA: University of Georgia Press, 1982), vol. xx. Julia Curtis speculates that the wellspring of the conversation was Henry Holt's Company in Charleston that was playing that winter.
35. Hallam's version of events was published in a public letter in the *New York Mercury*, July 2, 1753.
36. *George Gilmer Letterbook*, Colonial Williamsburg Foundation.
37. Williamsburg is the only County-town of James city County [York]; where the courts of common pleas are held monthly . . . The quarter sessions are also held quarterly . . . Besides these, there are two courts of oyer and terminer held annually . . . and likewise two general courts in April and October, which receive and determine appeals from every county, and all the interior courts, as well as try original causes for sums above twenty pounds. These, as also the courts of Chancery, courts of admiralty, and assemblies or parliaments, besides the college, occasion a great resort and concourse of people to Williamsburg; and are indeed the chief, if not the whole, support of the place: for her share of commerce is very inconsiderable, and she does not possess a single manufacture. From "Smyth's Travels in Virginia, in 1773," *Virginia Historical Register*, vol. VI, 14–15.
38. *George Gilmer Letterbook*, ms. in Colonial Williamsburg Foundation.
39. Lewis Hallam mortgaged the playhouse to John Stretch and Edward Charlton and defaulted on the arrears. Stretch was a printer in Williamsburg, and Charlton was a barber and peruke maker; both speculated in property. Both lost money to Hallam. Charles Bell, William Rigby, John Singleton, and Richard Scott, all actors in the company, all left debts to John Stretch, amounting to £28. Bell, Rigby, Singleton, and William Adcock all left another £14 in debts to Edward Charlton. Singleton, Rigby, and Bell left another £8.5s in debt to Alexander Craig for saddlery. Thomas Clarkson, another actor in the company, was in debt to Alex Finney, the tavern keeper, as was Charles Bell, both of whom defaulted on June 18, 1753. Stretch wrote on his account book below the actor's bills as follows: "if debts paid by 20 October, 1753, this is void." But accounts were not settled, bills were not paid, the actors defaulted, and on May 19, 1753, Hallam forfeited his playhouse to Stretch and Charlton for the company's debts. *Alexander Craig Account Book*

1749–1757, ms. Rockefeller Library; *York County Records, Judgements and Orders*, 1768–1770, vol. ii, 537–538.

40. Matthew Clarkson to "Dear John," New York Historical Society.

41. "Treatise by David Douglass," composed in New York in the winter of 1761–1762, published some years later in the *Pennsylvania Gazette*, March 5, 1767.

42. *Pennsylvania Gazette*, July 31, 1766.

43. Reprinted as "London News" in the *South Carolina Gazette* (Crouch), August 18, 1767.

44. "Letters of William Paine," *Proceedings of the Massachusetts Historical Society* (Boston: MA Historical Society, 1926), iii series, vol. 59, 422.

45. Kenneth Silverman, *A Cultural History*, 408.

46. *Nova Scotia Gazette*, August 11, 1768; August 18, 1768.

47. Ibid., August 11, 1768.

48. Ibid., August 25, 1768.

49. Ibid., August 18 and 25, 1768.

50. *The Royal Danish-American Gazette*, September 26, 1770.

51. *South Carolina Gazette*, August 9, 1773.

52. "Journal of Josiah Quincey, Jr.," *Massachusetts Historical Society Proceedings*, vol. XLIX (October 1915–June 1916): 441–442.

53. George O. Seilhamer, *History of the American Theatre* (Philadelphia: Globe Printing House), vol. I, 332.

54. *South Carolina Gazette*, September 20, 1773.

55. The petition was reprinted in the *South Carolina Gazette*, February 28, 1774.

56. Whitfield J. Bell, Jr., "Addenda to Watson's Annals of Philadelphia," in *The Pennsylvania Magazine of History and Bibliography* (Philadelphia: Historic Society of Pennsylvania, 1974), 143. Thomas Pike's life is summarized in Judith Cobau, "The Precarious Life of Thomas Pike, a Colonial Dancing Master in Charleston and Philadelphia," *Dance Chronicle*, 17:3 (1994): 229–262.

57. Thomas Wharton complained to Benjamin Franklin that the new governor of Pennsylvania, John Penn, was constantly at the theatre, and invited the players to dine with him. Thomas Wharton to B. Franklin, February 7, 1767. Cf. James H. Hutson, *Pennsylvania Politics* (Princeton, NJ: Princeton University Press, 1972), 81–82.

58. In Scotland, in mid-century, another patron, Edward Edlin, Scottish baron of the exchequer, wrote to Sir John Clerk on behalf of an unnamed actor from the Scottish stage who had applied for a government post. In a

prior letter, Clerk had cited legal objections that the players were to be regarded as alien, but Edlin lavished a long passage on both the merits of the actor and the unfounded legal objection to the profession itself. Sir John had also suggested that the player find an advocate, such as Robert Dundas (Lord Arniston, MP for Midlothian, and judge of the Court of Sessions); to both of these claims, Eldin countered,

> Players, I apprehend, have been in different Ages and Places in very different degrees of Repute. So that as we are disposed we may extol or despise them . . . As plays grew to be mixed with obscenities and Playhouses haunted by disorderly people, they have been discountenanced by all well disposed people of fashion and this to be sure gave rise to what is now rumaged out of the Civil Law from whence Lo. Coke no doubt takes, by way of Embellishment to his work the passage you send me. But it can no more be taken to be part of our Law than what he quotes in the same place out of Bracton, That an Alien born cannot be a witness. For I can assure you that a player can be as good a witness as the Bishop of Ross, though an alien born was allowed to be; for I myself saw Bowen [?] the player examined as a witness in a case of life and death before Lord Ch[ief] Justice Holt. The fate [state?] of players has been different in this country [Scotland]. The ministers have been furious against them. They are now greatly cooled. The Lord of Session [Robert Dundas] if I take it right have given them great countenance and they are now much encouraged by most sorts of people. But I hope will not any longer than they continue to act modest Plays, and their House is not infected with infamous women as the houses in London are. This, like many other things is of that nature that a man may take it in that light his inclination lead him to. But I say all this with regard to myself who would have him continue in the Profession he hath made a good Proficiency in. But as for him, he is desirous to quit it, and that is in the Reason of his present Application and therefore I make no doubt will leave the Stage directly if this objection swell so high as to make it necessary. National Archives of Scotland, ms. GD18/2919, Edward Edlin to Sir John Clerk.

The letter is undated but internal evidence suggests ca. 1750.

59. Devereux Jarratt, quoted in Rhys Isaac's *The Transformation of Virginia* (Chapel Hill, NC: University of North Carolina Press, 1982), 43.

60. *Edward Charleton Day Books*, August 19, 1770. The various designs of wigs and wig style could be further parsed to place the actor within the micro-hierarch: the physician's natty bob, the clergymen and scholar's "parson's wig," the merchant's bobbed wig with curled ends, or the merchant's brown wig, like the one Hugh Gaine wore and William Dunlap (*History of the American Theatre* [New York: J. Harper, 1832], 44) remarked on the industry it signified, were all part of a highly codified, if artificial, code of rank.

61. *Virginia Gazette* (Purdie and Dixon), April 30, 1772.

62. "The inhabitants of Philadelphia, like all citizens of the United States, are classified by their fortunes. The first class is composed of carriage folk." Charles Sherrill, *French Memories of Eighteenth Century America* (New York: Benjamin Blom, 1971), 47.

63. Reprinted as "London News" in the *South Carolina Gazette* (Crouch), August 18, 1767.

64. Kevin Sweeny, "High Style Vernacular: Lifestyles of the Colonial Elite," in *Of Consuming Interests*, 37.

65. I am indebted to Ed Chappel for the note on Elkanah Deane. See Edward Chappel's "Housing a Nation: The Transformation of Living Standards in Early America," in *Of Consuming Interests*, 188.

66. Bridenbaugh, *Itinerarium*, 122.

67. George Gilmore to Walter King, August 6, 1752, *George Gilmer Letterbook*, ms. Rockefeller library.

68. Edward Chappel, "Housing a Nation," *Of Consuming Interests*, 167–232 at 216.

69. When Douglass was called to defend the playhouse and its players against some detractors, he wrote this of himself for the *New York Mercury*, December 28, 1761: "Mr. Douglass, the director of the company, is of a good family, and has a genteel and liberal education; and if we may judge from behaviour, conduct, and conversation, has better pretensions to the name of a gentleman in every sense of the word, than he who so politely and generously lavishes the appellation of vagrant and stroller on him." Dunlap (*History*, 35) was probably thinking of the above passage when he wrote of him: "This man appears to have been by descent and education a gentleman." The charity donations are described in the *New York Mercury*, February 1, 1762.

70. *William Bradford ms*, books 14, file 1676, Historical Society of Pennsylvania; *Galt and Pasteur Account Book, 1770–1771*, 13, Rockefeller Library, Colonial Williamsburg. *New York Gazetteer*, June 30, 1774. See also the deed for the Southwark Theatre to Thomas Bradford cited above.

71. The following year when he remarried, the Kingston Parish Register recorded it: "David Douglass of the Parish of Kingston, Esq. and Mary Peters of the same Parish," Kingston Parish Register: Baptisms, Marriages, Burials, 1B/11/8/9:1.

72. T. H. Breen, "'Baubles of Britain': The American and Consumer Revolutions of the Eighteenth Century," in *Of Consuming Interest*, and the expanded treatment of the same idea in his *The Marketplace of Revolution*.

73. A summary of the articles of the Association is found in *The Virginia Gazette Extracts*, Barney Barnes, Colonial Williamsburg Foundation Library Research Report Series, 342, 3–5. For the full resolution, including the subscribers, see Julian Boyd, ed., *The Papers of Thomas Jefferson* (Princeton, NJ: Princeton University Press, 1950), vol. I, 43–47.
74. Worthington Ford, ed., *Journals of the Continental Congress 1774–1789* (Washington: U.S. Government Printing Office, 1904), vol. I, 78.
75. The *Pennsylvania Packet-Philadelphia*, October 17, 1778.

4 THE COUNTENANCE OF BROTHER DOUGLASS

1. William Dunlap, *History of the American Theatre* (New York: J. J. Harper, 1832), vol. i, 64.
2. Cadwallader Colden, *Letters and Papers of Cadwallader Colden* (New York: New York Historical Society, 1917), vol. 9, 236–237.
3. See Gordon Wood, *The Radicalism of the American Revolution* (New York: Vintage Books, 1991), 230ff.
4. Alfred Spencer, ed., *Memoirs of William Hickey* (London: Knopf, 1923), vol. ii, 22–23.
5. *Letters and Papers of Cadwallader Colden* (New York: New York Historical Society, 1917), vol. 6, 281–282.
6. Williamsburg, June 11 1761—The Company of Comedians under the direction of David Douglass have performed in this colony for near a twelvemonth; during which time they have made it their constant practice to behave with prudence and discretion in their private character, and to use their utmost endeavours to give general satisfaction in their public capacity. We have therefore thought proper to recommend them as a company whose behaviour merits the favour of the public, and who are capable of entertaining a sensible and polite audience. Published in *The Newport Mercury*, August 11, 1761.
7. See Introduction, n. 1.
8. "Mr. Douglass returns his most grateful thanks to the public, for the very generous countenance they have given to his Address. He begs leave to inform them, that the subscription is in great forewardness, and a considerable part of the money already collected, and deposited in the proper hands for carrying the design into execution; the receipts for which are lodged at Mr. Well's on the Bay, for the inspection of the subscribers," *South Carolina Gazette*, August 17, 1773.

9. Nathaniel Walthoe came to the colony of Virginia with Governor Dinwiddie in November of 1751 as the latter's secretary, and he served as secretary to Governor Botetout as well.

10. *The Treasure's Book of the Free and Accepted Masons*, ms. Colonial Williamsburg, Rockefeller Library.

11. Mark Leon has documented this great surge of the 1730s in "Georgian Order and Merchant Capitalism," in *The Recovery of Meaning, Historical Archaeology in the Eastern United States*, Mark Leon and Parker Potter, eds. (Washington: Smithsonian Institute Press, 1988). Particularly interesting is the table (7:1) that charts the percentage of wealth held by groups in Annapolis, from which he deduced by the early 1730s that 78 percent of the wealth was concentrated in the hands of 18 percent of the population.

12. William Moseley Brown, *Freemasonry in Virginia, 1733–1936* (Richmond, VA: Masonic Home Press, 1936), 14. The Queen Street Theatre hosted the Masons for an elaborate evening in Charleston, May 21, 1737, see the *South Carolina Gazette*, May 28, 1737.

13. Brown, *Freemasonry*, 15.

14. Paula Felder, *Fielding Lewis and the Washington Family: A Chronicle of 18th Century Fredericksburg* (Fredericksburg, VA: American History Company, 1998), 84.

15. See also his benefit, November 17, 1770, "After the play, an Epilogue in praise of Masonry, written and to be spoke by Mr. Verling, in Character of a Master Mason. Between the Acts will be introduced several Mason Songs, with a proper Chorus, &c. With entertainments of Dancing by Messers. Linck and Harris," *The Royal Danish-American Gazette*, November 14, 1770. We get a glimpse of the considerations of the lodge toward actor benefits from later in the century. From the *Columbian Herald*, March 23, 1795:

> Mr. Chambers having expressed a wish for the support of a fraternity of Ancient Masons on the occasion of his benefit, the present and past grand officers and the masters of several lodges being convened and taking into consideration the merits of that gentleman as a deserving brother and chaste actor and his superior talents in the vocal line . . . they recommend to the officers and members of the different lodges to countenance the said brother by their general attendance on the night of this benefit.

16. Richardson Wright started some work on the masonic connection of actors in the Caribbean. In Jamaica, David Douglass printed *The Elements*

of Freemasonry Delineated, 1782, which he and many other actors subscribed to. Wright's list includes Douglass, Hallam, Jr., Owen Morris, Stephen Woolls, Mr. Dermot, Isaac Morales, Richard Goodman, and Thomas Wignell—most of the male members of the American Company in Jamaica. See Richardson Wright, *Revels in Jamaica* (New York: Dodd, Mead, and Co., 1937), 175. The advantages to the membership is a study that still awaits an author.

17. The bylaws went even further to stipulate and fine for introducing such themes: "No discussions of Nation, religion, or politics are permitted to be introduced within the walls of a lodge." F. L. Brockett, *The Lodge of Washington* (Alexandria: George French, 1876), 41.

18. *New Hampshire Gazette*, November 13, 1772.

19. The most useful study is still Steven Bullock's *Ancient and Honorable Free Masonry in America*, 1730–1830, dissertation (Brown University, 1986). Thomas Wall would be listed as a "visiting brethren" in Fredericksburg, December 1770.

20. A photograph of a Masonic Certificate is preserved in the Massachusetts Historical Society.

21. Rivington advertised his *Pocket Companion* in the *New York Gazette* throughout November 1761 when Douglass and Company were on the boards at the Chapel Street playhouse. The text was probably based on one of the many "Pocket Companions" in circulation, like John Entick and William Smith's *Freemason's Pocket Companion* (Edinburgh: W. Cheyne, 1752).

22. Bullock, *Ancient and Honorable Free Masonry*, 54.

23. Ibid., 56.

24. Lawrence C. Wroth, *A History of Printing in Colonial Maryland*, 1686–1776 (Baltimore: Typothetae of Baltimore, 1922), 80–81.

25. Hugo Tatsch, *Freemasons in the Thirteen Colonies* (New York: Macoy, 1929), 60–61; see also Paul Leicester Ford, *The Journals of Hugh Gaine, Printer* (New York: Dodd, Mead, and Co., 1902), vol. i, 65. Abstracts of Wills, Liber 41 (New York Historical Society, 1905), vol. xiv, 281–282.

26. One could tease out the printer—Mason association and find a reputable list in the membership. Beyond Jonas Green, Hugh Gaine, and Robert Wells, there were Masonic Grand Masters Benjamin Franklin and Isaiah Thomas, both of whom had no little business in the print shop.

27. Philip M. Hamer, *The Papers of Henry Laurens* (Columbia, SC: South Carolina Historical Society, 1968), vol. ix, 332. Henry Laurens was also a mason and he records the great falling out the fraternity had with their Master over an illicit affair he had conducted with his sister-in-law.

See also Robert Mackey, *History of Freemasonry in South Carolina* (Columbia, SC: Wentworth Printing, 1998), 46–48.

28. Anne Cunningham, ed., *Letters and Diary of John Rowe* (Boston: W. B. Clarke, 1903), 190. For masonic dinners, see ibid., 223, 258, 259.

29. Douglass next moved up to Portsmouth, New Hampshire, and again availed himself of his masonic membership. He advertised his performances at the Staver's Inn, where the St. John Lodge regularly met. John Wentworth was the contact there, a Freemason and nephew to Governor Benning Wentworth. See Paul Wilderson, *Governor John Wentworth and the American Revolution: The English Connection* (Hanover, NH: University Press of New England, 1994).

30. Hallam arrived in Williamsburg in the first week of June and opened on September 15, but he also lost 11 days when the Georgian Calendar was adjusted on September 5, 1752.

31. The playhouse was certainly opened by October 2 when William Allason, a Falmouth merchant, noted in his daybook, "paid for play tickets at Fredericksburg and Williamsburg about 3 [£]."

32. John Watson, *Annals of Philadelphia and Pennsylvania in the Olden Time* (Philadelphia: J. B. Lippincott and Co., 1870), vol. I, 471.

33. Hornblow's version is admittedly the most extreme: "There was the most determined opposition on the part of the Quakers to any attempt to introduce play-acting. While the players had many warm friends and supporters in Philadelphia, the anti-theatrical party was in the majority. This hostile element did everything possible to check and harass the players, involving the existing statutes, causing new and more severe laws to be passed, and organizing meetings of protest." Arthur Hornblow, *A History of the Theatre in America* (Philadelphia: Lippincott, 1919), 2 vols, 52–53.

34. For their early history, see Hugo Tatsch, *Freemasons*. For the early Philadelphia Lodge, the St. John's Lodge, see Julius Sachse's "Roster of the Lodge of Free and Accepted Masons which Met at the Tun Tavern, Philadelphia," *Pennsylvania Magazine of History and Biography* (Philadelphia: Historical Society of Pennsylvania, 1896), vol. 20, 116–121. The Tun Tavern was also the meeting place of the Governor's Club, a sort of Philadelphian equivalent of the Annapolis' Tuesday Club.

35. Henry S. Borneman, *Early Freemasonry and Pennsylvania* (Philadelphia: The Grand Lodge of Pennsylvania, 1931), 98–99.

36. Julius Sachse, "Roster of the Lodge," 116–121.

37. Melvin Johnson "The Minutes of the Meeting of the Tun Tavern Lodge," reproduced in facsimile in *The Beginning of Freemasonry in America* (New York: George Doran Company, 1924) 358, 363.

38. Ibid., 363.
39. Sachse, "Roster of the Lodge," 116–121. Of the additional names, Mr. Moore is most interesting. William Moore, actor with the Murray–Kean Company in Philadelphia 1749, New York 1750–1751, would later join the American Company and travel with them to Jamaica. He would remain an active mason throughout his career and would deliver many prologues and poetic orations on masonry from the stage in Kingston. He would also author *The Elements of Freemasonry Delineated*, published by David Douglass and William Aikman, Jamaica, 1782.
40. Quoted in Marshall Wingfield, *History of Caroline County, Virginia* (Richmond, VA: Trevent Christian and Co., 1924), 101.
41. Bullock, *Ancient and Honorable Free Masonry*, 57.
42. *South Carolina Gazette*, December 28, 1754.
43. See e.g., his benefit in Philadelphia on November 2, 1759, as announced in the *Pennsylvania Gazette*, November 1, 1759.
44. *New York Gazette*, December 28, 1761.
45. *South Carolina and American General Gazette*, April 15–22, 1774.
46. In 1769, e.g., the Kilwinning Port Royal Lodge appointed a committee to visit lodges at Fredericksburg, Tappahannock, and Falmouth to solicit subscribers to aid in building a lodge. Sufficient subscribers were not found. Wingfield, *History of Caroline County*, 103.
47. *Pennsylvania Gazette*, October 14, 1772, and see below.
48. Lanaghan Flannigan, *Antigua and the Antiguans: A Full Account of the Colony and Its Inhabitants from the Time of the Caribs to the Present Day* (London: Saunders and Otley, 1844), 211–212.
49. *The Journal of a Lady of Quality*, Evangeline Andrews, ed. (New Haven, CT: Yale University Press, 1922), 122.
50. Richardson Wright has identified two editions of this text, the original published by Douglass and Aikman in Kingston and a second edition printed in Montego Bay. See Wright's "Masonic Contacts with the Early American Stage," *American Lodge of Research Transactions* (1936), vol. 2, 161–187.

5   MRS. WARREN'S PROFESSION

1. *Massachusetts Spy-Boston*, December 19, 1771.
2. Alexander Graydon, *Memoirs of His Own Times* (Philadelphia: n.p., 1846), 88.
3. I am working from the faintly preserved UMI microfilm edition. The author wishes to acknowledge the compilers of *The Performing Arts in*

Colonial American Newspapers database against which many of the following newspaper accounts have been checked. Although the database is probably wrong on this particular entry, this does not diminish its enormous usefulness.

4. *Pennsylvania Gazette* #307, April 29–May 6, 1736.

5. I am speaking collectively here of the *Boston News-Letter*, the *Boston Gazette*, the *New England Courant*, the *Boston Evening Post Boy, Boston Post Boy, Boston Chronicle*, and *Massachusetts Spy-Boston*. Some, like the *Boston News-Letter*, were very stable, but most were all under many editorships and printers. For particular editorships I would refer the interested to what is still the most thorough discussion of colonial newspapers: Isaiah Thomas, *The History of Printing in America* (1810, repr. New York: Weathervane, 1970).

6. The *Boston Gazette* was not alone in this strategy. See also *Pennsylvania Gazette* #307, April 29–May 6, 1736: "Friday last week the wife of a Shoe-Blacer in Fetter Lane came home so much intoxicated with Geneva, that she fell on the Fire and was burnt in a miserable manner, so that she immediately died, and her Bowels burst out."

7. See William Clapp, *Record of the Boston Stage* (Boston: J. Munroe & Co., 1853); Hugh Rankin, *The Theatre in Colonial America* (Chapel Hill, NC: University of North Carolina Press, 1960). For antitheatrical attitudes, see Edmund S. Morgan, "Puritan Hostility to the Theatre," *American Philosophical Society, Proceedings* 110 (October 1966): 340–347.

8. Some discussion about what constituted "news" may be helpful here: in the same paper, the same editor, John Campbell, some years later prided himself on the currency of his foreign intelligence by doubling the size of his sheet: "we were then [1718] 13 months behind with the Foreign News beyond Great Britain, and now less than Five Months, so that by the Sheet we have retrieved about 8 months since January last, and any One that has the News Letter since that time, to January next (life permitted) will be accommodated with all the News of Europe &c. contained in the Publick Prints of London that are needful for to be known in these parts" (*Boston News-Letter*, August 10, 1719).

9. *Boston Gazette*, November 29–December 6, 1736.

10. Ibid.

11. *Boston News-Letter*, July 14, 1757.

12. Ibid., August 17–24, 1719.

13. *Boston Evening Post*, October 29, 1764.

14. *Boston Post Boy*, May 21, 1770; *Boston Gazette*, June 12, 1750.

15. *Boston Evening Post*, July 31, 1749.

16. *Boston Gazette*, August 31, 1767.
17. *Boston Evening Post*, May 28, 1750.
18. *Boston News-Letter*, May 26, 1748.
19. George Willard, *History of the Providence Stage, 1762–1891* (Providence, RI: News Company, 1891), 4.
20. The Linonian Society was very active between 1754 and 1773. Several texts of plays from Dartmouth College produced during the 1770s have also survived. A full study of the impact of academic drama in colonial America, particularly in New England, is a field that is in want of a scholar.
21. Robert Brand Hanson, ed., *The Diary of Dr. Nathaniel Ames of Dedham, Massachusetts* (Camden, ME: Picton Press, 1998), 12–14.
22. Cf. *Records of the Massachusetts Colonial Society*, 48, 295.
23. Hanson, *The Diary of Dr. Nathaniel Ames*, 28–30.
24. *Boston News-Letter*, December 27, 1759.
25. The March 27, 1760 issue of the *Maryland Gazette* reprints a letter from "a late Boston Paper" that offers an account of a company of gentlemen who "amused themselves and their friends by a representation of . . . *Cato*." Cf. *Boston Post Boy*, January 7, 1760. Hanson, *The Diary of Dr. Nathaniel Ames*, 44–47.
26. Hanson, *The Diary of Dr. Nathaniel Ames*, 44, 45, 47.
27. How's Tavern, run at the time by Ezekiel How in Sudbury, was later immortalized as the Wayside Inn, where Longfellow recuperated after the death of his wife and composed his famous tales. It is still, the brochures tell us, the oldest operating inn in America.
28. Ames records his "General Prologue which I wrote for *The Toy Shop*, acted at Battles the 20th April 1772" in Hanson, *The Diary of Dr. Nathaniel Ames*, 244–245.
29. College Book, ms. Harvard College Library Archives, vol. vii (November 16, 1762), 101.
30. The full prologue is printed in Hanson, *The Diary of Dr. Nathaniel Ames*, 244.
31. Anne Cunningham, ed., *Letters and Diary of John Rowe* (Boston: W. B. Clarke, 1903), 77.
32. Heather Nathans, *Early American Theatre from the Revolution to Thomas Jefferson, into the Hands of the People* (Cambridge, UK: Cambridge University Press, 2003), 24.
33. *Boston Gazette*, April 13, 1767.
34. B. W. Brown, *The Colonial Theatre in New England* (Newport, RI: Newport Historical Society, 1930), 17.

35. Hanson, *The Dairy of Dr. Nathaniel Ames*, 63, 69.
36. Samuel Arnold, *History of the State of Rhode Island* (New York: D. Appleton and Co., 1878), vol ii, 238.
37. *Boston Evening Post*, April 6, 1767.
38. Ibid., March 13, 1769.
39. Ibid., March 20, 1769. Mounting theatricals was only one of the many grievances against the garrisoned troops. The conduct of the troops found its best expression in *The Journal of the Times*, a collection of articles and editorials compiled by Bostonians and published to make their condition known to Parliament and their fellow colonists. The same week of the military performances, the *Journal* recorded, "Instances of the licentious and outrageous behavior of the military conservators of the peace still multiply upon us, some of which are of such nature, and have been carried to so great lengths, as must serve fully to evince that a late vote of this town, calling upon the inhabitants to provide themselves with arms for their defense, was a measure as prudent as it was legal." *Journal of the Times*, March 17, 1769.
40. "Letters of William Paine," *Proceedings of the Massachusetts Historical Society*, 3rd series, vol. 59 (Boston, 1926), 442.
41. "A well regulated theatre has ever been held, by the wisest and most learned men of the present age, a matter of the highest utility; not only, as the most rational entertainment human nature is capable of enjoying, but, in being highly conducive to enlarge the mind, polish the manners, and while it entertains and improves, is as it were, to use the words of that great judge of nature, Shakespeare, to 'shew virtue her own image.' " New York, 1762; *Pennsylvania Chronicle*, January 26–February 2, 1767; *Maryland Gazette*, September 6, 1770; October 4, 1770; *South Carolina Gazette*, September 20, 1773; *Cornwall Chronicle* (Montego Bay, Jamaica), February 15, 1777.
42. Hugo Tatsch, *Freemasons in the Thirteen Colonies* (New York: Macoy, 1929), 34–35.
43. John Cary, *Joseph Warren, Physician, Politician Patriot* (Urbana, IL: University of Illinois, 1961), 55.
44. Hanson, *The Diary of Dr. Nathaniel Ames*, 18, n. 1.
45. *Boston News-Letter*, September 28, 1769.
46. "The Diary of John Rowe," *Proceedings of the Massachusetts Historical Society*, 2nd series, vol. X (Boston, 1896), 11–108 at 28.
47. *New Hampshire Gazette*, September 25, 1772. For Morgan's season in Portsmouth, 1772–1773, see Odai Johnson and William Burling, *The Colonial American Stage: A Documentary Calendar* (London: Associated University Presses, 2001).

48. Harold Rugg, "The Dartmouth Plays, 1779–1782," *Theatre Annual* (The Theatre Library Association, 1942), 55–69.
49. *Boston News-Letter*, April 1, 1773.
50. "The Diary of John Rowe," 23. Nicholas Cresswell, *The Journal of Nicholas Cresswell 1774–1777* (New York: Dial Press, 1924), 23.
51. *New York Mercury* (Gaine), October 12, 1772.
52. *Boston Gazette*, May 26, 1773.
53. For her career, see Jeffery Richards, *Mercy Otis Warren* (New York: Twayne, 1995).
54. Arthur Quinn, *A History of the American Dream from the Beginning to the Civil War* (New York: Harper, 1923).
55. John Leacock's *The Fall of British Tyranny; or, American Liberty Triumphant* was subtitled "A Tragi-Comedy in Five Acts, as Lately Planned at the Royal Theatrum Pandemonium at St. James" and was published in Philadelphia, 1776, but John Watson, in his *Annals of Philadelphia and Pennsylvania in the Olden Time* (Philadelphia: J. B. Lippincott and Co., 1870) suggests that the play was also performed. Watson quotes a correspondent as saying that Leacock "wrote a play with good humor called British Tyranny. The Fall of British Tyranny seems impossible to act, but apparently it was performed before it was printed, for there are a prologue and an epilogue with the names of the speakers. It was performed by amateurs in Philadelphia in 1776." Paul L. Ford ascribes its authorship to Leacock. The culminating moment in this modality becomes reified with the *Blockade of Boston* during which the theatrical vision is perforated, quite suddenly, by a surprise attack of the colonists. For a complete list, see Frank Pierce Hill, *American Plays Printed 1714–1830* (Stanford, CA: Stanford University Press, 1934). For discussion, see Jared Brown, *The Theatre in American during the Revolution* (Cambridge: Cambridge University Press, 1995).
56. "The Theatre of the Universe; or, The Great Assize," (Evans 13182), ascribed to Rowland Hill, broadside in the American Antiquarian Society. The broadside saw great circulation in early America with surviving copies issued in Boston (ca. 1775), Baltimore (1774), Vermont (1789), and New York (1798).
57. Hanson, *The Diary of Dr. Nathaniel Ames*, 132.

6 ASSUMING THE WALL

1. "Papers Relating to Provincial Affairs," Pennsylvania Archives, 2nd series (Harrisburg, 1878), vol. vii, 70–72.

2. These bills may have been printed locally by Andrew Bradford, the only printer in Philadelphia in 1723, or the performer carried a stock of them, like legal documents, with blanks for writing in the dates.

3. Outside the capitals, beyond the print shops, managers like Douglass carried blank playbills with the title, dates, place, and price of the evening's play to be penciled in. One such paybill is preserved in the Rockefeller Library, printed in Williamsburg for performances in Fredericksburg. Below the evening's play and farce, the next three evenings are handwritten.

4. Playbills in Colonial Williamsburg's Rockefeller Library.

5. Whitfield J. Bell, Jr. "Addenda to Watson's Annals of Philadelphia," *Pennsylvania Magazine of History and Biography* (Philadelphia: Pennsylvania Historical Society, 1974), vol. 158.

6. March 30, 1770 preserved in the Historical Society of Pennsylvania; December 16, 1772, found tucked in a file of old newspapers, is now preserved in the Library Company of Philadelphia. An inventory from the print shop of Douglass and William Aikman, Kingston, confirms that red ink was available and used, as red vials were among the items inventoried. *Inventories*, Liber 76, fol. 81r, Registry Office, Spanish Town, Jamaica.

7. *New York Evening Post*, May 4, 1752.

8. The brief list of surviving playbills is printed in Edwin Wolfe II, "Colonial American Playbills," *Pennsylvania Magazine of History and Biography* (Philadelphia: Historical Society of Pennsylvania, 1973), vol. 97, 99–106. Wolfe's list includes two playbills the originals of which can no longer be located.

9. Sybil Rosenfeld reprints such a list from the Kentish Circuit, 1739, in *Strolling Players and Drama in the Provinces, 1660–1765* (Cambridge, UK: Cambridge University Press, 1939), 232.

10. See C. William Miller, ed., *Benjamin Franklin's Philadelphia Printing* (Philadelphia: American Philosophical Society, 1974), 464.

11. See William Bradford's Account Books 1742–1775, *William Bradford ms.* 14, file 1676, Pennsylvania Historical Society for a list of plays advertised in Bradford's *Gazette* between June and August of 1759. The bill to Gaine is recorded in a published ledger printed in the *New York Mercury* for February 1, 1762. Later, the British military players in occupied New York published an account of their expenditures for the 1780–1781 season in which large unparsed sum went to Hugh Gaine for "Printing, Advertising, and Stationary" (British Military Theatre, 159).

12. *The Virginia Gazette Day Books of Joseph Royle, 1750–1752 and 1764–1766*, ms. Rockefeller Library, Williamsburg.

13. *New York Mercury*, February 1, 1762.
14. William Willcox, ed., *Papers of Benjamin Franklin* (New Haven, CT: Yale University Press, 1973), vol. 17, 129–131. The relationship between players and printers suffers no lasting damage as at the death of John Henry, then comanager of the American Company, Hugh Gaine was named an executor. Henry also made provisions in his will for three separate printers, Gaine, James Rivington, and Hugh Smith. *Abstracts of Wills*, Liber 41 (New York Historical Society, 1905), vol. xiv, 281–282.
15. Chapter XXXVII, 209–210.
16. *Pennsylvania Gazette*, November 17, 1773.
17. From Hird's *Annals of Bedale*, quoted in Mark Howell, "The Theatre at Richmond, Yorkshire," *Theatre Notebook*, vol. xlvi (1992), 1, 30–40 at 31.
18. *Pennsylvania Chronicle*, September 18–25, 1769.
19. *New York Mercury*, February 1, 1762. The same itemized account indicates that printer Hugh Gaine received £5.10s "for two sets of bills, advertisements, and commissions." One might also note in the same account that the company also employed a drummer to beat the street.
20. Undated clipping inserted in Joseph Ireland's expanded and extra-illustrated edition of *Records of the New York Stage*, prepared for Augustin Daly, with engravings and illustrations by Augustus Toedteberg (New York: T. H. Morrell, 1867), vol. i, 75, Harvard Theatre Collection.
21. E. G. Swem, "Notes from the Meeting of the President and Masters of the College," *William and Mary Quarterly*, 1st series, vol. v, 168–171.

PART II CARETAKERS OF MEMORY

1. *Pennsylvania Gazette*, December 22, 1768.
2. *Massachusetts Spy-Boston*, October 1, 1772.
3. Fredric Jameson reminds us that we never really confront a text as "a thing in itself. Rather, texts come before us as the always-already-read." *The Political Unconscious, Narrative as a Socially Symbolic Act* (Ithaca, NY: Cornell University Press, 1981), 9.

7 SPOILING NICE STORIES

1. *Accomac County Records*, vol. 1663–1666, fol. 102.
2. The performance was first noted by Philip Alexander Bruce in response to an article by William J. Neidig, "The First Play in America," published in *The Nation* (vol. 88) on January 28, 1909. Frederick Lewis responded in

the following issue (February 11) with early French plays in Quebec, and Philip Bruce furnished the details in the same journal of the Accomac County performance, pp. 135–136. Hornblow may have derived his information from these pages, though he cites J. C. Wise's work *Ye Kingdome of Accawmacke or the Eastern Shore of Virginia in the Seventeenth Century* (1911; repr. Baltimore: Regional, 1967).

3. William Dunlap wrote the first *History of the American Theatre* (New York: J. J. Harper, 1832), though as subsequent historians have pointed out, Dunlap's account is more properly an actor's memoir, as it is concerned primarily with his own contributions. Franics Wemyss produced an honorary volume, *The Chronology of the American Stage* (New York: Benjamin Blom, 1968), for the centennial of the opening of the Hallam Virginia season in 1852. George Seilhamer left an ambitious and well-researched *History of the American Theatre* (Philadelphia: Globe Printing House, 1889–1891), largely as a critique of Dunlap, a work Hornblow repeatedly dismisses. Charles Daly published a series of lectures, *The First Theatre in America* (New York: Burt Franklin, 1896). Many of these works are discussed below.

4. Hugh Rankin, opening *The Theatre in Colonial America* (Chapel Hill, NC: University of North Carolina Press, 1960), 1, would employ the same metaphor, modulating the subjects. He described the early settlers in colonial America as having no need for drama as they were themselves "actors in the more pressing true-life drama of carving homes out of the wilderness and the struggle for survival in hostile surroundings."

5. Inga Clendinnen, "Fierce and Unnatural Cruelty" in *New World Encounters*, Stephen Greenblatt, ed. (Berkeley, CA: University of California Press, 1993), 12–47.

6. Charles Durang, *The Philadelphia Stage from 1749 to 1821*, run as a serial in the *Philadelphia Sunday Dispatch*, 5.

7. Arthur Hornblow, *A History of the Theatre in America* (Philadelphia: Lippincott, 1919), vol. i, 21, 88, 223, and passim. Beyond the headlines, there is a ubiquitous assumption running throughout the work that theatre was essentially an oppositional space: "that so little should be known of the early beginnings of the acted drama in American [eighteenth century] is not surprising when one considers the intolerance of the age against the theatre and the player. In the face of almost general condemnation of the playhouse the journals of the day were not encouraged to give much, if any, space in their slender columns to the doings of player-folk" (ibid., 23). Glen Hughes in his *History of the American Theatre 1750–1860* (New York: Samuel French, 1951; 30–32), also retains many of Hornblow's title headings— "Douglass invades New England," "Douglass vs. New York," and the recent

compilers of the time line of Theatrical Events in America in *The Cambridge History of American Theatre*, vol. i, have also found the phrase "Douglass invades New England" (vol. i, 37) useful.

8. Hornblow, *A History*, 119.

9. Edmund Morgan, "Puritan Hostility to the Theatre," *American Philosophical Society, Proceedings* 110 (Philadelphia, 1966): 340–347 at 340.

10. Arthur Quinn, *A History of the American Drama from the Beginning to the Civil War* (New York: Harper, 1923), 1.

11. O. G. Sonneck, *Early Opera in America* (New York: Benjamin Blom, 1943), 44.

12. Ibid., 30, 31; Sonneck (32), speaking of the New York season of 1762: "Originally Douglass received leave only for sixteen performances, but such was the resourcefulness of this remarkable man that he forced a season of five months on the authorities."

13. Rankin, *The Theatre in Colonial America*, 108–111.

14. Ibid., 101 For more contemporary scholarship indebted to similar themes, see Kenneth Silverman's (*A Cultural History of the American Revolution* [New York: Thomas Cromwell, 1976]), Cynthia Adams Hoover's "Music and Theatre in the Lives of Eighteenth Century Americans," in Carson et al. *of Consuming Interest*, and, most recently, Heather Nathan's *Early American Theatre from the Revolution to Thomas Jefferson, into the Hands of the People* (Cambridge: Cambridge University Press, 2003), though an excellent study of emerging American identity in the Federalist period, nonetheless derives its model of American attitudes toward theatre from the opposition in Boston and Philadelphia and not from the support it received in the Southern colonies of Virginia, South Carolina, and Maryland, where the theatre was, as David Douglass wrote of it, "warmly countenanced and Supported by the publick."(*Virginia Gazette*, June 16, 1774). Parsing out cities like Williamsburg, Baltimore, Annapolis, and Charleston, where the patronage was historically warm, allowed Nathans a construction of America and its theatre based on the operational assumption that theatre arrived against its culture, and indeed even risks fetishizing the opposition.

15. Harold Shiffler, "Religious Opposition to the Eighteenth Century Theatre in Philadelphia," *Educational Theatre Journal*, October 1962, 215–223 at 218.

16. For the best summary of both the antitheatrical legislation and the politics that surround them, see Peter Davis, "Puritan Mercantilism and the Politics of Anti-Theatrical Legislation in Colonial America," in *The American Stage and Economic Issues from the Colonial Period to the Present* (Cambridge University Press, 1993).

17. Extract of a letter from Newport, dated September 10, 1761, and published in the *Boston Gazette*, September 21, 1761.

18. B. W. Brown, *The Colonial Theatre in New England* (Newport, RI: Newport Historical Society, 1930), 17–18. Brown qualifies the account with the following footnote: "This legend is generally accepted. It is not documented."

19. William Dunlap, *History*, 21.

20. Ibid., 38–39. Durang, *The Philadelphia Stage*, 10.

21. William Clark, *The Irish Stage in the Country Towns 1720–1800* (Oxford: Oxford University Press, 1965), 1.

22. James Dibdin, *Annals of the Edinburgh Stage* (Edinburgh, 1888), 20. Dibdin (20–25) summarizes the whole account in his study, including the conclusion that William Shakespeare was among the English comedians at Edinburgh.

23. *Pennsylvania Gazette*, October 4, 1753.

24. Peter Kalm, *Travels into North America* (Barre, MA, The Imprint Society, 1972) 28–29.

25. Whitefield's followers in Philadelphia were known as the New-lights, and in 1750 their body was large enough to build a church, the new Presbyterian church, in the northwestern part of the town.

26. Alexander Mackaby to his brother, June 20, 1770; Mackaby, *Extracts from the Letters*, 494.

27. Hugh Rankin, *The Colonial Theatre; Its History and Operations*, PhD thesis (Chapel Hill, NC: University of North Carolina Press, 1959), 278; cf. *The Theatre in Colonial America* (Chapel Hill, NC: University of North Carolina Press, 1960), 139.

28. Pennsylvania Archives, 1st series, vol. iii, Samuel Hazard, ed. (Philadelphia: 1853), 659–660.

29. *Boston Evening Post*, April 23, 1750; see also the *Act to Prevent Theatricals* printed in the same issue.

8   CASE STUDIES

1. John Watson, *Annals of Philadelphia and Pennsylvania in the Olden Time* (Philadelphia: J. B. Lippincott and Co., 1870), vol. I, 471.

2. Edward F. De Lancey, *Chief Justice William Allen, Pennsylvania Magazine*, vol. 1 (Philadelphia: Historical Society of Pennsylvania, 1877), 202–211 at 206.

3. Carl Bridenbaugh and Jessica Bridenbaugh, *Rebels and Gentlemen, Philadelphia in the Age of Franklin* (New York: Oxford University Press, 1965), 189.

4. Ibid., 12.
5. From *Votes of the Pennsylvania Assembly*, 8th series, vol. iv, Gertrude Mackinney, ed. (Philadelphia: Pennsylvania Historical Society, 1931), 3302–3303.
6. Ibid., 3310–3311.
7. In January of 1750, it was passed as a bill, but such a bill that carried with it little legislative force.
8. Paul Nelson, *William Tryon and the Course of Empire* (Chapel Hill, NC: University of North Carolina Press, 1990), 33.
9. Peter Davis, "Puritan Mercantilism and the Politics of Antitheatrical Legislation in Colonial America," in *The American Stage: Social and Economic Issues from the Colonial Period to the Present* (Cambridge, UK: Cambridge University Press, 1993).
10. *Minutes of the Common Council of the City of Philadelphia, 1704–1776* (Philadelphia, 1847), 512–523. The players' culpability in disorder of the streets was the same objection the Quaker-controlled Assembly would employ against David Douglass when he applied for permission to play ten years later: "the great numbers of disorderly persons drawn together in the night to the great distress of many poor families" (Act for Suppressing Lotteries and Plays, Bridenbaugh, *Rebels and Gentlemen*, 144).
11. From the *Gentleman's Magazine*, vol. XXII, April 1752, 190.
12. *Pennsylvania Gazette*, October 6, 1763.
13. Edward Shippen, writing from London to James Burd in Philadelphia, August 1, 1749: "You acquaint me of your acting a play last Winter to the Satisfaction of all Spectators . . . I am glad that Spirit is kept up, because it is an amusement the most useful of any to Young People and I heartily wish it would spread to ye younger sort, I mean School Boys."
14. When Dr. Hamilton passed through Albany he wearied of the place: "where was no variety or choise, either of company or conversation, and one's ears perpetually invaded and molested with volleys of rough sounding Dutch," Carl Bridenbaugh, *Gentleman's Progress: The Itinerarium of Dr. Alexander Hamilton* (Chapel Hill, NC: University of North Carolina Press, 1948), 69.
15. *Mrs. Grant's American Lady*, quoted in Joel Munsell, *Annals of Albany* (Albany, NY: Joel Munsell, 1869), vol. i, 116–117.
16. Ibid., 117.
17. Ibid., 118.
18. The full account can be found in Munsell's *Annals of Albany*, vol. i, 113–119.
19. Ibid., 120.

20. A mixed reception still awaited actors as late as 1784 when Mr. Allen brought a company up the Hudson. In December of that year the company leased the old hospital—the same site Douglass had played in—and refitted it once again to a playhouse. Munsell (*Annals of Albany*, vol. i, 295) relates how a local faction of detractors attempted to prohibit the players: "but the common council determined by a vote of 9 to 4, that they had no legal right to prohibit theatrical exhibitions in the city. A whole number of the *Gazette* is taken up with the controversy, to the exclusion of every other subject."

21. George Scull, ed., *The Montresor Journals* (New York: Collections of the New York Historical Society, 1881), 362.

22. Further discussion on the populist resistance to the Stamp Act is found in Gary Nash, *The Urban Crucible* (Cambridge, MA: Harvard University Press, 1979), 184–199.

23. William Sabine, ed., *Historical Memoirs of William Smith* (New York: Colburn and Tegg, 1956), 31–32.

24. Gaine announced his cessation of the *New York Mercury* on October 28, 1765, and reissued as a newssheet, November 4, 1765, with the header. Paul Leicester Ford, *The Journals of Hugh Gaine, Printer* (New York: Dodd, Mead, and Co., 1902), vol. i, 112–115. In Philadelphia, Franklin and Hall used the same device for their *Pennsylvania Gazette*.

25. E. B. O'Callaghan, ed., *Documents Relative to the Colonial History of the State of New York 1856–1887*, vol. vii, 806, 811.

26. Sabine, *Historical Memoirs*, 31.

27. Montresor records a few of their actions, including his entry of April 27, 1766: "Sons of Liberty will not suffer any Lamb to be brought to market nor eat, under penalty of having the offenders house pulled down" (362–363).

28. Capt. Montressor. "The Journals of Capt. Montessor," *Collections of the New York Historical Society for 1881*. G. D. Scull, ed. (New York: New York Historical Society), 357.

29. On April 26, 1766, Benjamin Kissam wrote to John Jay describing the uncertainty of New York: "We were last night strangely deluded with a mistaken account of the Repeal of the Stamp Act; and all the Bells have been ringing since Break of Day. Upon Enquirey We find That the Intelligence amounts to no more than that the Bill had passed the House of Commons on the 28 of February and was to be sent up to the Lords on the 3rd of March." Richard Morris, ed., *John Jay, The Making of a Revolutionary* (New York: Harper & Row, 1975), 81.

30. May 8, 1766; *Maryland Gazette*, May 22, 1766.

31. Nash, *The Urban Crucible*, 160.
32. Joseph Ireland, *Records of the New York Stage* (New York: T. H. Morrell, 1867), vol. i, 40–41.
33. Montresor, *Journal*, 364.
34. Ibid., 336.

9   THE BURNING OF THE LENA EDWIN

1. *New York Evening Post*, February 4, 1751.
2. *Gentleman's Magazine*, January 1749, 31.
3. Brooks McNamara, *The American Playhouse in the Eighteenth Century* (Cambridge, MA: Harvard University Press, 1969), 59–61.
4. T. Allston Brown, *A History of the New York Stage* (New York: Dodd, Mead and Co., 1902), preface, vii–viii.
5. Ibid., vol. i, 2. Brown claims that the plays were advertised in *Bradford's New York Gazette*, from the pages of which he extracts several notices of concerts as well. The notices have not survived.
6. *New York Times*, November 29, 1872, 8.
7. The map, *Plan of the City of New York*, is reprinted in Odell, vol. i, facing p. 12. McNamara, as well, reprints the map with a discussion (*The American Playhouse*, 8–12).
8. This habit exacerbates the problem of Brown's credibility. The opening passage that describes the Heady company in New York in 1732–1734, for example, misdates the Stamp Act riots by two years (1764), makes several alarming statements, the most glaring of which is his last in which he conflates John Moody's recruits traveling to Jamaica with the Murray–Kean Company arriving in Philadelphia: "In the winter of 1749 a company crossed the Atlantic. It consisted of Mesrs. Smith, Daniels, Douglass, Kershaw, and Morris, and their wives, and Miss Hamilton, the latter playing the leading business. This organization continued in New York for a season of eight months." On the following page Brown quotes the bill for the opening of the theatre, December 7, 1767, that concludes with a line that must have been simply inserted into the text: "Messrs. Douglas, Hallam & Henry, Managers." John Henry (21) had only joined the company three months earlier, and he and Lewis Hallam would not undertake the management of it until Douglass retired, a dozen years later. Brown, *History of the New York Stage*, 2, 7. The entry for David Douglass in Brown's *History of the American Stage* (repr; New York: Burt Franklin, 1969) erred by 35 years when claiming Douglass retired from the stage in 1812. None of which bolsters Brown's reputation for precision.

9. Quoted in Brown's preface to *A History of the New York Stage*, viii.

10. George Odell, *Annals of the New York Stage* (New York: Columbia University Press, 1927), 11.

11. Thomas Sharp, *A Dissertation on the Pageants or Dramatic Mysteries Anciently Performed at Coventry* (Coventry: Merridew and Son, 1825). A discussion on the reliability of Sharp's transcriptions is found in *The Cambridge Companion to Medieval English Theatre*, Richard Beadle, ed. (Cambridge, UK: Cambridge University Press, 1994), 28, 312–313.

12. John Bernard, *Retrospections of America, 1797–1811* (New York: Harper, 1887), 140.

13. Thomas Pollock (*The Philadelphia Theatre in the Eighteenth Century* [Philadelphia: University of Pennsylvania Press, 1933], 33), following Durang, also writes of him "for many years the caretaker of the Theatre in Southwark. Seilhamer, more prosaically, refers to North as "the janitor."

14. Charles Durang, *The Philadelphia Stage from 1749 to 1821*, run as a serial in the *Philadelphia Sunday Dispatch*, 22.

15. Ibid.

16. *New York Mercury*, September 27, 1773; *Virginia Gazette*, October 14, 1773.

17. *Pennsylvania Chronicle*, September 20–27, 1773; *Virginia Gazette, Supplement*, October 14, 1773.

18. *Boston Gazette*, August 31, 1767.

19. Richardson Wright (*Revels in Jamaica* [New York: Dodd, Mead, and Co., 1937], 62) reprints the Jamaican playbill; though earlier (43), he too inexplicably noted Mrs. Douglass's death in Philadelphia in 1774.

20. Odell (*Annals of the New York Stage*, 174) recorded the newspaper notice of Douglass's second marriage, also in Jamaica. Robert Myers and Joyce Brodowski, "Rewriting the Hallams," *Theatre Survey*, vol. 41 (May 2000), cite Reed's *Notitia Dramatica* 283r, "In April this year [1777] died Mrs. Douglass formerly Mrs. Hallam mother to Mrs. Mattocks at Spanish Town Jamaica," 20, n. 50. The legal account of both Mrs. Douglass's death and Douglass's marriage are found in the St. Catherine Parish Records, Births, Marriages, Burials, Jamaica Archives.

21. Her death in Philadelphia was picked up by many historians of the period, including T. Allston Brown, *History of the American Stage*, 157; Pollock, *The Philadelphia Theatre*, 33; George Seilhamer, *History of the American Theatre* (Philadelphia: Globe Printing House, 1889–1891), 338–340; Hugh Rankin, *The Theatre in Colonial America* (Chapel Hill, NC: University of North Carolina Press, 1960), 187; Joseph Ireland, *Records of the New York Stage* (New York: T. H. Morrell, 1867), vol. I, 63; Wright,

Revels in Jamaica, 43; Weldon Durham, *American Theatre Companies, 1749–1887* (New York: Greenwood Press, 1986), 14; the *Oxford Dictionary of National Biography*, vol. 24, 680. Susanne K. Sherman (*Comedies Useful: Southern Theatre History 1775–1812* [Williamsburg: Celest Press, 1998], 18) places her death in New York in 1774.

22. George Seilhamer, *History of the American Theatre*, vol. I, 339.
23. Durang, *The Philadelphia Stage*, facing p. 12.
24. Ibid., 12.
25. Arthur Hornblow (*A History of the Theatre in America* [Philadelphia: Lippincott, 1919], 85–86) published the *Virginia Gazette* version of the prologue in full; Seilhamer (*History of the American Theatre*, 41) and Ireland (*Records of the New York Stage*, 19) reprinted the Hallam version.
26. *Virginia Gazette*, September 22, 1752.
27. Lewis Hallam left the company in Montego Bay, Jamaica, in the spring of 1777. Presumably, his absence there suggests he was across the island with his mother and Douglass during her final days.
28. The manuscript has been published in an anthology, William L. Andrews, ed., *Journeys in New Worlds: Early American Women's Narratives* (Madison, WI: University of Wisconsin Press, 1990), 153. I am indebted to Tom Goyens at the Williamsburg Foundation for calling this journal to my attention. Note the low regard in which Ashbridge holds the players, she who would rather endure the servitude of "bondage" than emancipate herself through the means of the playhouse.

10   SILENT TRAVELERS, SILENT JOURNALS

1. *The Order Book and Related Papers of the Common Hall of the Borough of Norfolk, Virginia*, 1726–1798, Brent Tarter, ed. (Richmond, VA: Virginia State Library, 1979).
2. Josiah Quincy, *Journal*, 479–480.
3. "Josiah Quincy's London Journal," *Proceedings of the Massachusetts Historical Society*, 3rd series, vol. 50, 433–470 at 439, 449–450, 464.
4. "Deborah Franklin to Benjamin Franklin, 20–27 November 1769," in *Papers of Benjamin Franklin*, William Willcox, ed. (New Haven, CT: Yale University Press, 1972), vol. xvi, 231.
5. *Maryland Gazette*, August 20, 1772.
6. Thomas Warton to Benjamin Franklin, February 7, 1767. Cf. James H. Hutson, *Pennsylvania Politics* (Princeton, NJ: Princeton University Press, 1972), 81–82.

7. *New York Gazetteer*, September 23, 1773.
8. James Scott and Edward Wyatt IV, *Petersburg's Story* (Petersburg, VA: Titmus Optical Company, 1960), 40.
9. Elaine Forman Crane, ed., *Diary of Elizabeth Drinker* (Boston: Northeastern University Press, 1991), vol. i, 139.
10. Ibid., 145–146.
11. Arria Huntington, *Under a Colonial Roof-Tree: Fireside Chronicles of Early New England* (Syracuse, NY: Wolcott and West, 1892), 26–33.
12. Newton Mereness, ed., *Travels in the American Colonies* (New York: Macmillan, 1916), 403–404. Patrick McRobert, *A Tour of the Provinces of American, 1774–1775* (Edinburgh: n.p. 1776), letter II.
13. Ted Ruddock, ed., *Travels in the Colonies in 1773–1775* (Athens, GA: University of Georgia Press, 1993).
14. Nina Tiffany, ed., *Letters of James Murray, Loyalist* (Boston: Gregg Press, 1972).
15. Victor Hugo Paltsits, ed., "Journal of Benjamin Mifflin on a Tour from Philadelphia to Delaware and Maryland," *Bulletin of the New York Public Library*, 39 (1935): 432.
16. Elizabeth Cometti, ed., *The Journal and Letters of Count Francesco dal Verme 1783–1784* (Charlottesville, VA: University Press of Virginia, 1969), 46–47.
17. Hamilton has left a crude drawing of himself and his cronies from the Tuesday Club playing music at the theatre in Annapolis, ca. 1752, but the doodle includes nothing of the theatre itself. Reprinted in Cynthia Adams Hoover, "Music and Theatre in the Lives of Eighteenth Century Americans," in Carson et al., *Of Consuming Interests*, 311.
18. "Saturday 8th [Oct]—This day the races at Fredericksburg was finished and the night finished the Puppet shows, roape dancings [*sic*], &c, which has continowed every night this week in town. I only seed the purse of a hundred Guineas run for, and that day I hade the Misfortune to have my Horse, saddle, and bridle stole from me, while I was doing some Business in Town. And I never could hear, nor get any intelligence of either of them again." "Diary of John Harrower," *American Historical Review*, vol. vi (New York: Macmillan Co, 1901); 65–107 at 87.
19. Andrew Burnaby, *Travels through the Middle Settlements in North America in the Years 1759 and 1760* (Ithaca, NY: Cornell University Press, 1960), 46.
20. Fred Shelly, ed., "Ebenezer Hazzard's Travels Thru Maryland," *Maryland Historical Magazine*, vol. 46, 1951, 44–54 at 48.
21. James Wright, *Historia Histrionica: An Historical Account of the English Stage* (London: n.p., 1699), 32.

22. Narcissus Luttrell, *A Brief Relations of State Affairs from September 1678 to April 1714* (Oxford: Oxford University Press, 1852), vol. i, 449, July 10, 1688.
23. Evangeline Andrews, ed., *The Journal of a Lady of Quality* (New Haven, CT: Yale University Press, 1922), 122. This may have been William Verling's Leeward Island Company that was known to play in and around St. Croix between 1770 and 1772 at least. See Odai Johnson, "The Leeward Island's Company," *Theatre Survey*, May 2003.
24. *Alice Lee Letterbook*, ms. Virginia Historical Society, Richmond, VA.
25. Here is Burnaby on Newport, Rhode Island: "It is the capital city and contains about 800 or 1,000 houses, chiefly built of wood; 6 or 7,000 inhabitant. There are few buildings in it worth notice. The courthouse is indeed handsome, built of brick; and there is a public library, built in the form of a Grecian temple, by no means in-elegant. It is of the Doric order, and has a portico in front with four pillars, supporting a pediment; but the whole is spoilt by two small wings, which are annexed to it" (*Travels through the Middle Settlements*, 83).
26. William Young, *Documents of American Theatre History* (Chicago: American Library Association, 1973), vol. i, *Famous American Playhouses*, 6.
27. Alonzo May, Men and Women of the American Stage (Unpublished ms., Maryland Historical Society), lii.
28. McRobert, *A Tour of the Provinces*, letter ii.
29. Tiffany, *Letters of James Murray*, 110.
30. Susan Klepp and Billy Smith, eds., *The Infortunate, the Voyage and Adventures of William Moraley, an Indentured Servant* (University Park: Pennsylvania State University Press, 1992), 113. For wages and prices, see Billy Smith, "*The Lower Sort*": *Philadelphia's Laboring People, 1750–1800.*
31. *Columbian Centinel*, December 8, 1792.
32. New York printer James Parker wrote to Benjamin Franklin about an apprentice in a rival print shop (Hugh Gaine's) who had run off some counterfeit tickets to attend. The affair is described at some length in Willcox, *Papers of Benjamin Franklin*, vol. xvii, 129–132.
33. *Pennsylvania Gazette*, July 18, 1763, 33 (240).
34. John Watson, *Annals of Philadelphia and Pennsylvania in the Olden Time* (Philadelphia: J. B. Lippincott and Co., 1870), vol. I, 102.
35. *New York Gazette*, December 22, 1768.
36. *The Royal Danish-American Gazette*, July 21, 1770.
37. Jamaica National Archives, Deeds, Liber 364, fol. 37, dated August 24, 1788.
38. The map, "The British Governments in North America," was unsigned, published in the *Gentleman's Magazine*, xxxiii, London, 1763.

39. Cage wrote to Sir William Johnson on Christmas day, 1769: "It is a shocking alternative to let these savages destroy each other or by mediating peace turn their hatchets against our own heads. In such an extremity there is no doubt which to prefer, but humanity must make us regret that our affairs are in such a situation" Quoted in Gregory Dowd, *War Under Heaven* (Baltimore: Johns Hopkins, 2002), 264.

40. See Joseph Roach, "Feathered Peoples," in *Cities of the Dead, Circum-Atlantic Performance* (New York: Columbia University Press, 1996). There was one oddity worth noting. A university production at Dartmouth College, March 1779, of a dialogue between an Englishman and an Indian, was, its author wrote, "acted pretty naturally, as a real Aboriginal defended the part of the Indian." This was a commencement dialogue, unique in that an Indian undertook the brief role. A copy of the four-page text is reprinted in Harold Rugg, "The Dartmouth Plays," *Theatre Annual* (The Library Association, 1942), 55–69. I am grateful to Barry Witham for calling this to my attention.

41. Egerton Leigh wrote and published "The Man Unmask'd, a Comedy in Five Acts, Intended for the Press, and also for the exhibition on the stage" with a character Attakullakulla. But the "play" was nothing more than a tract defending a point of honor against his brother-in-law, Charleston merchant, Henry Laurens. *South Carolina Gazette*, May 25, 1769.

42. *New York Journal*, April 7, 1768.

43. Howard Zinn, in his *A People's History of the United States* (New York: Harper, 1995, 124), remarks of this: No wonder by the time of the Revolutionary War "almost every important Indian nation fought on the side of the British against the Americans."

44. Jean-Christophe Agnew, *Worlds Apart: The Market and the Theatre in Anglo-American Thought, 1550–1750* (Cambridge: Cambridge University Press, 1986), 150.

11   THE PERFECT STORM

1. I am indebted to Jean Marie Williams for calling this to my attention.

2. Carl Bridenbaugh, *Gentleman's Progress: The Itinerarium of Dr. Alexander Hamilton* (Chapel Hill, NC: University of North Carolina Press, 1948), 65, 9.

3. Hugh Rankin, *The Theatre in Colonial America* (Chapel Hill, NC: University of North Carolina Press, 1960), 201.

4. Alexander Graydon, *Memoir of His Own Times* (Philadelphia: n.p., 1846), 88.

5. Robert Earl Moody and Charles Crittenden, eds., "Letterbook of [Nathaniel] Mills and [John] Hicks," *North Carolina Historical Review* (Raleigh, NC: North Carolina Historical Commission, 1937), 48.

6. *New Jersey Gazette*, Trenton, November 15, 1780.

7. William Smith to Elizabeth Fergusson, March 2, 1781, Simon Gratz, "Some Material for a Biography of Mrs. Elizabeth Fergussun," *Pennsylvania Magazine of History and Biography* (Philadelphia: Historical Society of Pennsylvania, 1915), vol. 39:3, 257–321 at 309.

8. The military theatre of New York has been the subject of several studies, most notably, Ireland, Odell, and Jared Brown. The account books of the 1780 and 1781 seasons are preserved in the New York Historical Society.

9. February 27, 1781, Red Book No. 32, letter 36, Manuscript in Maryland Historical Society. An entry for February 1 (Red Book No. 28, letter 18) introduces him: "Walls once an Actor on the stage at Ann[apolis] draws for himself wife and children the British say he doth not belong to them; but he is their Country man."

10. *Journal of Correspondence of the State Council of Maryland, 1780–1781*, J. Hall Pleasants, ed. (Baltimore: Maryland Historical Society, 1931), vol. XLV, 446.

11. See David Ritchey, "The Maryland Company of Comedians," *Theatre Journal*, 24 (December 1972): 355–362.

12. Inserted with playbill in the Harvard Theatre Collection, where the play-bill came to rest. The acquisition number refers to the collection of Charles N. Mann, a collector of ephemera who died in 1907. There are 60 playbills from Wall's collection in the Maryland Historical Society Randall collection. Another volume, crudely bound, of 30 playbills and newspaper clippings lies in the NYHS, handwritten on a cover: "The Play-bills of Baltimore Theatre for the Years 1782 and 1782. Wall and Lindsay, manager." The New York collection has no acquisition notes, but Lynn Haims ("First American Theatre Contracts," *Theatre Survey*, 179–193 at 191, n. 6) noticed that George Seilhamer refers to them, who published his work in 1889.

13. Edwin Wolfe, II, "Colonial American Playbills," *Pennsylvania Magazine of History and Biography*, 97 (Philadelphia: Historical Society of Pennsylvania, 1973): 99–107 at 100.

14. Alonzo May, ms. Maryland Historical Society, 73.

15. Lewis Burd Walker, "Life of Margaret Shippen, Wife of Benedict Arnold," *Pennsylvania Magazine of History and Biography*, 24:4 (1900): 409–410.

16. These two lists, housed at the Maryland Historical Society, are published as an addendum to David Ritchey's work on the Baltimore stage.

17. New York Historical Society, Playbills from Maryland 1782–1783; undated [November 23, 1782?].

18. *Maryland Journal and Baltimore Advertiser*, undated clipping in the New York Historical Society, Playbills from Maryland 1782–1783 [November 27, 1782?].

19. Playbill in the NYHS.

20. *New York Journal*, June 2, 1768; *New York Gazette and Weekly Post-Boy*, June 27, 1768.

21. *Georgia Gazette*, June 22, 1768.

22. Richardson Wright, *Revels in Jamaica* (New York: Dodd, Mead, and Co., 1937), 46; Mrs. Reginald de Koven, *The Life and Letters of John Paul Jones* (New York: Charles Scribners and Son, 1930), vol. I, 12–13.

23. Kenneth Silverman, *A Cultural History of the American Revolution* (New York: Thomas Cromwell, 1976, 138) following Rankin, also concludes "With the close of the 1769 season, however, The New American Company apparently ceased to exist." Susanne Sherman, in her work on Southern theatre, similarly concludes, "After an ambitious five month season, the company lost its identity and the comedians scattered" (*Comedies Useful: Southern Theatre History 1775–1812* [Williamsburg: Celest Press, 1998], 5).

24. *The Royal Danish-American Gazette*, October 7, 1772. On the strength and promise of this letter, the young Hamilton was invited to New York, to King's College, to complete his education. It was a worthy investment; he went on to become the secretary of George Washington, and author of *The Federalist Papers*, and the first U.S. Treasury Secretary, among his many credentials.

25. From *The Royal Danish-American Gazette*, September 9, 1772.

26. *The Royal Danish-American Gazette*, September 9, 1772.

27. *New York Mercury*, October 12, 1772.

28. Waldo Lincoln, working at the American Antiquarian Society, published a brief list of occasional issues still preserved. See his "Newspapers of the West Indies and Bermuda in the Library of the American Antiquarian Society," *Proceedings of the American Antiquarian Society*, xxxvi (Worcester, MA, 1926): 130–135.

29. *Massachusetts Spy-Boston*, October 22, 1772.

30. Hugh Rankin (*The Theatre in Colonial America*, 150–151) itemizes some of the debts and suits brought against Verling's company. Whether Spencer was among the litigants he does not record. The performance information passim comes from Odai Johnson and William Burling, *The Colonial American Stage, 1665–1774: A Documentary Calendar* (London: Associated University Presses, 2001).

31. *The Pennsylvania Gazette*, October 14, 1772.

32. The American Company under Hallam and Henry were working Jamaica, between Kingston, Spanish Town, and Montego Bay. Bridgetown, Barbados, meanwhile, would see three separate theatrical ventures in the 1770s and early 1780s.

33. *The Royal Danish-American Gazette*, April 10, 1771.

34. National Archives of Scotland, ms GD/199/119 "Elizabeth Mackenie to Lady Pitcalnie, 8 October 1781." It reminds us what an infectious space the crowded theatre could be. The young George Washington attended the playhouse in Barbados, November 15, 1751; two days later he was down with the small pox.

35. The wills of John Henry and Stephen Woolls are abstracted in the New York Historical Society, *Abstracts of Wills*, vol. xv, 1906, Liber 43, 190–191; Liber 41, vol. xiv, 281–282.

36. Dennis Ryan capitalized on the memory of playgoers when he—erroneously—introduced his own upstart company to Charleston in 1785 as The American Company. Ryan was a fitting figure to evoke the memory of the American Company, having been its prompter in New York in 1773. It was his professional function to recall.

37. J. Whitfeld Bell, Jr., "Addenda to Watson's Annals of Philadelphia," *The Pennsylvania Magazine of History and Biography*, 98 (1974): 158.

38. "[The managers] surveyed and have taken the Measurements of both the playhouses in London, and have also engaged a draft of Drury Lane ho. And consulting a very ingenious Carpenter Mr. Saunderson the carpener of the ho. they have collected such Prints as they flatter themselves will be a means of saving some hundreds in Building ye intended ho. in Bristol." (*Minutes of the Proprietors of the Theatre Bristol*, quoted in Kathleen Barker, 8).

39. For the uniformity of language, see David Ross's "Proposal for Building a new Theatre Royal in Edinburgh" (1768), reprinted in David Thomas, ed., *Restoration and Georgian England 1660–1788* (Cambridge: Cambridge University Press, 1989), 249.

40. *Maryland Gazette*, March 6, 1760.

41. April 24, 1770, Extracts from the letters of Alexander Mackaby, 493.

42. "AN OCCASIONAL PROLOGUE. Spoken by Mr. Wall, on the opening of the Baltimore Theatre, January 15, 1782." Published in the *Maryland Gazette*, February 19, 1782.

Bibliography ❦

MANUSCRIPTS

Abstracts of Wills, vol. xv, 1906, Libers 41, 43. New York Historical Society.

Alexander Craig Account Book 1749–1757. John Rockefeller Library, Special Collections, Colonial Williamsburg Foundation, Williamsburg, VA.

Alice Lee Letterbook, ms. Virginia Historical Society, Richmond, VA.

Alonzo May, Men and Women of the American Stage. Unpublished ms. Maryland Historical Society.

College Book, vii. Harvard College Library Archives.

Deeds, Liber 364, folio 37. Jamaica Natural Archives, Spanish Town.

Diary of Jonathan Clark, unpublished manuscript held by the Filson Club.

Edward Charlton Day Book, ms. John Rockefeller Library, Special Collections, Colonial Williamsburg Foundation, Williamsburg, VA.

Elizabeth MacKenie Letters, LMS 60/199/119. National Archives of Scotland.

Galt and Pasteur Account book, 1770–1771. John Rockefeller Library, Special Collections, Colonial Williamsburg Foundation, Williamsburg, VA.

George Gilmer Letterbook, John Rockefeller Library, Special Collections, Colonial Williamsburg Foundation, Williamsburg, VA.

Humphrey Harwood Account Book, Ledger B, fol. 88. John Rockefeller Library, Special Collections, Colonial Williamsburg Foundation, Williamsburg, VA.

Inventories, Liber 76 folio 81r, Jamaica National Archives, Spanish Town.

James Winston Architectural Drawings, Theatre Museum at Covent Garden, Harvard Theatre Collection.

Matthew Clarkson to "Dear John." New York Historical Society.

"The Play-Bills of Baltimore Theatre for the Years 1782 and 1782. Wall and Lindsay, manager." The New York Historical Society.

Red Book No. 32, Manuscript in Maryland Historical Society.

Robert Southall Receipt Book. John Rockefeller Library, Special Collections, Colonial Williamsburg Foundation, Williamsburg, VA.

The Treasure's Book of the Free and Accepted Masons, ms. John Rockefeller Library, Special Collections, Colonial Williamsburg Foundation, Williamsburg, VA.

The Virginia Gazette Day Books of Joseph Royle, 1750–1752 and 1764–1766, ms. Rockefeller Library, Williamsburg, VA.

William Allason Daybook, ms. Virginia State Library, Richmond, VA.

William Bradford ms (Legal catalogue). Historical Society of Pennsylvania.

Woodfall, T., *James Winston—The Theatric Tourist*. London, 1805, Harvard Theatre Collection.

COLONIAL AND STATE PAPERS

Accomac County Records, vol. 1663–1666.

Anne Arundel County Judgement Records, State Archives, Annapolis, EB-2.

Calendar of Historic Manuscripts in the Office of the Secretary of State, Edmund B. O'Callighan, ed., Albany, NY: Weed Parsons, and Co., 1866.

Charleston County Land Records, Misc. Pt. 64, Book C5, 1779–1781.

Colonial Records of North Carolina, William L. Saunders, ed., Raleigh, NC: Trustees of the Public Library, 1886–1890, viii.

The Colonial Records of the State of Georgia, Kenneth Coleman, ed., Athens, GA: University of Georgia Press, 1982.

Documents Relative to the Colonial History of the State of New York 1856–1887, E. B. O'Callaghan, ed., vol. vi, i.

Journal of Correspondence of the State Council of Maryland, 1780–1781, J. Hall Pleasants, ed., Baltimore: Maryland Historical Society, 1931.

Linn, John B. and Egle, William H., eds, *Pennsylvania Archives*, 2nd series, Harrisburg, PA: Lane S. Hart, 1878, vol. VII.

Minutes of the Common Council of the City of Philadelphia, 1704–1776, Philadelphia: Pennsylvania Historical Society, 1847.

Minutes of the Executive Council, June 13, 1752.

The Order Book and Related Papers of the Common Hall of the Borough of Norfolk, Virginia, 1726–1798, Brent Tarter, ed., Richmond: Virginia State Library, 1979.

Pennsylvania Archives, 1st Series, vol. iii, Samuel Hazard, ed., Philadelphia: Pennsylvania Historical Society, 1853.

Proceedings of the Massachusetts Historical Society, 2nd series, Boston: MA Historical Society, 1896 (n.a.).

Records of the Colony of Rhode Island, 1757–1769, John Russel Bartlett, ed., Providence, RI: A. C. Greene, 1861.

Records of the Massachusetts Colonial Society.
St. Anne's Parish Vestry Book, 1767–1818, Maryland Historical Society.
The Treasury Book of the Theatre Royal, New York, 1780–1781, New York Historical Society.
Votes of the Pennsylvania Assembly, 1749, 8th series, vol. iv, Gertrude Mackinney, ed., Philadelphia: Pennsylvania Historical Society, 1931.
York County Records, Judgement and Orders, vol. ii.
York County Records, Judgements and Orders, 1768–1770.

RESEARCH REPORTS

Barney Barnes, *The Virginia Gazette Extracts*, Colonial Williamsburg Foundation Library Research Report Series.
David Wilmore, *The Georgian Theatre, Richmond*, Theatre Projects Consultants, 2003.
Jane McWilliams, *The Progress of Refinement, A History of Theatre in Annapolis*, Annapolis: Produced for the Colonial Players of Annapolis, 1976.
John S. Duvall and Stuart Schwartz, *Research and Archeology, Halifax, North Carolina, The Playhouse Site*, Raleigh, NC: State Department of Archives and History, 1970.
Mary A. Stephenson, *Second Theatre Historical Report, Block 7, Lot 21 and 22*, Williamsburg: Colonial Williamsburg Foundation, 1946.

PARISH RECORDS

Kingston Parish Register: Baptisms, Marriages, Burials, 1B/11/8/9:1.

NEWSPAPERS AND MAGAZINES

Barbados Mercury
Boston Chronicle
Boston Evening Post
Boston Evening Post Boy
Boston Gazette
Boston News-Letter
Boston Post Boy
Columbian Centinel
Columbian Herald
Cornwall Chronicle

Gentleman's Magazine
Georgia Gazette
Journal of the Assembly
Kingston Mercury
Maryland Gazette
Maryland Journal
Maryland Journal and Baltimore Advertiser
Massachusetts Spy-Boston
New England Courant
New Hampshire Gazette
New Jersey Gazette
Newport Mercury
New York Evening Post
New York Gazette and Weekly Post-Boy
New York Gazetteer
New York Journal
New York Mercury
New York Times
North Carolina Gazette
Nova Scotia Gazette
Pennsylvania Chronicle
Pennsylvania Gazette
Pennsylvania Packet-Philadelphia
The Royal Danish-American Gazette
South Carolina and American General Gazette
South Carolina Gazette Crouch
Virginia Gazette (Purdie and Dixon; Rind)
Virginia Gazette—Williamsburg

SOURCES

Agnew, Jean-Christophe. *Worlds Apart: The Market and the Theatre in Anglo-American Thought, 1550–1750.* Cambridge, UK: Cambridge University Press, 1986.

Andrews, Evangeline, ed. *The Journal of a Lady of Quality.* New Haven, CT: Yale University Press, 1922.

Andrews, William L., ed. *Journeys in New Worlds: Early American Women's Narratives.* Madison, WI: University of Wisconsin Press, 1990.

Armor, William, C. *Lives of the Governors of Pennsylvania.* Norwich, CT: T. H. Davis, 1874.

Arnold, Samuel. *History of the State of Rhode Island*. New York: D. Appleton and Co., 1878.

Barker, Kathleen. *The Theatre Royal Bristol, 1766–1966*. London: Society for Theatre Research, 1974.

Barret, Norris and Sachse, Julius. *Freemasonry in Pennsylvania, 1727–1907*. Philadelphia: Grand Lodge of Pennsylvania, 1908.

Bear, James A. Jr. and Stanton, Lucia C., eds. *Jefferson's Memorandum Books*. Princeton, NJ: Princeton University Press, 1997.

Bellamy, George Ann. *An Apology for the Life of George Anne Bellamy*. London: n. p., 1785.

Bennett, William. *Memorials of Methodism*. Richmond, VA: n. p., 1871.

Bernard, John. *Retrospections of America, 1797–1811*, New York: Harper, 1887.

Borneman, Henry Stauffer. *Early Freemasonry and Pennsylvania*. Philadelphia: The Grand Lodge of Pennsylvania, 1931.

Boucher, Jonathan, ed. *Reminiscences of an American Loyalist, 1738–1789*. Boston and New York: Houghton Mifflin, 1925.

Boyd, Julian, ed. *The Papers of Thomas Jefferson*. Princeton, NJ: Princeton University Press, 1950.

Breen, T. H. *The Marketplace of Revolution: How Consumer Politics Shaped American Independence*. Oxford: Oxford University Press, 2004.

Bridenbaugh, Carl. *Gentleman's Progress: The Itinerarium of Dr. Alexander Hamilton*. Chapel Hill: University of North Carolina Press, 1948.

Bridenbaugh, Carl, and Bridenbaugh, Jessica. *Rebels and Gentlemen: Philadelphia in the Age of Franklin*. New York, Oxford University Press, 1965.

Brockett, F. L. *The Lodge of Washington*. Alexandria: George French, 1876.

Brown, B. W. *The Colonial Theatre in New England*. Newport, RI: Newport Historical Society, 1930.

Brown, Jared. *The Theatre in American during the Revolution*. Cambridge, UK: Cambridge University Press, 1995.

Brown, T. Allston. *A History of the New York Stage*. New York: Dodd, Mead and Company, 1903.

———. *History of the American Stage* (reprint). New York: Burt Franklin, 1969.

Brown, William Moseley. *Freemasonry in Virginia, 1733–1936*. Richmond, VA: Masonic Home Press, 1936.

Browne, William Hand, ed. *Correspondence of Governor Horatio Sharpe*. Baltimore: Maryland Historical Society, 1890.

Bullock, Steven. *Ancient and Honorable Free Masonry in America, 1730–1830*. Dissertation. Brown University, 1986.

Burling, William. *Summer Theatre in London, 1661–1820, and the Rise of the Haymarket Theatre*. London: Associated University Presses, 2000.

Burnaby, Andrew. *Travels through the Middle Settlements in North America in the Years 1759 and 1760*. Ithaca, NY: Cornell University Press, 1960.

Bushman, Richard. *The Refinement of America, Persons, Houses, Cities*. New York: Alfred Knopf, 1992.

Carson, Cary, Hoffman, Ronald, and Albert, Peter J., eds. *Of Consuming Interests, the Style of Life in the Eighteenth Century*. Charlottesville, VA: University Press of Virginia, 1994.

Cary, John. *Joseph Warren, Physician, Politician, Patriot*. Urbana, IL: University of Illinois, 1961.

Clapp, William. *Record of the Boston Stage*. Boston: James Munroe & Co., 1853.

Clark, William. *The Irish Stage in the Country Towns, 1720–1800*. Oxford, Oxford University Press, 1965.

Colden, Cadwallader. *Letters and Papers of Cadwallader Colden*. New York: New York Historical Society, 1917.

Cometti, Elizabeth, ed. *The Journal and Letters of Count Francesco del Verme, 1783–1784*. Charlottesville, VA: University Press of Virginia, 1969.

Crain, Timothy M. *Music in the Colonial Charleston, South Carolina Theatre: 1732–81*. Dissertation. Florida State University, 2002.

Crane, Elaine Forman, ed. *Diary of Elizabeth Drinker*. Boston: Northeastern University Press, 1991.

Cresswell, Nicholas. *The Journal of Nicholas Cresswell, 1774–1777*. New York: Dial Press, 1924.

Cumming, William, P. *British Maps of Colonial America*. Chicago: University of Chicago Press, 1974.

Cunningham, Anne, ed. *Letters and Diary of John Rowe*. Boston: W. B. Clarke, 1903.

Cunningham, Noble, Jr. *In Pursuit of Reason, the Life of Thomas Jefferson*. Baton Rouge, LA: Louisiana State University Press, 1987.

Curtis, Mary Julia. *The Early Charleston Stage: 1703–1798*. PhD dissertation, Indiana University, 1968.

Daly, Charles. *The First Theatre in America*. New York: Burt Franklin, 1896.

Davis, Richard. *Intellectual Life in the Colonial South*. Knoxville, TN: University of Tennessee, 1978.

Deetz, James. *In Small Things Forgotten, the Archaeology of Early American Life*. Garden City, NY: Anchor Books, 1977.

De Koven, Mrs. Reginald. *The Life and Letters of John Paul Jones*. New York: Charles Scribners and Son, 1930.

Dibdin, James. *Annals of the Edinburgh Stage*. Edinburgh, 1888.

Dickason, David, Howard. *William Williams, Novelist and Painter of Colonial America, 1727–1791*. Bloomington, IN: Indiana University Press, 1970.

Dickerson, Oliver, Morton, ed. *Boston under Military Rule, a Journal of the Times*. Boston: Chapman and Grimes, 1936.

Dill, Alonzo. *Governor Tryon and His Palace*. Chapel Hill, NC: University of North Carolina Press, 1955.

Dorman, James, H. *Theatre in the Ante Bellum South*. Chapel Hill, NC: University of North Carolina Press, 1967.

Dowd, Gregory. *War Under Heaven*. Baltimore: Johns Hopkins, 2002.

Dunlap, William. *History of the American Theatre*. New York: J. J. Harper, 1832.

Durang, Charles. *The Philadelphia Stage from 1749 to 1821*, run as a serial in the *Philadelphia Sunday Dispatch*, vol. iii, May 21, 1854.

Durham, Weldon. *American Theatre Companies*. New York: Greenwood Press, 1986.

Easterby, J. H. *The History of Saint Andrew's Society*. Charleston, SC: Saint Andrews Society, 1929.

Ekirch, Roger. *Poor Carolina: Politics and Society in Colonial North Carolina*. Chapel Hill, NC: University of North Carolina, 1981.

Entick, John and Smith, William. *Freemason's Pocket Companion*. Edinburgh: W. Cheyne, 1752.

Eshleman, Dorothy, ed. *The Committee Books of the Theatre Royal, Norwich, 1768–1825*. London: Society for Theatre Research, 1970.

Felder, Paula. *Fielding Lewis and the Washington Family: A Chronicle of 18th Century Fredericksburg*. Fredericksburg, PA: American History Company, 1998.

Flannigan, Lanaghan. *Antigua and the Antiguans: A Full Account of the Colony and Its Inhabitants from the Time of the Caribs to the Present Day*. London: Saunders and Otley, 1844.

Ford, Paul Leicester. *The Journals of Hugh Gaine, Printer*. New York: Dodd, Mead, and Co., 1902.

Ford, Worthington, ed. *Journals of the Continental Congress, 1774–1789*. Washington: General Printing Office, 1904.

Graydon, Alexander. *Memoirs of his Own Times*. Philadelphia: n. p., 1846.

Hamer, Philip, M. *The Papers of Henry Laurens*. Columbia, SC: South Carolina Historical Society, 1968.

Handlin, Oscar, and Clive, John, eds. *Journey to Pennsylvania, by Gottlieb Mittelberger*. Cambridge: Harvard University Press, 1960.

Hanson, Robert Brand, ed. *The Diary of Dr. Nathaniel Ames of Dedham, Massachusetts*. Camden, ME: Picton Press, 1998.

Hill, Errol. *The Jamaica Stage, 1655–1900*. Amherst, MA: University of Massachusetts Press, 1992.

Hill, Frank Pierce. *American Plays Printed, 1714–1830*. Stanford, CA: Stanford University Press, 1934.

Hornblow, Arthur, *A History of the Theatre in America*, 2 vols. Philadelphia: Lippincott, 1919.

Hughes, Glen. *History of the American Theatre, 1750–1860*. New York: Samuel French, 1951.

Huntington, Arria. *Under a Colonial Roof-Tree: Fireside Chronicles of Early New England*. Syracuse, NY: Wolcott and West, 1892.

Huss, Wayne. *The Master Builders*. Philadelphia: Grand Lodge of Philadelphia, 1986.

Hutson, James H. *Pennsylvania Politics*. Princeton, NT: Princeton University Press, 1972.

Ireland, Joseph. Extra-illustrated edition of *Records of the New York Stage*, prepared for Augustin Daly, with engravings and illustrations by Augustus Toedteberg. New York: T. H. Morrell, 1867, Harvard Theatre Collection.

Isaac, Rhys. *The Transformation of Virginia*. Chapel Hill, NC: University of North Carolina Press, 1982.

Jameson, Frederic. *The Political Unconscious: Narratives in a Socially Symbolic Act*. Ithaca, NY: Cornell University Press, 1981

Johnson, Melvin. *The Beginning of Freemasonry in America*. New York: George Doran Company, 1924.

Johnson, Odai and Burling, William. *The Colonial American Stage, 1665–1774. A Documentary Calendar*. London: Associated University Presses, 2001.

Johnson, Robert. *The Struggle over Theatre in Colonial Pennsylvania*. MA thesis. University of Washington, 1950.

Judd, Jacob and Polishook, Irwin, eds. *Aspects of Early New York Society and Politics*. Tarrytown, NY: Sleepy Hollow Restorations, 1974.

Kalm, Peter. *Travels into North America*. Barre, MA: The Imprint Society: 1972.

Kidd, George. *Early Freemasonry in Virginia*. Richmond, VA: Dietz Press, 1957.

Klepp, Susan, and Smith, Billy, eds. *The Infortunate, the Voyage and Adventures of William Moraley, an Indentured Servant*, University Park: Pennsylvania State University Press, 1992.

Kornwolf, James D. *Architecture and Town Planning in Colonial North America*. Baltimore: Johns Hopkins University Press, 2002.

Kuntzleman, Oliver, C. *Joseph Galloway, Loyalist*. Dissertation. Philadelphia: Temple University, 1941.

Land, Aubrey C. *Letters from America*, William Eddis, ed. Cambridge: Harvard University Press, 1969.

————. *The Dulaneys of Maryland*. Baltimore: Maryland Historical Society, 1955.

Lemay, J. A. Leo. *Men of Letters in Colonial Maryland*. Knoxville, TN: University of Tennessee Press, 1972.

Leon, Mark and Potter, Parker, eds. *The Recovery of Meaning, Historical Archaeology in the Eastern United States*. Washington: Smithsonian Institute Press, 1988.

Little, Paul. Reactions to the Theatre: Virginia, Massachusetts, and Pennsylvania, 1969.

Luttrell, Narcissus. *A Brief Relations of State Affairs from September 1678 to April 1714*. Oxford: Oxford University Press, 1852.

MacNamara, Brooks. *The American Playhouse in the Eighteenth Century*. Cambridge, MA: Harvard University Press, 1969.

Mackey, Robert. *History of Freemasonry in South Carolina*. Columbia, SC: Wentworth Printing, 1998.

Maser, Frederick and Maag, Howard, eds. *The Journal of Joseph Pilmore, Methodist Itinerant for the Years August 1 1769 to January 2 1774*. Philadelphia: n. p., 1969.

McRobert, Patrick. *A Tour of the Provinces of American, 1774–1775*. Edinburgh: n. p., 1776.

Mereness, Newton, ed. *Travels in the American Colonies*. New York: Macmillan, 1916.

Miller C. William, ed. *Benjamin Franklin's Philadelphia Printing*. Philadelphia: American Philosophical Society, 1974.

Miner, Ward, L. *William Goddard, Newspaper Man*. Durham, NC: Duke University Press, 1962.

Capt. Montressor. "The Journals of Capt. Montessor." *Collections of the New York Historical Society for 1881*. G. D. Scull, ed. New York: New York Historical Society.

Morgan, Edmund and Morgan, Helen. *The Stamp Act Crisis: Prologue to Revolution*. Chapel Hill, NC: University of North Carolina Press, 1995.

Morris, Richard, ed. *John Jay, The Making of a Revolutionary*. New York: Harper & Row, 1975.

Munsell, Joel. *Annals of Albany*. Albany, NY: Joel Munsell, 1869.

Nash, Gary. *The Urban Crucible*. Cambridge, MA: Harvard University Press, 1979.

Nathans, Heather. *Early American Theatre from the Revolution to Thomas Jefferson, into the Hands of the People*. Cambridge: Cambridge University Press, 2003.

Nelson, Paul. *William Tryon and the Course of Empire*. Chapel Hill, NC: University of North Carolina Press, 1990.

Nester, William, R. *"Haughty Conquerors" Amherst and the Great Indian Uprising of 1763*. Westport, CT: Praeger, 2000.

Odell, George. *Annals of the New York Stage*. New York: Columbia University Press, 1927.

Paltsits, Victor Hugo, ed. "Journal of Benjamin Mifflin on a Tour from Philadelphia to Delaware and Maryland," *Bulletin of the New York Public Library*, 39 (1935).

Parramore, Thomas. *Norfolk, the First Four Centuries*. Charlottesville, VA: University Press of Virginia, 1994.

Phelan, Peggy. *Unmarked, the Politics of Performance*. New York: Routledge, 1993.

Pinckney, Eliza. *Letterbook of Eliza Pinckney, 1739–1762*. Chapel Hill, NC: University of North Carolina, 1972.

Pollock, Thomas. *The Philadelphia Theatre in the Eighteenth Century*. Philadelphia: University of Pennsylvania Press, 1933.

Price, Cecil. *The English Theatre in Wales*. Cardiff: University of Wales, 1948.

Quinn, Arthur. *A History of the American Drama from the Beginning to the Civil War*. New York: Harper, 1923.

Quincy, Josiah. The Journal of Josiah Quincy. Boston: Cummings, Hillard, & Co., 1825.

Rankin, Hugh. *The Colonial Theatre; Its History and Operations*. PhD thesis. Chapel Hill, NC: University of North Carolina, 1959.

———. *The Theatre in Colonial America*. Chapel Hill, NC: University of North Carolina Press, 1960.

Rice, Howard, C., Jr. *Travels in North American in the Years 1780, 1781, and 1782, by the Marquis de Chastellux*. Chapel Hill, NC: University of North Carolina, 1963.

Ricoeur, Paul. *Memory, History, Forgetting*. Chicago: University of Chicago Press, 2004.

Ritchey, David. *A Guide to the Baltimore Stage in the Eighteenth Century: A History and a Day Book Calendar*. Westport, CT: Greenwood Press, 1982.

Roach, Joseph. *Cities of the Dead, Circum-Atlantic Performance*. New York: Columbia University Press, 1996.

Rosenfeld, Sybil. *Strolling Players and Drama in the Provinces, 1660–1765*. Cambridge, UK: Cambridge University Press, 1939.

———. *The Theatre of the London Fairs in the 18th Century*. Cambridge, UK: Cambridge University Press, 1960.

Ruddock, Ted, ed. *Travels in the Colonies in 1773–1775*. Athens, GA: University of Georgia Press, 1993.

Sabine, William, ed. *Historical Memoirs of William Smith*. New York: Colburn and Tegg, 1956.

Scott, James and Wyatt, Edward IV. *Petersburg's Story*. Petersburg, VA: Titmus Optical Company, 1960.

Scull, George, ed. *The Montresor Journals*. New York: Collections of the New York Historical Society, 1881.

Seilhamer, George O. *History of the American Theatre*, 3 vols. Philadelphia: Globe Printing House, 1889–1891.

Sharp, Thomas. *A Dissertation on the Pageants or Dramatic Mysteries Anciently Performed at Coventry*. Coventry: Merridew and Son, 1825.

Sherman, Susanne K. *Comedies Useful: Southern Theatre History 1775–1812*. Williamsburg: Celest Press, 1998.

Sherrill, Charles. *French Memories of Eighteenth Century America*. New York: Benjamin Blom, 1971.

Showman, Richard, K. ed. *The Papers of General Nathanael Greene*. Chapel Hill, NC: University of North Carolina Press, 1976.

Silverman, Kenneth. *A Cultural History of the American Revolution*. New York: Thomas Cromwell, 1976.

Smith, Billy. *"The Lower Sort": Philadelphia's Laboring People*. Ithaca, NY: Cornell University Press, 1990.

Smith, William. *The History of the Province of New York*. New York: Thomas Wilcox, 1751.

Smith, Woodruff. *Consumption and the Making of Respectability, 1600–1800*. New York: Routledge, 2002.

Sonneck, O. G. *Early Opera in America*. New York: Benjamin Blom, 1943.

Spencer, Alfred, ed. *Memoirs of William Hickey*. London: Knopf, 1923.

Steurt, Colonel William. *History of Norfolk County, Virginia*. Chicago: Biographical Publishing Co., 1902.

Stockwell, La Tourette. *Dublin Theatres and Theatre Customs, 1637–1820*. Kingsport, TN: Kingsport Press, 1938.

Tatsch, Hugo. *Freemasons in the Thirteen Colonies*. New York: Macoy, 1929.

Thomas, David, ed. *Restoration and Georgian England 1660–1788*. Cambridge: Cambridge University Press, 1989.

Thomas, Isaiah. *The History of Printing in America*. New York: Weathervane, 1970.

Tiffany, Nina, ed. *Letters of James Murray, Loyalist*. Boston: Gregg Press, 1972.

Tinling, Marion, ed. *The Correspondence of the Three William Byrds of Westover, Virginia, 1684–1776*. Charlottesville, VA: University Press of Virginia, 1977.

Tuan, Yi-Fu. *Space and Place*. Minneapolis, MN: University of Minnesota Press, 1977.

Van Doran, Carl, ed. *The Letters of Benjamin Franklin and Jane Mecum.* Princeton, NJ: American Philosophical Society, 1950.

Van Horne, John. *The Correspondence of William Nelson, as Acting Governor of Virginia, 1770–1771.* Charlottesville, VA: University Press of Virginia, 1975.

Veblin, Thorstein. *Theory of the Leisure Class.* New York: Penguin, 1979.

Warren, Charles. *Jacobin and Junto, or Early American Politics as Viewed in the Diary of Dr. Nathaniel Ames, 1758–1822.* Cambridge, MA: Harvard University Press, 1931.

Watson, John. *Annals of Philadelphia and Pennsylvania in the Olden Time.* Philadelphia: J. B. Lippincott and Co., 1870.

Weatherill, Lorna. *Consumer Behavior and Material Culture in Britain, 1660–1760.* London: Routledge, 1988.

Wemyss, Francis. *The Chronology of the American Stage.* New York: Benjamin Blom, 1968.

Westergaard, Waldemar. *The Danish West Indies under Company Rule (1671–1754).* New York: Macmillan, 1917.

Wetenbaker, Thomas, J. *Norfork: Historical Southern Port.* Durham, NC: Duke University Press, 1962.

White, Hayden. *The Content of the Form: Narrative Discourse and Historical Representation.* Baltimore: Johns Hopkins University Press, 1987.

Whitelaw, Ralph. *Virginia's Eastern Shore, a History of Northampton and Accomack Counties.* Richmond, VA: Virginia Historical Society, 1951.

Wilderson, Paul. *Governor John Wentworth and the American Revolution: The English Connection.* Hanover, NH: University Press of New England, 1994.

Wilkinson, Tate. *The Wandering Patentee.* London: Scholar Press, 1973.

Willard, George. *History of the Providence Stage, 1762–1891.* Providence, RI: News Company, 1891.

Willcox, William, ed. *Papers of Benjamin Franklin.* New Haven, CT: Yale University Press, 1973.

Willis, Eola. *The Charleston Stage in the XVIII Century.* Columbia, SC: The State Company, 1924.

Wineman, Walter R. *The Landon Carter Papers in the University of Virginia Library. A Calendar and Biographical Sketch.* Charlottesville, VA: University of Virginia Press, 1962.

Wingfield, Marshall. *History of Caroline County, Virginia.* Richmond, VA: Trevent Christian and Co., 1924.

Wise, Jennings Cooper. *Ye Kingdome of Accawmacke or the Eastern Shore of Virginia in the Seventeenth Century* (1911; repr.). Baltimore: Regional, 1967.

Wood, Gordon. *The Radicalism of the American Revolution.* New York: Vintage Books, 1991.

Wright, James. *Historia Histrionica: An Historical Account of the English Stage.* London: 1699.

Wright, Louis, B. *The Cultural Life of the American Colonies.* New York, Harper, 1957.

Wright, Philip, ed. *Lady Nugent's Journal of Her Residence in Jamaica from 1801 to 1805.* Bridgetown, Barbados: University of West Indies Press, 2002.

Wright, Richardson. *Revels in Jamaica.* New York: Dodd, Mead, and Co., 1937.

Wroth, Lawrence, C. *A History of Printing in Colonial Maryland, 1686–1776.* Baltimore: Typothetae of Baltimore, 1922.

Young, William. *Documents of American Theatre History.* Chicago: American Library Association, 1973.

Zinn, Howard. *A People's History of the United States.* New York: Harper: 1995.

ARTICLES

"Abstracts from Norfolk Co. Marriage Bonds," na, in *Lower Norfolk County Virginia Antiquary*, Edward Wilson James, ed. (Baltimore: The Friedenwalk Co., 1902).

Bell, Whitfeld J., Jr. "Addenda to Watson's Annals of Philadelphia," *The Pennsylvania Magazine of History and Biography*, vol. 98 (Philadelphia: Historic Society of Pennsylvania, 1974).

Bielinski, Stefan. "The People of Colonial Albany, 1650–1800," *Authority and Resistance in Early New York*. William Pencak and Conrad Wright, eds. (New York: New York Historical Society, 1988).

Bruce, Philip Alexander. "Oldest Play," *The Nation*, 89 (February 11, 1909).

Cary Carson. "The Consumer Revolution in Colonial America: Why Demand?" in *Of Consuming Interests, the Style of Life in the Eighteenth Century.*

Chappel, Edward. "Housing a Nation: The Transformation of Living Standards in Early America" in Carson, Hoffman, Albert, eds., *Of Consuming Interests.*

Cobau, Judith. "The Precarious Life of Thomas Pike, a Colonial Dancing Master in Charleston and Philadelphia," *Dance Chronicle*, 17:3 (1994): 229–262.

Curtis, Julia, "Charlestown's Church Street Theatre," *The South Carolina Historical Magazine*, 70:3, Charleston, SC (July 1969).

Davis, Peter. "Puritan Mercantilism and the Politics of Anti-Theatrical Legislation in Colonial America," in Ron Engle and Tice Miller, eds., *The*

American Stage: Social and Economic Issues from the Colonial Period to the Present. Cambridge, UK: Cambridge University Press, 1993.

De Lancey, Edward F. "Chief Justice William Allen," *Pennsylvania Magazine*, 1 (Philadelphia: Historical Society of Pennsylvania, 1877): 202–211

"Diary of John Harrower," *American Historical Review*, vi (New York: Macmillan Co., 1901): 65–107.

Dye, William. "Pennsylvania Vs. the Theatre," *Pennsylvania Magazine of History and Biography*, 55 (Philadelphia: Historical Society of Pennsylvania, 1931): 333–371.

"Extracts from letters of Alexander Mackaby to Sir Philip Francis," *Pennsylvania Magazine of History and Biography*, 11 (Philadelphia: Historical Society of Pennsylvania, 1887): 2.

Gratz, Simon. William to Elizabeth Fergusson, March 2, 1781, "Some Material for a Biography of Mrs. Elizabeth Fergussun," *Pennsylvania Magazine of History and Biography*, 39:3 (Philadelphia: Historical Society of Pennsylvania, 1915): 257–321.

Haims, Lynn. "First American Theatre Contracts," *Theatre Survey*, 1: 79–193.

Henderson, Archibald. "Strolling Players in Eighteenth Century North Carolina," *The Carolina Play-Book*, Chapel Hill, NC: University of North Carolina, 1942.

Hoover, Cynthia Adams. "Music and Theatre in the Lives of Eighteenth Century Americans," in Carson, Hoffman, Albert, eds., *Of Consuming Interest.*

Howell, Mark. "The Theatre at Richmond, Yorkshire," *Theatre Notebook*, xlvi (1992): 1, 30–40.

———. "The 'Regular Theatre' at Jacob's Well, Bristol 1729–65," *Scenes from Provincial Stages: Essays in Honour of Kathleen Barker*, Richard Foulkes, ed. (London: Society for Theatre Research, 1994).

Jameson, J. Franklin, ed. "A Journal of a French Traveler in the Colonies, 1765," *American Historical Review* XXV (July 1921): 726–747.

Johnson, Odai. "Thomas Jefferson and the Colonial American Stage," *The Virginia Magazine of History and Biography*, 108:2 (2000): 139–154.

———. "The Leeward Island's Company" in *Theatre Survey*, May 2003.

"Josiah Quincy's London Journal," *Proceedings of the Massachusetts Historical Society*, 3rd series, 50 (1779–1782): 433–470.

"Journal of a French Traveler," in *American Historical Review*, xxvi (1921), 726–747.

"Journal of Josiah Quincey, Jr.," *Massachusetts Historical Society Proceedings*, XLIX (October 1915–June 1916).

"Letters of William Paine," *Proceedings of the Massachusetts Historical Society*, Boston, 1926, iii series, vol. 59.

Lincoln, Waldo. "Newspapers of the West Indies and Bermuda in the Library of the American Antiquarian Society," *Proceedings of the American Antiquarian Society*, xxxvi (Worcester, MA: 1926): 130–135.

Lovell, Margaretta M. "Painters and their Customers: Aspects of Art and Money in Eighteenth Century America," in Carson, Hoffman, and Albert, eds., *Of Consuming Interest*.

Mackaby, Alexander. "Extracts from the Letters of Alexander Mackaby to Sir Philip Francis," *Pennsylvania Magazine of History and Biography*. Philadelphia: Pennsylvania Historical Society, 1887.

Mays, David. "The Achievements of the Douglass Company in North America: 1758–1774," in *Theatre Survey*, xxiii: 2 (November 1982): 141–150.

Moody, Robert Earl and Crittenden, Charles, eds. "Letterbook of [Nathaniel] Mills and [John] Hicks," *North Carolina Historical Review* (Raleigh, NC: North Carolina Historical Commission, 1937).

Morgan, Edmund S. "Puritan Hostility to the Theatre," *American Philosophical Society, Proceedings* 110 (October 1966): 340–347.

Myers, Robert and Brodowski, Joyce. "Rewriting the Hallams," in *Theatre Survey*, 41 (May 2000).

Neidig, William J. "The First Play in America," published in *The Nation*, January 28, 1909.

Richards, Jeffery. *Mercy Ottis Warren*. New York: Twayne, 1995.

Ritchey, David, "The Maryland Company of Comedians," in *Theatre Journal*, 24 (December 1972): 355–362.

Rugg, Harold. "The Dartmouth Plays," *Theatre Annual* (The Library Association, 1942), 55–69.

Sachse, Julius. "Roster of the Lodge of Free and Accepted Masons which Met at the Tun Tavern, Philadelphia," *Pennsylvania Magazine of History and Biography* (Philadelphia: Historical Society of Pennsylvania, 1896).

Sauthier, Claude Joseph. *Architectura Civile* (Paris: n. p., 1763).

Shelly, Fred, ed. "Ebenezer Hazzard's Travels Thru Maryland," *Maryland Historical Magazine*, 46 (1951): 44–54.

Shiffler, Harold. 'Religious Opposition to the Eighteenth Century Theatre in Philadelphia," *Educational Theatre Journal* (October 1962): 215–223.

Simmel, Georg. "Fashion," *International Quarterly* 10 (1904): 130–155.

"Smyth's Travels in Virginia, in 1773," *Virginia Historical Register*, VI.

Sweeny, Keven. "High Style Vernacular: Lifestyles of the Colonial Elite" in Carson, Hoffman, and Albert, eds., *Of Consuming Interests*.

Swem, E. G. "Notes from the Meeting of the President and Masters of the College," *William and Mary Quarterly*, 1st series, v (1897): 168–171.

Tyler, Lyon. "Williamsburg Lodge of Masons," *William and Mary Quarterly*, vol. 1, 1st series (Williamsburg, 1892).

Walker, Lewis Burd. "Life of Margaret Shippen, Wife of Benedict Arnold," *Pennsylvania Magazine of History and Biography*, 24: 4 (1900).

Woolfe, Edwin II. "Colonial American Playbills," *Pennsylvania Magazine of History and Biography*, 97 (Philadelphia, Historical Society of Pennsylvania, 1973): 99–106.

Wright, Richardson, "Masonic Contacts with the Early American stage," *American Lodge of Research Transactions*, 2 (1936): 161–187.

Index